To my mother and father,
both teachers,
who instilled in me
a lifelong love of learning

Acknowledgments

I would like to thank all the editors of parapsychological journals who have guided my writing and given me a voice in parapsychology over the years, including K. Ramakrishna Rao, Dorothy Pope, Laura Dale, Betty Shapin, Rhea White, Stanley Krippner and John Palmer. Special thanks go to Rao, who got me started on the present book.

I would also like to thank J.B. and Louisa Rhine, my friends and mentors, as well as all the other teachers, students and colleagues who have helped shape my thought over the years. They have all contributed to this book.

Most of all, I would express my appreciation for their forbearance to my wife Iris and my daughter Rachel, who spent her formative years watching her daddy sitting at the word processor (although she learned to dance to the staccato of the printout and knew how to print out a document before she could spell).

THE NATURE OF MIND

Table of Contents

1. Introduction

We are complex collections of atoms, assembled at the whim of DNA molecules. Our beings are governed by the laws of physics, in which our minds play no part. Upon our deaths, our bodies will degrade, our assemblages of atoms will exist no more, and we will cease to exist, just as we did not exist before our physical bodies were assembled. For we are our physical bodies.

This is our modern self-portrait, as supplied by Western science. That science has no place for a mind or soul existing independently of the physical body. The ascendancy of Western science has led to the decline of many major organized religions and may be responsible for the increasingly materialistic outlook of our culture.

There are, however, a few chinks in the armor of the materialistic philosophy of Western science. We have hints of phenomena that defy explanation by modern theories of physics. These hints have been supplied by data collected by a handful of renegade scientists who call themselves parapsychologists. These data suggest that the laws of physics do not provide a complete description of the universe and that the mind may play a more fundamental role in the cosmos than is dreamt of in the philosophies of most modern scientists.

In the pages that follow, we will examine these data and their implications. We will begin with strange, almost transcendental experiences that suddenly intrude on the mundane reality in which we spend our day-to-day existence. These include cases suggestive of extrasensory perception, such as when a woman has a vivid dream of her husband being killed in a car accident the night before he is involved in a fatal collision with a drunk driver who has crossed into his lane. We will also examine cases suggestive of strange physical phenomena, such as those occurring in poltergeist outbreaks. More inflammatory topics, such as spontaneous human combustion, will not escape our notice.

The proof that such paranormal powers as ESP even exist will unfortunately lie elsewhere than in the pudding. Skeptics can always claim that there are plenty of nervous women who periodically dream about their husbands dying in car crashes. Sooner or later, they argue, one of these husbands is bound to be taken out by a drunk driver or to drive his Porsche through a department store window. Thus, nothing more than coincidence may be involved in such cases. For this reason parapsychologists have turned to experimental studies to prove the existence of such paranormal powers as ESP or psychokinesis (the power of mind over matter). In such experiments, subjects may guess the order of the cards in a shuffled deck that is hidden from their view. They may try to use their psychokinetic powers to influence the outcome of the roll of a pair of dice or to influence the motion of a group of balls cascading down a chute. Whether such experiments have succeeded in proving the existence of ESP and psychokinesis will not be an easy issue to resolve. We will be forced to look at science at its ugliest, from the prejudice of irrational skeptics to fraud and incompetence on the part of some (but by no means all) of the experimental workers in the field.

Following that, we will consider possible theories that have been proposed to account for such paranormal phenomena. These will include attempts to explain precognition (the apparent ability to foresee the future) in terms of physical particles that travel backward in time, such as tachyons, or in terms of warps in spacetime itself. We will see that modern theories of physics themselves carry the seeds of destruction of the Newtonian worldview that all things are composed of elementary particles existing independently of one another. Indeed, we will find that even two protons separated by light years of space cannot be viewed as separate entities under modern theories of quantum mechanics, but must be considered to be intimately interconnected. If even two simple protons can no longer be thought of as separate from one another, it follows that our seemingly isolated individual minds may be more intimately connected than we think. Like protons, our individual selves can no longer be thought of as encapsulated entities, shut off from the outside world and from each other.

We will also examine speculations (and evidence) that minds may comprise the "hidden variables" determining the outcomes of quantum processes. According to modern theories of physics, at any given moment of time an infinite number of different futures are possible. It may be within the power of our minds to determine which of those futures we experience. Finally, we will consider the possibility that psi phenomena (ESP and psychokinesis) point to the existence of a collective mind transcending the psyches of individual persons.

The book's final chapters will be devoted to a consideration of the mind's fate upon the death of the physical body. This discussion will force us to consider in detail the relationship between the conscious mind and the physical brain and will require us to delve rather deeply into the philosophical quagmire that has become known as the mind-body problem. We will then consider the evidence that our minds may survive the death of our bodies. This evidence ranges from the provocative to the frankly silly. It encompasses messages uttered by mediums allegedly possessed by the spirits of the dead, run-ins with ghosts, and people who claimed to have died, seen the other side and hustled back to life in New Jersey. We will discuss cases in which children spontaneously report seemingly accurate memories of previous lives at a distant location, as well as suburbanites who remember previous lives as Marie Bonaparte while undergoing hypnotherapy and massage. In fact, as we will see, the dead are thought by some to be not above placing occasional phone calls from the beyond or serving as disk jockeys on their own radio stations.

These discussions will force us to return to a consideration of the true nature of the self. We will examine the existing scientific evidence regarding the role of the brain in shaping our personalities and in storing our memories. One's true self, it will be suggested, may be at once infinitely more and considerably less than the cloak of particular emotions and idiosyncratic memories that we wear through this life. Finally, we will briefly consider the possibility that minds may play a truly grand role in the cosmic scheme of things, possibly even being responsible for the creation of the cosmos itself.

We will begin our journey with a consideration of some rather strange experiences happening to ordinary citizens as they go about their daily lives. These experiences will be the basis of all that is to follow.

2. Spontaneous Psi

The experience of psi phenomena in everyday life takes many forms. One woman in Wisconsin awoke from a nightmare in which she saw her husband standing in the bedroom door with his face all bloody and beaten up. His clothing was covered with blood. He told her not to be alarmed and said, "I just had a little accident." She jumped out of bed, turned on the light and found that there was no one there. An hour-and-a-half later, she was awakened again when her husband opened the bedroom door. The scene of the nightmare was repeated. His face and clothing were all bloody, and he told her not to be alarmed, saying "I just had a little accident." It turned out that two men had beaten him up over an old grudge.[1]

In most instances psi intrudes upon a person's life on only a few occasions. There are, however, some types of phenomena that tend to occur repeatedly within a relatively short time span. Most prominent among these are poltergeist effects.

In poltergeist outbreaks, objects may move inexplicably, seemingly of their own volition, and electrical apparatus may misbehave, starting, stopping and malfunctioning for no apparent reason. In one such case, reported by the parapsychologist A.R.G. Owen,[2] an 11-year-old girl living in the town of Sauchie in Scotland was beset by all sorts of strange phenomena. Loud knocks were repeatedly heard in her room, and a large, heavy linen chest rose from the ground and moved in a rocking motion over distances of up to 18 inches on more than one occasion while she was lying on the bed. Her pillow was seen to rotate beneath her while her head was resting on it. At school, the desk behind her reportedly rose about an inch in the air and then settled back down. Her teacher's desk began to vibrate to the extent that a blackboard pointer rolled off it, and the table itself began to rotate.

Poltergeist effects will be discussed more fully in Chapter 3. Other categories of spontaneous phenomena directly suggest that the mind or some part of the mind may survive the death of the physical body. These include the apparent sightings of ghosts, messages from the dead delivered by mediums, and cases in which children report apparent memories of previous lives. Discussion of these phenomena will be postponed until the final section of the book, which focuses on the evidence that there may be a life after death as well as the general role of conscious minds in a physical cosmos.

Encounters with the Paranormal

We will begin our study of spontaneous psi phenomena by examining such events as precognitive dreams, intuitions of danger and the sudden stopping of clocks at the time of a person's death. One of the foremost investigators of such strange happenings was Dr. Louisa Rhine, the wife and colleague of Dr. J.B. Rhine, the man who is widely regarded as the founder of the field of experimental parapsychology. Over a period of several decades, she amassed a vast collection of over 10,000 cases of apparently paranormal events, which were mailed to her, often in response to articles in the popular press, over a period of several decades. She partitioned the experiences suggesting the operation of an ESP capacity into four main groups: hallucinatory experiences, intuitive experiences, realistic dreams and unrealistic dreams. She established a fifth, "wastebasket" category of "indeterminate type" for experiences that were difficult to assign unambiguously to one of the four previously mentioned categories. Cases involving hallucinations while asleep (hypnagogic imagery) or waking up (hypnopompic imagery) might fall into this indeterminate category, along with cases involving mixed features.

Rhine's first category, hallucinatory experiences, comprises, as one might suspect, cases involving visual, auditory, olfactory or tactile hallucinations that seem to correspond to a distant or future event and in which the hallucinating person would seem to have no normal means of acquiring knowledge about the event. Such hallucinations suggest the existence of a channel of information transmission outside of the known physical senses.

The following is an apparent case of hallucinatory ESP taken from the early investigations of the Society for Psychical Research, an organization of prominent scientists and scholars founded in England in 1882 to study such anomalous events and which is still in existence today[3]:

On Thursday evening, 14th November, 1867, I was sitting in the Birmingham Town Hall with my husband at a concert, when there came over me the icy chill which usually accompanies these occurrences. Almost immediately, I saw with perfect distinctness, between myself and the orchestra, my uncle, Mr. W., lying in bed with an appealing look on his face, like one dying. I had not heard of him for several months, and had no reason to think he was ill. The appearance was not transparent or filmy, but perfectly solid-looking; and yet I could somehow see the orchestra, not through, but behind it. I did not try turning my eyes to see whether the figure moved with them, but looked at it with a fascinated expression that made my husband ask if I was ill. I asked him not to speak with me for a minute or two; the vision gradually disappeared, and I told

my husband, after the concert was over, what I had seen. A letter came shortly
after telling of my uncle's death. He died at exactly the time when I saw the
vision.

A second case involving a visual hallucination was provided to the Society by a Mrs. Bettany[4]:

I was walking along in a country lane at A, the place where my parents
then resided. I was reading geometry as I walked along ... when in a moment I
saw a bedroom known as the White Room in my home, and upon the floor lay
my mother, to all appearance dead. The vision must have remained some minutes, during which time my real surroundings appeared to pale and die out; but
as the vision faded, actual surroundings came back, at first dimly, and then
clearly. I could not doubt that what I had seen was real, so instead of going
home, I went at once to the house of our medical man and found him at home.
He at once set out with me for my home, on the way putting questions I could
not answer, as my mother was to all appearance well when I left home. I led the
doctor straight to the White Room, where we found my mother actually lying
as in my vision. This was true even to minute details. She had been seized suddenly by an attack of the heart, and would soon have breathed her last but for
the doctor's timely advent. I shall get my mother and father to read and sign
this.

In response to questioning, Mrs. Bettany stated that she was not feeling
anxious about her mother at the time of her death. She also noted that she
had found a handkerchief with a lace border beside her mother on the floor,
a detail which corresponded to her vision. Her father, upon being interviewed,
corroborated his daughter's statement and added that, so far as he was able to
tell, his wife was taken ill after his daughter had left the house. Of course, in
this case a determined skeptic could argue that the daughter might have subconsciously noticed subtle signs of cardiopulmonary distress before the full
blown heart attack occurred. Such a phenomenon is known as "sensory cueing" and will be discussed in more detail below.

Hallucinatory experiences frequently involve senses other than vision. A
typical auditory hallucination might consist of hearing your mother's voice
calling you at the exact time that she is experiencing some sort of physical
crisis at a distant location. Smell, kinesthesia (muscle sense), pain and other
sensory modalities may also be involved. The Finnish folklorist Leea Virtanen notes that cases involving the parallel experiencing of physical symptoms
of disease and injury are quite common and most often occur between parent
and child.[5]

One of my own students in a parapsychology course I taught as a graduate student at the University of Michigan told me that his father was knocked

off a bench he was sitting on by an invisible blow to the jaw. A few minutes later he received a call from the health club where his wife was working out informing him that his wife had just broken her jaw on a piece of gymnastic equipment. This story is admittedly thirdhand and based on what amounts to hearsay evidence; a very similar and much better documented case was, however, uncovered by the early investigators of the Society for Psychical Research. In that case a woman related how she had been awoken from her sleep at 7:00 A.M. by what she thought was a hard blow to her jaw. She in fact thought she had been cut and put her handkerchief to her mouth to stem the flow of blood. She was at first astonished to find that her mouth was not bleeding, but soon realized that it was extremely unlikely that she had really been struck by a hard object while she was alone in her bedroom sleeping. When her husband appeared for breakfast at 9:30, he sat far away from her and periodically put his handkerchief to his lip the way his wife had herself done two hours previously. She told him that she knew he had hurt himself and that she would tell him why shortly. He then admitted that he had gone for an early sail on the lake, and had been struck in the mouth by the tiller of the boat when a sudden squall had come up. When she asked him the time of the accident, he told her that it had happened around seven. She then told him of her dream. Both the husband and the wife made statements to investigators from the S.P.R. testifying to the veracity of the story.[6]

Intuitive ESP experiences are usually characterized by a sudden feeling that something is wrong with a particular person or place. This feeling is often accompanied by a compulsion to take some form of action. One such case is provided by Ian Stevenson, the former chairperson of the Department of Psychiatry at the University of Virginia and one of the most active modern investigators of spontaneous cases. A couple had gone to congratulate two of their friends on the birth of their child. While they were being shown blueprints of their friends' new house, the husband was seized by a feeling that something bad had happened at home. He asked his wife to call home. She said she would in a few minutes, but he insisted that she do so right away, saying "You'd better call now. Something is wrong." When the wife called, a neighbor answered the phone and she could hear both of her children screaming in the background. It turned out that the children's grandmother, who had been babysitting for them, had hurt her back a few minutes before the phone call, and the children were quite frightened about it. Stevenson obtained testimony from both the husband and the wife. The latter added that the husband had never before displayed strong anxiety about what might be wrong at home and had never previously asked her to telephone a babysitter.[7]

Intuitive experiences need not involve negative events such as the above. A "lucky hunch" might qualify as an intuitive experience, for instance. What sets intuitive experiences apart from the other categories of paranormal experience is the absence of visual imagery or other forms of hallucination.

The third major mode of ESP experience is that of dreams. Louisa Rhine divided dream cases into those involving "realistic dreams," which correspond closely in detail to the confirming event, and "unrealistic dreams," which she defined as containing "a bit of imagination, fantasy and even symbolism."[8] As one example of symbolism, she offered the case of a woman who tended to dream of heavy black smoke prior to tragic events.

The following account, taken from Rhine's collection,[9] is an example of a realistic dream. It was provided to Rhine by the district manager of a sheet and tin plate company. The experience occurred shortly before he and several business associates were to return home from a two week vacation in the wilderness, where they had been cut off from all news sources.

The night before they were to return home, the district manager had a dream, so clear, so vivid, he could not sleep afterward. In it, he writes, "one of our locomotive cranes that was unloading a car of scrap iron, together with the car, was on the track near the bank of a river alongside the water tower which served the locomotives. For some unaccountable reason, as the huge magnet swung around with a heavy load of scrap, it suddenly toppled over the river bank. The operator, whom I called by name, jumped clear of the crane and landed below it as it came bounding, tumbling and bouncing down the river bank, and he finally disappeared from view as the crane came to rest twenty feet below at the water's edge. I particularly noted the number of the crane and the number and positions of the railroad cars, and was able to tell how the crane operator was dressed. Furthermore, I noticed the approximate damage done to the crane. I did not know, however, what had finally happened to the operator. He had disappeared under or behind the crane after it had come to rest. In other words, I was observing the accident from somewhere in or across the river.

"Upon my return to the mill the following day, the first man I met was the master mechanic. He told me to come with him to inspect the crane of my dream, to talk with the operator who had emerged from the accident without a scratch. The operator explained his lack of injury by the fact that the crane had fallen over in front of him as he made his last jump and as it made its last bounce. The record showed the smallest detail to be as I had dreamed it, with one exception. The exception was that the accident had happened two hours after the dream."

Among Rhine's examples of symbolic dreams is a case in which a woman had a series of dreams in each of which the symbol of an avenue of trees seemed to be used to dramatize an impending death. The first such dream occurred when the woman was a 12-year-old girl. She had fallen asleep in a swing in the yard of her house and dreamed that she had seen her mother walking down a beautiful avenue of trees. She ran after her, realized that she was not going to be able to catch up to her and then called out to her. She turned, put up her hand and said, "Go back my daughter, your father needs you."

When she woke up, she immediately went into the house. Her father greeted her, embraced her and informed her that her mother had just died.

About 12 years after the first dream, the second dream occurred. Her brother was ill in a hospital in another state. She was herself ill and could not be with him. The night he died, she dreamed that he too was walking down the same avenue of trees. She tried to catch up to him but he told her to go back. (As we will see later, these dreams bear some resemblance to near-death experiences, in which the experiencing parties are told that it is not yet time for them to die and that they must return to life.) As it turned out, her brother died at the approximate time of the dream.

In the third dream, she saw her husband quickly walking down the same avenue of trees. He too put up his hand and said, "Our precious children need you—go back." The dream frightened her and she put her arms around her husband awakening him. He announced that he was feeling very sick, and he died a few minutes later.

Of course, the astute skeptic might note that in each of the above dreams, the woman might have had some reason to expect that the person's death was imminent. In the last case, she may have subliminally heard sounds of her husband's physical distress as she slept. Such objections would be more difficult to raise in the case of the fourth dream, in which the woman dreamed that her daughter and her girlfriend, who had gone to a dance, were involved in a fatal accident in front of her home. The same avenue of trees came into play in the dream. Needless to say, the woman was quite relieved when the girls returned safely home from the dance around 1:00 A.M. The very next night the daughters had a dance in their house. The girlfriend of her daughter that had appeared in the dream was in fact killed within a block of her house as she was on her way home. The woman noted that the accident was "just as I had dreamed it."[10]

It is of course possible that the woman had observed that the girlfriend was a reckless driver; Rhine's account provides us with no information on this point.

The psychiatrist Berthold Schwarz provides the following case, which incorporates both realistic and symbolic elements[11]:

Bartholomew A. Ruggieri, M.D., my friend and hardworking neighbor pediatrician wrote this memo: "On the afternoon of Sunday, June 2, 1968, I went up to my room to nap. I slept fitfully, from about 2:30 P.M. to 5–5:30 P.M. During this time I dreamed that I was at an upper story window facing Avenue B and Sixth Street in New York City, and saw a 'parade' of mourners approaching as pictured [diagram drawn by Dr. R]. It was more a mass of mourners than a parade. They carried a banner with a religious connotation and ending with the words: '...KENNEDY ASSASSINATION.' I know the area very well, having lived my youth there, but to my knowledge I have never lived on Avenue B. I awoke, vividly recalling all the words on the banner, felt I should get up and write them down, but did not do so. I lay in bed and, after a period of drowsiness, again fell asleep. Somehow in my mind I associated this to the imminent assassination of Robert Kennedy (Bobby). The Avenue B would support this. The same evening (6/2/68) sitting at my desk at 9:30 P.M., I phoned Dr. B. E. Schwarz, described the dream, and said I felt Bobby Kennedy would be assassinated on the 6th of June. Note 'Sixth' Street: June is the sixth month."

While it is true that Robert Kennedy was shot on June 5, 1968, he died on the sixth. Dr. Schwarz told his wife of Dr. Ruggieri's dream on the evening of June 2, 1968.

Rex Stanford has pointed to one possible type of psi experience that may be missed in Louisa Rhine's classification scheme. This category encompasses cases in which a person takes an action that is appropriate to a situation when the person has no normally acquired knowledge (or any conscious paranormally acquired knowledge) that the situation even exists. Presumably, in such cases the person is acting on the basis of information provided by ESP at an unconscious level. Stanford uses the term "psi-mediated instrumental response," or PMIR, to describe such events.[12] ("Psi" is a generic term parapsychologists use to refer to both ESP and PK.) As an example, he cites the case of a retired New York attorney who was traveling to Greenwich Village to drop in on two artist friends. He had to change subway trains, and upon leaving the first train, he claimed that he "absent-mindedly" walked out through the gate and was halfway up the stairs to the street before he realized that he had intended to switch trains. Not wishing to pay another fare, he decided to walk the additional six blocks south. He then ran into his friends, who had left their home and were walking north along the same route on their way to an appointment.

One reason why examples of PMIR may be relatively rare in collections of spontaneous cases may be that the people involved in such cases do not typically have any awareness of possessing paranormally acquired knowledge and are consequently likely to attribute their experiences to luck or coincidence rather than to the operation of ESP or PK (the usual abbreviation for psychokinesis). Stanford suggests that cases of PMIR may be occurring frequently without the people involved being aware that anything unusual is going on.

Rhine's second major category of paranormal experiences involves puzzling physical effects, such as the stopping of a clock at the time of the owner's death or a person's portrait falling off a wall at or near the time of the person's death. One of her cases involved a man in Wisconsin who died in an easy chair in his living room. The watch in his vest pocket and the large clock in the living were both found to have stopped, each at the approximate time of the man's death.[13]

Not all of Rhine's clock cases involved the stopping of timepieces. Occasionally, timepieces were reported to have behaved aberrantly at the time of a death. One woman gave an account of a case in which a clock that normally chimed only on the hour chimed once at 7:20 P.M., surprising the woman and her parents. Five minutes later, they received a phone call informing them that their mother's sister had died of a heart attack at 7:20. This was the only occasion on which the clock chimed at a time other than on the hour.[14] Ian Wilson describes a similar case involving the late Pope Paul VI. At the time of the Pope's death (9:40 P.M. on August 6, 1978), his bedroom alarm clock, which had always been set to 6:30 A.M., inexplicably rang.[15]

Objects are occasionally reported to fall or break at the time of a significant crisis to a person associated with the object, as in the following case from Louisa Rhine's collection[16]:

A woman in Nevada tells of an experience which centered on her elder brother Frank. He was an especially thoughtful boy who did many things to please his mother, to whom he was very close. She says: "One day he came home with a beautiful cut-glass dish. Mom thought it was just about the most wonderful thing that ever happened to her and put it on our sideboard.

"When the rest of us had chicken pox, my brother Frank was sent down to my grandmother's in Grand Haven, Michigan, which was about forty miles from where we lived, although Mother was reluctant to have him go. Two days after Frank left, Mom and our neighbor were having their morning coffee and talking, and we children were told to be quiet. All of a sudden, this cut-glass dish that Frank had given Mother popped and broke right in two. It was just sitting on the sideboard. Mother screamed and said, 'My God! Frank has just been killed.' Everyone tried to quiet Mother, but she said she just knew.

"About an hour after, or a little more, we received a telegram from Grandpa which said to come right away, something had happened to Frank. Mom said, 'I know.' She cried all the way going to Grand Haven, and Grandpa met us at the train. Before Grandpa could tell us what happened, Mom cried, 'At what funeral parlor is he?' Grandpa just stood there with his mouth open and Mom ran right up the street and went to the place Frank was without being told. The wouldn't let her see him because a terrible thing had happened.

"The boy next door to Grandfather was home from school and his parents were not at home, so he started playing with his father's shotgun, and came outside, showing it to Frank. The boy, not knowing it was loaded, pulled the trigger and killed my brother. The strange thing—Frank was shot at the same time the dish broke."

Cases involving physical effects are relatively rare. In an article written in the early 1960s, Rhine noted that her case collection at that point contained only 178 physical effect cases, in comparison to over 10,000 ESP cases.[17] Of those 178 cases, 65 involved falling objects, 49 involved the stopping or erratic movement of timepieces, 21 involved breaking or exploding objects, 17 involved lights turning on and off by themselves, 14 involved the sudden opening or closing of doors and 12 involved rocking and moving objects (half of which were rocking chairs). In 37 of the 49 clock cases, the clocks stopped at the time of death of a person associated with the clock. In 18 of the 65 cases involving falling objects, the object in question was a picture or portrait of a person undergoing a crisis, such as a serious accident or death, at the time of the object's movement. Thirteen other such objects bore a special relationship to a person undergoing a crisis at the time of the event.

Sometimes it is difficult to know whether a physical effect or an hallucination is involved. For instance, perceived raps or voices could simply be auditory hallucinations. On the other hand, they might be caused by real physical sound waves. One way to decide which is the case would be to see if such sounds can be collectively perceived (that is, can be heard by more than one person). In an attempt to resolve this issue, Louisa Rhine examined instances in which more than one person was present when the sound was heard. In 68 such cases involving vocal sounds, the sounds were heard by a second person only 28 percent of the time, whereas mechanical sounds, such as raps, were collectively perceived in 93 percent of the 63 cases involved.[18] In her study of Finnish cases, Virtanen also found voice sounds to be collectively perceived less frequently than "noisy" sounds such as bumps, thuds and rattles,[19] as did Rinaldi and Piccinni in their door-to-door survey of cases in the South Tyrol section of Italy.[20] Taken together, these data suggest that cases involving mechanical or "noisy" sounds involve real physical effects more often than do cases involving vocal sounds (which are more likely to be hallucinations).

A similar controversy surrounds cases in which someone experiences the apparition of a person near the time that the person was dying or experiencing a serious crisis at a location distant from the observer. In a case unearthed by the early investigators of the Society for Psychical Research, a man who was staying in Paris, and was consequently separated from his five-year-old son in London, was awakened by the sound of his son's voice at 7:30 A.M. He then saw a bright, opaque white mass before his eyes, and in the center of the light he saw the smiling face of his son. He later learned that his son had died at the exact time of the apparition.[21]

In this case the child's apparition could be interpreted as a telepathically induced hallucination or some sort of ghost existing in physical space. If several observers are present when an apparition appears and only one of them sees it, it would seem reasonable to assume that the apparition was an hallucination. On the other hand, if several of the witnesses simultaneously see the apparition, it would seem more reasonable to assume that some sort of physical ghost had put in an appearance. To see which was the case, G.N.M. Tyrrell, a prominent authority on ghosts and apparitions, looked at 1,087 apparitional cases collected by the researchers of the Society for Psychical Research.[22] He found that in 283 of those cases more than one person was present at the time the apparition was seen. In 95 of these 283 cases, the apparition was seen by more than one person.[23] In a later study, Hornell Hart found 46 cases in the literature satisfying the more restrictive criterion that the secondary witnesses present were clearly situated in such a manner that they would have been able to see the apparition had it been a physical object. In 26 of those cases, the apparition was seen by at least two observers.[24] In a more recent survey of apparitional experiences conducted through the mail, the Icelandic parapsychologist Erlendur Haraldsson found that a second potential observer was present in about half of the apparitional encounters reported. In about one-fourth of these cases, the respondent stated that the apparitional experience was shared by such secondary observers.[25] Thus, it is difficult to tell on the basis of collective perception whether such experiences involve mere hallucinations or physical ghosts.

The physical ghost theory was favored by the early psychical researcher Frederic W.H. Myers, who called his ghosts "metetherial presences."[26] Myers' contemporary Edmund Gurney believed that cases in which apparitions were sighted by more than one person could be explained by assuming that hallucinations could spread telepathically from one mind to another.[27] Myers argued against Gurney's theory that hallucinations can spread telepathically on the basis of the fact that the hallucinations of the insane are not in general particularly contagious. Other theorists, including Tyrrell and the philosopher H.H. Price, speculated that witnesses to apparitional cases share a deep region of the unconscious mind that may be termed the "collective unconscious" and that it is in this deep region of the mind that the apparitional image is constructed (which then emerges from the collective unconscious into the individual consciousness of the witnesses).[28] Finally, the American parapsychologist Karlis Osis has suggested that we call it a draw and assume that some apparitions are ghosts and others are hallucinations.[29]

Research Findings Relating to Spontaneous Cases

A large number of surveys have been conducted in an attempt to determine how many people have had experiences suggestive of ESP or PK. The results of these surveys, taken together, suggest that somewhere between one-third and one-half of the population claims to have had some sort of psi experience, and that this proportion seems to be fairly independent of culture and nationality.

Dreams appear to be the most common type of ESP experience, with intuitive experiences being the next most common and hallucinatory experiences the least common form. For instance, in one statistical analysis of her own collection reported by Louisa Rhine, 65 percent of the experiences were dreams, roughly a quarter were intuitive experiences and the remaining 10 percent were of the hallucinatory variety.[30] One finding that is fairly consistent across case studies is that dreams tend to be precognitive (that is to involve the apparent paranormal perception of future events), whereas waking experiences (including intuitive and hallucinatory cases) seem more often to refer to contemporaneous events.[31]

Dream experiences usually contain more detail and more complete information about the event than do intuitive experiences, whereas intuitive experiences tend to produce a greater sense of conviction that the experience refers to a real event and is more likely to lead the percipient to take some sort of action related to the event.[32]

A great many more women report having ESP experiences than do men. Whether this is due to enhanced sensitivity or psychic powers on the part of women or is due to a lesser reluctance on the part of women to report such experiences is not clear. As might be expected, spontaneous cases typically involve the anomalous knowledge of events happening to members of the percipient's immediate family rather than events happening to strangers or casual acquaintances. In general, the events that are perceived through ESP are negative ones involving death or serious injury to a close family member. Hardly ever does the experience relate to damage to material objects rather than to people.[33]

There has been a recent flurry of efforts attempting to relate activity of the Earth's magnetic field to the incidence rate of spontaneous psi cases as well as to success rates in parapsychological experiments. The chief element in this flurry has been the Canadian psychologist Michael Persinger, who has authored a series of papers on the subject.[34] In analyzing several case collections, Persinger has found global geomagnetic activity typically to be lower on the days of reported ESP experiences than on the days surrounding the day of the experience. This finding applies chiefly to cases in which the alleged psychic experience was nearly simultaneous with the confirming event. It does not hold in cases involving precognition nor does it hold for apparitional experiences which occur some days after the perceived person's death. There have been quite a few attempts to relate geomagnetic activity to obtained success in ESP experiments, but no unequivocal trend has emerged from these.[35]

Persinger[36] proposes two theories to account for apparent cases of spontaneous ESP. The first theory involves a direct signal transmitting information between the two parties involved in an apparent case of telepathy. In the second theory, it is assumed that some external factor causes the two people to have similar experiences. For instance, as a mathematics teacher, I know that on certain mornings, often rainy ones, my students all come to class in a stuporous mood. Would it not be possible that low barometric pressure might cause the "percipient" in an apparent case of spontaneous telepathy to be in a gloomy mood and also to cause one of the percipient's closest friends, who is a chronic depressive, to commit suicide by driving her car off a cliff? The percipient might then interpret his apparent gloom as being due to a paranormal awareness of his friend's death. Persinger's second theory is thus a theory of pseudo–ESP phenomena rather than of true ESP in that it denies the existence of an anomalous channel of information transmission. It is obviously conceivable that geomagnetic activity may have similar effects on the mood or behavior of two related persons and thus may generate a case of pseudotelepathy as suggested by Persinger's second theory.

With regard to the first theory, Persinger conjectures that geomagnetic activity may enhance the receptivity of the brain to extrasensory signals, noting in particular that sudden decreases in geomagnetic activity may decrease the likelihood of certain types of electrical seizures in the brain. Persinger contends that increases in geomagnetic activity tend to lower seizure thresholds and may even precipitate convulsions in epileptics. Some scientists have, however, expressed skepticism that changes in the geomagnetic field would have sufficient strength to produce any physiological effects on the human body at all.[37]

As a second possibility, Persinger suggests that lowered geomagnetic activity might enhance the signal carrying the ESP message, which he has speculated may consist in part of extremely low frequency electromagnetic radiation, which are also called (perhaps appropriately in this context) ELF waves.[38] Persinger's ELF wave theory of ESP will be discussed in more detail in Chapter 6, in which theories about ESP are explored.

Psychological Processes

Many parapsychologists have proposed that extrasensory perception is a two-stage process from a psychological point of view. Both G.N.M. Tyrrell[39] and Louisa Rhine[40] proposed that the information obtained through ESP is first received at an unconscious level of the mind and then emerges into consciousness in the form of an hallucination, dream or intuitive feeling that something is wrong. Rhine suggested that emotional reactions, impulses toward action, and feelings of conviction about the reality of the sensed situation may emerge into consciousness independently of the factual information relating to the sensed event, especially in intuitive cases. K. Ramakrishna Rao, J.B. Rhine's successor as director of the Institute for Parapsychology in Durham, North Carolina, observes that minor details may have more difficulty penetrating the barrier between the unconscious and conscious regions of the mind than more emotionally important elements might have. He indicates that this may be a reason for the failure of many experiments in the laboratory that require subjects to guess the identity of emotionally trivial targets such as ESP cards.[41] His views in this regard are similar to those of the psychoanalyst Jan Ehrenwald, who postulated that the weakness of ESP effects in the laboratory may be due to the fact that the ESP message is typically much less relevant to the needs of the subject in laboratory experiments than it is in spontaneously

occurring cases of extrasensory perception.[42] Thus, Ehrenwald suggested, laboratory cases of extrasensory perception depend for their success on flaws in
the "filter" that the French philosopher Henri Bergson proposed existed to
screen out noncrucial information so that the conscious mind could focus on
immediate problems relevant to the biological survival of the body.[43] After
all, it will not do to engage in clairvoyant voyeurism of an orgy down the
street if one's house is burning down around one.

Sigmund Freud, the founder of psychoanalysis, proposed a model of
telepathy similar to Tyrrell's and Rhine's. Freud had a lifelong interest in parapsychology, or psychical research as it was called at the time. He was a member of both the American and British Societies for Psychical Research, and
in 1921 he went so far as to write the American psychical researcher Hereward Carrington that, if he were at the stage of embarking on a career rather
than ending one, he would perhaps choose psychical research! The psychiatrist E. Fuller Torrey reports that Freud even claimed to have had telepathic
contact with his fiancée Martha Bernays.[44] Many of his thoughts on telepathy were, however, suppressed from publication during his lifetime under the
influence of his disciple Ernest Jones for fear of undermining the credibility
of the psychoanalytic movement.

Freud assumed that, if telepathy existed, the same dynamic processes
would govern the emergence of psi information into consciousness as governed
the emergence of other unconscious material. As an example, Freud reported
the case of a man who dreamed that his wife gave birth to twins at the same
time that his daughter gave birth to twins in real life. Predictably enough,
Freud attributed the distortion of the telepathic message to the man's unconscious wish that his daughter be his wife.[45]

The Australian psychologist Harvey J. Irwin likewise feels that repression may prevent ESP messages from emerging into consciousness. As a possible example of such suppression, he cites a case of Louisa Rhine's in which
a woman began to sob uncontrollably for 20 minutes before a huge decora-
tive vase fell off its shelf. Later she learned that her father had died about that
time. Presumably, as her conscious mind blocked out the ESP signal, her unconscious mind was forced to move the vase psychokinetically in order to dramatize the message and get it through to consciousness.[46]

Skeptical Explanations of Spontaneous Cases

Critics of spontaneous case investigations are quick to point out that
there are many explanations besides ESP and psychokinesis that might account
for apparent cases of paranormal phenomena. First, the cases may be due to
coincidence. For instance, consider a case in which a man is overcome by a
sense of impending doom, breaks out in a cold sweat and refuses to board an

airplane, and then later learns that the plane crashed upon landing at its destination. It might be quite plausible to assume that many people back out of imminent airplane flights because of sudden feelings of nervousness and anxiety. Occasionally, the planes involved in some of these flights may crash, thus producing what looks like a spontaneous case of intuitive ESP when really all that is involved is simple coincidence. Similarly, people may frequently dream of the death of one of their parents. When such a dream happens by chance to fall on the night preceding the parent's actual death, another spurious precognition case is generated.

Richard Broughton, a prominent parapsychological researcher who is currently the director of the Rhine Research Center in Durham, has noted that explanations in terms of coincidence are not particularly plausible when applied to experiences involving hallucinations or psychosomatic pain.[47] For instance, recall the case of my student's father who was knocked off a bench by an "invisible blow to the jaw" at the time that his wife broke her jaw on a piece of gymnastic equipment. Surely, it would be absurd to argue with regard to such a case that men are constantly being knocked off benches by invisible blows to the jaw and that sooner or later one of these events is bound to occur simultaneously with the breaking of the jaw of a member of the man's immediate family.

Despite the implausibility of coincidence explanations in hallucination cases, the early investigators of the Society for Psychical Research attempted to perform a statistical analysis to rule out the coincidence hypothesis in the case of crisis apparitions. They conducted what they called a "Census of Hallucinations" in order to find out how often people experienced apparitions of human figures. They found that, of the apparitions reported to them, 1 in 63 occurred within 12 hours of the death of the person whose apparition was experienced. Based on existing death rates, the investigating committee concluded that only 1 in 19,000 such hallucinations would occur so close to the death of the appearing figure by chance.[48] One could certainly quibble with this analysis. For instance, it could readily be imagined that cases in which a person's apparition was experienced in close proximity to the time of his death would make a deep impression on a person and might therefore be more easily remembered than other hallucinations of human figures, thus artificially inflating the proportion in the sample.

A second, more informal statistical argument is provided by the Italian investigators Rinaldi and Piccinini, who conducted a door-to-door survey related to psychic experiences in the South Tyrol region of Italy.[49] By interviewing informants about deaths in the family, they found that 1 in 12 deaths were accompanied by a paranormal experience related to the death. When only sudden deaths were considered, one in six deaths were the target event in a reported psi experience. It strains one's credulity, they argue, to assume that such a high proportion can be accounted for by chance coincidence.

A special form of the coincidence explanation is what the Dutch para-psychologist Sybo Schouten calls the "worry" hypothesis.[50] Schouten observes that the large number of psychic experiences that involve death or injury to members of the percipient's immediate family might be due to a combination of coincidence and the tendency of persons to think and worry about close family members. In a survey aimed at examining this hypothesis, Schouten found people's predominant worries to be about daily matters, material things, their present psychological situation and events happening to themselves rather than the traumatic events to others that are frequently the subject matter in spontaneous cases of ESP.

In general, any attempt to assess the actual probability that the evidence from spontaneous cases is due to chance coincidence, whether performed by the proponent of psi phenomena or the skeptic, is fraught with pitfalls. Such calculations rely on too many debatable and hidden assumptions, and the data are subject to too many distorting factors to allow any definitive assessment to be made. This is one of the reasons why parapsychologists have largely turned from the study of spontaneous cases to the study of psi processes in experimental situations, in which the probability that the results are due to chance can be more or less precisely calculated.

A second problem pointed out by critics of spontaneous case investigations is that what appears to be anomalously acquired knowledge may in fact represent information that has been consciously or unconsciously acquired through the normal sensory channels or may be based on unconscious inference from such information. For instance, a woman's husband may be exhibiting a depressed mood, increasingly reckless driving, and a decidedly morbid interest in automobile accidents on the evening news while polishing off his final two six packs of beer. She may then unconsciously infer that he is becoming suicidal or at least dangerously alcoholic, and her unconscious mind may present this conclusion to her in the form of a dream in which her husband is involved in a fatal car accident. If her inference is accurate and her husband is subsequently killed when his car collides with a pickup truck, an apparent case of spontaneous psi, which is really due to unconscious inference, is generated. Similarly, a trapeze artist may subliminally perceive a frayed wire and consequently have an apparently premonitory dream of her partner's fall to his death. I myself once had a dream that my wife had run out of gas in her car. About two hours after the dream, she called me up to tell me that she had run out of gas on her way to work. The gas gauge on her car was broken at the time, so it is quite possible that I had unconsciously inferred that she was about to run out of gas due to the fact that the gas tank had not been filled in quite some time. For the record, my most impressive precognitive dream involved an award I once received. I dreamed that one of my star math pupils and I were seated in a dark theater. The student was eating the inner core of a tootsie roll pop, and I was eating the outside layers, which had become detached from the core. I related this dream the next day to a dream study group I was sponsoring at school (which was patterned after the experiential dream sharing/interpretation groups developed by Montague Ullman[51]). I had also made a written record of this dream for the purpose of reporting it to the group. About ten minutes after the dream group ended, I received a phone call from a reporter from the *Philadelphia Inquirer* asking me for my comments about an honor I had received. It turned out that the student of my dream had been named a Presidential Scholar (very rare honor given only to about 140 students in the country) and that he had named me as his Distinguished Teacher (probably because he was a math whiz and I was his math teacher). We were both to travel to Washington at taxpayers' expense for a week of festivities, including a meeting with President Reagan. Thus, this was a very significant event in my life. The dream seemed to symbolize the fact that my student was getting the central award, whereas I was getting a satellite award. As it transpired, due to an aggressive action taken by one of the previous year's teachers against the reporter Sam Donaldson, only the students were invited in to see the President. So I never got to meet the Gipper, although I did have lunch with George Bush (and several hundred other people). My only compensation is that I did get to watch over two hundred hours of the television comedy *F Troop* with our current Vice President Al Gore when I was in college. (As I recall, Gore was especially fond of the episodes written by Arthur Julian.)

It would be hard to explain my "tootsie roll" dream on the basis of unconscious inference, as I had no way of knowing that my student was up for this award (in fact I did not even know what a Presidential Scholar was until the reporter called me). Also, no one at the school knew of the award prior to my receiving the phone call from the reporter.

Getting back to the subject, sometimes no direct signal may be involved in an apparent case of ESP, but rather a third factor may cause both the percipient's mood and the target event. For instance, the parapsychologist Ed Cox, famous for his invention of innumerable Rube Goldberg–like devices for testing for psychokinesis, found that trains involved in accidents tend to carry significantly fewer passengers than comparable trains not involved in accidents. Cox interpreted this finding as evidence that people use their precognitive powers (consciously or unconsciously) to avoid being involved in accidents.[52] Physicist John Taylor on the other hand points out that a third factor, such as bad weather, may contribute to both the passengers' decisions not to travel and to the increased probability of an accident.[53]

A third line of criticism of spontaneous case evidence centers around the possibility that the testimony provided by the informant may not be an accurate portrayal of the events as they occurred due to distortions of memory, delusions, conscious or unconscious embellishment of a case to make it seem more impressive, and possibly outright fabrication of a case in a conscious effort to perpetrate a hoax. For instance, in the fictional case considered above, the woman may merely have dreamed of a car accident, but reported that she dreamed of her husband being killed in a collision with a pickup truck because she viewed her dream as a premonition of that event and wished to communicate that fact. Alternatively, she may have consciously added the details regarding the truck to make the dream more impressive to the researcher, a form of falsification which she may take to be benign. A third possibility is that her memory of the dream and the actual event may have been confused, so that she came to believe that she saw a pickup truck in the dream when in fact she had not. This process is known as confabulation.

In some instances, the testimony of independent witnesses can help bolster one's confidence that the experience occurred as the informant described it. For instance, a percipient may have related a precognitive dream to her family before news of the confirming event was received. In such a case, the family members may be interviewed to obtain independent confirmation that the dream in fact occurred. Such independent testimony would then constitute evidence against the hypothesis that the percipient simply made up the precognitive dream after hearing of the confirming event or that she came to believe falsely that she had had such a dream through a memory distortion process. It was the practice of the early psychical researchers, who sought to prove the existence of ESP through the analysis of spontaneous cases, to obtain such independent testimony when available, and that is still the practice of a large proportion of case investigators today. As a result, there are many cases on record in which such independent testimony corroborates the existence of the ostensible psi experience.

Memory distortion can also be minimized if written descriptions of the experience are made as soon as possible. This criterion is met by dream diary studies in which the dreams were immediately recorded, such as those reported by Schriever[54] and Sondow.[55] The subject in Schriever's study sent all her dream reports to a research institute, and Schriever eliminated all reports that did not reach the institute before the confirming event occurred. This method carries the advantages both of allowing corroboration by witnesses and of immediate recording of the experience.

Sybo Schouten found that the number of details in case reports and the length of such reports fell off as the time interval before reporting the case increased. He attributes this effect to the percipients' forgetting of details over the course of time.[56] This finding could be cited as evidence against the hypothesis that spontaneous case informants tend to "improve" their testimony or embellish their reports over time.

Psychologist Elizabeth Loftus has observed that witnesses' testimony and possibly even their memories may be distorted by leading questions posed by an interviewer. Loftus and her associates have obtained evidence in support of this view from several studies they have conducted. In one study, they found that subjects' memories could be biased by questions about a stop sign when in fact a yield sign had been presented to them. In another study, subjects were misled by questions about a nonexistent mustache.[57] Clearly, psychical researchers must be wary about altering their informants' testimony and possibly even their memories through the use of leading questions.

A less innocent possibility is that the informant may fabricate the case. Melvin Harris notes that one story, in which British troops were said to have been helped in battle by an apparition of St. George and some accompanying angels, was shown to be a falsification concocted by persons not present at the battle.[58] In his study of reported premonitions, Keith Hearne found that his respondents had elevated scores on the Lie-scale of the Eysenck Personality Inventory, which is designed to detect dissembling subjects. Furthermore, the Lie scores correlated with the alleged accuracy of the reported premonition.[59] These findings will give comfort to skeptics wishing to ascribe much of the spontaneous case evidence to fabrication.

Of course some cases of reported psi phenomena are the product of delusion or even outright insanity, as in the case of a schizophrenic man who believes that his garbageman is the reincarnation of Noah and is telepathically commanding him to build a second Ark. There is no doubt that some cases of this type are reported to parapsychological laboratories. During the year that I worked in J.B. Rhine's lab in Durham, I fielded many reports of this type. I conducted one interview with a woman who held a clear umbrella over her head the whole time in order to screen out the thoughts that were being beamed into her brain by aliens sitting in UFOs well above the planet. I talked to one couple in my office who had just traveled to the planet Pluto during the previous week. One gentleman from Yugoslavia sent us an envelope containing a series of photographs of the coffee grounds in the bottom of his cup. It turned out that aliens were creating their own self-portraits in these grounds. While cases like this may be reported to research centers, they are unlikely to find their way into the case collection of a rational parapsychologist.

Conclusions Regarding Spontaneous Cases

Most parapsychologists today do not feel that the existence of ESP and psychokinesis can be proven on the basis of spontaneous cases, as skeptics can always explain away such cases by ascribing them to coincidence, sensory cues, delusion, memory distortion, and outright falsification. While the construction of such skeptical explanations for any given case is frequently possible, often such constructions involve so many mental gymnastics that the brusque dismissal of spontaneous case material seems far too cavalier an approach to take. It is sometimes argued that, while each individual spontaneous case is like a twig that may be broken by counterexplanations in terms of normal processes, when taken as a whole the spontaneous case evidence constitutes an unbreakable bundle of sticks. Tyrrell called this the "faggot" theory.[60] (Tyrrell was using the word "faggot" as the British often do to denote a bundle of sticks.) It is true that spontaneous cases follow certain patterns (the events foreseen in precognition cases are predominantly serious health crises to close relatives, for instance) and that they do not resemble the consciously invented ghost stories that appear in the fictional literature. It could still be maintained, however, that the similarities are simply due to common patterns of human thought and behavior rather than reflecting the characteristics of an anomalous channel of information transmission.

Louisa Rhine herself initially rejected the position that the existence of psi powers (ESP and psychokinesis) could be established on the basis of spontaneous case evidence. She maintained that the existence of psi abilities had already been established through the program of experimental research led by her husband, J.B. Rhine. She saw spontaneous cases as being valuable primarily for the insights they might provide into the psi process and particularly for any suggestions they might yield for experimental work. However, JoMarie Haight, one of Rhine's coworkers, has noted that case investigations and experimental work have become essentially separate approaches to the study of psi, with very little interaction between them.[61] Rhine herself became less confident in her later years that spontaneous cases would have much of an impact on experimental approaches. She came to see the study of spontaneous cases, not as an enterprise subordinate to experimentation or as justified primarily in terms of its suggestions for experimental work, but as an independent means of investigating paranormal abilities that had value in its own right. In her words:

> Instead of isolated and concrete suggestions for experiments, the continued study of the [spontaneous] material permitted a more fundamental concept of the psi process than I could have anticipated.[62]

The brusque dismissal of spontaneous case material by many parapsychologists does a grave disservice to the field. Surely naturalistic observation is of inestimable value in any science. Much remains to be learned from the observation and study of psi phenomena as they occur in their natural setting.

Two Types of Miscellaneous Effects

I have held off until now discussing two types of phenomena that do not fall unambiguously into the category of human ESP experiences. These are déjà vu experiences and "psi-trailing" in animals.

Déjà vu. Déjà vu is the fairly familiar experience of having lived through a current situation before. For instance, a woman may be engaged in a conversation with two friends when a diminutive girl scout cookie salesperson appears at her door. She then gets the eerie sense that this exact sequence of events has happened to her before. Surveys show that the vast majority of people have had such a déjà vu experience.[63]

One explanation of the déjà vu experience would be that one has experienced a very similar situation in the past and the resultant feeling of familiarity gives one the misleading impression that one has experienced the *exact* sequence of events before (as opposed to merely a similar sequence).

Robert Efron has proposed a neurological explanation for the sense of déjà vu. Specifically, he proposes that one hemisphere of the brain may receive information about an event slightly before the other hemisphere does. The second hemisphere will consequently find information regarding the second event stored in memory by the time it becomes aware of the event, leading to the conclusion that the event has occurred previously.[64] Memory storage is still a poorly understood physiological process (if it is an entirely physiological process), so Efron's hypothesis is largely speculation with little in the way of solid data to support it. Also, it takes considerable time for a long term memory trace to consolidate. For instance, if you elect to have electrical shock applied to your brain in order to treat a recalcitrant case of severe depression, you may wake up from the treatment to find that your memories for events that occurred in the hours preceding your treatment may be gone. You may even have spotty amnesia for significant events occurring days, weeks or even years before the treatment. A similar memory loss may occur following a traumatic head injury. For instance, one of my students suffered a severe concussion when he wrapped his car around a telephone pole. He told me that he had no memory of even leaving his house to get into the car. Neuropsychologists attribute such retrograde amnesia to the disruption of the process by which long term memories are consolidated in the brain. Thus, full consolidation of a long term memory trace may take years; it certainly involves more than the few milliseconds proposed by Efron. At best Efron can assert that the memory trace is merely the sort of short term trace normally ascribed to short term memory or the very short term sensory "buffers" proposed by cognitive psychologists. It would seem likely, however, that such a short term memory trace would be recognized as referring to an immediately recent event, and would not evoke the sense of déjà vu that a long term memory trace would.

A second type of explanation of the experience of déjà vu is that one has in fact experienced the exact situation before, mainly through a precognitive experience such as a dream that has subsequently been forgotten but is still available at a subconscious level. Louisa Rhine in fact proposed an explanation of this type.[65] Some writers, such as Ian Stevenson[66] and Joe Fisher,[67] have proposed that some cases of déjà vu might be explained on the basis of reincarnation. For instance, a feeling of familiarity on entering a strange city might be due to having lived in that city in a previous life. (A variant of this type of explanation is the "eternal return" proposed by the philosopher Friedrich Nietzsche; under this hypothesis one lives one's present life over and over again.) Stevenson sees most cases of déjà vu as being susceptible to other kinds of explanations, although he notes that the few instances of déjà vu on record in which a person displays knowledge of a location he has not visited before suggest an explanation in terms of some anomalous process such as precognition or reincarnation. It is also possible that such cases might be explained in terms of cryptomnesia, or forgotten knowledge (for instance, a person may have seen a travelogue about the place in question but does not remember having seen it). In any event, instances in which a person displays detailed anomalous knowledge of a strange or unique site or situation, such as by describing what is around the next corner, go beyond the mere sense of familiarity that constitutes the experience of déjà vu and perhaps should be classed as a probable case of ESP. The experience of déjà vu itself, which involves only a strange sense of familiarity and not the anomalous possession of knowledge, is probably best not classified as a paranormal phenomenon at all (although it remains possible that such cases may involve forgotten precognitive dreams, as we have seen).

Psi-trailing. In psi-trailing cases, it is animals rather than humans who display the apparent extrasensory ability. A typical case of psi-trailing involves a pet getting lost and then apparently making its way to its owner at a distant and unfamiliar location. J.B. Rhine and his daughter, Sara Feather, compiled a collection of 48 cases of psi-trailing.[68] Of these cases, 22 involved dogs, 22 involved cats, and 4 involved birds. In one case, a business executive and his family were moving from Tulsa, Oklahoma, to a new home in Memphis, when their pet cat, Smoky, jumped out of the car 18 miles into the journey. Neighbors reported seeing Smoky two weeks later in the vicinity of the old Tulsa home. A year later, Smoky reportedly arrived on the front porch of the Memphis home. The cat was identified on the basis of its physical appearance, including a distinctive tuft of dark red hair under its chin as well as unusual behavioral characteristics, such as the cat's jumping on the daughter's right side and putting his paws on the keyboard when she was playing the piano. In a similar case, a cat was identified on the basis of a deformity in the hip joint. In yet another case, a dog apparently found its way from Aurora, Illinois, to its owner's new home in East Lansing, Michigan. In this instance, the dog was identified on the basis of its physical appearance as well as its distinctive collar. Rhine and Feather point out that in many cases the identification of the pet cannot be considered definitive. Also, the majority of their cases (18 of the 22 dog cases, 10 of the 22 cat cases, and 1 of the 4 bird cases) involved fairly short distances (less than 30 miles), raising the possibility that the animal might have been guided by its sense of smell or may have used some other sensory cue to find its owner.

3. Chasing the Poltergeist

A poltergeist disturbance typically involves strange physical events that occur repeatedly in a specific location or in the vicinity of a specific person or group of people. These physical phenomena generally include inexplicable movements of objects, such as a glass spontaneously flying off a kitchen table and hitting the kitchen floor at a considerable lateral distance from the table. Sometimes quite large objects such as heavy cabinets are involved in such movements. Frequently the motion of the object is described as being unusual in terms of curved trajectories or abnormal slowness of flight. Levitation effects have also been reported. In such cases, the beginning of the object's motion is hardly ever observed. This is sometimes called the "shyness effect," and it has been interpreted by some observers as evidence for an inhibiting effect of observation, while for others it suggests the possibility that the motions may have been fraudulently produced. William Roll, perhaps the world's foremost investigator of poltergeists, attributes the failure to observe the beginnings of movements to the fact that people do not typically attend to an object until after it is already moving.[1] Apparent materialization and teleportation effects are also reported. Occasionally, rocks are reported to materialize inside a room and drop to the floor. An apparent teleportation event might involve the sudden disappearance of an object at one physical location and its reappearance at another. Objects in poltergeist cases are usually inferred to have been teleported when they are found at an unexpected location. Again, the actual moments of disappearance and rematerialization are almost never witnessed.

Another frequently occurring poltergeist effect is the aberrant behavior of electrical apparatus. In some instances, machines such as radios, lights, and dishwashers are inexplicably turned on or off. One famous case that centered on electrical apparatus was the Rosenheim poltergeist, investigated by the German parapsychologist Hans Bender.[2] The events in this case occurred in a lawyer's office in the town of Rosenheim, Bavaria, in 1967. Neon lights were frequently found to be nonfunctioning and occasionally to have been unscrewed from their sockets. Electrical light bulbs exploded, bangs were heard, and electrical fuses blew for no apparent reason. The developing fluid in the copying machine was repeatedly found to have been spilled. The office telephones became disturbed, calls were cut off, and occasionally all four phones would ring simultaneously, with no one on the line. The telephone bills were inordinately high and reflected large numbers of calls to the number announcing the time of day. Large deflections in the power supply were found to coincide with some of the phenomena, and these continued even after a special power supply was installed to circumvent the problem.

The phenomena seemed to center around a 19-year-old girl named Annemarie Schneider. The power supply surges often occurred when she arrived for work. When she walked down the corridor, the electrical lights would start swinging behind her as she passed, a phenomenon that was successfully videotaped. When light bulbs exploded, the fragments tended to fly toward her. In general the phenomena tended to occur only in close proximity to her.

Two physicists from the Max Planck Institute were called in to monitor the power supply. They observed electrical surges accompanied by loud cracks, such as those produced by electrical sparks. They were able to rule out several normal causes, but were unable to explain the surges.

Paintings began to swing and rotate. These motions were also captured on videotape. Drawers came out by themselves, documents were found to have been displaced, and at one point a 175 kilogram cabinet moved 30 centimeters from the wall.

Toward the end of the manifestations, Annemarie was getting more and more nervous and began to display hysterical contractions in her arms and legs. When she was on leave from the office nothing happened, and when she departed for another job, the phenomena ceased altogether (although they started up at her new place of work!).

Strange sounds, most prominently including rapping, are sometimes heard in poltergeist cases. Less frequently, apparitions or disembodied voices are perceived, although these are more commonly a feature of hauntings, as will be discussed below. Truly strange phenomena such as showers of rocks or even frogs on or toward a house, as well as the spontaneous ignition of fires, have been reported. However, despite what you may have seen in the movies, people are not generally sucked into their television sets by poltergeists.

The term "poltergeist" means literally "noisy ghost," and poltergeist phenomena were sometimes suspected to be caused by such entities. (Some writers still assert that spirits of the dead may be involved in some poltergeist cases, as will be discussed below.) It has been discovered that poltergeist phenomena generally tend to center around a single person or group of persons in that the phenomena only occur in their presence and in their immediate spatial vicinity. Such a person is called a focal person or, less commonly nowadays, a "poltergeist agent." The prevailing view among those parapsychologists who believe that some poltergeist effects are truly paranormal is that the focal person or persons cause the poltergeist phenomena through the (largely unconscious) use of their psychokinetic powers. For this reason, many para-psychologists use the term "recurrent spontaneous psychokinesis" or "RSPK" to describe such outbreaks. Skeptics, on the other hand, maintain that the focal person produces such effects through fraud and trickery. They also believe that some residual effects may be due to the witnesses' misinterpretation of normal physical events.

Let us now examine in detail a fairly typical poltergeist episode that was reported by Arthur Hastings.[3] The phenomena occurred in a business office in Oakland, California, and seemed to center around John, a 19-year-old typist. The reported phenomena included the malfunctioning of telephones and typewriters, the breakage of coffee cups and glasses, and the movement of heavy objects.

Many of the anomalous movements involved falling objects. Phones and a glass ashtray fell off desks, usually with no witness present to observe the motion. One 15-year-old witness claimed to have seen (out of the corner of his eye) a stapler move off the left side of a table and fall to the floor, landing about three and a half feet from the table. A fluorescent tube from a light fell, although the only one present at the time of this event was the focal person, John. A second tube fell when another witness was in the room but was distracted by a phone call. John was present on this occasion also. A large number of other objects were discovered to have fallen. In some instances, the objects were heard to fall by someone outside of the room involved. When these witnesses entered the room, no one was present. A floor plan of the office, however, reveals that most rooms had multiple exits.

Exploding coffee cups also figured prominently among the events. In one case, a witness saw a cup explode without John touching it (he was adjusting a clip-on bow tie at the time). No trace of explosives was found.

Cabinets were seen to undergo strange movements on two occasions. In one instance, a cabinet was observed to rotate 90 degrees and then to fall over. Witnesses claimed that John was six feet outside of the room at the time of the incident. In all of the above incidents, John was either present or in an adjoining room at the time of the event.

At one point a water cooler fell over. John claimed to have been in the adjoining room at the time; however, his trouser cuffs were wet, and he was later observed to be picking glass fragments from them. The police took John to the station for questioning, whereupon the phenomena ceased except for a brief resurgence on one occasion. John confessed to the police that he had used tricks to produce the effects, such as pushing over the water cooler and throwing light bulbs behind his back.

Psychological testing showed John to be under a great deal of tension. Personality testing, including the California Personality Inventory and the Thematic Apperception Test (TAT), revealed prankster tendencies, with the TAT indicating a large amount of projected aggression. John was also under

a great deal of stress. He was a slow worker and was constantly being repri-
manded by his bosses. In addition, he was newly married and making double
payments on his car.

Arthur Hastings, the case's investigator, felt that some events were
unlikely to be explained by fraud and may therefore represent true psi phenomena. These events include the above-mentioned movements of the stapler and the cabinet. Furthermore, Hastings observed that the smallness of
the fragments of the "exploding" coffee cups make it seem unlikely that they
were broken by impact.

As already mentioned, one of the most prominent investigators of poltergeist cases has been William G. Roll. In a series of publications,[4] he has
provided statistical analyses of a sample of 116 published poltergeist cases. Roll
estimates that parapsychologists in the United States learn of approximately
five promising poltergeist cases per year, of which two or three are investigated and about one per year reaches the professional literature in the United
States. On the other hand, in Palmer's mail survey of the greater Charlottesville, Virginia, area, 6 percent of the student respondents and 8 percent of the
townspeople claimed to have experienced poltergeist phenomena, suggesting
that many more cases may exist than reach the attention of professional parapsychological investigators.[5]

Among Roll's findings was that in the vast majority of cases (92 percent)
the phenomena appeared to focus on the same object or area, inasmuch as the
same object or area of the house was repeatedly involved in the effects. The
average duration of a case was about five months, although half of the cases
lasted for less than two months. In 41 percent of the 105 cases that involved
moving objects, the objects displayed unusual trajectories of movements, such
as wavering, zigzagging and hovering. In 17 percent of the cases, the apparent teleportation of objects was reported. Such teleportation might involve an
object previously inside a house suddenly appearing outside the house or the
apparent passing of objects through ceilings or walls. Some of the poltergeist
cases displayed features that are more commonly associated with hauntings.
Twenty-three percent of the Roll's 116 cases involved apparitions or "hallucinations." These visual hallucinations included human figures, animals, demons
and amorphous shapes. In 11 percent of the cases intelligible voices were heard,
often these were associated with apparitions. In five cases, one or more persons were wounded or slapped by an unknown agency or displayed stigmata
(spontaneously appearing wounds). In five cases people were pulled or lifted
by an unseen force. In most instances the victim was the poltergeist agent (or
focal person).

The British researchers Alan Gauld and Tony Cornell used a statistical
technique called cluster analysis to examine reported cases of recurrent anomalous events, such as those in poltergeist cases and hauntings. Their computer
analysis indicated that the cases did tend to fall within two primary "clusters,"

meaning that the cases tended to group into two types with distinctive characteristics. Furthermore, these clusters seemed to correspond to the traditional categories of hauntings and poltergeist cases. Haunting cases were longer lasting than poltergeist cases and tended to center on a house or location rather than a person. Haunting phenomena were primarily nocturnal, as opposed to poltergeist phenomena, which are more likely to occur during the day, when the focal person is awake. (No RSPK phenomena occurred with the focal person asleep in Roll's 116 case sample.) Hauntings are more likely to involve raps, imitative noises, voices, phantasms, luminous effects, and movements of doors and door handles. Poltergeist cases were found to be shorter in duration, especially if the focal person is quite young. Finally, poltergeist cases were more likely to involve thrown objects, displaced objects, and objects carried through the air.[6]

Still, there are a few cases that display mixed features. George Zorab and Andrew MacKenzie report a haunting case in which the phenomena seemed to center around two focal persons. Zorab speculates that some hauntings may, like poltergeist outbreaks, center around a focal agent and suggests that haunting apparitions may represent actual physical objects that are materialized by the focal person's psychokinetic powers.[7] A similar theory has been proposed by D. Scott Rogo.[8]

H.W. Pierce also reported a case which seemed to display features of both poltergeist and haunting cases.[9] This case involved a split-level house. The upstairs apartment was occupied by Ellsworth Cramer, an industrial engineer, his wife Naomi, a psychiatric nurse, and their child. The downstairs flat was occupied by Peter Henry, a nuclear training engineer, and his wife Claire. All four were in their mid-twenties, and the men described themselves as cynical or skeptical about the existence of psychic phenomena. Most of the events were witnessed by Naomi Cramer. She found her lights on repeatedly when they should have been off. At one point she heard a switch click as the living room lamp turned on. She found that the radio station had been changed when no one was in the apartment, and at one point she heard the radio come on spontaneously (it was tuned to a 24-hour broadcasting station at the time). She then saw an "oblong white cloud" for five or six nights in a row sitting in a chair in the dining room table. The cloud was about four feet tall. She was not initially disturbed by it, thinking that it was an illusion caused by light passing through the drapes, but after the third or fourth night, it "began to bother her." She also reported hearing the cupboard doors in the downstairs apartment opening and closing when no one was supposed to be there. At one point, she went to answer the phone after disassembling a salt shaker, leaving the pieces of the shaker on the table. The pieces came flying at her, hitting the floor just behind her, traveling about nine feet laterally in the process. This scared her because she thought the manifestations were becoming hostile.

Later, she heard a thump and saw a "shadow" dart into the baby's room. Once, when she was downstairs, she heard a lot of noise in her apartment. When she went up to her apartment, the furniture had all been moved around. She thought it unlikely that an intruder had entered, as a ladder would be required to enter the apartment without going through the front entrance.

Once, when she was rocking in her chair, it started to rock more violently, causing her to jump up so that her baby would not be harmed. Three days later, she heard "childlike laughter" while changing her baby. It seemed to came from her baby, although the baby was definitely not laughing. The sound was loud enough to wake her husband.

At one point, Naomi was in bed when she heard the dog barking. She ran into the living room where the dog continued to bark. There was a dancing cloud in the middle of the room, from which emanated a laugh "more eerie than childlike."

Her husband, Ellsworth Cramer, confirmed that he had heard the childlike laughter which woke him. He also testified that he too found lights turned on and off unexpectedly and said that he saw a light in the lower hall seemingly turn itself off on one occasion. He also reported seeing a mist, which was somewhere between three and four feet high, standing at the foot of his bed and that he saw it pass right through the door.

Claire Henry testified to finding lights on in both her apartment and Naomi's when they should have been off. She also saw a chair rocking by itself on two occasions.

Peter Henry stated that he saw a three-dimensional shadow. He believes he was the first to see such a form, but says he did not mention it to the others. He confirmed that he and his wife Claire both saw a rocking chair moving "several inches" up and down with no deceleration. He lit a match and circled the chair to test for air currents and found none. Later, he saw a rocking horse moving up and down in the closet. He deemed it too dangerous to light a match on this occasion. He also heard a child's giggle, which he described as "musical," and had no doubt that it was the voice of a little boy. No one focal person existed in this case, as no particular person's presence seemed to be required in order for the phenomena to occur. Pierce speculated that the agent could be the ghost of the son of the building's former owner. The son had manifested symptoms of childhood schizophrenia and hyperactivity. He also was reported to have displayed strong hostility and frustration in expressing his needs and was subject to nocturnal roaming. These are all features that one might associate with a living poltergeist agent, as will be discussed below.

Ian Stevenson has also argued that some poltergeist phenomena may be caused by deceased agents,[10] and Harvey Irwin feels that it may be premature to adopt the theory that poltergeist cases are necessarily characterized by one living focal agent. He argues that sometimes several agents may be involved and that the rejection of the discarnate (dead) agent theory is just a special case of modern parapsychologists' antipathy toward the idea of the existence of ghosts.[11]

The Poltergeist Agent

Focal persons were involved in 92 of the 116 poltergeist cases examined by Roll. Most of the agents (61 percent) were female, although Roll notes that this proportion has declined over time and that the sexes are nearly equally represented in recent cases. Poltergeist agents are also typically young. Half the focal persons in Roll's sample were under thirteen years of age.

Roll found that slightly more than half of the agents suffered from some form of "debilitating ailment." These ailments were often psychological or neurological in nature. About a quarter of the agents had disorders involving seizures or dissociative states, including muscular contractions, convulsive disorders, fits, trances and so forth. In 41 percent of the cases with focal persons, a change or problem in the home preceded the onset of the RSPK phenomena. (Such changes might include a move, illness or death.)

Roll conjectures that RSPK incidents may substitute for medical symptoms in some cases. He and his co-investigator Steven Tringale report a case with features of both typical haunting and poltergeist phenomena in which there was an inverse relation between the RSPK phenomena and migraine attacks in the focal person.[12] The witnesses in this case involved a married couple, Mr. and Mrs. Berini, and their two children. This family experienced some rather bizarre phenomena in their house which lasted from the time they moved in (May of 1979) until late August of 1981. The phenomena began when Mr. and Mrs. Berini heard a voice at night which seemed to belong to a young girl, who gave her name as Serena and who was crying for her mother. Mr. Berini's father later informed him that his sister Serena had died in the house at the age of five. Three of these voice incidents occurred on the night preceding a death or an illness (respectively, the daughter's tonsillectomy, a stroke suffered by Mrs. Berini's grandmother and her later death).

In March of 1981, Mrs. Berini awoke and saw the figure of an eight- to nine-year-old boy, dressed in white. Mr. Berini thought it might be Giorgi, his father's brother, who had died at eight and was buried in a white communion suit. Four days later Mr. Berini saw a similar apparition, which seemed to be trying to pick up the rug in the hallway. They later removed the rug and the floor boards and found a medallion of the Virgin Mary underneath the floor. The apparition continued to appear sporadically, two or three times a week. It occasionally made short statements, sometimes in response to questions. On some of these occasions only one of the Berinis saw the figure. The apparition seemed to cause physical movements, including the repeated open-ing and closing of the closet door. After two attempts by Catholic priests to exorcise this ghost, it seemed to depart. Unfortunately, it was soon replaced by another less savory figure, a dark, caped and humpbacked entity. This figure was first seen by Mr. Berini, with Mrs. Berini seeing it a few nights after its initial appearance. On one occasion when Mr. Berini and his mother were in the bedroom, he saw it twice, but she saw nothing. This bestial figure was not particularly well-behaved during its week's tenure in the Berini household, and it had the temerity to say "really disgusting things" in a gruff male voice, usually when Mrs. Berini was attempting to pray. When they inquired as to its identity, it replied "I am a minister of God." Lest we conclude on this basis of this last remark that the exorcisms had been successful, it should be noted that the RSPK phenomena started up soon after this ethereal "minister" appeared. In fact, the night after his arrival, the bedside phone kept flying across the room and the bedside lamp fell on Mrs. Berini's head several times. Further incidents involved the breaking of dishes, crosses and religious stat-ues. The furniture then seemed to get restless. A china cupboard turned over four times, and a bookcase on the top landing moved downstairs twice. The daughter's desk meandered out of her room and down the stairs. The retractable staircase to the attic opened and slammed shut repeatedly, causing the ceil-ing in the hall to crack. The incidents continued until the daughter's birth-day in August, when a carving knife was found stuck in the kitchen table. The family then moved out, and a priest performed a third exorcism. This final exorcism attempt was apparently successful, as the phenomena finally ceased.

Some of the events were witnessed by outside observers, including a friend of the son's, a neighbor, and Mr. Berini's sister. These include the flight of a candle, the movement and toppling over of a table lamp, the levitation of a comb, and one of the bookcase's frequent sojourns down the stairs.

This was a particularly nasty poltergeist which frequently attacked peo-ple. Mr. and Mrs. Berini and their son were all hit by moving objects. On four separate occasions when they were in bed, Mr. Berini saw his sleeping wife lifted from the bed and moved out into the room, where she was dropped to the floor. In fact the poltergeist seemed to have a particular aversion to Mrs. Berini. Once she experienced a burning sensation, and three bleeding scratches were found on her chest and an upside down cross was found to be scratched on her back. She was scratched twice more. On one of these occasions, her sister was present and was on the phone to the police. Her sister experienced a burning sensation on her face and found a scratch on her own cheek.

The phenomena seemed to center around Mrs. Berini. Virtually all the incidents took place when she was in the house, and she tended to be the per-son closest to any strangely behaving object. She was also the one who expe-rienced the first two apparitions. She had suffered from migraine headaches and vomiting since she was a child. The phenomena tended to occur during periods when she was free of migraine attacks. Roll and Tringale speculate that the RSPK manifestations could have served as a substitute for the migraine symptoms. They compare the apparitions in this case to the visual "auras" that frequently precede epileptic attacks and speculate that such apparitions may be an externalized form of such auras. In fact, Roll had earlier postulated that both apparitions and voices in such cases may represent externalized hallucinations.[13]

In an article written with Elson de A. Montagno, Roll draws further parallels between RSPK phenomena and the symptoms of epilepsy. Both types of phenomena are most frequently exhibited by people in their teens. Knocking and rapping sounds in poltergeist cases may be analogous to the rhythmic tonic-clonic movements of epilepsy. Sudden movements and the existence of visions and apparitions constitute other similarities. Finally, Montagno and Roll note that the onset of RSPK phenomena frequently coincides with the abatement of hysterical or epileptic symptoms in the agent.[14] These facts, combined with the high incidence of convulsive-dissociative disorders in poltergeist agents, lead Roll to suspect that some forms of brain dysfunction may play a role in causing RSPK phenomena. Harvey Irwin has, however, recently argued that Roll's epilepsy theory of RSPK phenomena may be premature. He notes that only 4 percent of Roll's agents manifested clear-cut symptoms of epilepsy per se, and that this may not represent much of an elevation above baseline rates in the general population.[15]

Many other investigators have postulated that psychopathology or aggression in the agents may be responsible for the generation of the psychokinetic phenomena. Indeed, for years the stereotypical picture of the poltergeist agent was that of the disturbed adolescent girl, which formed the basis of *Carrie*, Stephen King's first best-selling novel. The psychoanalyst Nandor Fodor saw RSPK phenomena as being analogous to hysterical conversion symptoms resulting from emotional tension.[16] The late D. Scott Rogo, a writer of popular books on parapsychology, postulated that RSPK phenomena are due to projected hostility and constitute a psychokinetic form of the "acting out" of displaced aggression. In support of this contention, he cites a case in which RSPK phenomena (raps) occurred during a psychotherapeutic session with a 32-year-old man who claimed to be persecuted by a poltergeist.[17] A.R.G. Owen cites a number of poltergeist cases in which the focal person displayed signs of hysteria.[18]

Alfonso Martinez-Taboas and Carlos Alvarado have criticized the body of research indicating psychopathology in poltergeist agents. They argue that much of this evidence has been produced through clinical interviews in which the interviewer knew that the subject was a suspected poltergeist agent. The interviewer may thus have been biased by this knowledge and his own stereotypical ideas about poltergeist agents. They also fault the researchers for their use of unreliable projective psychological tests, such as the Rorschach inkblot test, which are open to multiple interpretations, as well as the fact that the researchers may be seriously underestimating the prevalence of psychological disorders in the general population.[19]

The Problem of Fraud

Skeptics contend that most, if not all, poltergeist effects are produced by trickery on the part of the apparent poltergeist agent, often in an attempt to gain attention. In some cases direct evidence of such fraud on the part of the focal person has been obtained. Roll used a one-way mirror to observe a 12-year-old focal person in another room together with his grandmother.[20] His coworker (J.G. Pratt) saw the agent hide two measuring tapes behind his shirt and then later throw them after his grandmother. The grandmother then reported this as another poltergeist incident, evidencing no suspicion of any fraudulent activity. The boy was later administered a polygraph test. That test indicated that he was telling the truth when he was in fact lying in denying that he had thrown the tapes (which shows you why the results of polygraph tests are not admissible as evidence in most courts). Roll reports another case in which the poltergeist agent was found to be producing "knocks" by stamping his foot.[21]

More recently, James "the Amazing" Randi, a skeptical magician who has written several books debunking parapsychology, has presented photographic evidence suggesting that Tina Resch, the focal person in a poltergeist case in Columbus, Ohio, threw a phone when no one was looking and produced an apparently anomalous movement of a couch by hooking it with her right foot. A videotape also suggested that she pulled a lamp toward her in order to make it fall.[22] Roll has, however, continued to argue for the genuineness of the RSPK phenomena in this case, noting that Tina was not in the area when many of the events occurred. He also documents an apparent attempt by the prominent skeptic Paul Kurtz to doctor the evidence in this case by implying that two photographs that were actually taken an hour apart were taken within seconds of each other.[23] On the other hand, the fact that Resch was recently sentenced to life in prison for the murder of her daughter does nothing to enhance her credibility as a poltergeist agent.[24]

Roll does note that the focal person was detected in fraud in 19 of the 92 poltergeist cases in his sample in which a focal agent could be identified.[25] Gauld and Cornell report a somewhat lower incidence rate of detected fraud. Fraud was detected in 41 of the 500 poltergeist cases in their sample, yielding an incidence rate of 8 percent. In this context, Gauld and Cornell note that the initial stages of object movements are rarely observed, which would be consistent with the fraud hypothesis.[26] Roll notes that, in 105 cases involving anomalous object movements, visual fixation of objects by witnesses seemed to have an inhibiting effect in 47 cases and no effect in 43 cases. (In the remaining 15 cases, the effect of visual fixation could not be determined.)[27]

Several writers, while admitting the existence of fraud in some cases, suggest that the fraudulent activity is merely the agent's way of maintaining the attention he received when genuine phenomena were occurring. In particular, Jeffrey Munson attributes fraud in poltergeist cases to the agent's "owning" of impulses (such as aggressive impulses) that were previously projected into the environment via PK.[28]

Theories About Poltergeists

Several writers have offered theories about how poltergeist effects are produced, assuming they are not the result of deliberate fraud. G.W. Lambert proposed that reported poltergeist phenomena may be due to motion of underground water and the resulting stress on houses.[29] While it is easy to imagine that poltergeist raps and creaks might be due to such motion of underground water, it is hard to believe that such motion could produce the large horizontal movements of objects frequently reported in RSPK outbreaks. In order to test Lambert's theory, Gauld and Cornell conducted an extraordinary experiment in which houses were mechanically shaken. They concluded that serious structural damage to, and even collapse of, such houses would in all likelihood occur well before any substantial lateral movements of objects were induced. They also feel that such jolting and vibrations would be immediately apparent to anyone inside the house. With regard to Lambert's observation that poltergeist cases tend to cluster around bodies of water, Gauld and Cornell note that this may simply be due to the fact that the population in general tends to congregate in such locations.[30]

William Roll, Donald Burdick, and William Joines have postulated that RSPK agents produce a type of force field in the area surrounding their bodies. Based on an analysis of the locations, directions and magnitudes of movements of objects relative to an ostensible poltergeist agent, they suggest that these movements could have been produced by three rotating "beams" of force emanating from portions of the agent's body. They do not hazard a guess as to the type of force involved or as to how the field is generated. As arbitrary models can rather easily be constructed to "retrodict" observed patterns of movements, their model must await confirmation with new poltergeist agents.[31]

Michael Persinger and Robert Cameron have proposed that some poltergeist episodes may be a product of electromagnetic fields produced by geological stresses. They postulate that extremely low frequency (ELF) components of such fields may directly stimulate the brains of persons involved in such cases and induce apparitional experiences or hallucinations of an olfactory or auditory nature. They further suggest that electromagnetic transients may be responsible for such phenomena as current surges, anomalous telephone rings and light bulb failures. They report on a case in Sudbury, Ontario, which they feel might support such an interpretation.[32]

Summary

Poltergeist cases constitute a dramatic and striking category of possible spontaneous psi phenomena. The number of agents who have been detected in fraud together with the "shyness effect," wherein the beginnings of motions are rarely observed, suggest that RSPK phenomena will have to be approached cautiously and investigated thoroughly from a skeptical viewpoint before they can be accepted as genuinely anomalous phenomena. Investigations of the personalities and other characteristics of poltergeist agents will have to be conducted more rigorously and with more appropriate experimental blinds before they can be considered definitive. Finally, theories to account for poltergeists will have to be constructed that are fully capable of predicting new phenomena rather than merely "retrodicting" phenomena that have already occurred. Theories failing to meet this criterion may well have to be considered as no more scientific than one of Rudyard Kipling's "Just So" stories.

A Personal Postscript

My own life has not been entirely poltergeist free. When I was in high school and fast asleep in my bed, I was struck on the head by a book at about 3:00 in the morning. The book had apparently fallen from the bookcase that was mounted on the wall above my bed. I doubt that any book had been dangling out of the bookcase before I went to bed, and I had been asleep for several hours at that point. The book was *The Art of Loving* by Erich Fromm. Years later, when I was in graduate school and browsing through a bookstore, three books fell and hit me on the head. They were all copies of *The Art of Loving* by Erich Fromm. In this case, as the books fell from the upper shelf of the bookcase I was perusing, it is quite possible that I had slightly jarred the bookcase and that nothing more than gravity was responsible for the fall of the books. Nevertheless, I finally decided to take the spook's literary recommendation and bought and read a copy of the book. I was ultimately forced to conclude that, whatever this invisible book-throwing agent might have been, it did not share my taste in literature.

4. Astral Wanderings

We now turn to the subject of out-of-body experiences, in which people are apparently able to leave their physical bodies and wander about the physical universe wrapped in some sort of "astral body." The abbreviation "OBE" is frequently used by parapsychologists to denote the out-of-body experience, and we will follow that convention here in order to save some paper and thus minimally retard the rate of global warming.

Some people experience but one OBE in their lifetimes, whereas others experience OBEs repeatedly. In some cases, the OBE occurs without any conscious effort to induce it; in others, the OBE occurs as a result of a deliberate induction or incubation process. The following is an example of the former type of OBE and is taken from the collection of Susan Blackmore, an unusual researcher who is at once one of parapsychology's harshest critics and at the same time a prominent investigator of OBEs[1]:

I crossed the road and went into a well-lit wood. My distant vision began to blur and within five or ten seconds I could only see a distance of a few feet, the rest was "fog."
Suddenly my sight cleared and I was looking at the back of myself and the dogs from a position eight or ten feet behind myself and about a foot higher than my height. My physical self had no sight or other senses and it was exactly as if I was simply walking along behind some-one, except that some-one was me...

Involuntarily experienced OBEs can occur for no apparent reason, as in the above case, or they can be the result of fatigue, drug intoxication, sensory deprivation, and psychological or physical stress. A most dramatic form of out-of-body experience occurs when a person is rendered nearly unconscious and near death but is able to witness attempts to revive or resuscitate her physical body from a perspective well above the body. Often such a person feels herself being pulled back into the body at the moment of successful resuscitation. Such cases may be regarded as one form of the near-death experience. Near-death experiences will be discussed in greater detail in Chapter 9.

Obviously, there may be nothing paranormal about OBEs in and of themselves. They may simply be a kind of delusion, hallucination or dream in which one experiences oneself outside of one's body. The OBEs have been of interest to parapsychologists for at least two reasons. First, they suggest the existence of a mind or soul that is capable of traveling beyond the confines of the physical body in ways that are not explainable by current theories of physical science. Also, many people experience themselves as being encased in a secondary body while in the OBE state. Often this secondary body takes the form of a duplicate of the person's ordinary physical body. This has suggested to many researchers that there may exist a nonphysical or quasi-physical "astral body" in which the soul or mind may be housed during its extrasomatic sojourns. If so, this body would be of a type unknown to current theories of science. Of course, the fact that people experience themselves as possessing astral bodies could be explained in terms of hallucination and fantasy, unless some means of detecting such astral bodies with physical instruments could be devised. Several parapsychologists have in fact attempted to use some sort of physical measuring device to detect astral bodies, as will be discussed in greater detail below. Many parapsychologists remain skeptical about the reality of astral bodies due to the fact that people generally perceive themselves as being clothed while in the astral state. This would seem to indicate that astral bodies are merely hallucinations (at least as literally perceived), unless one wishes to assume that clothes have astral bodies too!

A second reason parapsychologists have become interested in the OBE is that there are many anecdotal reports of persons becoming aware of information during out-of-body travel to remote locations that would have been inaccessible to them at the location of their physical bodies during the OBE. For instance, the well known psychiatrist and consciousness researcher Stanislav Grof describes a case in which a woman who was undergoing cardiac arrest felt herself leaving her body and exiting from her hospital room. She then seemed to travel in the out-of-body state to a point outside of the hospital, and she felt herself rise to a point near a tennis shoe that was sitting on a ledge near a third floor window. A subsequent search revealed that there really was such a shoe on the ledge.[2] (A determined skeptic, could of course always argue that the patient might have caught a glimpse of the shoe when she was admitted or when entering the hospital on a previous occasion, as her admission took place at night.)

Cases such as these have led parapsychologists to perform experiments in which people have tried to travel to a remote location in the out-of-body state in order to identify target materials placed at that location. These experiments will be discussed later in this chapter. Of course, if these experiments are no more successful than ordinary ESP experiments, it would not be necessary to assume that the subjects literally traveled out of their bodies; instead, one could simply assume that the subjects used their ESP abilities to identify the target.

On rare occasions, witnesses present at the location to which an OBEr has traveled in the out-of-body state may experience an apparition of the OBEr or otherwise become aware of the OBEr's presence. Such cases are sometimes given the (somewhat prejudicial) label "reciprocal hallucinations," because both the OBEr and the witness have mutually consistent experiences. Perhaps the most famous instance of reciprocal hallucination in the annals of psychical research is the Wilmot case. It has in fact become almost obligatory to cite the Wilmot case in an introductory work on parapsychology. The events in this case occurred in the 1860s, so it is a very old case indeed. A Mr. S.R. Wilmot was sailing from Liverpool to New York when his boat passed through a severe storm. During the storm, he had a dream in which he saw his wife come into the door of his stateroom, hesitate and then bend down to kiss and caress him. Upon awakening, his fellow passenger William Tait said to him, "You're a pretty fellow to have a lady come and visit you in this way." When Wilmot pressed him for an explanation, Tait said that, as he lay awake in the upper bunk, he saw a woman enter, hesitate and then kiss Mr. Wilmot.

When Mrs. Wilmot greeted him upon his arrival in Watertown, Connecticut, she almost immediately asked him if he had received a visit from her on the night in question. She said that she had been anxious about the severity of the weather and the reported loss of another vessel. She had lain awake for a long time and at about 4:00 A.M. she had the sensation of leaving her physical self and traveling across the stormy sea until she reached her husband's stateroom. She said she saw a man in the upper berth looking right at her and so for a moment she was afraid to go in. But she did enter, kissed and embraced her husband and then departed.

One major drawback to this case is that the principal informants did not give their testimony until about twenty years after the events in question.[3]

Alan Gauld provides a more recent case of reciprocal hallucination. He quotes from a statement sent to the American Society for Psychical Research by a 26-year-old woman from Plains, Illinois.[4] This woman experienced a dream on the morning of January 27, 1957, in which she seemed to travel to the home of her mother in northern Minnesota, 926 miles away:

After a little while I seemed to be alone going through a great blackness. Then all at once way down below me, as though I were at a great height, I could see a small bright oasis of light in the vast sea of darkness. I started on an incline towards it as I knew it was the teacherage (a small house by the school) where my mother lives.... After I entered, I leaned up against the dish cupboard with folded arms, a pose I often assume. I looked at my Mother who was bending over something white and doing something with her hands. She did not appear to see me at first, but she finally looked up. I had sort of a pleased feeling and then after standing a second more, I turned and walked about four steps.

Gauld also quotes a letter the woman received from her mother:

I believe it was Saturday night, 1.10, 26 January, or maybe the 27th. If would have been 10 after two your time. I was pressing a blouse here in the kitchen…. I looked up and there you were by the cupboard just smiling at me. I started to speak and you were gone. I forgot for a minute where I was. I think the dogs saw you too. They got so excited and wanted out—just like they thought you were by the door—sniffed and were so tickled.

Your hair was combed nice—just back in a pony tail with the pretty roll in front. Your blouse was neat and light—seemed almost white. [Miss Johnson confirmed in correspondence that this was an accurate description of her subjective appearance during the OBE.]

It is difficult to decide whether to classify this experience as a dream or as an OBE. Philosopher Michael Grosso suggests that the OBE is just one in a continuum of states of consciousness encompassing schizophrenic, meditative, drug, reverie and dream states. He further argues that ESP, "travelling clairvoyance" (in which a person seems to project his mind to a distant location and to become aware of events happening at that location), and the OBE may merely represent three aspects of the same process.[5]

There are a few other states of consciousness that also bear a resemblance to the OBE. Psychiatrists use the term "depersonalization state" to refer to instances in which a person feels himself to be detached from his emotions, actions and even his body. A person undergoing feelings of depersonalization may describe himself as hovering over his body and watching his body perform actions without really being a part of them himself. Janet Mitchell argues that depersonalization states differ from OBEs in that depersonalization states, unlike OBEs, may involve feelings of derealization (in which one's environment is felt to be unreal).[6] It should also be noted that the flattening of affect (that is, diminished emotional reactions) that is often a characteristic of depersonalization states is not usually reported by people undergoing OBEs.

Autoscopy is a state in which one perceives a double or apparition of oneself in the external environment, such as across the street. Autoscopy thus differs from the OBE in that the person's location of consciousness seems to remain located in the physical body rather than in the double. Tyrrell reports the case of Archbishop Frederic, who saw an apparition of himself after awakening from a deep sleep. He stated that the apparition was "luminous, vaporous and wonderfully real" and that the apparition was looking at him. This state lasted for a few seconds, after which the apparition disappeared. A few seconds later, the specter reappeared, only to vanish once again after a few more seconds.[7]

Closely related to autoscopy is the experience of the "doppelganger." *Doppelganger* is a German word used to refer to the apparition of a living person who is not present. In many reported cases, the doppelganger presages the arrival of the person and is often reported to perform acts later performed by the real person. Andrew MacKenzie cites the case of Canon J.B. Phillips, whose wife had gone with an ambulance to the hospital to see after an injured person. Phillips reported hearing a car driving up the road to his chalet. He then heard his wife's voice saying "Thank you very much, goodnight," and he said he then "distinctly" heard the slamming of the car door. He ran out to welcome his wife, but there was no one there at all. About an hour later, these auditory events were replayed, but this time for real.[8] Like autoscopy, the doppelganger experience differs from the OBE in that the person's consciousness remains in the physical body, not in the appearing double.

The phenomenon that will perhaps most strain the reader's credulity is that of bilocation, in which a person, often a Christian, Hindu or Buddhist saint, is experienced as being physically present at two distinct physical locations at the same time. For example, on one night in 1774, the monk Alphonso de Liguori was reported to have been seen simultaneously in his cell and at the bedside of the dying Pope Clement XIV about 100 miles away.[9] Sue Blackmore relates the case of a schoolteacher in the 1840s who evidently frequently appeared in duplicate. The students would see two copies of her standing side by side at the blackboard and also at dinner. Two copies of her would also be seen performing activities at different locations around the school. Blackmore reports that this teacher was fired from her job. One would have thought the administration was getting quite a bargain![10] Finally, Osis and Haraldsson report on two Indian swamis, Sai Baba and Dadajai, who have been reported to bilocate in more recent times.[11]

Bilocation is a very infrequently reported phenomenon and few parapsychologists would put much credence in it. Bilocation appears to differ from the OBE in that the double appears to be a solid physical object that does not vanish into thin air and that is capable of physical interaction with its environment. Also as both copies of the self are reported to be capable of performing complex acts, bilocation would seem to involve a duplication of consciousness as well as of the body. It might of course be possible to explain such phenomena by assuming that the person's mind is at least temporarily split into two distinct subpersonalities. This would be a type of mental, as well as physical bilocation that is not usually reported in OBE cases.

Explanations of the OBE

Theories concocted to explain OBEs may be divided into roughly two types. Theories of the first type postulate that the OBE involves an "exteriorization" or projection of some (possibly nonphysical) aspect of the person outside of the physical body. This projected aspect is variously conceptualized as the mind, the soul, or some form of quasi-physical "astral body." Theories of this type date back to at least 5000 B.C., the time of the creation of portions of the Egyptian *Book of the Dead*.[12] The ancient Egyptians postulated the existence of a *ka*, a form of astral body inhabited by the *ba*, or soul, after death. Likewise, the *Tibetan Book of the Dead* postulates the existence of a *Bardo-body* to house the soul after death. Some Mahayana Buddhists subscribe to the doctrine of *kayatraya*, postulating three bodies. This multiple body principle was later adopted by the religion of Theosophy, which has its roots in Buddhism. Non-Western shamanistic traditions also incorporate the notion of out-of-body travel, as in the case of the Australian aborigines, whose "clever men" are alleged to be able to project themselves at will.

Based on his analysis of a large number of reported out-of-body experiences, Robert Crookall was led to propose that the astral separation takes place in two stages. In the first stage, the soul or "soul body" is housed in a quasi-physical "vehicle of vitality." When in this state, the OBEr experiences a gloomy Hell-like environment. The second stage, which occurs after the soul body is successful in shedding the vehicle of vitality, is characterized by a great sense of peace, beauty and tranquility.[13] Several writers in the early days of OBE research were led, based on anecdotal reports, to postulate the existence of a "silver cord," or sometimes cords, connecting the astral and physical bodies, often through the head or solar plexus.[14] Modern OBErs are much less likely to see such cords, however.

Janet Mitchell has proposed that dreams in which one is falling are related to the process of reentry of the astral body into the physical body.[15] She also suggests that sudden jerkings of one's body when falling asleep may be due to the astral body's suddenly moving back into "coincidence" with the physical body, an idea that had been earlier proposed by Sylvan Muldoon.[16] It should be noted, however, that such sudden jerkings are commonly called myoclonias and that several normal explanations have been proposed to account for them. One such explanation ascribes myoclonias to the withdrawal of the cerebral cortex's control over spinal motor neurons (this withdrawal is a necessary component of the development of the "sleep paralysis" that prevents your body from acting out your dreams at night).

The OBE has been taken by many to suggest that some portion of the human personality may be capable of surviving outside of the physical body and hence capable of surviving the death of that body. William Roll has warned that such survival may be sharply limited in time, as the number of reported crisis apparitions declines steeply with the time interval since the death of the appearing person (assuming that such apparitions are perceptions of astral bodies).[17] Rodger Anderson observes that the OBE does not constitute unequivocal evidence for the mind's survival after death, as the site of consciousness might occasionally extend beyond the body yet still perish with the body. He also notes that the silver cord need not be thought of as a means of animating the physical body, as some advocates of astral projection believe, but may instead be a means of animating the astral body by serving as a conduit for the delivery of energy from the physical body.[18]

Perhaps the most devastating argument against the interpretation of the OBE as the literal projection of an astral body is that people are generally unable to identify stimuli placed at locations to which they have supposedly traveled in the out-of-body state in experimental situations, as will be discussed in greater detail below. Attempts to detect a quasi-physical astral body at its projected location through the use of physical instruments will also be discussed below.

The second category of theories includes those that propose a largely psychological explanation for the OBE. The psychiatrist Jan Ehrenwald viewed the OBE as an attempt to assert the reality and autonomous existence of the soul and as a psychological defense against the threat of extinction at death.[19] Russell Noyes likewise sees the OBE as a form of psychological "negation of death."[20] On the other hand, the existing evidence indicates little relationship between anxiety about death and the reporting of OBEs.[21]

D. Scott Rogo, Carl Sagan, and Barbara Honegger have each suggested that the OBE (and the closely related phenomenon of the near-death experience or NDE) may be based on a rebirth fantasy or a reliving of the birth process.[22] Some of the evidence they cite in support of this hypothesis includes the experiencing of tunnel-like passageways during OBEs and NDEs, as well as the cord-like connection between the physical body and the astral body reported by some OBErs (this cord being taken as reminiscent of an umbilical cord). There is some reason to be skeptical of this hypothesis. First, there is considerable doubt in the scientific community that the process of birth can be remembered in any detail, due to the incomplete myelinization of the neonatal brain. Second, Susan Blackmore has attempted to test the hypothesis that persons born by Cesarean section (and hence who have not experienced a classical birth process to relive) will report fewer OBEs than persons born by vaginal delivery. She found no relationship between the reporting of OBEs and type of birth in her survey.[23] It remains possible of course that OBEs may be related to fantasy or archetypal ideas about birth even if they do not involve a literal reliving of the birth process.

John Palmer has proposed that OBEs may be triggered by changes in the body concept arising from altered patterns of feedback from nerves monitoring the positions of muscles and limbs.[24] Such altered proprioceptive feedback might occur in sleep, in conditions involving physical trauma or following the administration of anesthetics. In Palmer's view, these changes in body concept may threaten the normal concept of the self. As a result, the person's unconscious defenses are activated in order to reestablish a sense of identity, and this reestablishment may take the form of an OBE. When the normal body concept is reestablished, the OBE ends.

Susan Blackmore proposes a psychological model of the OBE that is quite similar to that proposed by Palmer.[25] Like Palmer, she suggests that the OBE represents a mental model of the world that is constructed in response to a breakdown in the usual body-centered model of the world. This breakdown may be due to reduced sensory input or to a diminishment of proprioceptive feedback under conditions of reduced bodily movement. This secondary model of the world is often constructed from a "bird's eye view," suggesting to the person that he or she is located in the air above the physical body. Blackmore contends that such a bird's eye view is frequently adopted when remembering a scene from one's past and is thus a characteristic of mental models of the world constructed on the basis of memory. While it is true that in her own research she found that OBErs (that is, people who claim to have had an OBE) were no more likely than non–OBErs to recall scenes from an overhead vantage point, she did find that OBErs were able to switch viewpoints in such imagined scenes more easily than were non–OBErs. Blackmore further conjectures that if a dreaming person becomes aware that he is sleeping, he may construct a model of himself lying in bed and thus come to see himself as located outside of his body. In her view, this might explain why the reporting of OBEs tends to go hand-in-hand with the reporting of lucid dreams (a term used to denote dreams in which one becomes aware that one is dreaming).[26]

A somewhat more outlandish theory to explain the OBE has recently been proposed by Persinger and Munro. They suggest that OBEs may be produced when the left hemisphere of the brain gains a glimpse of the independent workings of the right hemisphere. This may lead the left hemisphere to perceive itself as separate from the rest of the body. They cite an observed correlation between such a sense of detachment and mismatches in the electrical activity of the two cerebral hemispheres as evidence in support of this theory.[27]

Research Findings Relating to the OBE

Incidence rates. A great many surveys have been conducted to determine how frequently people in the general population report OBEs.[28] The estimates of the incidence rate vary widely, from a low of 8 percent reported by Haraldsson and his coworkers[29] to a high of 54 percent reported by Kohr.[30] Most surveys, however find that somewhere between 10 percent and 20 percent of the general population report having had an OBE at some time in the past. Blackmore found that 85 percent of the people who reported any OBE said that they had experienced out-of-body travel on more than one occasion. She also found that 85 percent experienced some sort of strange sensation before entering the OBE state; these sensations included vivid imagery, disorientation, shaking and vibrations, and the seeing of tunnels and doorways.[31] Carlos Alvarado asked college students reporting OBEs whether they experienced themselves as being housed in any sort of second body during the OBE. Thirty-five percent said they experienced themselves as not having any sort of body, 23 percent experienced themselves as located in a second body similar to the physical body, 13 percent experienced themselves as a cloud, mist, ball of light or point in space, 8 percent had no recollection, and 20 percent reported some other form of existence. Alvarado found that 81 percent of the students who reported having an OBE claimed to have had more than one OBE, a figure similar to Blackmore's.[32]

All of the above-mentioned surveys were conducted with modern, Western populations. This raises the question of whether the OBE is a universal experience or is peculiar to Western culture. To address this issue, Dean Shiels conducted a study of 70 nonwestern cultures. He found belief in some form of out-of-body travel in 95 percent of these cultures. Sometimes these beliefs do not correspond to the classical OBE as described above, but may encompass such doctrines as the travel of the soul to nonphysical realms during dreams.[33]

Psychological factors. A large number of studies have been conducted to see if there is any relation between the reporting of OBEs and mental imagery ability.[34] (Such a positive relationship might be taken as support for the idea that the OBE is largely a fantasy experience.) The net result of these studies is that there is little evidence for a relationship between the reporting of OBEs and the experienced vividness of mental images, a person's ability to control her mental imagery, or the tendency to adopt any particular perspective when recalling or imaging a visual scene. There is, however, a fairly consistent body of evidence indicating that OBErs have a greater ability to switch perspectives when viewing imagined scenes than do persons not reporting OBEs.[35] There is also a fairly consistent body of evidence indicating that persons who report OBEs tend to fit the profile of a "fantasy-prone" personality.[36] This would lend some support to the view that OBEs may simply be the product of an overactive imagination.

One fairly consistent finding is that OBErs tend to report having lucid dreams more often than do non–OBErs.[37] Rex Stanford has interpreted this to mean that people tend to confuse OBEs with lucid dreams.[38] Another possibility is suggested by the fact that some people have reported that they are able to deliberately launch OBEs from the lucid dream state. (Lucid dreams, it will be recalled, are dreams in which the dreamer is aware of the fact that he or she is dreaming.) One such person was the late D. Scott Rogo. Rogo trained himself to control his hypnagogic imagery (the imagery one has when first falling asleep) in order to enter a state of lucid dreaming. While in the lucid dream state, Rogo like many other lucid dreamers was able to manipulate his dream imagery. He used this ability to "order up" a car, which he then drove and crashed, producing an OBE. Perhaps other lucid dreamers have learned similar techniques.[39]

Experimental Studies of the OBE

There have been several attempts to determine whether people can identify target items placed at a location to which they have allegedly projected during an OBE. Of necessity, these experiments have focused on deliberately produced OBEs, sometimes using special subjects who claim to be able to enter an OBE at will and sometimes using ordinary people as subjects. In the latter case, the subjects typically undergo some sort of training procedure that supposedly will allow them to experience an OBE in the experimental situation. Such induction techniques usually involve the subject entering a state of relaxation, possibly through the use of auditory tapes. Occasionally visual input is restricted by placing ping-pong balls over the subject's eyes, producing a "ganzfeld" or blank field of homogeneous visual stimulation. John Palmer and his colleagues used such techniques in an attempt to induce OBEs in a group of ordinary citizens, who were then asked to travel to another room in the OBE state and to identify an ESP target placed there. While 45 percent of the subjects claimed to experience literal separation from their bodies, they were not successful in identifying the target.[40] A second experiment was a little more successful, with the subjects reporting OBEs having greater success in identifying the target than subjects not reporting OBEs.[41] In a similar experiment, Smith and Irwin found a positive relationship between degree of experienced out-of-body separation and success in identifying a target.[42] One problem with their experiment is that the same materials, a small sheep skull and potted palm, served as targets for all the subjects. Thus, their results could be due to a tendency for people who claim to experience OBEs to also report death-related or plantlike imagery.

Several studies have been made of special subjects who claim to be able to produce OBEs at will. One of the most famous of these is Charles Tart's study of the subject he refers to as Miss Z.[43] In the one reported trial with Miss Z, she was asked to identify a five digit number that had been placed on a shelf above her while she lay on a cot with EEG electrodes affixed to her scalp. She was able to identify all five digits successfully, a feat which would occur by chance only one time in one hundred thousand. Unfortunately, no one was in the room observing her at the time. Tart conceded that it might be possible that Miss Z could have seen a reflection of the number in a clock that was present in the experimental chamber. Sue Blackmore has pointed out that Tart placed the number on the shelf when Miss Z was already in the room, so that it is possible that she was able to get a glimpse of it then.[44] Thus, this experiment was far from perfect. Unfortunately, Miss Z moved away from Tart's area and was not available for further testing (although one might have thought that, given her level of success, Tart would have moved his lab to her new location!). Tart attempted a similar experiment with Robert Monroe, a well-known OBEr who has written several books on the subject, but without success.[45]

Janet Mitchell conducted a very similar experiment with another prominent OBEr, the artist Ingo Swann. Swann did have some success identifying the target materials, but once again he was allowed to be in the room with the target materials with no one observing him. While his movements were restricted by the EEG electrodes attached to his head, it is conceivable that he could have used a device such as an extensible mirror to identify the targets, which were placed on a platform near the ceiling of the room.[46]

Osis and McCormick conducted an experiment in which the special subject Alex Tanous attempted to identify a target displayed in an "Optical Image Device" (OID) while in the OBE state. Although Tanous had little overall success in identifying the target, a strain gauge placed in the vicinity of the OID showed greater activity when Tanous correctly identified the target than when he did not.[47]

There have been several other attempts to detect some sort of physical effect at the site to which a person has allegedly projected during an OBE, using both animate observers and physical instruments as detection devices. Such physical effects could be interpreted as signs of an astral body. Perhaps the most elaborate such attempt was conducted with the special subject Keith Harary at the Psychical Research Foundation in Durham, North Carolina.[48] (Harary has since gone on to write several popular books about parapsychology.) In this study, Harary attempted to project himself from the experimental room to an adjacent building during a voluntarily produced OBE. He was unable to identify target materials placed in the second building. No behavioral changes were observed in a snake or small rodents located in the second building during Harary's projection, although a kitten was less active and cried less during Harary's OBE than during control time periods.

This effect was not, however, obtained in two follow-up studies. No consistent responses from human detectors were observed, although one witness claimed to have seen Harary on a video monitor during one of his projections. Several instruments were used to measure physical effects in the area to which Harary had projected. These included devices to measure several electromagnetic effects and a delicate thermistor to measure temperature changes. No physical effects related to Harary's OBEs were observed with these devices.

There have been many attempts to detect the astral body by weighing or photographing the soul as it leaves the physical body upon death or by photographing the human aura, which is sometimes identified with the astral body. Because these attempts have not been performed with the subject explicitly in an OBE state, they will be discussed later in the book, when we come to the subject of the survival of death.

Conclusions

Most people are unable to identify target materials while claiming to be located in the vicinity of those target materials during an OBE. In fact, the overall results from these types of OBE experiments are in general no more impressive than the fairly weak effects obtained in ESP experiments, and thus it is plausible that even these minimal successes are due to simple ESP. This failure to reliably identify target material during OBEs constitutes fairly strong evidence against the view that some aspect of the person has literally projected from the body and is perceiving the remote location. This body of evidence would thus support the view that OBEs are simply the product of fantasy or hallucination.

5. Healers, Shamans, Saints and Seers

In this chapter we will examine a variety of phenomena that occur for the most part outside of the parapsychological laboratory but which fall beyond the scope of the previous three chapters. These phenomena include such deliberate practices as dowsing, psychic prognostication, psychic healing, and the work of psychic detectives. We will also examine a few instances of truly strange phenomena, including the alleged ability of certain Christian saints, to levitate, an instance of possible weather control by a Tibetan shaman, and even that old favorite, spontaneous human combustion. We will begin, however, with the more mundane topic of psychic predictions.

Psychic Predictions

Every year, several tabloids, including the *National Enquirer* and the always entertaining *Weekly World News*, publish the predictions of "leading psychics" for the upcoming year. It is not easy to perform a statistical analysis on such predictions to see whether or not they come true more often than one would expect by chance. Nevertheless, it is safe to say that such predictions are not in general very accurate. Several skeptical writers, among them James Cunliffe[1] and John Booth,[2] have delighted in pointing out some of the more conspicuous failures among such predictions. Recently, Gene Emery, a science writer at the *Providence Journal-Bulletin,* has compiled a list of failed predictions for 1995.[3] Emery observes that Hugh Hefner did not give up his Playboy empire to become a cultivator of sunflowers, as predicted by psychic Shawn Robbins. No child genius constructed a working time machine from parts of a microwave oven as an entry in a seventh grade science fair, as predicted in the *National Enquirer;* nor did Tonya Harding seek to open the nation's first all-nude ice skating rink, as forecast in the same publication.

In some cases, an apparently successful prediction may be fabricated. Quite a splash was made several years ago by a videotape of an apparently accurate prediction of the assassination attempt on President Reagan by John Hinckley that was allegedly made by psychic Tamara Rand on a talk show. President Reagan, it will be recalled, was shot in the chest on March 30, 1981, by John Hinckley, a blond-haired former member of the American Nazi party. Hinckley claimed that he made the assassination attempt in order to impress actress Jodie Foster, who had played the subteenage flame of a psychotic assassin in the movie *Taxi Driver*. The tape of the alleged prediction was broadcast on NBC's *Today* show and ABC's *Good Morning America* as well as on Ted Turner's Cable News Network, on April 2, 1981. The tape showed Rand, a Los Angeles area psychic who catered to Hollywood celebrities, making the prediction that Reagan would be shot in the chest by a sandy-haired young radical having the initials "J.H." and that the assassin's name would be something like "Jack Humbley." Rand further predicted that the assassination attempt would take place during the last week in March or the first week in April. The tape had supposedly been aired on March 28, 1981, two days before the actual assassination attempt took place. It turned out that no such tape had been aired and that the tape was in fact made the day after the assassination attempt but was fraudulently dated to make it appear to have been made before the attempt. Dick Maurice, the host of the talk show in question, confessed to involvement in the hoax.[4]

Sometimes predictions may be worded so vaguely that many events may be interpreted as fulfilling them. This is particularly true of the poetic quatrains of the sixteenth century prophet Nostradamus, as has been pointed out by magician and writer Milbourne Christopher. One of Nostradamus' most prophetic quatrains begins, "The King-King will be no more, of the Gentle One destroyed."[5] This was taken (after the fact) to be a prediction of the slaying of Henry III, King of both Poland and France, by a man named Clement (a synonym of "gentle"). Nostradamus' quatrains are, however, like Rorschach inkblots, onto which the reader may project any message she wants. For instance, Paul Kurtz cites the following quatrain:

An emperor shall be born near Italy
Who shall be sold to the Empire at a high price
They shall say, from the people he disputed with,
That he is less a prince than a butcher.

As Kurtz points out, this particular quatrain is so vaguely worded that it could be taken as a prediction of the reign of Napoleon, Hitler or even Ferdinand II, the king of Bohemia and Holy Roman emperor.[6] Such vague predictions as are contained in Nostradamus' quatrains are effectively no predictions at all; as no dates or specifics are given, they can be interpreted to fit any suitable event in the last four centuries.

Occasionally, formal divination systems such as the *I Ching* or tarot cards are employed to make predictions, read a person's character, or offer advice. As the message of the cards, yarrow stalks or stars may be interpreted in several ways, there is an opportunity for the reader or diviner to select the appropriate interpretation by means of intuition or even ESP. There is also the "Barnum" effect, the tendency for people to believe that a vaguely worded statement holds a deep message meant specifically for them. Most studies that have been conducted to test the efficacy of such divination systems have yielded null results. For instance, in a test of divination with tarot cards, Sue Blackmore found people unable to distinguish between tarot card readings meant for them from readings meant for other people.[7] Serena Roney-Dougal repeated Blackmore's experiments and got essentially the same results.[8] Two similar experiments with the *I Ching* divination system also produced null results.[9]

Psychic Detectives

There are frequently accounts in the popular press of cases in which psychics have been able to use their powers to help the police solve crimes. Unfortunately, newspaper accounts are not always noted for their accuracy. Studies of psychic detectives from a skeptical vantage point have been published by Melvin Harris and Piet Hein Hoebens.[10] Hoebens has focused his investigations on the Dutch psychic Gerard Croiset and his prime investigator from a parapsychological point of view, Professor Wilhelm Tenhaeff. According to popular accounts, Croiset has displayed an astonishing success in helping the police find bodies and solve crimes. Yet when Hoebens interviewed the Utrecht police, they denied that any of Croiset's attempts to locate missing persons or to solve crimes had been successful. Hoebens also notes certain inconsistencies in Tenhaeff's accounts of Croiset's successes. In addition, Tenhaeff distorted many of Croiset's statements in his summaries of them. Initially vague statements were made to seem much more detailed and accurate than they really were. Errors made by Croiset were deleted. Tenhaeff also distorted his descriptions of confirming events to make them better conform to Croiset's predictions. Hoebens also reviews one instance of an apparent gross falsification by Tenhaeff. Thus, what you read in the popular press may not necessarily correspond to the facts when it comes to the area of psychic detection.

Arthur Lyons and Marcello Truzzi have recently published a semipopular, semiskeptical book on psychic detection called *The Blue Sense*. In it they document the fairly impressive case of psychic Greta Alexander, who was called in by police to find the missing body of Mary Cousett, a woman who had disappeared in April 1983. Alexander correctly predicted that the body would be found near the intersection of several roads, that it would be missing a leg or foot, that the head would not be found with the body, and that it would be found by a man with a crippled hand. In fact, the body was found in such a location by an officer who had had several fingers on his left hand damaged in a drill press accident. It should be noted, however, that these statements were embedded in a fairly large number of other statements that were either too vague to be called predictions or were in fact incorrect. Further, the body was found outside the area on the map circled by Alexander.[11]

What is clearly needed are more rigorous and skeptical field investigations of psychic detectives. It would also be possible to conduct laboratory studies in a forensic format with such persons. To date, only a handful of studies have been conducted, and these preliminary results indicate that "readings" provided by psychic detectives are no more accurate than those provided by normal persons claiming no psychic ability.[12]

Dowsing

Dowsing is a technique in which the practitioner (called a "dowser") employs a device such as a forked stick or dowsing rod to locate some object (usually a body of underground water, although other sorts of objects such as buried mines have served as target objects). When the dowser is located over the target object, the dowsing rod signals that fact by making a movement. Most scientists believe that the movement of the rod is caused by unconscious muscular movements on the part of the dowser, although A.B. Kaufman has reported strain gauge measurements on dowsing rods that he claims reveal a force unexplainable by gravity, muscular jerking or thumb pressure.[13] As the dowser is in physical proximity to the target object, it is possible that some physical signal serves as a sensory cue to guide him to the object. Thus, dowsing may not involve the operation of ESP at all. Kaufman, for instance, notes that many geological features are associated with magnetic anomalies and that human beings have been shown to be capable of detecting such magnetic fields. Such sensory cueing may be less prominent in cases of "map dowsing," in which the practitioner holds his apparatus over a map of the area rather than walking over the area itself. Even maps, however, provide clues as to the geophysical makeup of an area.

George Hansen has conducted a thorough and detailed review of the literature relating to dowsing.[14] In his view, many of the studies of dowsing that have been conducted have used quite sloppy experimental procedures and in many cases the reporting of the methodology that was used is unclear. Despite these shortcomings, many of the studies showed dowsing techniques to be ineffective. Since Hansen's review, Hans-Dieter Betz has reported a massive field study of dowsing in several countries.[15] Betz' results indicate that the use of dowsing can enhance the efficacy of searches for underground water sources. As with virtually any field study, Betz' methodology is not adequate to rule out the hypothesis that the dowser may be responding to physical cues. Because of the poor reliability of the dowsing procedure and the methodological inadequacies of field studies, it is not clear that dowsing offers a more effective means of demonstrating the existence of ESP than do more traditional ESP experiments.

Psychic Healing

"Psychic healing" is a generic term employed to describe a variety of techniques whereby diseases and other ailments are healed or alleviated by an apparently paranormal process. Stanley Krippner has proposed a typology of practitioners of such healing techniques, which he calls "folk healing."[16] Krippner's first category of folk healers is that of shamanic healers. Shamans are persons, usually in "primitive" cultures, who are ostensibly able to enter a trance and visit the world of spirits, a vocation typically entered as the result of a "calling" in youth. Their healing rites may consist of literally retrieving lost souls or departed animal spirit guardians that have deserted the ailing patient. Spiritist healers are distinguished from shamanic healers by the fact that the former undergo possession by a spirit in the course of performing their healing rituals. The Condomble and Umbanda sects of Brazil are examples of this tradition. Krippner's next two categories are esoteric healers, who follow an occult tradition such as alchemy, astrology, tarot-reading or tantric Buddhism, and religious ritual healers, whose healing takes place in the context of a religious ritual, such as a Mexican sacred mushroom ceremony. Krippner would classify faith healers, such as Kathryn Kuhlman, who operate in the context of a Christian religious service, as religious ritual healers. Krippner's final category is that of intuitive healers, who (unlike shamans) undergo no special training or initiation but who chose their vocation based on an inner sense of a calling (sometimes described as a "call from God"). Such practitioners frequently employ the technique of laying-on-of-hands, which has been the subject of much parapsychological investigation (to be discussed below) and often describe themselves as tuning in to a "universal energy field." As examples of this type of healer, Krippner offers Olga Worrall and Oscar Estabany, both of whom have been extensively studied by experimental parapsychologists.

For the purposes of the present analysis, we will subdivide psychic healing by the type of technique employed rather than by the type of practitioner, as there is considerable overlap in the techniques employed by practitioners of different Krippnerian types.

Faith healing. The term "faith healing" will be used primarily to refer to healing carried out in the context of a (usually Christian) religious meeting in which ailments are ostensibly cured by the power of God or the patient's own religious faith rather than the cure being ascribed to any "energy" emanating from, or physical manipulation performed by, the healer. Faith healing may be accomplished with or without any physical contact between the patient and the healer. Extensive physical contact between the healer and the patient would probably result in the classification of the technique as either psychic surgery or the laying-on-of-hands (to be discussed below). Examples of modern day faith healers would be Kathryn Kuhlman, Oral Roberts, Peter Popoff, Ernest Angley, noted Christian broadcaster and former presidential candidate Pat Robertson, and the somewhat more infamous Jim Jones.

Some cures that occur in the context of faith healing may be due to the fact that the original ailment was psychogenic in origin. Some apparently serious conditions, such as paralysis and blindness, may have no organic basis but may merely be hysterical symptoms that reflect the patient's psychological distress. Even apparently genuine physical conditions such as visible rashes, ulcers and asthma attacks may be aggravated or even caused by psychological factors. Such illnesses are typically referred to as psychosomatic illnesses to distinguish them from hysterical ailments. Obviously, as both types of conditions are at least partially caused by psychological factors, it would not be surprising if a religious ritual, which may have a considerable emotional impact on the patient, had the effect of alleviating these symptoms.

Sometimes people with a genuine physical illness may experience a surge of excitement, possibly involving the release of endorphins (the brain's "natural opiates"), during a religious ritual and may overcome their symptoms for a brief time. (The alleviation of pain through the administration of placebos or hypnosis is a well-known effect and is thought to be governed by the release of endorphins in many cases.) The symptoms may, however, return once the fervor of the ritual has waned. Cases in which documented serious physical illnesses, such as cancer and lupus, were cured through faith healing do exist, although they are extremely rare; however, cancer and other serious illnesses do sometimes improve without medical intervention, in a process known as spontaneous regression. What is needed in order to document the efficacy of faith healing are controlled studies showing that such spontaneous regression occurs more frequently among patients undergoing religious rituals than for control patients not undergoing such rituals. Such studies have not been done.

The activity of the immune system and the course of diseases are known to be affected by psychological conditions such as stress. It is well established that physical diseases occur more frequently following traumatic life events such as the loss of a job or the death of a spouse. There are cases on record of voodoo death, in which a victim who learns that he has been cursed by a witchdoctor suddenly dies. It is commonly thought that this is an example of what is known as parasympathetic death or "death by helplessness," as described by Martin Seligman.[17] In such a death, a person facing what he perceives to be a hopeless situation essentially relaxes himself to death, stopping the heart. The central nervous system is also known to interact directly with the immune system through the hypothalamus, and immune responses in animals have been conditioned to occur in response to certain tastes or even in response to the presence of particular persons.[18] Thus, it might not be too surprising if participating in a faith healing ritual served to bolster a patient's immune system. This would not be a paranormal or supernatural phenomenon, however, as the bolstering of the immune system could be due to the brain's normal channels of influence over the immune system operating in response to suggestion. Some evidence against the hypothesis that all forms of psychic healing are placebo effects or due to suggestion is provided by a survey conducted by Haraldsson and Olafsson, in which they found that prior belief in the efficacy of psychic healing did not correlate with the perceived benefit the patient received from the healing session.[19] Their study was not specific to faith healing, but encompassed healing in general.

Several faith healers have been exposed in using fraud to aid their practices. James Randi's book *The Faith Healers* contains an extensive documentation of such fraudulent activity.[20] Perhaps the most common ploy used by faith healers is to "heal" a stooge sitting in the audience who is only faking an illness. Robert Morris describes how the Reverend Jim Jones used such stooges and other forms of deception to dupe his followers into believing he had magical powers.[21] Some of these people later followed Jones into death in the infamous Jonestown massacre in Guyana, in which hundreds of Jones' followers drank cyanide-laced Kool Aid at his command.

In general, there is no compelling evidence that any paranormal process is involved in faith healing. The more spectacular miracles are chiefly the result of fraud, and other cures may be due to the effects of suggestion and normal psychosomatic and psychoimmunological processes.

Psychic diagnosis. Some healers claim the ability to diagnose illness by psychic means. One such person was Edgar Cayce. Given the name and address of a patient, Cayce would enter a trance, diagnose the patient's ailment and prescribe a (typically unorthodox) method of treatment. Cayce's recommended cures have been the subject of study by physicians at the Association for Research and Enlightenment, an organization dedicated to the study of Cayce's readings based in Virginia Beach, Virginia. James Randi has provided a skeptical analysis of Cayce's diagnoses, pointing out that Cayce was often inaccurate and even provided diagnoses of people who were in fact already dead.[22] However, this negative evidence may not prove much, as Cayce's proponents concede that he was accurate in only about one-third of the cases he attempted to diagnose. A well-controlled statistical study might have settled the issue of whether Cayce displayed any paranormal ability in his diagnoses, but unfortunately Cayce died before any such study was conducted.

Randi has cast more definitive doubt on the paranormal diagnostic capability of the faith healer Peter Popoff. In his services, Popoff claimed the ability to obtain the names and medical conditions of people in his audience through paranormal means (described as a revelation from God). Randi and his associates were able to intercept a radio signal transmitted from Popoff's wife to an earpiece worn by Popoff giving him names and medical data for various audience members. In this instance at least, the psychic diagnosis was achieved through fraud.[23]

Psychic surgery. In the technique of psychic surgery, the healer purportedly enters the patient's physical body, sometimes using only his bare hands, as in the case of the Philippine healer Tony Agpaoa, and in other cases using an unorthodox implement such as the rusty knife wielded by the Brazilian healer Arigo.[24] In a typical psychic surgery session, the healer might massage the patient's stomach muscles, seemingly penetrate the abdominal cavity with his bare hands, and apparently remove a "tumor" (which is frequently immediately destroyed because of its "evil" nature). Although bleeding may be profuse during the surgery, the alleged incision usually heals immediately, without a trace of a scar.

Psychic surgery is now widely regarded by scientists both within and outside the parapsychological research community as a fraudulent activity. The illusion of an incision is thought to be produced by kneading the patient's skin. The illusion of bleeding is achieved by the psychic surgeon's releasing blood or some other red liquid from a source he has palmed as if performing a cheap magic trick. The tumors removed by the surgeons are thought to be samples of animal tissue that have also been palmed by the surgeon. An early investigation of psychic surgery by the American physician William Nolen failed to uncover even one case in which a physical illness that had been documented to exist before a psychic surgery session was found to be absent following the session. Nolen also detected many instances of fraudulent activity on the part of the psychic surgeons he observed. In one case, a "kidney stone" was found to be composed of sugar.[25] In an earlier investigation, Granone had found such "kidney stones" to consist of table salt and pumice stone.[26] David Hoy also describes sleight-of-hand techniques he witnessed during psychic surgery sessions, including the palming of objects.[27] Lincoln and Wood identified "blood" produced from a patient during psychic surgery as pig blood rather than human blood.[28] Finally, Azuma and Stevenson analyzed two more kidney stones removed from patients during psychic surgery and found them to be pebbles.[29] By now it should be apparent that the rampant fraudulent activity on the part of psychic surgeons casts extreme doubt on the hypothesis that any paranormal effect has been demonstrated in this procedure.

Laying-on-of-hands and remote healing. In both the technique known as the "laying-on-of-hands" and in the technique I will call "remote healing," the healer is conceptualized as being the source or channel of a healing effect or healing "energy." The chief difference between the two techniques is that the laying-on-of-hands involves more or less direct physical contact between the patient and the healer, whereas the healer is isolated from the patient in remote healing. In practice the distinction between the two techniques becomes blurred by the fact that many experimental studies of healers who would normally use the laying-on-of-hands in their daily practice have of necessity used experimental protocols that remove the healer from direct physical contact with the patient to be healed or from the biological system to be influenced. Unlike other forms of healing, a great many experimental tests of the efficacy of these two techniques have been performed. A surprisingly high proportion of these experiments have yielded evidence of some sort of healing effect. Healers have been found to be able to retard the growth of goiters in mice and to accelerate the recovery of such goiters,[30] to speed the healing of experimentally induced wounds in mice,[31] to accelerate the recovery of mice from anesthesia without physical contact,[32] to speed the regeneration of salamander forelimbs,[33] to heal malaria in rats (remotely and retroactively!),[34] and to facilitate the healing of surgically induced wounds in humans.[35] A large number of studies have shown that the growth of plants may be accelerated when they are irrigated with water previously held by healers or when they are grown from seeds held by healers.[36] There have also been claims of changes in the light absorption properties of samples of water held by healers.[37] Healers have also been found to produce effects on the activity levels of enzymes.[38]

Experiments have shown that even ordinary citizens may be able to influence biological systems at a distance. Ordinary subjects in such bio-PK experiments have been found to be capable of affecting the growth rates of fungal and bacterial cultures,[39] the mutation rates of bacterial genes,[40] the electrical activity of plants,[41] the electrodermal and brainwave patterns of human subjects,[42] the firing rate of individual neurons of the sea snail *Aplysia*,[43] and the rate of hemolysis of red blood cells,[44] to name only a few of the effects that have been reported. To be sure, not all investigators who have looked for such effects have found them, but the success rate is rather substantial. In a "meta-analysis" of 149 psychokinesis experiments using living organisms as targets, Braud, Schlitz and Schmidt found that 53 percent of them produced significant evidence of a psi effect.[45] As in any other area of research, the methodological quality of the studies is uneven. While the procedures in many of the studies are quite sound, others suffer from various defects. One common defect is that the person caring for or measuring the target organisms may not be blind as to which experimental group the organisms are in. If the person watering a plant or placing a fungal colony in a incubator knows whether the plant or fungus is in the "healed group" or the control group, this may affect his treatment of the organism. This was in fact a problem in some of the plant and fungus experiments.[46] Another defect occurs when the target and control organisms are not housed in the same areas or under comparable conditions, as was the case in some of the wound-healing experiments with mice,[47] or when the healing and control procedures are carried out at different times or locations, as was the case in some of the mouse anesthesia experiments, some of the enzyme studies, and some of the human wound experiments.[48] In such cases the target organisms or systems may simply be responding differently to different locations or times of day rather than to the treatments. A third defect occurs when the healer is allowed to be in close physical proximity to the patient or target organism, as the possibility then arises that any effects may be due to suggestion or to the comforting of an animal. Nonetheless, there do remain a large number of seemingly methodologically sound studies that appear to show that humans are capable of affecting biological systems at a distance, and that therefore there may well be reason to believe that there could be some validity to the claims of laying-on-of-hands or remote healing. The reason this evidence is largely ignored by the medical and scientific community is probably related to scientific community's general rejection of psi research; the data just do not fit into established theories. On the other hand, while there may be prejudice against this research, any person seeking treatment should understand that the magnitude of the healing effects found in these studies tends to be far less than the effects produced by orthodox medical treatment, and they are also much less reliable.

Acupuncture. A form of medical treatment that is occasionally linked with psychic healing is the Asian practice of acupuncture. There are two reasons for this link. First, there is no agreed upon orthodox explanation for acupuncture's effects. Second, acupuncture is based on an ancient Asian theory involving the flow of a type of energy called *ki* through a network of channels called *nadi* or meridians. These channels are conceived to be part of a subtle or astral body in some traditions. The *nadi* and *ki* are paranormal in the sense that they do not correspond to any networks or energy known to Western science. The Japanese scientist Hiroshi Motoyama has claimed to measure the flow of *ki* through the *nadi* by placing electrodes along the meridian lines described by acupuncture theorists.[49] However, as I have pointed out in a previous publication,[50] Motoyama's evidence is less than compelling due to his failure to place any control electrodes outside of the meridian system for the purpose of comparison.

One prominent use of acupuncture or the related technique of acupressure is as an analgesic. Needles inserted at specified points on a patient's body may evidently produce anesthetic effects at remote and seemingly unrelated body locations. Several orthodox explanations have been offered to explain these effects, including suggestion and the placebo effect. One suggestion is that acupuncture causes the release of endorphins, the "brain's natural opiates." In fact, there have been reports that acupuncture can cause the release of endorphins into the cerebrospinal fluid[51] and that naloxene, a morphine antagonist that blocks the effects of endorphins, also blocks the effects of acupuncture.[52] Thus, it is possible that orthodox explanations for the effects of acupuncture are forthcoming.

Summary of healing studies. In conclusion, there is not much solid evidence for the existence of paranormal effects in the areas of faith healing, psychic diagnosis, psychic surgery or acupuncture. With regard to the techniques of laying-on-of-hands and remote healing, there are hints from the existing experimental evidence that some sort of paranormal effect could be involved in these techniques.

Psi Phenomena in Nonwestern Cultures

Several anthropologically-oriented investigators have explored beliefs about and practices relating to psi phenomena in cultures markedly different from our modern Western civilization. These studies may be broken into roughly two types: (a) those that merely seek to describe such practices and beliefs, and (b) those that seek to evaluate the hypothesis that psi phenomena are actually involved in such practices.

With regard to studies of the first type, we have already mentioned Dean Shiels' survey indicating the widespread belief in out-of-body experiences among nonwestern or "primitive" cultures. Renee Haynes notes that witches' brews and ointments frequently contain hallucinogenic chemicals that could produce sensations of flying and hence precipitate OBEs.[53] Magical or psi-like powers are frequently attributed to shamans or medicine men in "primitive" cultures. The belief of the Australian aborigines that their "clever men" may project themselves at will has already been discussed. Richard Reichbart describes how Navajo hand tremblers are thought to be able to find lost objects and to diagnose the causes of illnesses.[54] In a general essay on shamanic practices,[55] Reichbart notes that the following powers have been attributed to shamans: (a) the ability to direct the movements of game animals, (b) healing abilities, (c) the ability to find lost objects, and (d) the ability to predict and control the weather. He notes that shamans frequently do rely on sleight-of-hand techniques and use normally acquired information in their practices. He suggests that the use of such fraudulent practices may facilitate the occurrence of actual psi phenomena, and he compares it to the technique developed by Kenneth Batcheldor and employed by Colin Brookes-Smith of using fraudulently-produced table movements to create an atmosphere in which paranormally produced table movements may be more likely to occur in a seance situation.[56] (Unfortunately, there is little in the way of hard evidence that any of the table movements produced using Brookes-Smith's technique were in fact genuinely paranormal.) Michael Winkelman has traced several similarities between techniques used in experimental parapsychology to elicit psi and shamanic practices. Like parapsychologists, shamans may use altered states of consciousness and visualization techniques to facilitate psi. Shamans and other nonwestern diviners may use random processes, such as tossing coins when using the *I Ching*, as a part of their divination practices. It is possible that such random devices could be susceptible to psychokinetic influence by the shaman, allowing the production of meaningful messages.[57] (On the other hand, we have of course already seen the lack of effectiveness of such techniques when subjected to experimental test.)

Studies of the second type go beyond mere description and attempt to evaluate the paranormality of the purported effects. Some investigations are essentially anecdotal in nature. Richard McKee describes a case involving voodoo-like effects on the wife of the manager of a Ford agency in Swaziland. This woman had been experiencing migraine headaches for a period of time before a clay effigy was discovered hidden in an unused cupboard. The woman had told her maid that she could work for her if she were sick. Her headaches went away after a ritual in which the effigy was destroyed and prayers were said.[58] This cure could of course, like the cases of voodoo death discussed previously, be purely psychosomatic in nature and no more paranormal than the usual placebo effect.

Some experimental investigations of the psi powers of nonwestern shamans and healers have been reported. In an investigation of the psychokinetic powers of the practitioners of an Afro-Brazilian healing cult, Patric Giesler found that such practitioners were more successful in an experimental test of their PK abilities than were control subjects. Their scoring was facilitated when a cult-relevant form of feedback (the display of a deity figure) was used to signal success in the PK task.[59] The significance of Giesler's results may, however, be questioned due to the large number of statistical tests he performed on his data. Alok Saklani found Himalayan shamans to be successful in using PK or "healing energies" to accelerate the growth of plants.[60] In this context, it would be good to keep in mind the previously discussed negative verdict on psychic surgery.

Firewalking is a technique practiced by people in diverse cultures, ranging from fakirs in India to account executives in California. The ability to walk on fire is often taken as an indication of the firewalker's mental discipline, spiritual development or faith. In back-to-back articles in *The Skeptical Inquirer*, Michael R. Dennett and Bernard Leikind and William McCarthy observe that many of the materials used in such firewalking escapades, such as wood, coal and volcanic pumice, are noted for their low heat capacity or poor thermal conductivity.[61] Leikind and McCarthy also suggest that the "leidenfrost effect" may protect the feet of firewalkers. Water vapor is a poor conductor of heat, and sweat from the feet of the firewalker may form an insulating layer, or leidenfrost, protecting the feet from burning. Thus, there may be nothing paranormal about a person's ability to walk on fire for reasonably short distances at a fast enough pace. Thus, a high degree of spiritual development may not be a prerequisite for successful firewalking, and so our account executive need not balk at treading the coals.

Probably the most outlandish anecdotal case in the professional literature is David Read Barker's claim to have witnessed a possible instance of weather control by a Tibetan shaman.[62] This shaman was commissioned by the Dalai Lama to perform a rite designed to stop a huge storm long enough for a mourning ceremony to take place. The storm was reduced to an area of cold fog within a radius of 150 meters of the site of the ceremony, although the rain continued to pour elsewhere. Of course, this is an isolated observation, so a coincidence explanation cannot be ruled out.

While anthropological investigations have yielded tantalizing hints of dramatic phenomena such as Barker's anecdotal report of weather-engineering, such studies have been sparse indeed. A more systematic effort may be needed to sort the wheat from the chaff in this area. Such an effort would of course cost money, and, given the present state of funding in parapsychology, it is not likely to happen soon.

Forteana

There is a wide variety of truly strange phenomena that are sometimes linked, albeit tangentially, with phenomena that form the subject matter of more "orthodox" parapsychology. These bizarre occurrences are sometimes designated "Forteana," in honor of the early twentieth century paradoxer Charles Hoy Fort, who amassed a large catalogue of anomalies that seem to fly in the face of modern science. Forteana include such diverse subjects as UFOs, sightings of Bigfoot and the Loch Ness monster, weeping statues, the Bermuda triangle, and spontaneous human combustion. While none of these topics have been given extensive consideration by mainstream parapsychologists, relationships between these phenomena and more typical psi phenomena have been drawn by several "fringe" writers. Therefore, for the sake of completeness (as well as the reader's entertainment), a very brief discussion of Forteana is given in the paragraphs to follow, with an emphasis on the connections that have been alleged to exist between Forteana and the psi phenomena more typically studied by parapsychologists.

In cases of spontaneous human combustion, people are alleged to burst into flames for no apparent reason, with their bodies being more or less completely incinerated. While this might seem to be intimately related to the spontaneous ignition of fires that occur in some poltergeist cases, parapsychologists have shown remarkably little interest in spontaneous human combustion. A skeptical explanation of this phenomenon has been provided by Joe Nickell and John Fischer, writing in the pages of *The Skeptical Inquirer*.[63] In their view, many cases of ostensible spontaneous combustion death may be explained in terms of careless cigarette smoking by intoxicated persons of high body fat content. The body fat and the alcohol provide the fuel for the fire, with the body fat liquefying in what the authors colorfully term "the human candle effect."

Paranormal phenomena are frequently linked with Christian saints and holy men (and women) of other religions; indeed, such phenomena often constitute the miracles prerequisite to the canonization of such saints. Among the psi phenomena that have been ascribed to Christian saints are the materialization of food, the ability to prophesy, bilocation, levitation (as in the famous cases of St. Joseph of Copertino and St. Teresa of Avila, both of whom frequently ascended into the air in fits of religious ecstasy), and immunity from the damaging effects of fire.[64] Berthold Schwarz has described cases of fire immunity, fire handling and apparent immunity from snakebites among Pentacostal worshippers,[65] and Carlos Alvarado notes that luminous auras have often been reported around both saints and mediums.[66] All of these cases are of course anecdotal in nature, and many of them rely on testimony that is quite old. Certainly, reports of bilocation and levitation in the modern era are few and far between, notwithstanding the construction of a levitation hall at Maharishi International University in Iowa to accommodate an ever-increasing host of "levitating" transcendental meditators. (To anyone who has watched films of allegedly levitating TMers, the word "bouncing" will seem a more apt description than "levitating.")

Carlos Alvarado has also reported on a case in which faces kept appearing on a kitchen floor as well as on a mirror and on the hearth of a house. When the offending spot on the kitchen floor was cut out, bones were discovered under the site of the face.[67]

The list goes on and on, and encompasses bleeding statues, sightings of the Virgin Mary, UFOs, Sasquatch and cattle mutilations. It would take us too far afield to give a comprehensive review of such fields as ufology and cryptozoology here. Readers interested in such phenomena are invited to consult such specialty journals as the *Journal of Scientific Exploration* and *The Skeptical Inquirer*.

D. Scott Rogo hypothesized that many strange, seeming external and physically objective phenomena such as flying saucers and Bigfoot are really materialization phenomena or psychic projections that are produced by the minds of the observers themselves.[68] As such, these would be analogous to the "thought forms" that are alleged to be projected by Tibetan shamans, as described by Alexandra David-Neel.[69] Because there is little in the way of scientifically rigorous evidence for the existence of materialization phenomena and because many of the cases that Rogo cites in support of his theory are of dubious credibility, the parapsychological community has not exactly rushed to embrace his theory.

General Summary of Field Investigations

The evidence discussed thus far in this book has been largely of an anec-dotal nature. A determined skeptic might be inclined to dismiss all of it on the basis of coincidence, unconscious inference, memory distortion, delusions, hallucinations and outright fraud. It is largely because of these counterexplanations that parapsychologists have turned to experimental investigations as the primary means of establishing the existence of psi phenomena and investigating their modus operandi. These investigations form the subject of the next chapter. It should be noted, however, that these experimental studies have themselves been subject to repeated attacks by skeptics on the basis of methodological errors, lack of repeatability, and possible experimenter fraud. Sometimes spontaneous case material may be more convincing than an array of experiments. I have talked to several skeptics who, while dismissing experimental investigations, were left with a nagging feeling that psi might be real after all due to their own personal psi experiences or those of their acquaintances.

A summary dismissal of the evidence from spontaneous cases as nonrigorous and hence unworthy of serious consideration is not appropriate. Not only may spontaneous cases provide unique insights into the operation of psi in naturalistic settings, which may not be obtainable from contrived and artificial experimental situations, but they may provide important clues as to possible productive lines of experimental investigation. Also, many skeptical counter-explanations of spontaneous cases are quite implausible. Thus, spontaneous cases form an important body of evidence for psi in their own right, and supplement the evidence obtained by experimental parapsychologists. A past president of the Parapsychological Association, Rhea White, has even gone so far as to urge the abandonment of the experimental approach in psi research in favor of the study of spontaneous cases.[70] She has contended that reliance on statistical and laboratory methods may lead to a suppression of awareness of clues to the nature of psi arising from spontaneous experiences and informal practices, and she suggests adopting a "depth psychology" approach to the investigation of parapsychological phenomena. She has further contended that sounder data have arisen from surveys of spontaneous experiences than from unreliable laboratory effects. In all probability, however, it will take evidence of both types to convince a skeptical scientific community of the existence of psi. A total abandonment of the experimental approach would probably disqualify parapsychology from any claim to be a real science in the eyes of the scientific establishment. Experimental approaches must be an integral part of any science of parapsychology. It is to an examination of such laboratory studies that we now turn.

6. Is Psi Real?

Psychical researchers soon came to realize that spontaneous cases could not provide a "clean proof" of the existence of psi due to the various possible skeptical explanations of these cases, such as those invoking coincidence, delusion, unconscious inference and fraud. Therefore they turned to experimental approaches to establish the reality of psi effects. In the early days of parapsychology, such experiments typically involved attempts by human subjects to use their powers of extrasensory perception to discern the identity of a playing card hidden from their view or to use their psychokinetic abilities to influence the fall of mechanically thrown dice. When a subject is guessing a randomly selected card held in a separate room, the problems of sensory cues and unconscious inference are presumably removed. If contemporaneous records of the experiments are made, one need not rely on the fallible memory (or deceiving testimony) of the people involved, save of course for the experimenters themselves. Thus, the problems of memory distortion or fraudulent testimony on the part of informants in spontaneous cases are likewise eliminated when the experimental approach is adopted.

Perhaps the chief benefit of the experimental approach is its ability to deal with the objection that apparent cases of psi are simply due to coincidence. For instance, suppose an experiment is run in which a subject tries to guess in advance the outcomes of a series of tosses of an unbiased coin. If the subject guesses the outcomes of four tosses, his probability of getting them all right by chance may be easily computed. If a coin is tossed four times, one of the following events must occur:

HHHH HHHT HHTH HTHH THHH HHTT HTHT HTTH
THHT THTH TTHH HTTT THTT TTHT TTTH TTTT

(Here HHTH, for instance, denotes the event in which the coin comes up heads on the first, second and fourth tosses, while the third toss comes up tails.) As these events are all equally likely, the probability that the toss outcomes correspond exactly to the subject's sequence of guesses is 1 in 16. In other words the subject would be expected to obtain perfect success through sheer luck in about one out of every sixteen experiments. Similarly, if a subject guesses twenty-five flips of a coin and gets twenty of them right, standard statistical formulas may be applied to determine that the probability of guessing twenty or more flips correctly by chance is approximately .002. In other words, one would expect this level of success to occur in only two out of every thousand experiments by chance. As it would be unlikely that this level of success could be achieved through sheer luck (that is, in the absence of ESP), one would take the step of rejecting the "null hypothesis" (that the results can be ascribed to chance) and state that the results are significant at the .002 level, meaning that the probability of attaining such an extreme score by chance would be less than .002 in the absence of ESP. Similarly, if a person attempts to guess the order of the cards in a well-shuffled and hidden deck of ESP cards and guesses 13 of the cards correctly (as opposed to the five she would be expected to get right on the average by chance), the mathematical theory of probability can be invoked to show that this would happen in fewer than 1 in 10,000 such experiments by chance. We would conclude that it is very unlikely that we would have obtained such a result by chance unless we were to run thousands of such experiments.

The philosopher Francis Bacon was perhaps the first on record to suggest that psi phenomena could be investigated through the statistical analysis of card-guessing and dice-throwing experiments.[1] Charles Richet was the first to initiate anything approaching an actual research program in this area. Richet's card-guessing experiments were conducted in the 1880s in France.[2] In the early part of the twentieth century, experimental studies of ESP involving the guessing of cards were performed by Leonard Troland and George Estabrooks at Harvard University and J.E. Coover at Stanford University.[3] Estabrooks' very successful experiment was conducted while completing his doctorate under William McDougall, a prominent psychologist who had an interest in psychical research.

In 1927, McDougall moved to Duke University to assume the chairmanship of the psychology department. He was followed soon thereafter by an enthusiastic young psychical researcher, J.B. Rhine, and his wife, Louisa. During the academic year 1929-1930, Rhine began his program of experimental research on psi phenomena. This program eventually evolved into the sustained and continuous research tradition that has become known as experimental parapsychology. For this reason, Rhine is usually regarded as the founder of the field of parapsychology (in the sense of the experimental study of psi phenomena). Rhine in fact was responsible for the adoption of the name "parapsychology" to describe his field of inquiry, although it should be noted that Max Dessoir in Germany was the first to use the term "parapsychologie" to describe the investigation of the "border" region between normal and abnormal psychological states.[4] Rhine can, however, lay sole claim to coining the term "extrasensory perception," or ESP, to describe the receptive form of psi (as opposed to PK).

Rhine's initial methods for investigating ESP relied heavily on the standard "ESP cards," which were designed for Rhine by the Duke perceptual psychologist Karl Zener. (This deck was known for a long time as the "Zener deck," somewhat to the consternation of Zener, who later abandoned parapsychological research for work in more mainstream and less controversial areas of psychology.) The ESP deck consists of 25 cards, with five cards representing each of the following five symbols: circle, star, cross, square and wavy lines. When a subject guesses the order of the cards in a well-shuffled ESP deck, he has a one-fifth chance of guessing any particular card correctly, and it can be shown mathematically that the average score he would expect to achieve by chance is five correct guesses.

In 1934, at the suggestion of a young gambler, Rhine began to investigate psychokinesis (PK), or the power of the mind to influence matter directly, without the involvement of the musculoskeletal system, using dice as target objects. Initially, Rhine investigated the ability of human subjects to influence dice to roll in such a way that a given "target" face would come up. Later, other investigators had subjects attempt to influence the direction or speed of mechanically thrown dice so that they come to rest at specific target locations. Such tests became known as "placement tests." Because of the controversy surrounding his ESP results, Rhine withheld publication of his PK research until 1943.

In the modern era the targets of psychokinetic influence have expanded to include living organisms, red blood cells, thermistors, and quantum-mechanically based random event generators (REGs). The latter devices have also been used to generate ESP targets. In ESP research, there has been a move in the direction away from forced-choice experiments (in which the subject's response on each trial is restricted to a finite set of specified alternatives, as in guessing a deck of ESP cards) and toward free-response experiments, in which a subject is free to describe his impression of the target in any terms he chooses. A free-response methodology is employed in modern ganzfeld experiments, in which a subject is typically seated in a comfortable chair with ping-pong balls placed over his eyes to produce a uniform visual field and frequently with white or "pink" noise played in his ears to produce a homogeneous form of auditory stimulation as well. The subject may then try to describe a target picture that is being viewed by a human sender or agent, this target having been randomly selected from a target pool consisting of, say, four potential target pictures. The subject or an outside judge then ranks the pictures in the target pool against the subject's descriptions. Obviously, given the random nature of the target selection, the probability that the subject's description will be matched against the correct target by chance is one-fourth. Other examples of free-response experiments include remote viewing studies, in which a subject attempts to describe the location to which a human sender has been sent, and dream studies, in which a subject's dream reports are matched against, say, art prints viewed by a human sender attempting to influence the subject's dream.

Forced-choice Experiments

Perhaps the foremost forced-choice ESP experiment performed in the heyday of the card-guessing era of Rhine's early research group at Duke University was the Pearce-Pratt series conducted on the Duke campus during the 1933-1934 academic year.[5] In this experiment, the subject, a divinity student named Hubert Pearce, attempted to guess the identity of cards held in a separate building by J.G. Pratt, a graduate student in psychology. In each session, the men would synchronize their watches, and then Pearce would leave for a cubicle in the stacks of the library. Pratt then shuffled a deck of ESP cards and placed one card face down each minute on a book on a table in his building, which was either the Physics Building (100 yards distant from the library) or the Medical Building (250 yard distant). Pearce attempted to guess the identity of the card located on the book at the specified time. Two decks were guessed per session. In all, 1850 cards were guessed, and Pearce averaged 7.54 cards guessed correctly per deck, where 5 would be expected by chance. These results were significant at the $p < 10^{-22}$ level, meaning that this level of success would occur by chance fewer than once in 10 sextillion such experiments. Clearly chance coincidence cannot account for these results, and they have been taken as strong evidence of ESP.

A more modern form of forced-choice experiment was pioneered by physicist Helmut Schmidt in his study of the precognition of radioactive decay, a quantum process that is in principle unpredictable under modern theories of physics.[6] Schmidt's study relied on a type of quantum-mechanically based random event generator (REG) that has since become known as a "Schmidt machine" and is now a widely-used and basic tool in parapsychological research. With Schmidt's original machine, the subject was confronted with an array of four differently colored light bulbs. The subject's task was to guess which bulb on the display was going to be the next to light up. The subject signaled his or her guess by pushing a button in front of the chosen bulb. During this process, an electronic counter was constantly cycling through the values 1, 2, 3, 4, 1, 2, 3, 4, 1, 2, 3, 4… at the rate of a million steps a second. After the subject pressed a button indicating his or her guess, the counter stopped when a Geiger counter detected a decay electron emitted from a sample of strontium 90 and the corresponding lamp was lit. The subject's task could thus be construed as one of predicting the time of future radioactive decay of a strontium 90 atom to within an accuracy of a millionth of a second. (However, more plausibly from a psychological and sensory-motor point of view, the subjects were simply foreseeing which lamp would be lit). The subjects' guesses and the lamps actually lit were automatically recorded on counters and punch tape, eliminating the possibility of directional errors by human recorders. Extensive randomness tests were run on the REG to ensure that its output was indeed random. In Schmidt's first experiment, three subjects made a total of 63,066 guesses and scored 691.5 more hits than they would have been expected to by chance. This level of success could be achieved through sheer luck in only two out of every billion such experiments. In a confirmation study, Schmidt had the subjects attempt to achieve high scores in some prespecified trials and low scores in others. 20,000 trials were run, and the subjects obtained 401 more hits (in the prespecified direction) than they would have expected to by chance. Results this good would be expected only once in 10 billion such experiments. It certainly seems as though some other than chance, or "coincidence," is operating in Schmidt's experiments. Presumably, that something is ESP.

Free-response Experiments

In free-response experiments, the target is generally not chosen from a small pool of targets known to the subject, but instead may be drawn from a small pool of targets unknown to the subject or, much more rarely, may be created uniquely for each trial. The subject in turn does not simply select a guess corresponding to one of a fixed number of alternatives but rather describes her impressions of the target, which may be in the form of dreams, visual imagery, or a free-association monologue. The subject typically uses verbal descriptions or drawings to communicate these impressions.

Some of the earliest free response experiments involved the telepathic transmission of drawings.[7] In these studies, the sender, or agent, generally constructed a drawing and the percipient attempted to draw a picture corresponding to the sketch made by the agent. In these early studies, some very striking correspondences were obtained, even when the sender and the percipient were located on opposite sides of the Atlantic Ocean. However, as the targets were not selected randomly from a fixed set of alternatives, statistical evaluation of these correspondences proved difficult and a quantitative estimate of the probability that these similarities between the agent's drawings and the percipient's impressions would arise by chance could not be obtained, despite the subjectively striking nature of these correspondences.

The most commonly used techniques in modern free-response experiments are the ganzfeld and remote-viewing procedures. A highly successful series of remote-viewing trials was conducted in the late 1970s by the team of Targ and Puthoff at Stanford Research Institute.[8] To give the reader the flavor of the remote-viewing procedure, a single trial from a five-trial long-distance series will be described. Unlike most of Targ and Puthoff's trials, the target was not chosen randomly but rather was selected by a skeptical scientist. The scientist then took the remote-viewing team to the target site, which was a series of underground chambers in Ohio Caverns in Springfield, Ohio, which were filled with stalagmites and stalactites. The subject remained behind in New York City and was told only that the remote-viewing team was located somewhere between New York City and California. After the remote-viewing team had spent 45 minutes touring the caverns, the skeptical scientist then called the subject in New York, whereupon a transcript of the subject's impression of the target area was read to him. The opening passage of the transcript was as follows[9]:

1:50 PM before starting—Flat semiindustrial countryside with mountain range in background and something to do with underground caves or mines or deep shafts—half manmade, half natural—some electric humming going on— throbbing, inner throbbing. Nuclear or some very far out and possibly secret installation—corridor—mazes of them—whole underground city almost—Don't like it at all—long for outdoors and nature. 2:00 PM—[Experimenters] R and H walking along sunny road—entering into arborlike shaft—again looks like man helped nature—vines (wisteria) growing in arch at entrance like to a wine cellar—leading into underground world. Darker earth-smelling cool moist passage with something grey and of interest on the left of them—musty—sudden change to bank of elevators—a very manmade [sic] steel wall—and shaft-like inserted silo going below earth—brightly lit.

The above correspondence is of course quite impressive. But it is important that targets in free-response experiments be chosen randomly (as they were in most of Targ and Puthoff's research). For instance, a depressing global event (or increasing sunspot activity, etc.) may have caused both the skeptical scientist and the percipient in this experiment to be in a gloomy mood, and that may account for both the scientist's selection of a dark underground cave as a target area and for the percipient's descriptions.

In the early 1970s, Montague Ullman and Stanley Krippner conducted an experimental study of "dream telepathy" at the New York Maimonides Medical Center. This research employed a fully-equipped sleep laboratory and was designed to investigate the possibility that a subject's dreams could incorporate elements of an art print chosen as an ESP target. The subject went to sleep in the laboratory, with the usual EEG electrodes affixed to his head. He was then awakened toward the end of each rapid eye movement (REM) period, which is known to be associated with dreaming, and asked to give a dream report. Several such reports would be elicited from a given subject in a typical night. The art print to serve as the ESP target was randomly chosen from a set of possible targets. A person who served as sender or "agent" then attempted to "send" the picture to the sleeping subject, so that the latter might incorporate the target material into his or her dream. Usually, one art print served as the target for an entire night. After the subject's sleep period was concluded, the subject's dream reports were compared to the target as well as to a set of control art prints, which served as foils. The pictures were then ranked as to degree of correspondence with the dream reports, both by the subject and by outside judges. In several series, the foil pictures consisted of the remaining targets in a small target pool from which the actual target was chosen. Some subjects obtained highly successful results. For instance, a woman named Felicia Parise obtained 34 "direct hits" (meaning that the target picture was rated first among the pictures in an eight target pool in terms of correspondence with the subject's dream) out of 66 trials, as determined by her own ratings of the targets. Only 8.25 direct hits would be expected by chance, so this is a clearly significant result. Strangely enough, the independent judges gave Ms. Parise only nine direct hits (about what would be expected by chance). Another subject, Dr. Robert van de Castle, himself a dream researcher, spent eight nights in the laboratory as a subject and scored a "hit" (target print ranked in the top half of the eight-target pool) on each night by his own evaluations. The independent judges gave him only six hits, but five of these were direct hits, where only one direct hit would be expected by chance. Many other subjects were less successful.[10]

Sometimes rather striking correspondences between the target print and the subject's dream were obtained. For instance, on one night the art print chosen as target was Goya's *The Duelers*, which portrays two Spaniards engaged in a duel with swords. One of the participants has succeeded in making a thrust into the other's abdomen. The first dream report of the subject, Dr. Robyn Posin, a psychologist, was as follows:

[I was] in the office of a man who is sort of waiting for this woman to arrive. He's actually ... talking about her in the sense that the venom and anger that I experience in him is reserved for her ... And he has this thing that's like a bullwhip ... and he hits the wall with the whip and makes a crack ... and then thinks of a woman. There was something very impotent about this man's rage ... It wasn't a bullwhip that he had, it was really a cat-o'-nine tails ... It had its origins ... in Spain ... It was a very frightening experience.[11]

The researchers go on to report that

In her seventh dream, she was at a Black Muslim rally. "They were really raging, and all of a sudden some doors from an auditorium opened and out came Elijah Mohammed and a bunch of his followers ... He had on this huge flaming torch with which to set some more stuff on fire, and I got very scared." Her associations to this were "It was like a real chaos scene ... the terrorism, that same kind of lack of control, I guess, that seemed to me to be anger and hostility and acting out in it ... It's some sort of conflagration, either symbolically or realistically ... something rather violent."[12]

PK *Tests*

PK tests may be divided into roughly two types: "micro-PK" tests, in which the evidence for PK is primarily based on deviations from statistical distributions expected by chance (such as those governing the fall of dice) and "macro-PK" tests, in which the subject attempts to create a macrophysical change in the target object (such as by bending a spoon).

In the early days of parapsychology, dice typically served as the target objects in micro-PK experiments. In the modern era, quantum-mechanically based random event generators (REGs) and living systems have been the most frequently used target objects. In one typical experiment, Helmut Schmidt enclosed his pet cat in a cold shack.[13] In the shack was a 200 watt lamp, which served as a source of heat for the cat. Once each second, a quantum-mechanically based REG of the type described previously sent either an "on" or "off" signal to the lamp. The REG was designed in such a way that the probability of an "on" signal was 50 percent. Thus, the cat could obtain more heat by using its psychokinetic abilities to influence the REG to output more "on" signals than would be expected by chance. In fact, in 9000 trials, 4,615 "on" signals were generated, indicating that the cat may have used its PK to increase the probability of an "on" signal from 50 percent to 51.2 percent, admittedly a very slight increase, but one which would occur by chance in only eight of a thousand such experiments. To check the randomness of the generator, Schmidt ran the REG over a period of 24 nights without the cat in the shack and found no departures from chance levels in a total of 691,200 signals generated.

Some micro-PK experiments are designed to detect a psychokinetic influence on living organisms. For instance, William Braud conducted a study in which human subjects attempted to influence the spatial orientation of a knife fish (*Gymnotus carapo*). The fish generates its own electrical field, which Braud monitored through two parallel copper plates placed in the fish's tank. When the fish swam parallel to the plates, a weak signal was recorded; the signal became stronger as the fish rotated its position to become perpendicular to the plates. The human subject's task was to increase the strength of these signals during certain time periods designated as conformance epochs. The strength of this signal was then compared with that generated in other time periods that served as controls. The signal was found to be stronger during the conformance epochs than during the control epochs, indicating that the subjects were successful in influencing the fish to adopt an orientation perpendicular to the plates.[14]

The subject of macro-PK is much more problematic. Macro-PK, which may involve the bending of metal specimens, the ostensibly paranormal production of images on photographic film, or the movement of small objects across the surface of a table, usually involves special subjects having the status of semiprofessional psychics. Because the psychic himself to a large extent determines the nature of the phenomena he may produce and the conditions under which he feels comfortable in producing them, the investigator does not have the same control over the experimental procedure that he would have in a micro-PK experiment instigated and designed by himself. In fact, in macro-PK research, experimental procedures and conditions often must be negotiated with the psychic if he is to perform at all. Consequently, proper procedures are much less well-defined in macro-PK research than they are in micro-PK research. As most special macro-PK subjects are suspected of, and accused of, fraud by skeptical scientists and writers, the suspicion arises that these psychics will not perform unless they have succeeded in negotiating conditions and procedures that will allow them to produce the alleged macro-PK phenomena fraudulently. Thus, there is considerable debate, both within and outside the parapsychological community, over the adequacy of the methods and safeguards taken in macro-PK research. In fact, several macro-PK subjects have indeed been detected in fraud, as will be discussed in greater detail in the section on subject fraud below.

Separation of Psi Modalities

In the beginnings of experimental parapsychology, it was thought possible to separate psi abilities into several component subtypes: telepathy (the ability to read the mind of another person or being, usually assumed to involve direct contact between minds at the mental, rather than physical, level), clairvoyance (the paranormal ability to acquire information directly from objects, such as when a subject is able to identify a card which has been hidden in a container and whose identity is known to no one at the time), precognition (the ability to foretell events that are yet to happen), retrocognition (the direct paranormal knowledge of past events), and psychokinesis (the ability of mind to influence matter directly). To this list could be added retroactive psychokinesis, the rather outlandish ability to influence events that have already occurred in the past. This seemingly implausible psi power was first proposed to exist by Helmut Schmidt,[15] who has since gone on to amass a considerable amount of experimental data in its support.[16] In a typical retroactive-PK experiment, a subject may be asked to use his mental abilities to increase the rate at which one of two lights comes on. Unknown to the subject, the behavior of the lights is governed by the output of a random event generator (REG) of the "Schmidt machine" type that was generated two weeks previously. Thus, the subject's covert task is to extend his PK influence backward in time to influence the behavior of the REG two weeks in the past. Schmidt has actually provided a fairly plausible account of why such retroactive PK effects might be expected to occur, based on his reading of quantum mechanics. Essentially, Schmidt, along with many other theorists, believes that the outcome of a quantum process does not take on a definite value until it is observed by a conscious being (even if a considerable period of time elapses before the observation takes place). We will examine this view of quantum mechanics further in the next chapter.

Early on in parapsychology, it became apparent that it was difficult to establish the existence of any of these pure forms of psi in a definitive manner. For instance, in Schmidt's four-button precognition experiment, rather than using precognition to guess the identity of the correct lamp, the subject may rather be pushing a button and then using her psychokinesis to cause the correct lamp to light up. Similarly, in a telepathy experiment in which a percipient attempts to guess what card an agent is looking at, it is quite possible that the percipient may use his clairvoyant powers to read the card directly rather than reading the mind of the agent. Alternatively, if the agent is merely thinking of a card, the identity of which he will announce later, the percipient might use precognitive clairvoyance to access whatever physical record of the target is later made. Also, even if a seemingly pure test of telepathy could be devised, any alleged telepathy on the part of the percipient could be interpreted as clairvoyant perception of the brain state of the agent. Such considerations led J.B. Rhine to call the existence of telepathy an "untestable hypothesis" and to recommend that the problem of proving the existence of pure telepathy be "shelved."[17]

It is also possible that much of the evidence for PK, especially that arising from micro-PK experiments with random event generators as targets, might be explained in terms of precognition. Specifically, consider Schmidt's experiment with his cat, described above. Rather than assuming that the excess of "on" signals is due to the cat's PK abilities, it might be argued that Schmidt used his precognitive ability to initiate the experiment (e.g., by pushing a button) at the precise time that a series containing an excess of "on" signals was about to be generated.

Because of the difficulty of obtaining an experimental separation of the various types of psi phenomena, the parapsychologists Robert Thouless and B.P. Wiesner suggested adopting the neutral term "psi" to designate parapsychological phenomena of unspecified type. They further suggested that psi might be broken into psi-gamma, the receptive type of psi seen in clairvoyance, telepathy and precognition experiments, and psi-kappa, the active type of psi generally seen in PK experiments[18] (although as we have just seen, it may be difficult to distinguish between these two types of ability in practice). The British psychologist John Beloff has argued for the retention of the traditional categories of psi in general and of telepathy in particular. Beloff feels that interpretations of phenomena suggestive of telepathy in terms of clairvoyance of brain states is questionable, as it is doubtful that a person could interpret the idiosyncratic "neural code" employed by another person's brain.[19]

Parapsychologists do continue to use terms such as precognition, clair-voyance and psychokinesis in describing their own experimental procedures, but these typically refer to the experimental task as described to the subject rather than implying that a particular set of experimental results is definitely due to, say, precognition rather than PK.

We will now turn to an examination of the controversies surrounding experimental work in parapsychology, the lessons that may be learned from them regarding proper methodology and the reasons for the continuing resistance of the scientific establishment to experimental psi research.

Criticisms of Psi Research

Irrational motives. Before plunging into a discussion of the various "rational" criticisms that have been made of experimental methodology such as charges of statistical and methodological errors in psi research and allegations of fraud by subjects or experimenters, it may be instructive to consider first the possible irrational thought processes that may account for the fact that some people seem to rush to embrace a belief in psi phenomena while other people summarily dismiss the possibility that psi phenomena may exist, often before examining the evidence for such phenomena. The irrational bases for both belief and disbelief in psi may include emotional and religious motives, metaphysical prejudices and the various types of illogical reasoning that often underlie the formation of attitudes in general.

To begin with, at least some skeptics have indeed manifested a fairly closed-minded and prejudiced attitude against psi research. Such an attitude is evident in the following quotations from two eminent scientists, the psychologist Donald Hebb and the physicist Hermann von Helmholtz.[20] First Hebb:

Why do we not accept E.S.P. as a psychological fact? Rhine has offered us enough evidence to have convinced us on any other issue … I cannot see what other basis my colleagues have for rejecting it … My own rejection of [Rhine's] views is in a literal sense prejudice.

Now Helmholtz:

I cannot believe it. Neither the testimony of all the Fellows of the Royal Society, not even the evidence of my own senses would lead me to believe in the transmission of thought from one person to another independently of the recognized channels of sensation. It is clearly impossible.

In part this rejection is based on the perception that the existence of psi phenomena would be incompatible with known scientific principles. Certainly it is true that it would be hard to explain ESP and PK on the basis of currently understood physical processes. This does not, however, imply that psi phenomena are necessarily in conflict with any known laws of physics (except perhaps for certain types of psychokinetic phenomena). In fact, not only are many of the theories proposed by parapsychologists to account for psi compatible with known scientific principles, a large number of them are even based on such principles (these theories will be discussed more completely in the next chapter). It is probably true that the ultimate explanation of psi phenomena will require the postulation of new entities or processes that are not part of current scientific theories, but this does not mean that psi phenomena need violate any established law of science, as will be made clear in the succeeding chapter.

In this light, the (a priori) resistance of orthodox scientists may be based more on a desire for closure or a tendency to see the work of science as being completed than on any real logical contradiction between psi phenomena and established theories. This attitude is exemplified in the following statement by the physicist A.A. Michelson, which he made twenty years *after* his paradigm-shaking experiment on the velocity of the Earth relative to the luminiferous ether, an experiment that led to the downfall of Newtonian mechanics and to the eventual acceptance of the special theory of relativity:

The more important fundamental laws and facts of the physical universe have all been discovered and these are now so firmly established that the possibility of their ever being supplanted in consequence of new discoveries is exceedingly remote.[21]

Michelson added that, although there were apparent exceptions to most of these laws, these were due to the increasing accuracy of measurement made possible by modern apparatus and that the system of known physical laws would be adequate to deal with the "apparent exceptions." He went on to assert that "Our future discoveries must be looked for in the sixth place of decimals."[22] What is most amazing about these statements is that they preceded rather than followed the publication of Einstein's paper on special relativity, a paper which of course caused a revolution in science that received its main immediate empirical support from the results of Michelson's own experiment!

With such a desire on the part of some scientists to see the picture of the world constructed by science as finished and final, it is not surprising that there is antagonism toward psi phenomena, with their implication that current scientific pictures of the world are incomplete.

A more modern version of this tendency toward closure is provided by the biologist Sidney Fox, who argues that, if new laws are required to explain the emergence of life, then they lie "outside the realm of science."[23] Fox thus equates science with established scientific theories rather than with the process of scientific discovery.

This "principle of closure" was recognized by the Gestalt psychologists as a common psychological tendency arising from the pressure to achieve a solution to a problem-solving task. One way a person may reduce such psychological pressure is to enter a state of premature closure, in which the problem is viewed as having been solved when in fact it has not been.

Religious motives. There is no doubt that the same psychological needs that promote belief in various religions (including desires for control over the elements, knowledge of the future, protection from natural forces and the vagaries of chance, power over disease, and a life after death) are also responsible for the widespread belief in parapsychological phenomena. Modern science has discredited naive and literal interpretations of many religions, and for many people parapsychology fills the void thus created. Parapsychology not only has all the accouterments of science itself but also promises to satisfy most of the psychological needs underlying religious belief through its alleged demonstration of such paranormal phenomena as psychokinesis, precognition, psychic healing, and the survival of death.

Religious motivations and a desire to overthrow what they regarded as the depressing mechanistic cosmology proposed by nineteenth-century science formed an explicit and openly acknowledged part of the motivations of the founders of the Society for Psychical Research. Prominent among these concerns was unquestionably the fact of death with its promise of total annihilation of the human personality. This great concern of the early psychical researchers with the problem of the survival of death was undoubtedly in part attributable to the biological instinct for survival as well as a desire to be reunited with lost loved ones. It is well known, for example, that the public's interest in mediums and seances, with their offer of a chance to communicate with deceased loved ones, tends to increase markedly during and after times of great tragedy, such as world wars. As psi phenomena seemed to contradict the exclusively materialistic outlook of nineteenth century physics and to point to a mental realm over and above the physical world, they were readily embraced by persons seeking scientific support for the concept of a spiritual realm. Indeed, as recently as 1982, upon the occasion of the centenary of the founding of the S.P.R., the prominent British parapsychologist John Beloff asserted in his presidential address to the Parapsychological Association that the survival of death was contingent upon the existence of psi.[24] This is probably a questionable assertion, as it is quite conceivable that the mind could survive death even if it did not possess the powers of ESP and PK, but it does show how closely related the issues of the existence of paranormal powers and the survival of death are in the minds of many parapsychologists.

The scientific community may in turn have feared (and may still fear) a trend toward irrationalism and a possible reemergence of religious persecution with an accompanying attempt to suppress scientific doctrines. Certainly the memory of the Christian resistance to the heliocentric (sun-centered) model of the solar system has never been far from the consciousness of the scientific community. Certainly, the credulous attitude of many elements of the public and even some self-proclaimed parapsychologists toward various purported paranormal phenomena has done little to lessen the skeptics' fears. The skeptics, however, do a disservice to the enterprise of rational inquiry when they misleadingly classify parapsychologists who adhere to the principles of science in their investigations of purported paranormal phenomena together with wide-eyed believers in cattle-mutilating UFO pilots and channelers of the Loch Ness monster.

Psychodynamic factors. Paranoid mechanisms undoubtedly account for some portion of the belief in psychic powers, especially one's own psychic powers, and these mechanisms are particularly apparent in many persons who visit, write, or call parapsychological laboratories. Paranoid delusions of persecution, for instance, commonly include the belief that one's enemies are paranormally monitoring and manipulating one's thoughts. James Alcock is among several skeptics who contend that such "magical thinking" also underlies parapsychologists' belief in psi.[25]

On the other hand, ardent disbelief in psi phenomena could be construed as a form of defense against paranoid thoughts (and the causal efficacy of unconscious wishes) or as fear of the uncanny and unknown. Charles Tart has attributed skepticism toward psi phenomena to a "primal repression" of threatening telepathic interactions between mother and child.[26] In an attempt to document such a widespread fear of psi, Tart asked subjects to imagine that they possessed extraordinarily strong psi powers that were effective within a 100 yard radius. He found that the reactions of the subjects in this "belief experiment" were predominantly negative.[27] Harvey Irwin found fear of psi to correlate negatively with sympathy for psi research,[28] lending support to Tart's contention that such fear forms a motivational basis for skepticism. Such fears of psi are sometimes explicitly stated by skeptics. For instance, in a recent debunking of hypnosis and associated psi phenomena printed by Prometheus Books, the publishing arm of the Committee of the Scientific Investigation of the Claims of the Paranormal, an organization of skeptics, Robert Baker has this to say:

Think what a horrible world it would be if psychokinesis were a fact and could be used at will by anyone. The slightest angry thought could propel a brick, a stone, a chair, a bottle with deadly force. Cars would be washed from the highways and planes wiped out of the skies by someone's whim. If telepathy were common or universal, privacy would be a thing of the past and the mental effort we would be required to exert to monitor our own as well as other people's thinking processes would leave use little time for ordinary cognitive chores. We would be faced with a world made up of human monsters and creatures that would no longer appear to be human. Rather than the boon and blessing that proponents of the paranormal have foreseen, universal access to such full-blown mental powers could destroy civilization as we know it and bring us down more quickly than the most deadly of our nuclear devices.[29]

Social and attitudinal processes. Obviously, the subfield of social psychology known as "attitude theory" may have much to tell us about how attitudes toward parapsychology are formed. According to Hovland, Janis and Kelly's reinforcement theory of attitude formation, one tends to hold beliefs that one has been rewarded for expressing and to extinguish beliefs for which one has been punished for expressing.[30] To express a belief in psi phenomena or to pursue psi research may result in a loss of tenure and funding and a general ostracism from the orthodox academic community. Thus, as the reward structures within the academic community tend to favor anti-psi beliefs, one would expect them to engender skepticism. This would, however, neglect the propensity of some members of the lay public to provide monetary support and sometimes even adulation to investigators expressing belief in psi powers.

According to Leon Festinger, the author of "cognitive dissonance" theory, one method of avoiding the stress arising from an inconsistent belief system is to avoid exposure to high-quality communications and arguments that run counter to one's own position on a given issue.[31] This might explain the tendency of some parapsychologists to ignore or repress legitimate and constructive criticisms of their methodology. Sometimes this can result in disaster, as has often happened in research on paranormal metal-bending, most notably in the case of Project Alpha, in which researchers at Washington University in St. Louis were deceived by stooges of critic James Randi posing as psychics, primarily because the researchers failed to employ safeguards suggested by Randi (Project Alpha will be discussed in more detail in the section on subject fraud below).

On the other side, critics often fail to heed (or at least discuss) the better-conducted studies in the field of parapsychology. Occasionally, critics write books and articles debunking the weakest claims in the field, such as Arthur Conan Doyle's alleged pictures of fairies[32] and Kreskin's stage performances,[33] while at the same time claiming to have debunked the entire field of parapsychology. This may be understandable in light of the fact that the scientific community's main concern may be directed toward a possible trend toward irrationalism (and the concern of magicians such as Randi may be directed at possible dishonest and attention-stealing uses of conjuring techniques). The primary concern of such critics may thus not be so much with "legitimate" parapsychology, but with clearly quack science and charlatanism. To the extent that this is the case, parapsychologists should applaud their efforts (but not their claim to have debunked the entire field of parapsychology).

Another technique for avoiding a sense of cognitive dissonance is to reduce the psychological importance of an issue about which there is conflict. I recall the remarks of one prominent cognitive psychologist who told me that, although he did not know whether parapsychological phenomena existed or not, he did not see why they were of any importance (perhaps reflecting his concern as a psychological rather than a physical theorist). A related strategy for reducing the stress of cognitive inconsistency is to "stop thinking."[34] To some extent, this has been the traditional response of academic psychology to the claims of parapsychology, which are almost never discussed in any detail in the academic curricula of psychology departments. Because of this "heads in the sand" approach, departments of psychology have in many instances failed in what should be their responsibility to provide a responsible (even if skeptical) discussion of alleged parapsychological phenomena, a topic that is of great interest to students and to the public in general.

Lack of social support for one's beliefs is another source of cognitive dissonance, according to Festinger. Certainly, the tendency of people to conform to group opinion, the pressure put upon people to conform to majority opinions by groups, and the tendency of people to obey authority figures have been amply demonstrated in classic psychological experiments by Asch, Schachter, and Milgrim.[35] Within the academic community, one would expect such pressures to favor skepticism with regard to psi phenomena. One way to decrease the cognitive dissonance arising from lack of social support is, according to Festinger, to decrease the perceived attractiveness of the disagreeing parties (which might result in a skeptic classifying all parapsychologists as fairy-worshipping lunatics or a parapsychologist classifying all skeptics as unimaginative, narrow-minded bigots). It would be expected that this strategy would be especially prevalent among persons scoring high on scales of dogmatism.[36]

In closing, it should be noted that the denial of funds and professional opportunities is not confined to parapsychologists but is a problem faced by non-mainstream scientists in general. Eliot Marshall, for instance, recently wrote an article in *Science* in which he discussed the denial of telescope time to heterodox plasma theorist Halton Arp, thus depriving him of the opportunity to make even basic observations. By restricting telescope time to supporters of orthodox views, Marshall notes, the process of science is thereby distorted and the potential for dialogue between opposing views closed off. (Indeed, the possibility of observationally-supported heterodox views even arising is virtually eliminated). As a resolution to this problem, Marshall recommends that some funds be allocated to non-mainstream scientists, without requiring the process of "peer review" by advocates of orthodox positions.[37]

Rational Bases

We will now consider more rational grounds for the rejection of psi phenomena that are based on legitimate concerns regarding proper methodology, the issue of the replicability of the effects and the possibility of fraud.

Sensory cues. When one is attempting to establish the existence of an ability to identify target material that lies outside of the normally recognized channels of the physical senses, it is obviously important to exclude the possibility that the subject's knowledge of a target is based on "sensory cues" (that is, information acquired through the usual physical senses). The early days of experimental parapsychology were not characterized by the stringent safeguards against sensory cues that are (usually) employed today. For instance, an "agent" might sit at one end of a table, pick up an ESP card and attempt to project its identity into the mind of a percipient seated at the other end of the table. Under these circumstances, the percipient might learn the card's identity by seeing the card reflected in the agent's eyes or by picking up on cues unconsciously provided by the agent (such as tilting the head when viewing a "star," etc.). The behaviorist B.F. Skinner pointed out that the cards in the Zener ESP deck used by Rhine in his early experiments could be read from the back under certain lighting conditions, invalidating any experiment in which the percipient could see the backs of the cards. Parapsychologists were quick to respond to such critiques by totally isolating the subject from the targets (such as by having them in a separate building, as was done in the Pearce-Pratt series discussed previously, for instance). Most forced-choice experiments in parapsychology today are characterized by adequate shielding of the target from the percipient. Exceptions do of course still occur, as no field is immune from methodological errors committed by its practitioners. For instance, Don, Warren, McDonough and Collura report an experiment in which the ESP cards used as targets were placed directly on the hand of the special subject (Olof Jonsson), allowing him access to possible sensory cues arising from the back of the cards, as well as possible glimpses of the fronts of the cards. The random number table used to generate the targets was also in the room with the subject and could be a source of additional cues.[38]

As another example, the archskeptic Martin Gardner has pointed out that a light system that was used by the "sender" to signal the beginning of the next trial to the percipient in Charles Tart's experiments on training ESP ability might allow the sender to provide cues as to the identity of the next target through the conscious or unconscious use of a time delay code.[39] As a rule of thumb, in a parapsychological experiment no person with knowledge of a target's identity should be allowed to communicate with the subject attempting to guess that target until after the subject has made his guess.

The mathematician Persi Diaconis points out the danger of giving trial-by-trial feedback to a subject guessing a target pool that is being sampled without replacement, such as might occur if the subject is guessing a deck of ESP cards and being shown each card after every guess.[40] Such feedback would enable the subject to improve his chances by avoiding guesses corresponding to already sampled targets (e.g., if the subject guessing an ESP deck has already seen all five circle cards, he can improve his chances by not guessing "circle" again). This is of course correct, but Diaconis' implication that this is a typical testing procedure in parapsychology is misleading. In fact a search by Tart[41] revealed only four studies using such a procedure, three of them appearing in an unpublished master's thesis. Tart had labeled all four studies as methodologically defective in his review of the literature pertaining to studies employing trial-by-trial feedback.

While it is rare for forced-choice experiments to employ trial-by-trial feedback with such a "closed deck" procedure, this does occur more often in free-response experiments, in which subjects give their subjective impression of a target rather than guessing it directly. In one type of procedure, these subjective impressions are ranked or matched against all the targets used in the experiment. For instance, Puthoff, Targ and Tart conducted an experiment in which a subject attempted to use her ESP to describe ten different target objects. Because the subject was shown the target object after each trial, she could, on subsequent trials, avoid giving descriptions corresponding to previously seen targets, thus artifactually inflating the probability that her descriptions would be correctly matched to the targets by the judges.[42] Diaconis' criticism is clearly applicable to this sort of free-response experiment. In a similar vein, Marks and Kammann have argued that in Targ and Puthoff's main remote viewing research the subjects' remarks contained clues as to trial order (by referring to "two previous targets," for example) and target identity (by explicitly referring to previously seen targets, which the judges would then know not to match with the present transcript).[43] Tart, Puthoff and Targ attempted to respond to Marks and Kammann's critique by conducting an analysis showing that the results were still statistically significant even after these cues had been edited out of the transcripts.[44] One can of course quibble about the efficacy of the editing process, and Marks and Scott have argued that statements left in the transcripts after the editing that referred to the subject's location could constitute residual order cues that might be used by judges.[45] For instance, in one trial Targ asked the subject if he noticed "any difference being in a shielded room rather than in the park." This was the first trial done in a shielded room. In any event, the basic problem (namely, the avoidance by the subject of responses descriptive of previously seen targets) that arises from use of trial-by-trial feedback under conditions of sampling without replacement remains, no matter how effective one assumes the editing process was.

A related problem in free-response experiments involves the nonverbal sensory cueing of judges. For instance, in remote viewing experiments conducted by Bisaha and Dunne, judges were provided with pictures of the target location taken on the day of the remote-viewing trial.[46] Thus, cues as to weather conditions, seasonal variations (e.g., foliage conditions), time of day, and so forth, could have been present in both the subject's transcripts and the pictures, and the judges could then use these cues, consciously or unconsciously, to match the transcripts to the targets. Bisaha and Dunne deny that such cues exist, but in the only two picture sets they reproduce from their first experiment, the leaves are still on the trees in one, whereas the trees are bare in the other. Also, David Marks has pointed out that, in Bisaha and Dunne's experiments, the decision as to whether the subject's drawings of his or her impressions of the target site would be presented to the judges was made on an ex post facto basis (that is, after examination of the drawings), which may have biased the information presented to the judges in favor of correct transcript-target matchings.[47] Marks goes on to note that the choice of which photographs of the target site to present to the judges may have been a further biasing factor.

As another example of how sensory cues may be inadvertently provided to judges in free-response experiments, one can cite the transoceanic remote-viewing experiment reported by Marilyn Schlitz and Elmar Gruber. In the first judging of the experiment, the agent's impressions of the target site were included among the material provided to the judges.[48] This may have resulted in cues as to target order being given to the judges (e.g., the agent and the percipient might both refer to a news event occurring on a given day). Schlitz and Gruber themselves pointed out this problem and reported a rejudging of the experiment with the cues deleted; the results were still significant.[49] The skeptic Ray Hyman has since detected a further possible source of sensory cues to judges arising from the fact that Gruber, who served as agent and hence knew the identity of the target for each trial, was responsible for translating the remarks of Schlitz, the percipient, into Italian for presentation to the judges. His translation might have been biased by his knowledge of the target site.[50]

A very similar problem exists in two dream telepathy experiments reported by Child, Kanthamani and Sweeney.[51] In each experiment, an agent attempted to send a different target picture into the dreams of a percipient on each of eight different nights. The eight sets of dreams and impressions were then ranked by the agent against the eight targets. However, as the agent knew which target was used on which night and as the percipient's dreams would be expected to incorporate certain "day residues" reflecting the events of the prior day, the agent could have used this knowledge to match the dreams against the targets.

Most of the just discussed problems arise from the fact that the experiments involved used a procedure involving sampling without replacement from a finite target pool, often combined with judging the entire set of transcripts for a series against the actual targets used in that series. Most free-response experiments have the responses judged against a different target pool for each trial and do not suffer from the problem of sensory cueing of judges to the extent that the above-discussed studies do. That is not to say that these experiments have been immune from such problems. For instance, in the early ganzfeld experiments, the subject often judged his own transcripts against the same physical target pool used by the agent. Thus, it is possible that the subject could obtain cues as to which target was actually sent by the agent by examining the target pictures for fingerprints, crumpling effects and so on. In an initial attempt to test this "greasy fingers" hypothesis, John Palmer found no evidence that subjects in fact used such cues to identify the picture held by the agent, although the results of this study were to some extent contradicted by a later study by Palmer and Kramer indicating that subjects could indeed use such cues to identify the target picture when they were specifically instructed to do so.[52] This problem has been eliminated in recent ganzfeld experiments through the use of duplicate sets of pictures, one to be used by the agent and the other by the judge.

It is obvious that the problem of sensory-cuing can be a subtle one. While the problem of eliminating sensory cues to subjects has long ago been resolved, procedures for the elimination of sensory cues to judges are still evolving. How prevalent is the problem of sensory cuing in parapsychological research? In order to find out, Charles Akers conducted an analysis of a sample of 54 parapsychological experiments. Among his criteria for inclusion were that each experiment have produced significant evidence of psi and that the experiment be from a relatively repeatable line of research Consequently, Akers' sample included a large number of ganzfeld experiments, as this is one of the lines of parapsychological research that have come the closest to producing a repeatable parapsychological experiment. Of the 54 experiments, Akers cites 22 studies as possibly providing sensory cues regarding the target's identity to subjects or judges. One would suspect, however, that, had Akers' sample included a greater proportion of (less repeatable) forced-choice studies, the proportion of studies with methodological flaws involving sensory cues would be reduced. Now we turn from the problem of sensory cues in ESP experiments to the related problems of motor artifacts in PK experiments.

Motor artifacts. In certain types of psychokinesis experiments, it is very important to ensure that the subject cannot use his or her motor skills to influence the target apparatus. For instance, in a "placement PK" experiment in which a subject is attempting to use psychokinesis to influence a series of balls rolling down a chute to go into the left or right side of a collection bin, it is important to ensure that the subject cannot influence the balls by breathing on them, rocking the table, altering the air currents by changing his or her body position, and so forth. Also, it is important to ensure that the balls be placed in the apparatus in the same way at the beginning of each trial, otherwise the experimenter may subconsciously learn how to place the balls in such a way that the desired result occurs.

As an example of such artifacts, consider an experiment reported by George Egely in which a subject attempted to influence the motion of objects floating in liquid in a Petri dish. The subject was allowed to put his hand into the shielded box and next to the Petri dish. Thus, it is quite possible that the obtained motions of the target object might have been due to air currents set in motion through the moving of the subject's hand.[54] As another example, John Taylor has contended that the movement of small objects by the Russian psychic Alla Vinogradova was due to an electrostatic effect. Specifically, he contends that a repulsive force may have been induced by electrical charges on her hands and the object to be moved. Indeed motion pictures taken of this type of "psychokinetic" motion do suggest this possibility, as the objects are typically a short distance from the psychic's fingertip and moving away from it, much like a peanut one centimeter in front of the nose of a contestant in a peanut race. Taylor also cites the fact that Vinogradova typically rubbed her hands together prior to her performances as further evidence that an electrostatic effect was responsible for the motion of the objects.[55]

Experiments that involve an attempted psychokinetic influence of living targets should also include precautions against normal sensory-motor influence. For instance, in an experiment reported by Jean Barry, subjects sat for fifteen minutes at a distance of one and a half meters from a set of ten Petri dishes, attempting to inhibit the growth of the fungus in five experimental dishes while "ignoring" the control dishes.[56] Under these conditions, it might be possible for a subject to influence the growth by, for instance, breathing on the dishes. In the early 1950s, Nigel Richmond reported an experiment in which he was successful in influencing paramecia to swim to a specified target quadrant as he viewed them through a microscope. As Richmond was obviously close to the microscope, he could have influenced the paramecia through his breath or by jiggling the slide.[57] Another problem in this experiment is that, while the target quadrant was randomly selected, Richmond did not use a random process to select the paramecium to be influenced; thus he may have selected paramecia already predisposed to move to the desired quadrant, as has been pointed out by Mark Johnson.[58]

Pleass and Dey report an experiment in which subjects attempted to use their PK abilities to influence the motion of specimens of the marine alga *Dunaliella*.[59] A problem with this experiment is that the subjects were allowed to select which time periods would be the PK influence periods rather than having these periods specified in advance. Thus, it is possible that the subjects may have been able to choose favorable periods based on sensory cues derived from observations of the algae or of environmental factors that were associated with the motion of the algae.

Fortunately, most PK experiments reported in the modern literature are relatively free from such artifacts. Indeed, the bulk of the literature uses quantum-mechanically based Schmidt REGs as target objects, and radioactive decay is hardly subject to sensory-motor influence!

Violations of blindness. It is important in parapsychology, as in other disciplines, that measurement of certain variables be done by a person who is blind as to the values of other variables. For instance, if an experimenter who is rating a person's extraversion based on clinical observation during an interview already knows that person's score on an ESP test, the experimenter may consciously or unconsciously tend to give higher extraversion ratings to persons with high ESP scores, thus artifactually producing another confirmation of the generally-obtained positive relation between ESP and extraversion.

It is also important that anyone interacting with a subject prior to his description of an ESP target be blind as to the identity of that target. For instance, Palmer and Lieberman report an "out-of-body experience" study in which an experimenter who knew the identity of the target was in the room with the subject.[60] This experimenter might have been able to exert some sort of subtle influence to predispose the subject to give a description corresponding to the target, without even being aware of doing so.

Persons physically interacting with PK target materials should also be kept blind as to the target. For instance, in an experiment reported by Carroll Nash,[61] the experimenter placing fungus samples in an incubator was not blind as to which funguses were to be psychokinetically inhibited and accelerated and which were controls. Thus the experimenter might have been able to influence the outcomes in the desired direction by selective placement of the funguses in the incubator. Obviously, in such an experiment it is important that the person measuring the fungus growth also be blind as to the experimental condition.

An artifactual correlation between ESP scores and a personality trait may result if the subject has knowledge of his ESP score prior to taking the personality test, as the subject's responses to the latter test may be biased by his knowledge of his ESP scores. That this possibility is a legitimate concern is evidenced by results reported by Palmer and Lieberman.[62] They found a positive relationship between imagery score and ESP score for subjects who took the Betts Imagery Scale after getting feedback about their ESP scores, but not for subjects who took the imagery test prior to the ESP test. On the basis of these results, they conclude that a previously reported positive relationship between imagery and ESP[63] was probably due to the same artifact.

A "meta-analysis" of experiments exploring the relationship between ESP ability and extraversion by Honorton, Ferrari and Bem strongly suggests that much of the evidence for a positive relationship between these two variables might be due to a similar artifact.[64] In particular, these authors found no evidence for a positive relationship between ESP and extraversion in forced-choice studies in which the extraversion measurement preceded the ESP test. The evidence for a positive relationship in forced-choice experiments thus appears to be an artifact of the subjects' knowledge of their ESP scores when responding to the extraversion test. In 11 of 14 free-response studies, the extraversion test preceded the ESP test, and a positive relationship between the two variables was still found in these studies, which is apparently not due to the artifact in question. In an attempt to test whether this artifact is indeed a problem, Krishna and Rao gave subjects false feedback as to their ESP scores in order to see if such feedback would indeed bias their responses on a personality test. They did not find a significant difference in extraversion scores between subjects given positive and negative false feedback, in opposition to the bias hypothesis. It should, however, be noted that there was no significant relation between extraversion and (real) ESP scores in this study.[65]

As a general principle, recording or measurement of experimental conditions and targets and of the related psi effects should be carried out under conditions of mutual blindness in both PK and ESP experiments.

Due to the defensive stance parapsychologists must take in light of criticism by a community of hostile skeptics, parapsychologists tend if anything to be more careful about blindness violations than most scientists. In his analysis of 54 parapsychological experiments, Akers cited nine for having flaws involving the nonblind measurement of personality variables.[66] As Akers' sample included a large number of studies relating personality variables to ESP, this is probably an overestimate of the rate at which blindness violations are committed in parapsychology.

Nonrandom target selection. In order to eliminate the hypothesis of chance coincidence, it is important that the targets in parapsychological experiments be selected randomly. It will not do, for instance to have a person select a target by thinking of a number between 1 and 10, as certain numbers are more likely to pop into his mind (and the guesser's) than are others, raising the probability to a correct guess above the chance level of .1. For instance, in an experiment by Tyrrell,[67] the subject had to guess which of five targets lamps would be lit on each trial. In the initial stages of the research, Tyrrell himself selected the targets, attempting to be "random" but not employing any formal randomization procedure. Thus, the subject could quickly learn Tyrrell's favorite targets and guess these more frequently than the others. She could also increase her score by not calling lamps that had just been lit or by calling the same lamp again if it had not been lit on the previous trial (as people attempting to produce a random sequence of targets tend to avoid repetitions, thus producing sequential dependencies in the target series). Therefore, the subject could expect to do much better than the twenty percent hit rate expected by chance. This sequential dependency problem was pointed out to Tyrrell by G.W. Fisk, and the experiment was continued using random numbers to select the targets. Under these conditions, the subject was still able to achieve a highly significant score.

More recently, Susan Blackmore criticized a study by Ernesto Spinelli on the basis that the children who served as agents in Spinelli's experiment were simply allowed to choose which picture they wished to "send" to the percipient via ESP.[68] This is Tyrrell's initial flaw in a modern guise.

Randomization of target selection has also been a problem in some free-response experiments involving the drawing of pictures, including the classic initial experiments reported by Upton Sinclair and Rene Warcollier.[69] In recent times, this problem has been exemplified in the picture-drawing experiments with Uri Geller at Stanford Research Institute conducted by Targ and Puthoff.[70] In these experiments, the target was generated by opening a dictionary "at random" and drawing the first "drawable" word on the page. (Which words are to be considered "drawable" is an arbitrary decision that may itself disqualify the target selection process as a truly random procedure.) The investigators allowed considerable latitude in the interpretations of the word in the target drawing. For instance, the one target selection that Targ and Puthoff describe in detail involved the word "farmer." In the target drawing, the farmer is equipped not only with a pitchfork, but also with horns and an elaborate tail; in addition, the label "Devil" appears above the figure. If Geller and the target preparer had just been viewing *The Exorcist*, for instance, that common experience could account for both the target drawing and Geller's religiously oriented response. This amount of latitude in interpretation destroys any claim to random selection of the target.

Nonrandom target selection has also plagued some recent remote viewing research. For instance, in the "volitional mode" technique employed in the remote-viewing studies by Jahn and Dunne,[71] the target to be visited was merely selected by the agent rather than chosen randomly from a prepared target pool (no such pool even existed on these trials). Also, in Jahn and Dunne's experiments, the agent was frequently allowed to wander from the assigned target area, to take photographs and to write descriptions of the target area. As these materials were provided to the judges, they essentially constitute the target. The agent was therefore free to construct a target that might match the verbal transcript likely to be provided by the percipient on that particular day. Hansen, Utts and Markwick estimate that in 211 of Jahn and Dunne's 336 formal remote-viewing trials the agent was free to choose or construct the target in a nonrandom manner.[72]

In his analysis of a sample of 54 ESP experiments, Akers concluded that target randomization was informally done (e.g., hand-shuffling of cards) or inadequately described in about half of the studies.[73] Some of these randomization flaws may be debatable (e.g., the fact that an "untrained agent" prepared targets from a random number table). He also found that randomness tests were not conducted on the apparatus used in 10 out of a sample of 27 psychokinesis experiments. He further notes that control runs are done infrequently in PK experiments and calls for an increased use of control runs as well as for more frequent randomness checks on the equipment to be performed during the experiment and within the actual experimental environment.

Statistical controversies

The use of improper statistical tests. In parapsychology as in any other science, researchers do occasionally apply inappropriate statistical tests to their data or commit other statistical errors. As universal perfection is not likely to be achieved in any field of study, the rate at which such errors occur is not likely to be reduced to zero. In recent years, however, parapsychologists have been fairly meticulous about ensuring that the statistical tests they perform are appropriate to their data. They have been held to higher standards than the practitioners of other disciplines due to unrelenting and vigorous attacks by critics. Thus, the statistical practices of parapsychologists tend, if anything, to be a little more rigorous than those of many other scientific disciplines. Some researchers will always be more competent than others, and some errors are bound to occur from time to time.

Attacks on probability theory itself. There have been some critics who have gone so far as to suggest that basic tenets of probability theory should be given up in order to avoid swallowing the bitter pill of the existence of psi. Among them are George Spencer Brown, J. Barnard Gilmore, and James Alcock.[74] This would be more than throwing out the baby with the bathwater. The whole family tree would be getting the toss, because virtually all branches of science reply on statistics and probability theory to reach and justify their conclusions.

In this context, it should be noted that there are other writers, such as Arthur Koestler and Alister Hardy, who have also argued for the existence of basic flaws in probability theory.[75] They differ from the critics mentioned above primarily in terms of motivation. They see such flaws as supporting the theory of synchronicity or meaningful coincidences promulgated by Carl Jung. Jung's theory of synchronicity will be taken up again in the next chapter.

Specifically, Koestler argued that the "law of large numbers" constitutes a paradox in probability theory. This law asserts, for instance, that if an unbiased coin is tossed a large number of times, the obtained proportion of heads will be very nearly equal to the value of 1/2 that would be expected by chance. Koestler contended that this requires an "acausal connection" or conspiracy among parts of the series such that an initial run of, say, heads will be balanced by a later run of tails. However, the law of large numbers is mathematically derived from the precise assumption that no such conspiracy exists, that is to say, that the outcome of one trial has no effect on the outcome of any other. Thus there is no need for, and indeed no room for, Koestler's proposed mysterious acausal connections. After all, the fact that the laws of probability theory are obeyed in the law of large numbers hardly constitutes evidence against those laws!

There have been several critics who have objected to parapsychologists' comparison of their data to theoretical distributions derived from the theory of probability rather than to empirical control groups.[76] In this context, the skeptic James Alcock has contended that the comparison of experimental with control groups "makes artifact only a minor problem" in "normal" science.[77] However, in a crude (and methodologically unacceptable) PK experiment in which coins are tossed by hand, motor skills could be used to increase the number of heads in the "heads" condition and the number of tails in the "tails" condition. Thus, the use of a control group would hardly eliminate all artifacts in this case, as it would not in the case of a psychology experiment in which violations of blindness could lead a researcher to treat subjects in his experimental and control groups differently, perhaps in the process consciously or unconsciously using subtle means to make them behave in such a manner as to confirm his hypothesis. Use of a control group does not automatically eliminate all sources of experimental error, as Alcock seems to assume.

Some critics have even chastised parapsychologists for their use of control groups. C.E.M. Hansel has criticized Helmut Schmidt for using a high-aim condition (in which subjects try to guess which of four lamps will be lit) and a low-aim condition (in which subjects try to guess a lamp that will not light) in the second experiment in his investigation into the precognition of a quantum process, which was discussed at the beginning of this chapter.[78] In Schmidt's experiment, the subject indicated his or her response by pushing a button on the machine, and the guess and target for each trial as well as the type of condition (high- or low-aim) were recorded on tape. Schmidt's low-aim condition thus served as an excellent control for his high-aim condition (and would guard against some types of possible machine artifacts). Hansel makes the point that the overall results were not significantly different from chance. However, when the results are scored in the *intended* direction (that is, high- or low-aim), they are highly significant. Hansel also recommends that different machines be used for the high- and low-aim conditions. However, as the machines could each be mechanically biased in the desired directions, this would negate the advantage of using the same machine as a control for itself.

Thus, parapsychologists are caught in a double bind, as critics have castigated them both for their employment of a control condition and for their failure to employ one. They use theoretical distributions to attack parapsychological work (as Hansel did in attacking Schmidt) but disapprove of parapsychologists' use of the same distribution (Alcock). Hansel also uses a theoretical distribution to attack results showing differences in psi scoring rates between groups of subjects (such as extraverts and introverts, for example) when he notes that, although the groups differ from one another (one scoring above chance and one below), the overall score does not differ significantly from chance.

It should also be noted that the traditional statistical tests of differences between experimental and control data themselves rely on theoretical distributions (such as the *t* distribution). In any event, Charles Akers points out that, in his analysis of a sample of 54 ESP studies, the statistical tests used were directed at a comparison between empirically obtained means in about two-thirds of the cases, so the use of purely theoretical distributions is by no means as rampant as these critics have charged.[79]

Multiple analyses. It is possible for a parapsychologist to conduct so many statistical tests on his data that some of them would be expected to be significant purely by chance. If you try hard enough to find patterns in random data, you will be successful. These patterns will be meaningless, however, as they represent nothing but the fluctuations that would be expected to occur by chance. There are mathematical corrections that may be used to take the number of analyses performed on the data into account, and these are increasingly being used by parapsychologists.

A related problem is that of post hoc analysis. Suppose a researcher glances at her data and happens to notice that female subjects tended to get higher ESP scores in her experiment than did male subjects. If she runs a test to see if this difference is statistically significant, we once again run into the problem of multiple analyses, as we have no way of how many potential patterns of this type might have "caught her eye" had they been present in the data. In this case, it is impossible to correct for the number of analyses performed, as it is unclear how many different patterns could have been noticed by the experimenter. The proper thing to do in this case would be for the researcher to label her finding as "post hoc" and as only providing a suggestion that an effect might be present. The demonstration of the effect's reality would have to involve further experimental testing to see if the effect occurred again. It is crucial in parapsychology as in all areas of scientific investigation that the hypotheses that are to be tested in an experiment be stated before collecting and examining the data.

In his review of 54 ESP experiments, Charles Akers cites only two studies for flaws involving multiple analyses.[80] He disputes skeptic Ray Hyman's contention that 39 of 42 ganzfeld studies suffer from flaws involving multiple analyses,[81] based on the fact that which analysis should be regarded as the primary analysis in these studies could be inferred from the author's previous practices. One of the tasks I routinely perform is to review the proceedings of the annual meetings of the Parapsychological Association for the *Journal of Parapsychology*. In the course of doing so, I regularly tabulate problems involving multiple analyses of the data, and it is my impression that the real rate lies somewhere between Akers' and Hyman's estimates. It is also my impression that parapsychologists have become increasingly aware of this problem and more vigilant about avoiding it in their research in recent years.

Data selection. If only a portion of the data of a parapsychological experiment is singled out for analysis on an ex post facto basis (e.g., because the hitting rate was particularly high for this portion of the experiment), a spurious psi effect may be generated, as improbable subsequences will exist in any sufficiently long series of random events. Victor Stenger, for instance, claims that data selection took place in the picture-drawing experiments conducted with Uri Geller at Stanford Research Institute, insofar as many unsuccessful trials were never reported or included in the overall analysis.[82] Data selection within a single study has become a less frequent problem in parapsychology over the years (except for the data selection inherent in many post hoc analyses, as discussed above). Charles Akers, for instance, classified only 4 of the 54 ESP studies in his sample as having results that could be attributed to data selection.[83]

One special type of data selection involves what is known as "optional stopping." This occurs when a researcher is monitoring the data of the experiment and waits until an opportune time to stop the study ("quitting while he is ahead," so to speak). To avoid this problem, it is important that the length of any study be specified in advance or at least prior to any examination of the data.

Another form of data selection occurs when only significant results are published or selected for analysis, with insignificant studies being ignored. This form of data selection has long been a standard allegation of the critics. James Alcock for instance charges that parapsychologists only tend to publish significant studies, intimating that the overall evidence for psi might be due to this type of data selection.[84] In rebutting Alcock, Rex Stanford notes that the Parapsychological Association has long had a policy of encouraging the publication of nonsignificant studies,[85] and indeed it does appear that negative results have been published with greater frequency in recent years. To gauge the extent of selective reporting in one specific area of psi research, Susan Blackmore sent a questionnaire to members of the Parapsychological Association asking about unpublished ganzfeld studies. She uncovered 20 such studies, 37 percent of which were significant, as opposed to 57 percent of published studies. (One of the twenty studies could not be evaluated as to significance.) A statistical test indicated this slight difference in success rate between published and unpublished studies was not a statistically significant one. Thus, selective reporting does not appear to be a major problem in this area of research. Also, the high significance levels obtained in some parapsychological studies argue against a data selection explanation for those particular results. If an experimenter obtains an ESP scoring rate in his study that would only be expected to occur in one in a billion such studies by chance, we may conclude that the result is not due to data selection, as it would be absurd to assume that a billion such studies have been conducted and have gone unreported.

Also, using the technique of meta-analysis (to be discussed below) it is often possible to estimate the number of nonsignificant studies that must have gone unreported in order that a particular line of experimentation might be attributed to data selection. Often the number of unpublished studies that must be postulated is unreasonably high, as we shall see.

The Problem of Fraud

One reason for critics' reluctance to accept the experimental findings of parapsychologists is the possibility that they may be the result of fraud, either by subjects or by the investigators themselves. We will discuss each in turn, beginning with the former.

Fraud by subjects. In certain types of parapsychological experiments, fraud by subjects is a possibility that must be carefully guarded against. This is especially true of experiments employing "special subjects," a term used to designate persons with a reputation for having extraordinary paranormal abilities and whose livelihood often depends on the exhibition of such abilities. Subject fraud is much less of a concern in situations in which a group of supposedly average citizens participates in an experiment initiated and designed by the parapsychological investigator, although even in this type of experiment it is prudent to take precautions against the possibility of deceit by subjects.

Several instances of subject fraud occurred in the very early investigations of "mind-reading" teams. C.E.M. Hansel describes how such fraud occurred in the S.P.R.'s investigations of the mind-reading team of Douglas Blackburn and G.A. Smith, which were conducted over the time period from 1882 to 1894. Blackburn served as the telepathic agent in a series of apparently successful picture-drawing experiments in which Smith was the receiver. Blackburn confessed in 1908 that these results had been due to fraud. He as agent had transferred the target drawings onto cigarette paper and then was able to get this paper to Smith when Smith reached for his pencil. Smith himself never admitted to his involvement in the fraud.[87]

The subjects in another one of the S.P.R.'s investigations, the Creery sisters, likewise admitted six years after the investigation that they had use auditory and visual codes to transmit the identity of playing cards to one another.[88] Similarly, Hansel describes how two Welsh schoolboys, Glyn and Ieuan Jones, used signals involving coughs and leg movements to transmit the identity of cards from one to another during experiments run by the British parapsychologist S. G. Soal and his coworkers.[89] The alleged telepathic effects ceased when the door joining the boys' rooms was closed, illustrating the importance of eliminating the possible use of sensory codes by members of alleged mind-reading teams. This is of course merely a special case of the elimination of sensory cues, which is a necessary feature of any properly designed parapsychological experiment.

Hansel has also charged that the results of the Pearce-Pratt experiment, discussed above, were due to subject fraud.[90] Specifically, Hansel proposes an implausible scenario that involved Pearce's sneaking out of the library and peering through the transom at the top of the door to Pratt's room to learn the identity of some of the cards as Pratt recorded the order of the target deck. In presenting his hypothesis, Hansel distorted the architectural plan of the building in which Pratt was located, as has been pointed out by Ian Stevenson.[91] Also, the rather obvious possibility of detection would surely have acted as a strong deterrent to such a scheme. Nevertheless, the fact that Pearce's whereabouts were not well monitored renders this experiment less than definitive. Harvey Irwin has recently argued that declines in Pearce's scoring rates over the course of each session that were discovered after the experiment was concluded, are further evidence for the authenticity of the data, as such decline effects are commonly observed in ESP scoring.[92] A determined skeptic could of course argue that these decline effects may be due to subjects' tendency to cheat early in a session and then "rest their case."

Subject fraud becomes a central concern in experiments on "macro-PK." Macro-PK experiments involve the production of macrophysical effects, as opposed to subtle influences on random event generators that may only be detectable through statistical analysis. Such macrophysical effects include the bending of metal specimens, the levitation or anomalous movement of macrophysical (that is, nonmicroscopic) objects, the starting or stopping of watches, and the apparently paranormal production of photographs. Macro-PK experiments typically but not always involve "special subjects" (persons with prior reputations regarding their ability to manifest extraordinary physical effects of an apparently paranormal nature). It is of course quite possible that such subjects may use fraudulent means to simulate paranormal effects, and it is thus very important that every precaution be taken to eliminate the possibility of such fraud. Unfortunately, macro-PK experiments have frequently lacked the kind of rigorous conditions that would enable the fraud hypothesis to be definitively ruled out. For instance, in the research on metal-bending conducted by physicist John Hasted, the subjects were allowed physical contact with the target object.[93] One subject, Masuaki Kiyota, was even allowed to carry a spoon he was attempting to bend psychokinetically around with him in his pocket. Such lax conditions allow the subjects the opportunity to bend the metal specimens through covert muscular action. Hasted eschewed the use of a video camera, as he felt that such a device with its implied mistrust would decrease his rapport with the subject.

Martin Gardner has criticized macro-PK researchers for their failure to employ traps such as a one-way mirror to detect cheating.[94] That such devices may be effective in detecting fraud is borne out by the research of Pamplin and Collins, who used a one-way mirror to observe several young subjects using fraudulent means to bend metal specimens.[95]

James Randi, who is a professional magician as well as being a prominent critic of psi research, sent two young magicians to a parapsychological laboratory in St. Louis to pose as special macro-PK subjects in an operation Randi dubbed "Project Alpha."[96] Randi found that the researchers had ignored his own advice as to what precautions should be taken against subject fraud. Objects were marked with tags that could be switched. The subjects were allowed to handle sealed envelopes containing ESP targets when they were alone and unobserved. They were able to remove the targets and return them, replacing the staples on the envelope. They were able to remove metal specimens and other target objects from containers supposedly designed to prevent their removal. They were also able to introduce a gap in the sealing of a bell jar, allowing movement of a rotor inside to be produced through air puffs.

Another area in which subject fraud has frequently been charged is that of psychic photography or "thoughtography," in which a psychic is allegedly able to impress his mental images directly onto film, often through a sealed camera or a camera in which the lens has been removed. Several investigations of thoughtography have been reported by Jule Eisenbud and his coworkers.[97] Eisenbud's most prominent subject was Ted Serios, an alcoholic who was consistently intoxicated throughout the experiments and often insisted that the other people present at the experimental sessions drink with him. A party atmosphere often prevailed, with many people milling about. Needless to say, this did not make for the best observational conditions. Serios used a "gizmo," a cylindrical device that he held up to the camera when the pictures were taken. Many skeptics have contended that this gizmo provided Serios an opportunity to engage in sleight-of-hand, such as by secreting a photographic transparency and lens in the gizmo. A gizmo-like device was also used by another of Eisenbud's subjects, stuntman Willie Schwanholz. It is also unclear in many of the experiments how closely guarded the camera and filmpacks were during the sometimes lengthy proceedings. Another subject, the aforementioned Masuaki Kiyota, was allowed to take the camera in the room by himself and to unload the film by himself.

Thus, it is clear that investigations of special macro-PK subjects have all too often fallen short of ideal standards of rigor and sometimes lack necessary precautions against subject fraud. It is important that the control of experiments reside with the experimenter; the subject simply must not be allowed to dictate conditions to the extent that all precautions and safeguards are abrogated.

Akers cited 12 of his 54 experiments for allowing the possibility of subject fraud.[98] Again, subject fraud is not usually so great a concern in experiments involving unselected subjects as it is in experiments with special subjects.

Experimenter fraud. There remains the possibility that the experimenters themselves might engage in fraud. Certainly, some parapsychological researchers have been caught red-handed in such activity. Experimental studies of telepathy by S.G. Soal,[99] long regarded as among the most impressive evidence for ESP, have been demonstrated through statistical analyses by Scott and Haskell[100] and a computer analysis of Soal's target series by Betty Markwick[101] to be due to a crude form of fraudulent alteration of the experimental data by Soal.

The second major scandal involving investigator fraud in parapsychology involved Walter J. Levy, a young medical school graduate, who had recently been appointed as director of J.B. Rhine's research institute and whom many people regarded as Rhine's heir-apparent. When I joined Rhine's research staff in 1974 shortly after completing my own doctorate, one of the primary things that lured me to the lab was Levy's active and hugely successful program in investigating the psi powers of animals, including the precognitive abilities of jirds (a fancy name for what are essentially gerbils) and the psychokinetic powers of rats and chicken embryos. The hapless little jirds had to use their ESP to avoid getting zapped by an electrical shock by moving to the part of their cage or exercise wheel that was going to get spared the electricity. The chicken embryos (still of course encased in their eggs) had to use their PK powers to get a random event generator (REG) to turn on a light to warm them up in lieu of a hen. The rats had to use their PK to convince an REG to send them a jolt in the pleasure center of their brains. The rat experiment proved to be Levy's undoing. I recall one night when he showed me a live data feed indicating that a rat was getting about 25 jolts to his pleasure center in a row. This was most remarkable, as the rat should have been getting a joy burst on only about half the trials by chance. Levy asked me what I thought, and I told him he should check to see if his equipment was functioning properly. Unfortunately he took this hint a little too much to heart as we shall see.

Perhaps we should have suspected Levy as being involved in fraudulent activity earlier than we did. He used to take the laboratory staff out to lunch and excitedly read us passages about the faking of cancer research by William Summerlin, which was big news in the pages of *Science* and *Nature* at the time. We should have known that Levy's enthusiasm about this subject indicated something amiss, but then hindsight is, as they say, always 20-20. I occasionally asked the research team at lunch what they thought of the possibility that one member of the research team might be doing something to fake all the spectacular results they were getting. I never suspected Jay Levy himself, as he seemed to work too hard. Having newly arrived in Durham, I was Levy's roommate for a period while I searched for my own apartment. He worked day and night. He read constantly. It is still not clear to me why a person engaged in fraudulent activity would put in such long hours at it. If I were to perpetrate a fraud myself, I suspect I would work much less arduously at it.

As I said, Levy seemed to take my recommendation to check his equipment a little too seriously. His fellow researchers noticed him frequently puttering around the equipment when experiments were in progress and there would normally be no reason to be interacting with the experimental apparatus. To see if he were up to some monkey business, they secretly wired up the computer to make a duplicate record of the output of the REG. This second record showed the output of the REG to be perfectly random, while Levy's official record showed that the rat was getting jolt after jolt to his pleasure center and obtaining truly prodigious PK scores in the process. It transpired that Levy was disconnecting the wire that recorded the trials on which the rat was unsuccessful and shorting it out on the side of the computer for brief periods of time, thus making it seem as though the rat was achieving remarkable PK success. Some of the members of the research staff told me that they knew that something must have been amiss, as the rats continued to obtain high scores after the electrode that was implanted in their brain had obviously deteriorated and was no longer delivering to the rat its fix of ecstasy. Similarly, Doug Richards told me that he should have known something was wrong with the chicken embryo experiments when the eggs continued to get good scores even though they were quite malodorous (that is, the embryos had long since died). Confronted with the evidence of his crimes, Levy was forced to resign as the director of Rhine's lab and returned to the practice of medicine.

Some critics, including Hansel, have alleged fraud in a great many other investigations.[102] Hansel provides lengthy analyses of experiments showing how significant results could have been produced by fraud on the part of one or more members of the investigating team. His postulation of honesty on the part of some of the participants increases the fun of his analyses, but of course any significant result could be the result of collusion on the part of everyone concerned. Occasionally, Hansel goes somewhat overboard, such as when he fishes through the data of the famous Pratt-Woodruff experiment[103] until he finds an anomalous pattern in the data and then proceeds to use that pattern as evidence for a fraud hypothesis—a hypothesis that was itself undoubtedly constructed on the basis of the pattern in an ex post facto manner (although Hansel does not present it that way). Such flagrantly circular reasoning and unwarranted inferences from post hoc analyses are no more appropriate when they are employed by a skeptic like Hansel than when they are employed by the parapsychologists he criticizes.

It should be borne in mind that parapsychology is by no means unique in having had investigators exposed in fraudulent activity. Few areas of science have escaped the problem of experimenter fraud, as is evident to anyone reading the pages of *Nature* and *Science* these past few years. Among the recent books documenting how rampant fraud has become in established, orthodox areas of science are William Broad and Nicholas Wade's *Betrayers of the Truth* and Alexander Kohn's *False Prophets*.[104] As these authors note, even such great scientists as Galileo, Newton and Mendel apparently succumbed to the temptation to fudge their data from time to time. It must stand to parapsychology's credit that the major instances of fraud in parapsychology have been unearthed by the parapsychologists themselves. Like most areas of science, parapsychology is self-policing and most parapsychologists wish simply to get at the truth underlying ostensible psi phenomena rather than having any dogmatic pro-paranormal ax to grind. Even archskeptic Martin Gardner has stated that he believes that such cheating by experimenters is not much more of a problem in parapsychology than it is in more orthodox areas of science.[105] Given my own failure to obtain reliable experimental evidence for psi and given the scarcity of investigators who can, I myself continue to wonder.

One method of minimizing the possibility of experimenter fraud, which was endorsed by J.B. Rhine, is to run experiments in such a way that the integrity of the procedures and data is under the control of several observers. Experiments can (and have been) designed in such a way that no one member of an investigating team could fraudulently generate a significant result. In such experiments, a determined skeptic would have to postulate a conspiracy among all the members of the investigating team, which is of course much less plausible than the allegation of fraud against a single person.

Psi-mediated experimenter effects. It is certainly true in parapsychology that some investigators seem to be able to obtain significant psi effects on a fairly regular basis, while other investigators (including me) almost never obtain significant evidence of psi despite years of prodigious effort spent in the laboratory. Experimenter fraud is of course one possible explanation for this state of affairs. Another possibility is a difference in personality traits and social interaction style between so-called "psi-facilitory" and "psi-inhibitory" experimenters. J.B. Rhine, for instance, contended that it takes a great deal of skill, personal warmth and enthusiasm on the part of an experimenter to elicit psi from subjects in a laboratory situation. A third possibility, suggested by Jim Kennedy (a member of the research team that exposed Levy) and Judy Taddonio among others, is that the "psi-facilitory" experimenters are themselves the real source of psi in their experiments.[106] In their view, such experimenters might subconsciously use their own psi powers to generate significant results, such as "PK-ing" extroverts to score above chance and introverts to score below chance in an ESP test in order to confirm a pet hypothesis, or by using their precognitive powers to select an appropriate entry into a random number table to ensure that the targets will coincide with the subjects' guesses. For instance, Helmut Schmidt once ran an experiment to see if cockroaches could use their psychokinetic powers to avoid getting electrical shocks. Instead, he found that they got more shocks than they would have been expected to by chance. Does this mean that cockroaches are masochistic? Not necessarily. It seems that Schmidt may have rather enjoyed the sight of the cockroaches popping up from their grid floor like so much popcorn whenever a shock was delivered. He may have been the real source of the PK effect.[107]

Some studies have shown that psi-facilitating experimenters outperform psi-inhibiting experimenters in tests of their own psi ability.[108] There is even evidence that the person who tabulates the data of an experiment after it has been completed may influence the outcome of the experiment (the "checker effect"), possibly through the use of retroactive psychokinesis.[109] Some writers, including Brian Millar, have suggested that psi ability may be compara- tively rare in the population and that successful experimenters may represent some of the few available "psi sources."[110] Of course, if these psi-facilitating experimenters are using their own psi abilities to force the data to conform with their own theories, it would be wise to be cautious about such experi- mental "confirmations" of hypotheses.

The repeatability problem. One of the reasons why parapsychology has not been embraced by the scientific establishment is that many people (includ- ing myself) have been unable to obtain reliable evidence of psi. In the critic's mind, this raises the suspicion that the evidence for psi may be due to unde- tected methodological errors or possibly even fraud on the part of the exper- imenters. Parapsychologists have been quick to point out that many naturally occurring phenomena, such as ball lightning and meteorite landings, are not reproducible on demand but are nonetheless real. Also, some psi proponents suggest that the mere presence of a skeptic may inhibit the manifestation of psi, in a kind of reverse psi-mediated experimenter effect. Interestingly, the noted physicist A.J. Leggett has described the principle of the repeatability of observations in science as the "no ghost" hypothesis (that is, that scientific results are not dependent on the presence or absence of certain observers or on the mental state of the observer).[111] This is a not-so-veiled jab at parapsy- chology. David Ray Griffin, on the other hand, contends that the repeatabil- ity problems of parapsychology are due to the fact that "purposive elements" do not behave with same regularity as the billiard balls of Newtonian physics.[112] Indeed, results in the field of orthodox psychology are rarely as repeatable as are well-established findings in physics.

John Beloff has concluded that "strict repeatability" ("repeatability by any competent observer who adopts the prescribed procedures") is what is needed to convince the critics of the validity of psi.[113] Beloff contends that one form of repeatable observation would be the examination of a film of a strong macro- PK performance or of a "permanent paranormal object" (PPO), such as two interlocked rings of differing composition (e.g., different types of wood). Beloff notes that precisely the latter form of evidence was allegedly produced by the medium Margery in the 1930s, although the rings later became mysteriously unlocked.[114] Possibly in response to Beloff's call, Bernard Wälti has recently reported the existence of a PPO, consisting of two interlocked frames of paper and aluminum that was presented to Wälti by the psychic Silvio Meyer.[115]

Martin Gardner, however, has discussed methods suggested to him by his readers whereby Meyer might have fraudulently produced the object. One of the methods involved manufacturing the paper square around the aluminum frame.[116]

Meta-analysis. Recently a statistical technique known as "meta-analysis" has played an extraordinarily active role both in parapsychological research and debates about the reality of parapsychological effects. A meta-analysis consists of a statistical examination of a group of experimental studies, sometimes consisting of an entire line of research, in order to determine the strength, direction and statistical significance of any overall effects as well as the possible influence of moderator variables (e.g., barometric pressure or the sex of the experimenter) on the size and direction of the effect in question.

One of the earliest uses of meta-analytic techniques was in the now classic debate over the significance and replicability of the ganzfeld line of research between the parapsychologist Charles Honorton and the critic Ray Hyman.[117] Since that time, meta-analyses of a great many lines of parapsychological research have been reported, including forced-choice precognition experiments, free-response ESP experiments, bio-PK studies, PK experiments with REGs, PK experiments with dice, and experiments investigating the effects of hypnosis on ESP, the relationship between ESP scores and the psychological trait of defensiveness, and the relationship between ESP and extraversion, to name just a few.[118]

Among other things, meta-analysis offers a means of deciding whether a given line of research has produced overall results that differ significantly from what would be expected by chance. For instance, in a vote-counting type of meta-analysis (that has now gone out of fashion), Radin, May and Thomson analyzed 332 PK experiments with random event generators that had been published between 1969 and 1984, finding 71 of them to have produced statistically significant evidence of psi. They compute the probability of this happening by chance to be less than 5.4×10^{-43}. For those not versed in scientific notation, this means that it is virtually impossible that these results could be due to chance coincidence. Meta-analysis also provides a means for answering the charge of data selection. For instance Radin, May and Thomson note that, to reduce the overall REG-PK effect to nonsignificance, it would have to be assumed that 7,778 nonsignificant studies had been conducted but not reported.[119]

Meta-analysis can go a long way toward settling the question of whether the significant results reported in a line of research could have arisen by chance or as a result of data selection (by computing the size of the "file drawer" of unreported nonsignificant studies that must be assumed to exist in order to reduce the reported results to nonsignificance). There are, however, other ways significant effects could arise and still not be due to psi. Procedural errors and fraud are two possibilities. What might satisfy the critics would be something approaching repeatability upon demand. If virtually anyone could produce psi effects under conditions he or she found acceptable, there would probably no longer be much debate about their reality. Perhaps, if a certain minimal proportion of all investigators could obtain evidence of psi, then the critics would be satisfied. Or possibly if certain individual critics obtained evidence for ESP the battle for the acceptance of psi would be won. Replication may well be at heart a political process rather than an issue that can be decided by statistical analysis.

Conclusions

To answer the question that is the title of this chapter is not easy. Neither the critics nor the parapsychologists have delivered a knockout blow to the other side. The parapsychologists' claim to have demonstrated the existence of psi in statistically evaluated experiments has not been demolished by any convincing argument on the part of the skeptics. At the same time, the inability of many if not most people to obtain evidence of psi in their own experiments raises questions. Is psi real? I do not know. If I had to base my answer on my own experimental work, I would, like Susan Blackmore, have to say no. But many people have told me some fairly compelling stories about their spontaneous psi experiences, and I have had a few of my own. If psi is real, it carries with it profound implications about the nature of the relationship between the mind and the physical world, as we shall see in the next two chapters. It is to space, time, matter and the brain and their relation to the conscious mind that we now devote our attention.

7. Time, Space and Mind

We will now examine the various theories that have been proposed to explain psi phenomena. Many of these theories involve extensions of our current views of space and time, hence the title of this chapter. Other (mostly failed) attempts have been made to give an account of psi phenomena in terms of more orthodox theories of physics. A third genre of theories proposes the existence of a collective unconscious or collective mind. We will consider each of these theoretical genres in turn.

No one theory has gained general acceptance within the parapsychological community. As K. Ramakrishna Rao has pointed out, the lack of any agreed-upon theory of psi is one reason for the general skepticism of the scientific establishment regarding the existence of parapsychological phenomena.[1] Indeed, some skeptics, such as Antony Flew, have explicitly cited the lack of such a theory as their reason for rejecting the evidence for psi.[2] The lack of a viable theory has hindered the acceptance of hypotheses in other areas of science as well. For instance, Alfred Wegener's ideas regarding continental drift were rejected for decades by the scientific community of geologists, despite an impressive array of geophysical evidence supporting them. It was not until the theory of plate tectonics had been developed and the vast amount of physical evidence for sea-floor spreading had accumulated that Wegener's theory was finally accepted by the majority of geologists.[3]

Thus, a powerful theory may be sorely needed if the science of parapsychology is to gain general acceptance by the scientific community. Of course, the very elusiveness of psi phenomena makes it very difficult to test and refine such a theory. So long as psi effects manifest themselves so capriciously in experimental situations, it will be hard to construct a well verified theory of psi.

Characteristics of a good scientific theory. One of the commonly accepted criteria for classifying a theory as scientific (or in some circles as meaningful at all) is that the theory should make specific predictions about the outcomes of experiments or of other forms of scientific observation. In other words, the theory must be capable of being falsified should the predictions prove erroneous. This is the criterion of "falsifiability" propounded by the philosopher

Karl Popper.[4] Theories that do not yield any predictions regarding possible scientific observations are held to be unfalsifiable and are generally rejected as being unscientific. A large number of "crackpot" theories have been proposed to explain psi phenomena. These theories have invoked new fields or particles, such as "psi fields," "psi-info waves," "psychical fields," "omnipotent consciousness fields," and "bioplasma" (to name but a few recently proposed constructs), in order to explain ESP or PK. The authors of these theories have typically offered no reliable means of detecting or measuring their hypothetical fields, particles or energies, nor do they specify the properties of these entities in a sufficiently exact way that testable predictions can be derived from their theories. Thus, these theories do not qualify as scientific (or even as meaningful) under Popper's falsifiability criterion, and they will therefore not be further considered in this chapter.

Before dismissing all such theories entirely, however, it should be noted that not all scientists and philosophers of science insist on strict adherence to the falsifiability criterion. For instance, physicist David Bohm and F. David Peat have argued that insistence on immediate falsifiability may stifle creative thought and innovation and discourage the creative playing with ideas that may eventually give rise to falsifiable theories. In this context, they cite Democritus' postulation of the existence of atoms, which stood as an untestable idea for millenia before giving rise to modern theories of the atom.[5]

Two theories that make exactly the same predictions are said to be "operationally equivalent" and are often considered to be merely different verbal or mathematical formulations of the same theory. (Of course, it may be a bit chauvinistic on our part to regard two theories as identical simply because they make the same predictions regarding our possible experiences. Just because we with our limited senses and powers of investigation can't distinguish between two theories does not necessarily mean that some privileged observer may not be able to distinguish between them. For instance, the hypothesis that reincarnation occurs but that one carries no trace of one's previous personality or memory of one's previous lives may be operationally equivalent for us to the hypothesis that no soul exists and that consciousness is totally extinguished at death, but to some observer capable of perceiving disembodied souls, the two hypotheses may be not at all equivalent.)

In instances in which two theories appear to be operationally equivalent, the theory that is more conservative in terms of postulating new entities and processes is usually held to be preferred over any less conservative rival. This injunction "not to multiply entities beyond necessity" is commonly known as Ockham's Razor (after the fourteenth century philosopher William of Ockham). Thus, if a medium becomes apparently possessed by the spirit of someone's dead uncle and proceeds to relate accurately details of that uncle's life, it is more conservative to assume that the medium used his or her powers of telepathy (or even better yet from the conservative point of view, fraud) to obtain this information than to postulate the existence of disembodied spirits. This "super-ESP" hypothesis is preferred to the discarnate spirit hypothesis by most parapsychologists on the basis of Ockham's Razor (which is ironically the same principle invoked by the skeptics to support their preference of the fraud/error/delusion hypothesis over the ESP hypothesis).

In some instances, hypotheses that at first glance appear to be unfalsifiable, and hence metaphysical rather than scientific in nature, can be rendered falsifiable through the use of an "operational definition." Consider the question of "consciousness" in animal and computers. Are, for instance, dogs to be regarded as conscious? Amoebae? How about computers? Or thermostats? The famous neurophysiologist W. Grey Walter constructed mechanical "tortoises," which ambulated about his house randomly until they ran low on power, at which point they would proceed to the nearest electrical socket to recharge themselves. Were Walter's tortoises conscious? Did they feel a passion for communion with electrical sockets or a sense of anxiety and depression when their power became low? In order to resolve one of these questions, the mathematician Alan Turing proposed to define a computer as conscious if it could successfully imitate a human being to the extent that a person communicating through a teletype terminal could not discriminate between the computer's remarks and those of the human being.[6] Turing's "imitation game" provided a means whereby the apparently metaphysical hypothesis of consciousness in computers could be given an operational definition and become subject to scientific test.

Alternate forms of rationality. A small minority of parapsychologists have on occasion called for a reexamination of the appropriateness of the traditional methods of science for the investigation of psi phenomena. In some cases, they have called for the abandonment of such methods in favor of alternate forms of rationality. Willis Harman, for instance, has recently questioned the ontological assumption of the separation of the observer from what is observed that he sees as underlying the modern scientific method. He calls for the adoption of "other ways of knowing," such as intuition and mysticism, that are based on the assumption of an underlying "oneness" between the knower and the known.[7] Earlier, at the close of the "consciousness revolution" of the sixties (which included the early 1970s, by the way), Charles Tart noted that different states of consciousness (such as dreaming, marijuana intoxication, and religious ecstasy) are characterized by different forms of information processing and cognition, and he called for the development of "state specific sciences," each to be based on the form of rationality characteristic of a particular state of consciousness.[8] In making such suggestions, both Tart and Harman reflect a recent trend among historians, sociologists and philosophers of science to question whether there is one demonstrably correct form of rationality.[9]

Traditional scientific methods have enjoyed a history of success in the prediction and control of nature. They have led to a convergence of thought that is unprecedented (with the possible exception of the occasional "pseudo-consensus" achieved through the ruthless exercise of religious or other author-ity). Mystical insight and religious inspiration have rarely led to consensus about the nature or number of gods or the purpose of the universe. Neither have the variant thought processes of the intoxicated or the schizophrenic led to a consistent alternative picture of realty. Of course, it may be argued that consistency is the hobgoblin of the unimaginative and that reality may not correspond to the consensus of the majority of scientists. It is also true that certain central issues have proven themselves relatively impervious to scientific investigation. Science has for instance no good explanation of why certain types of brain activity should be associated with or give rise to conscious expe-rience. Neither is it able to offer an explanation of why the universe should have been created with its particular set of properties (it can only elucidate what those properties are). Thus, alternate forms of rationality may have their place and may even be necessary to address questions that are (at least at pre-sent) not answerable by science. However, if parapsychologists were to depart from traditional scientific methodology and adopt some form of alternative rationality, it is not clear that they would any longer be practicing science in any conventional sense of the term. It is clear that such action would result in the rejection of parapsychology as an unscientific enterprise by scientific establishment. This rejection would be legitimate under any standard use of the word "scientific."

In order to preserve itself as a scientific enterprise, parapsychology must adhere to the recognized principles and practices of science. As noted above, alternative forms of rationality may have their place and may even be neces-sary to address certain issues that lie beyond the present domain of scientific inquiry (such as the nature of the soul). Yet, by definition these alternate forms of rationality cannot form a part of any science of parapsychology.

We will now turn to an examination of some of the theories that have been proposed to account for ESP and PK. Theories that are primarily directed to the problem of the relationship of the mind to the physical brain—and to the possible survival of the mind (or some portions thereof) of the death of the physical body—will be addressed in later portions of the book.

Spacetime Theories

Several theorists have invoked "warps" in spacetime or even extra dimen-sions of spacetime in order to explain psi. It is for instance difficult to explain apparent cases of telepathy between two people who are separated by thou-sands of miles on the basis of the exchange of any physical signal over such distances. If it could be assumed that the people are really in much closer proximity than they seem to be due to the presence of a warp in spacetime or to a spacetime "wormhole" directly connecting them, then such long-range psi may not seem quite so problematic. Similarly, highly curved spacetimes may offer a means a getting a signal from a future event into the present, which might help to explain precognition.

"Spacewarp" theories. Gertrude Schmeidler has proposed that the universe may contain an extra dimension in addition to the familiar four dimensions of space and time that might permit the "topological folding" of spacetime to occur.[10] As a result of such folding, two regions that appear to be widely separated in space and time might actually be very close to one another in the higher-dimensional spacetime, much as two points on a towel that are normally far apart may be adjacent once the towel is folded.

One of parapsychology's archenemies, the physicist John Wheeler, has proposed that at a microscopic level, quantum effects may act to produce a spacetime structure containing "wormholes" or "bridges."[11] (The handle on a coffee cup might be thought of as a wormhole or bridge in the surface of the cup.) Wheeler proposed that such wormholes might connect pairs of oppositely charged particles such as electrons and positrons, and his proposed spacetime structure is sometimes referred to as the "quantum foam." As Barry Parker points out, however, Wheeler's quantum foam theory is not accepted by most scientists today.[12] Several other scientists have speculated that such wormholes may exist on a macroscopic scale and that in some cases rotating black holes may generate wormhole tunnels to other regions of our own spacetime or even to a different universe that exists outside of the spacetime regions to which we have access.

Wormhole theories of psi have been proposed by Gardner Murphy[13] and Bob Toben and Fred Wolf,[14] although these theories are not spelled out in much mathematical detail. Richard Morris points out that any attempt to travel through a wormhole or to send a signal through one will result in frustration, as the traveler or signal will emerge from the wormhole within the event horizon of another black hole, from which no escape is possible. Morris does point out that there may exist a type of wormhole called a Schwarzschild wormhole and that, if one were to travel through a Schwarzschild wormhole one might be able to avoid emerging inside a black hole.[15] It is, however, extremely doubtful that Schwarzschild wormholes exist. Another loophole may be provided by J.L. Friedman's observations that naked singularities may exist.[16] A naked singularity is essentially a black hole that does not have an event horizon, so that escape would be possible from it (that is, it is an oxymoronic nonblack black hole).

In 1949, the famous mathematician Kurt Gödel demonstrated that Einstein's theory of general relativity allows the existence of universes containing closed time lines.[17] The notion of a closed time line is perhaps best explained by a spatial analogy. If a person were to begin walking due east and continue until she has circumnavigated the globe (obviously some water skiing would come into play), she would eventually return to her starting position, but from a westerly direction. Similarly, in a closed time line, if one were to travel far enough into the future, one would eventually return to the present moment (via the past).

One could readily imagine the perplexing experience of a transsexual traveler traversing a closed time line in a large spacecraft. He meets a woman who seems strangely familiar, who reminds him of his mother, but is obviously much younger. Being of an Oedipal nature, he marries her, impregnates her, but soon abandons her because he hears a group of transsexuals talking about their experiences on the Phil Donahue XI show on holovision. He realizes at that point that he has been living a lie, that he is a woman in a man's body. He has the newest, most advanced form of transsexual operation, which renders him a fertile woman. Just for kicks, he has them do a rejuvenation procedure on him at the same time. A few years later, she meets a man at a bar who reminds her of her younger self. Soon, she realizes that it is her younger self. Being narcissistic as well as transsexual, she marries herself (himself?), all the while keeping her fairly large secret from her husband. She becomes pregnant and has a little boy. The birth is traumatic and she develops a white streak in her hair as a result. As she sits in the recovery room, she catches a glance at herself in the mirror. She recognizes her new look and realizes that she is her own mother. She has just given birth to herself.

If time were to be closed for the universe as a whole, everything would recur over and over again, the ultimate form of the philosopher Friedrich Nietzsche's "eternal return." The universe might collapse to a black hole and bounce back in a repeat of the Big Bang. We would all live the same lives over and over again on each iteration of the process. The Stoic philosophers of ancient Greece in fact believed in such a doctrine of eternal cyclic recurrence, which they termed palingenesia.

Several theorists have suggested ways in which anomalous spacetime regions might allow a physical particle to traverse a closed time line and arrive at its own "past." Frank Tipler has proposed that a time machine could be constructed by rotating an extremely long cylindrical mass at an extraordinarily high speed, but observes that such a time machine would unfortunately collapse along its axis due to its own gravitational self-attraction before it could be put into service.[18] Nick Herbert has observed that a very rapidly rotating Kerr black hole would contain a naked ring singularity that would make travel from the Kerr hole to any location in spacetime (including one's own past) possible.[19] Michael Morris and Kip Thorne have suggested that a time machine might be produced by taking one of the two mouths of a wormhole, moving it rapidly back and forth and then returning it to the vicinity of the second mouth of the wormhole. After this process, travel through the wormhole would enable one to reach the past.[20] More recently, J. Richard Gott of Princeton

University has proposed that closed time loops may be created when two cosmic strings hurtle past each other at a high velocity. A rocket ship looping around both strings could arrive at its own past. Of course, the very existence of cosmic strings remains speculation at this point. Also, Gerard t'Hooft of the Institute for Theoretical Physics in Utrecht has pointed out that, if there were enough mass in the universe to construct a time machine along Gott's lines, the universe would necessarily have to be closed (that is, would eventually collapse back upon itself due to its gravitational self-attraction). He further points out that any closed universe would necessarily collapse to a size smaller than any closed time path under Gott's model, making the existence of a Gott time machine impossible. Furthermore, physicist Stephen Hawking has argued that any closed time line would destroy itself by generating a feedback loop leading to the build-up of an infinite amount of energy, destroying any time machine that might be created. Gott proposed a variant version of his theory involving a rapidly shrinking "loop" type of cosmic string, but the equations have proven difficult to solve for this case.[21]

If closed time lines exist, it might be possible to account for precognition in terms of a signal being emitted from the precognized event and arriving at the past by traveling along a portion of a closed time line.

"Spacewarp" theories of psi face several difficulties. The huge curvatures of spacetime that would be required to explain psi phenomena occurring over the typically cosmically small space-time separations involved in spontaneous and experimentally-produced psi effects would undoubtedly involve the presence of very large gravitational fields under any standard interpretation of Einstein's theory of general relativity. For the "spacewarp" explanation to be useful, it would probably be necessary to assume, say, that the participants in a case of telepathy were in closer proximity to a rotating black hole than they were to each other. In such a case, the gravitational tidal forces of the black hole would probably reduce a person to a molecular gas long before it conferred any paranormal powers upon him.

Similarly, the closed time lines generated in rotating universes under Gödel's model are gigantic in size.[22] Also, it is doubtful that a precognitive message could remain intact throughout the universe's collapse in the "Big Crunch" and reemergence in a "Big Bang."

Multidimensional models. Several parapsychologists have proposed spacetime models with additional dimensions beyond the usual four in order to explain psi phenomena. The postulation of additional dimensions is one way to avoid the large gravitational fields required to produce wormholes and large curvatures of spacetime in standard interpretations of Einstein's theory of general relativity. Gertrude Schmeidler's postulation of an extra dimension of spacetime in order to permit "topological folding" to occur is essentially a theory of this type. The postulation of extra dimensions of spacetime may no longer be the radical move it once was, as physicists nowadays think nothing of toying with as many as 11 spacetime dimensions in "supersymmetric" theories of gravity (although most of these dimensions are thought to be curved so severely that they become microscopic circles that are not noticeable at a macroscopic level).

Two versions of what is essentially the same multi-dimensional theory of spacetime have been proposed apparently independently by the team of Russell Targ, Hal Puthoff and Ed May, and by physicist Elizabeth Rauscher.[23] Both posit eight dimensions of space and time, although Rauscher proposed an alternative model employing six dimensions. Essentially what they propose is that events that seem to be widely separated in space and time may in fact be quite close together in the higher dimensional space. As they propose no means of measuring an object's coordinates on their new dimensions, they are free to adjust these coordinates as they please to make things come out right. As the theory seems to be capable of explaining anything, it should be regarded as unfalsifiable and not worthy of consideration as a serious scientific theory.

One writer who has expressed a virtually mystical enthusiasm for the possibility that the mysteries of the mind and psi might be explained in terms of higher dimensional space is the mathematician and sometimes science fiction writer Rudy Rucker. In his book *The Fourth Dimension*,[24] he reviews the history of the use of higher-dimensional models to explain psi phenomena and mystical experiences. He notes that the seventeenth century philosopher Henry More postulated that spirits are four-dimensional beings. He cites J.C.F. Zöllner's experiments with the medium Henry Slade, who was supposedly able to tie a knot in a closed loop of string by transporting it to a higher dimensional realm.[25] Zöllner further proposed that a miraculous object such as interlocking rings composed of different types of wood would provide evidence of the existence of a higher dimensional reality. It will be recalled that John Beloff has also contended that such a "permanent paranormal object" might provide convincing evidence of the reality of psi phenomena, if not of higher dimensional realms.

Rucker himself takes an almost mystical view of higher dimensional geometries. He seconds Ouspensky's view that dreams may afford a glimpse into our four-dimensional nature.[26] Rucker suggests that seemingly separate individual persons may simply be parts of a higher unity, much as five seemingly independent circles on a two-dimensional plane may be the cross-sections of the fingers of a single three-dimensional hand.

Models of Time

There are quite a few spontaneous cases on record that seem to indicate that one can foresee an unpleasant event in the future and then perform some action to avoid that event. Thus, it seems that one might be able to change the future. This raises interesting philosophical and scientific questions about the nature of time. Louisa Rhine published a collection of such cases,[27] and we will cite two of her cases here to give the reader a better sense of nature of such experiences. The first case is taken from her book *Hidden Channels of the Mind*[28]:

In Washington State a young woman was so upset by a terrifying dream one night that she had to wake her husband and tell him about it. She had dreamed that a large ornamental chandelier which hung over their baby's bed in the next room had fallen into the crib and crushed their baby to death. In the dream she could see herself and her husband standing amid the wreckage. The clock on the baby's dresser said 4:35. In the distance she could hear the rain on the windowpane and the wind blowing outside.

But her husband just laughed at her. He said it was a silly dream, to forget it and go back to sleep; and in a matter of moments he did just that himself. But she could not sleep.

Finally, still frightened, she got out of bed and went to the baby's room, got her and brought her back. On the way she stopped to look out the window, and saw a full moon, the weather calm and unlike the dream. Then, though feeling a little foolish, she got back into bed with the baby.

About two hours later they were wakened by a resounding crash. She jumped up, followed by her husband, and ran to the nursery. There, where the baby would have been lying, was the chandelier in the crib. They looked at each other and then at the clock. It stood at 4:35. Still a little skeptical they listened—to the sound of the rain on the windowpane and wind howling outside.

In another case in Rhine's collection, a streetcar operator braked as he approached a one-way exit in order to avoid an accident that he had dreamed about that morning. At that moment, a truck containing the very same people who had been injured in the dream shot out into the street, having gone the wrong way through the one-way exit.

In both of these cases, it would seem that two different futures were involved. In the first, precognized future a negative event took place. In the second future, the one that actually occurred, the negative event was avoided.

Multidimensional time models. In order to account for such cases of precognition followed by intervention to prevent the precognized event from occurring, J.W. Dunne proposed the existence of additional dimensions of time.[29] Dunne invoked a second time dimension (Time 2) to "clock" a person's progress on the first, ordinary dimension of time (Time 1). Thus, in Dunne's theory a person is conceived of as "moving" along the Time 1 dimension and occupying later and later moments on that dimension as Time 2 elapses.

Suppose for instance that a man named Harry has a vivid dream of being killed when the giant Snoopy balloon collapses during the annual Macy's

Thanksgiving Day Parade. Suppose, that on the basis of this dream, he cancels his annual visit to his cherished parade and goes to Fire Island instead. As his wife roasts up the turkey, he turns on the T.V. only to witness the horrible destruction as the beloved Snoopy character descends on the assembled multitude. We could conceptualize this situation under Dunne's theory as follows. The future, as it existed at the moment (in Time 2) before Harry went to bed contained the event of Harry's demise in the great Snoopy massacre, but the future after Harry made the decision to go to Fire Island (at a later moment in Time 2) did not contain his imminent death. Harry precognized the future as it existed before he took his evasive action.

There are several problems with Dunne's theory. One major problem is that, in order to clock an observer's progress on the second time dimension, Dunne felt compelled to invoke a third time dimension. To clock his progress in Time 3, Dunne invented Time 4. In fact, continuing in this manner, Dunne was forced to postulate the existence of an infinite number of time dimensions. This is what is known as the problem of an "infinite regress," which is usually as a sign that something is severely wrong with a theory. This infinite regress seemed to bother just about everyone but Dunne, who was happy to talk about "the observer at infinity." This regress is probably a result of Dunne's failure to employ the notion of a "timeless array" of events in spacetime rather than his dynamic model involving the "motion" of an observer along a time axis.

Some later theorists, such as C.D. Broad and D.F. Lawden, tried to save Dunne's theory by constructing models that involved "only" two time dimensions.[30] One basic problem remains with all these models, however. What is to prevent someone in the past from precognizing something that we are doing now and performing an act that would pop us all out of existence? Or perhaps we have all just been popped into existence by such an act. If the latter is the case, we remember having lived for years, but these memories are illusory. We have really only existed for a few seconds (of Time 2) and may be popped out of existence in a few more moments if someone in the past has a visionary experience. It would be at least somewhat discomforting to think that our existence could be so ephemeral. One way out of this quandary might be to attempt to construct a model in which only observers at some specified coordinates in Time 1 and Time 2 would be allowed to alter the future. This would be equivalent to defining a unique moment in time as "the present" and only allowing observers in the present to alter the future. Unfortunately, as we shall see later, Einstein's theory of relativity implies that there is no unique set of events called the present that is the same for all observers. Rather, the set of events that one experiences as being simultaneous with oneself varies depending on one's state of motion. Unless the problems arising from this "relativity of simultaneity" could be overcome, it would seem impossible to rescue Dunne's theory by appealing to a unique present.

The philosopher C.W.K. Mundle points out that when Dunne speaks of precognizing "probable futures," he is essentially abandoning his own model, which assumes that a single future exists at any given moment (of Time 2).[31] Thus, Dunne may himself have been striving for a model something like the branching time models to be described below.

Branching time models. In branching time models, it is assumed that at the "present" moment many possible futures exist. For instance, in the case of the baby and the chandelier, in one possible future (the one that was precognized) the baby was killed by the falling chandelier, whereas in a second possible future (the one that actually occurred) the baby escaped injury.

In the classical, Newtonian view of the universe that prevailed until early in this century, it would be unthinkable that two different alternative futures could both be possible. Under the Newtonian worldview, the universe was seen as governed by laws that preordained the state of the future. This deterministic outlook of classical physics led the famous mathematician and cosmologist Pierre Simon Laplace to propose that a Divine Calculator who knew the position and velocity of every particle in the universe could deduce the entire history and future of the universe down to the last detail.

The development of the modern theory of quantum mechanics has overthrown this deterministic outlook. Under modern theories of physics, given the present state of the universe, many different futures are possible. An atom of radioactive material may or may not decay during a given time period. It is impossible *in principle* to predict whether it will or not. Under quantum theory, different futures may have different probabilities assigned to them. For instance, it may be more likely that the above-mentioned radioactive decay will occur during the next half-hour than that it will not.

While most scientists hold that only one of these alternative futures is actually realized, the physicist Hugh Everett has proposed that all the possible futures are actualized, albeit in alternate universes.[32] Everett's theory has become known as the "many worlds" interpretation of quantum mechanics. For instance, assuming no violations of the laws of physics are entailed, there may well be an alternate universe in which Sonny Bono is now President of the United States.

The branching time model is easily capable of accommodating cases of precognition followed by intervention. One could assume, say, that in our "chandelier" case the mother foresaw the most probable future, that her baby would be killed, but was able to act in such a way as to ensure the occurrence of a less probable future.

The linear time model. It is also possible to account for such cases with a model postulating only one time dimension and one future, should one prefer such a pedestrian and colorless approach. One could simply state that the mother accurately foresaw that the chandelier was going to fall. Her premonition of her baby's death was simply an error, as that death never occurred.

The mother's unconscious mind was merely dramatizing to her the consequences of not moving the baby out from under the chandelier.

The downright cynical model. Under this view, there is no such thing as ESP. The mother probably subliminally perceived some dust falling from the unstable chandelier support as she was about to go to bed and then dreamed the probable consequences.

Signal Theories

Several attempts have been made to explain psi phenomena in terms of the exchange of some type of physical signal. Some theories assume that ordinary physical particles carry the psi message. Such particles are typically conceived of as "traveling forward in time." To explain cases of precognition, some theorists have resorted to more exotic particles that travel backward in time. We will consider each in turn.

Theories employing "orthodox" signals. Several theorists have proposed that the transfer of information in cases of ESP is accomplished through the exchange of some signal already known to contemporary physicists, such as electromagnetic radiation[33] and neutrinos.[34] There are many problems with theories of this type. Successful telepathy experiments have been reported in which the subjects were electromagnetically shielded from one another, ruling out the exchange of most electromagnetic signals.[35] Some theorists, including Michael Persinger and I.M. Kogan, have proposed that psi signals are carried by extremely low frequency electromagnetic radiation, also known as ELF waves.[36] ELF waves would be able to penetrate some of the electromagnetic barriers used in these experiments. One of the disadvantages of ELF waves is that they have a very low information-carrying capacity, so that it would take an unreasonably long time to transmit a psi message by ELF radiation.[37]

Neutrinos of course have the attractive feature that they could sail right through such barriers and right through any barrier, for that matter. They could sail right through the Earth. This is the chief problem with neutrinos. The vast majority of them would also sail right through one's brain without interacting with it in any way. Thus, a person would be unable to receive any psi message sent by neutrinos. In order for an agent to transmit enough neutrinos to ensure that her message was received, her brain would probably have to use up enough energy to power several small cities for months.

The brain also does not have enough power to transmit electromagnetic radiation with any intensity. In fact, electromagnetic radiation produced by the brain is practically undetectable a few inches from the head.

Both neutrino and electromagnetic signals weaken as they travel over distances, as they spread out in space and become diluted. The existing evidence would seem to indicate that psi signals do not weaken appreciably over distance, if at all.[38] Also, many successful ESP and PK experiments have been conducted over distances of thousands of miles, whereas the brain simply does not have enough power to transmit a detectable signal over such distances.[39]

Retrocausal signals. Some theorists have proposed that phenomena such as precognition and retroactive psychokinesis, in which the future appears to influence events in the present (or, as in the case of retroactive PK, events in the present appear to influence events in the past) may be explained on the basis of physical signals that travel backward in time.

Advanced waves. One such signal is what is known as "advanced waves." The differential equation that governs the motion of electromagnetic and sound waves is time-symmetric and admits of two solutions. The first corresponds to the normal "retarded" wave, which propagates outward from a source and travels forward in time. The second is a mirror image of the first and consists of an "advanced" wave, which travels backward in time. Such a wave might be experienced by an observer "traveling forward in time" as a contracting shell of light that converges on a light bulb at the instant it is turned on.

Advanced electromagnetic (and sound) waves suffer from all the same inadequacies of normal "retarded" electromagnetic waves when it comes to explaining psi. The brain simply does not possess enough power to send a signal via advanced waves over any substantial distance in space and time. Another disadvantage of advanced waves is that, although they are theoretically possible, they have never been observed to exist.

Antimatter. Another possible retrocausal signal is antimatter. Antimatter, despite its provocative name, is not an esoteric form of matter out of science fiction but is an ordinary form of matter that is observed daily in particle accelerators around the world. Every particle of matter has its corresponding antiparticle. The antiparticle of the electron is called the positron; it has the same mass as the electron but carries a positive electrical charge, whereas the electron is negatively charged. When an electron meets a positron, they annihilate one another. Their mass is converted to pure energy in the form of photons. If a substantial quantity of matter were to meet up with a corresponding amount of antimatter, a powerful explosion would occur. (This is the source of power for the propulsion drive of the spaceship *Enterprise* in the popular *Star Trek* series).

The Nobel winning physicist and legendary character Richard Feynman noted that antimatter could be regarded mathematically as ordinary matter traveling backward in time. Thus, a positron could be conceived of as an electron traveling into the past. Consider a case in which a high-energy photon creates a positron-electron pair at spacetime location *A*. Assume the positron then meets up with a second electron and annihilates with it at spacetime location *B*, producing a second photon.[40] Under Feynman's interpretation, this process could be regarded as the trajectory of one electron. The electron would be regarded as traveling forward in time to event B, reversing its direction through the emission of a photon, traveling backward in time to event A, where it reverses its direction once more through the emission of a photon traveling backward in time (photons are their own antiparticles) and returns to its normal forward trajectory in time. This would be analogous to the more usual case in which an electron zigzags back and forth in space, emitting and absorbing photons to change direction. In fact, as Feynman related in his Nobel prize acceptance speech, the physicist John Wheeler once suggested to him that the reason why all electrons have the same mass is that they are all the same particle, zigzagging backward and forward in time (Wheeler was only joking).

What would antimatter-based time travel look like to us if we were to encounter an instance of it while walking down the street? We might notice a big burst of light in front of the drug store. Out of the explosion, two seemingly identical men would emerge, one walking forward and one walking backward. If we were to examine the one walking backward under a microscope, we would see that he was getting seconds younger with each step and that his beard was retreating into his skin. Suddenly, we see a third copy of the man across the street. The man walking backward crosses the street, miraculously avoiding all the oncoming traffic even though his head is turned away from it. He then seems to back into the third copy of the man that is walking on the other side of the street. There is a giant explosion, after which both men have disappeared. (Actually, most towns would have been destroyed in this process, but we will assume that this one was particularly well constructed.) What really happened? This man has the ability to reverse his direction in time by emitting photons and changing himself into antimatter. As he was walking down the street, he thought he heard someone in front of the drug store across the street make disparaging remarks about his toupee. Just to make sure, he reversed direction in time and walked over to hear what was really said. After crossing the street, he again reversed his direction in time in order to eavesdrop more effectively. (It is much easier to interpret sound waves when one is going forward in time. Did you ever try to listen to a record played backwards? No, don't tell me. If you're reading this book, you probably have.)

In trying to account for precognition on the basis of antimatter signals, one runs into all the usual problems of signals weakening with distance (and time) and the difficulties of trying to account for how the brain could generate and decode such a signal, especially in view of the scarcity of antimatter in our region of the universe. With antimatter, there is the additional problem that any message sent by antimatter particles would quickly degrade as the antimatter would rapidly annihilate with matter, which constitutes the predominant form of material particles, at least in our region of the universe.

The final problem is that antimatter need not be regarded as matter traveling backward in time. This interpretation is really based on a cheap mathematical trick on Feynman's part. It is perfectly legitimate to regard a positron as a positively charged particle traveling forward in time rather than a negatively charged particle traveling backward in time.

Tachyons. Some parapsychologists, including Martin Ruderfer and Adrian Dobbs, have proposed that tachyons carry the psi signal in cases of precognition.[41] Tachyons are particles that travel faster than light and therefore have the ability to go backward in time, as will be explained below. Dobbs' theory is in fact quite elaborate and essentially involves the emission of tachyons from one of the alternative futures in a branching time model.

The existence of tachyons has been postulated by such physicists as E.C.G. Sudershan and Gerald Feinberg. (Feinberg, incidentally, has proposed his own version of an "advanced wave" theory of precognition.[42]) Tachyons always go faster than the speed of light. Paradoxically, the less energy a tachyon has, the slower it goes. You would have to apply an infinite amount of energy to slow a tachyon down to the speed of light, however. Tachyons' ability to travel backward in time depends on something called the relativity of simultaneity. In Einstein's theory of relativity, two events that are perceived as simultaneous by one observer may not be perceived as simultaneous by another observer. This can be explained most easily by using Einstein's famous train example. Suppose you are standing on the ground and your friend is standing on top of a freight train that is hurtling past you. Suppose further that she is standing in the exact middle of the train. At the precise time she passes you on the ground, two lightning bolts hit the front and back of the train. The light from the two bolts reaches you at the same instant, and so you judge the bolts to be simultaneous. Your friend, on the other hand, has been traveling toward the bolt on the front of the train and away from that on the rear; consequently, she sees the bolt at the front of the train first. To her, however, both bolts have traveled the same distance, namely half the length of the train; therefore, she concludes that the bolt at the front occurred before the bolt at the rear of the train. Her conclusion is based on the fact that the laws of physics are the same for observers in states of relative motion under Einstein's theory. The speed of light, which is a consequence of those laws, is also the same for all observers. It doesn't matter if you run away from a photon, it will still pass you at the same speed it would have had you remained motionless.

Here is how communication into the past via tachyons might be achieved. Suppose that a man has been sent to jail because he has been caught in an embezzling scheme. Over the course of few months, he is able to construct a crude tachyon transmission device out of soap flakes, pipe cleaners and discarded razor blades. He uses the device to send a signal to his friend Jimmy "the Weasel" Peterson, as the Weasel hurtles through space away from the authorities in his souped up getaway ship. The transmission instructs the

Weasel to send a message to the prisoner's girlfriend, Susan Wayward, telling her to remove a crucial piece of evidence from his apartment and to plant it in the apartment of his despised rival at the accounting firm where he used to work. Due to the relativity of simultaneity, because the Weasel is moving rapidly away from the prisoner, portions of the prisoner's past lie in the Weasel's future. Thus, the Weasel is able to use a tachyon signal to get the message to Susan a full month before he is caught and convicted of embezzlement. Consequently, he was never sent to jail in the first place and is now a free man.

This of course brings up the subject of changing the past. It seems logically contradictory that the prisoner could both have been sent to jail and not sent to jail. These sorts of causal paradoxes are one of the reasons why many philosophers and scientists regard time travel as being inherently impossible. It would, however, be possible to avoid the paradoxes by adopting a branching time model. Once Susan has received the Weasel's signal, a new time branch has been created, one in which the embezzler will not be sent to prison. This does not help the prisoner, however, as the version of the embezzler that should be most important to the prisoner is still sitting in jail on the first time branch. All he has succeeded in doing is freeing many of his twins in Everett's parallel universes. (Although his message in fact created these alternate universes, no mean feat in itself!)

The ability of tachyons to travel backward in time appears to be based on the assumption that judgments regarding simultaneity will continue to be based on light signals. Because light is the fastest known signal, it is used to define simultaneity in the special theory of relativity. If an observer takes a snapshot of an event, the event photographed is defined to occur at a time halfway between the time of the emission of light by the camera's flashbulb and the time of the reception of the light back at the camera's lens (as the light travels equal distances in both directions and is assumed to travel at a constant speed). Yet if tachyons exist, light would no longer enjoy its privileged status as the fastest available signal, and simultaneity might have to be defined in terms of tachyon signals instead. In fact if infinitely fast signals were available, the relativity of simultaneity might disappear altogether. Of course, such a redefinition of simultaneity might have unforeseen repercussions on the laws of physics (affecting the assumption of the constancy of the speed of light in all reference frames, for instance). Nevertheless, if an absolute simultaneity could be established using tachyonic signals, tachyons might be deprived of their retrocausal properties, as has been pointed out independently by physicists John Bell and Basil Hiley and by the writer.[43]

Another drawback to the tachyon theory of psi is that tachyons have never been observed to exist; they remain purely theoretical constructs. In the 1970s, physicists Roger Clay and Philip Crouch claimed to have detected evidence for tachyons in the form of anomalous particle events that preceded the main showers of particles caused by cosmic rays; however, later experimenters were unable to repeat this observation.[44]

Tachyon theories suffer from all the usual difficulties confronting signal theories of psi, including the fact that tachyon signals would be assumed to rapidly weaken over distance (and time). There is also the problem of accounting for how the brain could encode, generate and receive a tachyon-based psi message. This problem is even worse in the case of tachyons than it is for the other signal theories, as there is no good theory of how tachyons could interact with the tardyons of which human observers are composed (tardyons are particles that travel slower than the speed of light). In fact physicist Nick Herbert has outlined several mathematical obstacles confronting any attempt to construct a theory of tachyon-tardyon interaction.[45]

Precognitive attrition. In all the retrocausal signal theories we have discussed, the signals involved would be expected to spread out and weaken as they travel backward in time. Thus, one would expect a "precognitive attrition" effect to occur, whereby precognition would be more effective over short time intervals than over long time intervals.

Many case investigators claim to have detected a decline in the number of precognition cases with increasing time intervals between the precognitive experience and the confirming event. In his analysis of Louisa Rhine's collection, Sybo Schouten found 33 percent of the precognitive experiences to involve intervals of less than 24 hours, 67 percent to involve intervals shorter than two weeks, and 95 percent to involve intervals less than one year. Schouten found no significant relation between the form of the experience and time interval, although he notes that virtually all cases involving intervals greater than one year were dreams.[46] Other investigators have also found evidence for a precognitive attrition effect in analyzing collections of reported spontaneous experiences.[47]

These findings of a precognitive attrition effect in spontaneous case collections might be explained on the basis of selective reporting of cases. Cases involving relatively short time intervals may seem more impressive if the confirming event occurred one day after the dream than if it occurred fifteen years later. Also, people may forget precognitive dreams over long time intervals and be unable to recall them at the time of the confirming event. For these reasons one might expect a decline in the number of reported cases as the time interval between the experience and the confirming event increases, even in the absence of any real precognitive attrition effect.

Nancy Sondow reports a decline in the number of her own precognitive dreams with increasing time interval.[48] Her analysis is based on a diary of her own dreams, which contained 943 entries. She argues against the hypothesis that the decline effect is due to increased forgetting of dreams over longer time intervals, noting that when she "overlearned" the dreams through repetitive study there was no reduction in the slope of the decline. There remains, however, the possibility that the decline effect could be an artifact of dismissing a dream from consideration after encountering an apparently confirming event, thus preventing the matching of the dreams with later events. For instance, precognition of one's grandmother's funeral one week from now might be interpreted as precognition of her death two days hence, reducing the "real" interval of one week to an apparent interval of two days. Schouten, in a review of the history of parapsychology in the Netherlands, notes that both J.M.J. Kooy and J.C.M. Kruisanga kept diaries of precognitive dreams and that Kruisanga's data showed a pronounced decline effect with time, although the exact nature of this decline effect is not made clear in Schouten's paper.[49]

Restricting their analysis to "coincidence" cases (in which the experience and the confirming event were separated by less than 24 hours in time), Rinaldi and Piccinini found 5.2 percent of the cases to fall within the interval of 12-24 hours before the event, 10.8 percent within 1-6 hours before the event, 62.7 percent to occur within an hour of the event, 1.9 percent to fall within 1-6 hours after the event, 1.9 percent within 6-12 hours after the event, and 1.2 percent to fall within 12-24 hours after the event. This may constitute evidence for precognitive attrition that is not so easily explainable by the above counterhypothesis of forgetting and dismissal after premature matching. Rinaldi and Piccinini attribute the clustering of cases within an hour of the event to a possible "improvement" of testimony. However, as will be seen below, Charles Tart found higher scoring rates in ESP experiments employing real-time rather than precognitive targets, which would be consonant with Rinaldi and Piccinini's finding. Rinaldi and Piccinini also report an analysis of forgetting artifacts in spontaneous case collections. They note that the number of cases reported declines as the amount of time that has elapsed since the experience increases. They found 168 cases per year for intervals of less than 6 months between the experience and interview, 47 cases per year for intervals from 6 months to 2 years, 33 cases per year for intervals from 2 to 5 years, and 27 cases per year for intervals from 6 to 10 years. Dream and intuition cases appeared to be forgotten at a faster rate than were the possibly more striking hallucination and physical effect cases. Cases involving death were not forgotten so quickly as cases not involving death. This forgetting factor may possibly bias the composition of spontaneous case collections to some degree. In any event, if already confirmed cases can be forgotten over time, it stands to reason that as-yet-unconfirmed dreams and hunches might well be forgotten if a long time interval separates them from the confirming event.[50]

Turning to experimental evidence, Charles Tart found no evidence of a correlation between time interval and rate of psi information transmission in an analysis of published precognition experiments employing forced-choice ESP targets.[51] He does note that the rate of information transmission was higher in "real-time" ESP experiments than in precognition experiments (his analysis being restricted to experiments obtaining significant evidence of psi). Tart suggests that real-time ESP and precognition may represent different abilities, although he concedes that the difference in scoring rates could be due to psychological barriers to the acceptance of precognition that would undermine the subject's performance. He does not address the issue of whether methodological flaws in some real-time experiments (such as the existence of sensory cues allowing the subject to identify the targets) may be responsible for the high hit rates in some of the real-time ESP experiments.

On the other hand, in a more recent meta-analysis of forced choice precognition experiments published during the years 1935–1987, Honorton and Ferrari found significant evidence of a decline in the size of the obtained psi effect with increasing time intervals. This decline seemed to be due to studies with average citizens as subjects; studies using subjects preselected for their psi abilities actually showed a positive relationship between effect size and time interval. Honorton and Ferrari suggest that these effects may be due to differences in motivational factors between the two types of subjects.[52] The experimental evidence for precognitive attrition is thus somewhat equivocal.

A second means of testing the hypothesis of precognitive attrition is to determine whether the overall accuracy and number of details in the precognitive experience declines over time. Schriever found no difference in the time intervals involved in highly accurate and less accurate dreams in her analysis of the dream diary of an actress.[53] Sondow found no significant decrement in the accuracy or number of details in her own precognitive dreams over increasing time intervals. She suggests a possible psychological explanation for her evidence for precognitive attrition (discussed above), namely that people may largely restrict their precognitive monitoring to the near future.[54] Haight likewise found no relation between temporal interval and completeness of information, conviction or importance of the confirming event in her study of experiences reported by high school students.[55] Even if the number of details in precognition cases were to decline as the time interval increased, such a decline could be explained on the basis of forgetting. For instance, Schouten found that the number of details reported in experiences in the Sannwald case collection fell off as the amount of time that had elapsed before reporting the case increased.[56] The length of the report also declined. Schouten attributes these effects to forgetting. These effects are also evidence against the critics' charge that such cases will be improved or embellished over time; the evidence suggests instead that the cases deteriorate as details are forgotten.

In summary, the evidence for precognitive attrition is equivocal. It is possible to argue that many reported declines in frequency of cases over increasing time intervals may be due to forgetting as well as the premature matching of experiences to events. The experimental evidence, as reviewed by Tart and Honorton and Ferrari, is also equivocal. There is no compelling evidence for a weakening of psi signals, in the form of a decrease in the number or accuracy of the details in an experience, over increasing time intervals. (Of course, to the extent that people will be more reluctant to report less detailed cases, it might be possible that a reduction in the number of details would be reflected indirectly in a decline in the number of cases reported over increasing time intervals rather than directly in the composition of the reported cases themselves.)

In any event, as the evidence for precognitive attrition is so equivocal, it is impossible to come to a firm decision about the viability of theories ascribing precognition to retrocausal signals on the basis of precognitive attrition.

Mind and the Quantum

The "signal" theories of psi that have been just discussed are all based on the assumption that some relatively localized particle or wave carries the psi message. As we have seen, these theories all have rather severe drawbacks. As it turns out, developments in the field of quantum mechanics indicate that the universe does not consist exclusively of discrete, mutually isolated and localized particles and objects. In fact, as we shall see, the theory of quantum mechanics paints a picture of the universe that is not at all hostile to psi phenomena. Indeed the principle of nonlocality in quantum mechanics, which we will discuss shortly, would almost lead one to anticipate the existence of psi. Prior to the development of quantum mechanics, the dominant worldview in physics was the classical, Newtonian cosmology in which the universe was thought to consist of isolated, localized particles. This aspect of Newtonian physics was actually little affected by the development of the theory of relativity. In this cosmology, objects (and people) are seen as separate and autonomous from one another, interacting only indirectly through the exchange of physical signals. Such a universe is hostile to the existence of psi phenomena. This psi-hostile cosmology constitutes the outlook of many laypersons and even most practicing scientists today, who have not entirely assimilated the fact that this worldview has been demonstrated to be absolutely false in a series of experiments testing the implications of quantum mechanics.

Consider the case of two protons that are initially united in a state of zero spin (what physicists call the singlet state). Suppose that the protons become separated from each other and are moving in opposite directions through space. If the spin of one of these protons is measured along a spatial axis and the proton is found to be spinning "upward" along that axis, the other proton must be spinning "downward" along that axis (as their total spin on any axis must sum to zero). In other words, the protons must display opposite spins along any measured axis. Thus it seems that when you measure the spin of one proton and find it to be "up," the second proton is somehow instantly informed that it should adopt the "down" state on that axis. Wait, the reader might protest, surely the Newtonian outlook can accommodate that! All you have to assume is that when the protons separated one of them possessed some property that made it spin down on the axis and the other one had some property that made it spin up. There is no need to assume any mysterious interconnection between the protons. This is the doctrine known as "local realism."

It can be shown that if such protons really do possess such local properties, the numbers of proton pairs exhibiting various combinations of spins on certain predefined spatial axes must satisfy a class of inequalities known as Bell inequalities, named after the physicist John Bell. The theory of quantum mechanics, on the other hand, predicts that Bell inequalities will be violated if certain combinations of spatial axes are chosen. Experiments have been performed to determine which theory is correct, local realism or quantum mechanics. The results clearly support quantum mechanics rather than the doctrine of local realism.[57] What this means is that the protons are not two isolated objects separated from each other in space. Instead, they form one united system even if they are separated by light years of space. The protons do not have defined spins on a spatial axis until a measurement of their spin along that axis is made, at which point the proton adopts a spin. After the first proton "chooses" a spin along the axis, the second proton then is somehow mysteriously informed that it should adopt the opposite spin if measured along that axis. It cannot be true that the first proton manages to send a message to the second proton telling it what state to adopt, as the protons may be sufficiently far apart that no such signal could be sent between them unless it exceeded the speed of light, which is regarded as impossible in most current theories of physics. The protons, two seemingly separate and isolated little billiard balls, turn out not be separate from one another after all.

Thus, mathematical results in another area of science, physics, have major implications for the metaphysical underpinnings of any parapsychological theory. If not even two protons separated by light years can be conceptualized as separate objects, perhaps it is also incorrect to consider persons as encapsulated, spatially isolated entities. Seeming separate persons may in fact merely be different facets of a higher nonlocal entity. The mysterious connections between apparently isolated elementary particles revealed in the violations of Bell inequalities make the prospect of psi interactions between people much more palatable.

(Incidentally, the reader who is interested in the mathematical details of Bell inequalities or in the mathematical details of any of the theories we have discussed, and many that we have not, should consult some of my more technical previous publications.[58])

Quantum holism. Science has generally proceeded by the analysis and dissection of complex systems into their parts, the ultimate parts being of course elementary particles such as electrons and quarks. Higher order phenomena, such as the activities of the mind, are to be explained in terms of lower order entities such as molecules and electrons, at least according to the "orthodox" (that is, outmoded, Newtonian) view of the world. This type of explanation is known as "upward causation." The philosophy upon which it is based is called "reductionism," as it assumes that the properties of complex systems, such as people, can be reduced to the properties of their components (such as atoms). Several parapsychologists have called for an abandonment of the exclusive reliance on upward causation in science, basing their arguments in part on quantum nonlocality. In his Presidential Address to the Parapsychological Association, Dean Radin proposed quite strongly that instances of "downward causation" also occur and are neglected by orthodox science.[59] Such downward causation might consist of an influence of the mind on the behavior of molecules, for instance. Indeed, as we have seen, even the behavior of our two entwined protons, seemingly the simplest of physical systems, is not governed by their local properties but rather by the more encompassing system that includes them both.

Hoyt Edge has called for the abandonment of the localized "entity" metaphysics and the adoption of an "activity meta-physics," in which reality would not be seen as separated into physical or mental atoms and the dichotomy between the observer and what is observed would be abandoned.[60] Stephen Braude has also criticized the "small-is-beautiful" bias of reductionistic science, and William Roll even recommends extending the traditional biological hierarchy beyond atoms, cells, organs and organisms to encompass a superorganismic level of description.[61] Even such an orthodox mathematician and scientist as Roger Penrose has suggested that the unity and global quality of consciousness may be related to nonlocal quantum connections governing the activity of neurons in the brain.[62] It should also be noted that Sir John Eccles, a Nobel prize winning neurophysiologist, likewise finds the conscious integration of visual experience impossible to account for in terms of known neural processes (in view of the fact that the nervous impulses related to visual experience appear to be fragmented and sent to divergent areas of the brain). This difficulty led Eccles to postulate the existence of a "self-conscious mind" existing separately from (or in addition to) the physical brain.[63] Indeed, a mind conscious of a complex array of stimuli at one time and existing through substantial periods of time has no place in a cosmology permitting only the existence of isolated elementary particles having only the most rudimentary of interactions with the rest of the universe and the most ephemeral of existences.

With its penchant for dissection it is almost no wonder that reductionistic science cannot explain the unity of mental experience or indeed give any account whatsoever of why certain firing patterns of neurons in the brain should give rise to conscious experience. Rather than admit this basic failure, reductionists such as the behaviorists in psychology have even gone so far as to deny the very existence of the mind, often placing themselves in absurd positions in the process of doing so, as we shall see in the next chapter.

The physicist David Bohm has referred to the universe as a "holomovement," invoking an analogy to a hologram (a three dimensional photograph in which the entire picture may be reconstituted from each part). Bohm has termed the world of manifest phenomena or appearances the "explicate order" and the hidden (nonlocal) reality underlying it the "implicate order." Bohm laments the tendency of modern science to fragment and dissect the universe and to focus on parts rather than wholes. He proposes a new mode of speaking in which "thing" expressions would be replaced by "event" expressions (this is reminiscent of Edge's call for an activity rather than an entity metaphysics, as discussed above).[64]

In a Presidential Address to the Parapsychological Association, K. Ramakrishna Rao noted the similarity of both Bohm's concept of an implicate order (in which all events are interconnected) underlying the manifest world and Karl Pribram's view of the world as a hologram, in which the whole universe is seen as somehow contained in or related to each of its parts,[65] to the Vedantic doctrine of the identity between *atman* (or a person's individual consciousness) and *Brahman* (the Supreme Self or World Mind). Transcendental and mystical states of consciousness may involve the direct experience of *Brahman* in Rao's view. He sees the implicate organization of the world as mediated by psi. Rao suggests that the practice of yoga may facilitate the occurrence of psi phenomena, as it enables the self to sink back into a primordial condition of unity with the rest of reality.[66] In his recent book *Soul Search*, astrophysicist David Darling proposes that our individual, encapsulated egos are illusions and that, when a person dies, this illusory self is dissolved and the person's consciousness merges with the world consciousness (or Brahman, in Rao's terminology).[67]

Psi and the quantum. Several parapsychological theorists have explicitly proposed that psi phenomena may due to nonlocal quantum connections between the elementary particles in someone's brain and particles in another person or object.[68] This hypothesis runs into difficulties on several fronts. First, it is difficult to believe that pairs of particles could be maintained in a coherent quantum state while residing in separate physical objects for any reasonable amount of time. Second, this hypothesis assumes an ability of a person or brain to track the past history of particles that is far more miraculous than the psi powers it is invoked to explain. Third, no psi message can be sent through such nonlocal connections under standard interpretations of quantum mechanics, as the behavior of both particles in a pair is apparently random at each site (although they are correlated with each other). The only way a psi message could be sent or a PK influence exerted would be for the mind to force the quantum process to occur in a preferred manner (such as by sending a message in Morse code by making protons spin up or down with respect to a selected spatial axis). This would implicitly equate the mind with the so-called "hidden variables" that determine the outcome of quantum processes. As these variables must necessarily be nonlocal, why not simply assume that the mind exerts its influence on the object directly rather than through particles in the brain that happen to be correlated with particles in the target? The latter view seems to be mired in a view of the mind as a localized entity, despite its explicit appeal to quantum nonlocality.

Several theorists, including Helmut Schmidt, Harris Walker and Richard Mattuck, have in fact taken the position that the mind should be equated with the hidden variables of quantum mechanics and that the mind should be seen as capable of directly influencing the outcome of quantum events.[69] Their theories are collectively known as the "observational theories." This term derives from the fact that attributes of quantum particles, such as the position of an electron, only take on definite values when an act of observation is made to determine what those values are. For instance, an electron is usually observed to be a point-like particle when its actual position is measured. Between measurements, however it appears not to have any particular position, but to exist in a state known as a probability wave (a mathematical function that specifies the probability that the electron will be detected in a particular location should an act of observation occur). The probability wave of a single electron is capable of passing through two separate microscopic windows simultaneously, something that would be impossible for a localized electron. The very act of measuring the electron's position seems to cause it to adopt a particular position, with the probability wave determining the relative likelihoods of particular positions being adopted. The sudden adoption of a particular position in response to an act of observation is called the collapse of the state vector, and there is no explanation within the mathematical theory of quantum mechanics itself of how or why such state vector collapse occurs. It seems almost as though the electron prefers to exist as a ghostlike probability wave existing in an abstract, almost mind-like mathematical space when we are not looking, but quickly appears to be a definite particle when we peek at it (which makes the seemingly solid world of physical objects seem like a giant hoax).

If being observed by a conscious mind somehow causes the electron's position to assume a definite value, the observational theorists reason, perhaps the conscious mind can also somehow determine what particular position the electron will adopt. There is already ample evidence that the mind may be able to influence the outcomes of quantum processes in the form of significant PK influences on quantum mechanically based random event generators. So the observational theories are not without experimental support. Specific mathematical versions of the observational theory have been proposed by Schmidt, Mattuck and Walker, but it would not be appropriate to delve deeply into them in a book for the general reader. Any reader interested in hearing my discussion of the technicalities of these models is referred to my previous publications on the subject.[70]

The Collective Mind

If individual persons cannot be thought of as separate and autonomous from one another, perhaps it would make sense to abandon the assumption that their minds are entirely separate from one another and to raise the possibility that individual psyches may be aspects of a group mind or collective unconscious. In fact, several parapsychological thinkers have postulated the existence of a collective mind in order to explain telepathy and other forms of psi phenomena. Some of these theorists, such as Tyrrell and Jung, have postulated that individual minds may share common regions at a deep level of the unconscious. More recently William Roll has suggested that the Iroquois' concept of the "long body" (a kind of collective mind encompassing one's family and other intimate acquaintances) might usefully be employed in attempting to understand psi phenomena.[71] We will consider several of these theories in turn, beginning with that of Jung.

Jung's theory of synchronicity and the collective unconscious. Carl G. Jung was one of Freud's most prominent disciples in the early psychoanalytic movement; indeed, he was regarded as Freud's "crown prince" until he broke with Freud to found his own school of Analytical Psychology. To account for similarities in the hallucinations and delusions of his psychotic patients (as well as the presence of apparent references to classical mythology in the delusional productions of apparently uneducated schizophrenic patients), Jung was led to postulate the existence of a "collective unconscious." Jung proposed that this collective unconscious existed at a deeper level of the psyche than the "personal unconscious" discovered by Freud. He also invoked the collective unconscious to explain the many similarities among the mythological and religious traditions of apparently unrelated peoples. Not only was the collective unconscious conceived to be basis for the common primordial images (archetypes) that appear in various mythological traditions, it was also conceived of as containing "racial" or "inherited" memories of the entire history of humankind. (Freud had also propounded the doctrine of inherited memory in his own theorizing.)

Some of Jung's followers have invoked the work of such ethologists as Konrad Lorenz and Niko Tinbergen on "innate releasing mechanisms" (indicating that, for instance, a bird of a given species has an apparently genetically-based tendency to sit only on eggs of a certain type) as evidence for the existence of inherited memory images or at least of primordial or archetypal imagery. While the inheritance of this sort of tendency to respond to a particular "sign stimulus" is not in dispute, the doctrine of the inheritance of specific memories has fallen into general scientific disrepute along with the rest of the Lamarckian doctrine of the inheritance of acquired characteristics. (Lamarck thought, for instance, that giraffes' necks might have become longer through generations of being stretched in order to reach leaves on tall trees, whereas the modern neo–Darwinian theory holds that giraffes that inherited random mutations that made their necks longer were able to outcompete their rivals for food.)

Jung also proposed the existence of an "acausal connecting principle," which he called the principle of "synchronicity." This principle acts to produce "meaningful coincidences." An example of a synchronistic occurrence is provided by the case of one of my friends in graduate school, who, not being prepared for the preliminary examination for his doctoral degree, postponed the examination after much soul-searching. That night, he went to eat in a Chinese restaurant. When he opened his fortune cookie, it said, "It is best to put off until tomorrow that which you may botch today."

Jung viewed the collective unconscious as being capable of extending its influence to the external physical world. In fact, he regarded all reality as being "psychoid" in nature (meaning that even seemingly inanimate objects have a psychic component). For instance, in one oft-discussed incident, Jung was in the middle of having an argument with Freud when loud raps were heard, seemingly coming from a nearby bookshelf. Jung attributed this coincidence to the "exteriorization" of an archetype (a doctrine that he also invoked to explain sightings of ghosts).

Several parapsychologists have objected to Jung's use of the term "acausal" to describe synchronistic occurrences. First of all, many of Jung's examples of synchronistic effects could be explained on the basis of ESP or PK. For instance, Jung might have unconsciously used his own psychokinetic powers to produce the raps in the bookcase (he described feeling intense symptoms of anger in his abdomen just preceding the incident). Also, it seems that Jung implicitly assumed that synchronistic events are in some sense caused by factors in the collective unconscious. As John Beloff has noted, Jung seems to confuse causation with mechanical causation.[72] What Jung probably wanted to deny was the existence of ordinary physical causes for synchronistic effects.

Rogo's materialization theory. As we have already discussed in Chapter 5, D. Scott Rogo proposed a "materialization theory" of anomalous events that is closely related to Jung's concept of exteriorization and to his notion that physical reality is psychoid in nature. As the reader will recall, Rogo proposed that all sorts of strange events, including such things as sightings of Bigfoot, UFOs, the Virgin Mary and maybe even Jimmy Swaggart, are due to psychic projections or materializations produced by the human mind.[73] In other words, a witness might create a quasi-physical UFO through psychokinesis, and then that UFO would be able to be seen by other observers insofar as it enjoyed a semipermanent physical existence. (Rogo-type theories of UFO abductions have proliferated in recent years. Many UFO enthusiasts no longer assume that UFOs are spacecraft from another planet. Now they are more often assumed to be projections from the human mind or from another dimension of psychic reality.)

It should be noted, however, that the evidence for many of the phenomena upon which Rogo constructed his theory is very shaky. For instance, one of Rogo's percipients of multiple UFO sightings was twice hospitalized for schizophrenia; thus, in the eyes of an orthodox scientist her sightings might be more parsimoniously explained in terms of psychotic hallucinations rather than psychic projections.

One piece of evidence that might be taken to support Rogo's theory has been provided by psychiatrist Morris Schatzman, whose patient "Ruth" was reportedly able to create hallucinatory figures or visual apparitions at will.[74] When such an apparition was interposed between Ruth and a flashing light, the evoked potential in her EEG (brain wave) record that was normally produced by the light was suppressed. On two occasions, Ruth was apparently able to create apparitions seen by other members of her family. In one case, a projected apparition of Ruth herself was seen by her husband; in the second, a projected apparition of her husband was seen by her father. In a review of Schatzman's book, T.C. Goodsort suggests that voluntarily projected apparitions of this kind may take on an objective existence,[75] in this way being analogous to the "thought forms," or tulpas, that Alexandra David-Neel described being produced by Tantric Buddhists in Tibet.[76] Goodsort's hypothesis is remarkably similar to Rogo's materialization theory. This similarity becomes less surprising once one realizes that the name "T.C. Goodsort" is an anagram of "D. Scott Rogo" and that Rogo had to author the review under a pseudonym because the journal's editor, Laura Dale, had banned Rogo's further contributions to her pages.

Tyrrell's theory of subliminal selves. It will be recalled from our discussion of collectively perceived apparitions that the parapsychologist G.N.M. Tyrrell proposed a theory of the collective unconscious that bears a certain resemblance to Jung's theory. Essentially, Tyrrell believed that people share regions of their minds at a deep unconscious level. He sees these regions of the mind as possessing "in some degree both the qualities of selfhood and of otherness from self."[77] It is in these regions that our dreams and hallucinations are constructed, which is why witnesses are consistent in their descriptions of collectively perceived apparitions. Also, as this deep region of the unconscious has no organization in space or time according to Tyrrell, it makes telepathy possible.

James' "cosmic consciousness." William James, one of the pioneers of both American psychology and American psychical research, postulated the existence of a "cosmic consciousness" into which individual minds merge during mystical experiences. James saw the everyday, normal state of consciousness as being a circumscribed form of awareness designed for adaptation to the "external earthly environment."[78] James' vision of a cosmic consciousness corresponds closely to Rao's depiction of an implicate order bearing a resemblance to the World Mind or Brahman of Hinduism.

Myers' metetherial world. F.W.H. Myers, one of the discoverers of the unconscious mind and a leader in the early psychical research movement, also postulated the existence of a deep region of the unconscious or "subliminal self" capable of accounting for paranormal events (although he was somewhat vague as to the mechanism underlying psi).[79] He also proposed the existence of a "metetherial world," which he conceived to be a world of images lying beyond the normal world of ether (the substance once thought to be the medium in which light waves propagated, but which is now generally regarded as nonexistent by physicists). On the basis of the fact that apparitions are frequently seen by more than one observer, Myers was led to conjecture that apparitions are not mere hallucinations but have a real existence in the metetherial world. He called such apparitions "metetherial presences" and conjectured that they represented modifications in regions of physical space, thus implying some sort of coextension between normal physical space and the metetherial world. Myers compared the metetherial world to a dream world, noting that phantoms often appear to behave in a dreamlike manner. Thus, Myers' metetherial world might be considered to be a form of collective unconscious. (We have already reviewed the debate between Myers and his contemporary Edmund Gurney over whether apparitions have a "real" external existence or whether they are due to the telepathic spread of hallucinations from one mind to another in Chapter 2, and so will not do so again here.)

Price's dream world. The philosopher H.H. Price also argued for the existence of a collective unconscious, noting that the possible existence of continuous telepathic rapport between minds makes it foolish to argue for a total separation of minds.[80] Like the philosopher Henri Bergson, he assumed that a repressive mechanism acts to prevent biologically irrelevant telepathic information from entering consciousness while the person is awake. He suggested that this suppressive mechanism may be relaxed in the dream state and in the states of dissociation associated with mediumship, making these states particularly conducive to the occurrence of psi phenomena.

Price proposed that one survives death in a dreamlike afterlife, whose characteristics are determined in part by a person's wishes and beliefs (and in part by telepathic impulses from other minds). Price assumed, like Myers, that the images persisting in the psychic "ether" may acquire a life of their own and may be responsible for experiences of hauntings and apparitions. In particular, Price argued that cases in which persons undergoing out-of-body experiences have been perceived at the locations to which they have projected (that is, "reciprocal hallucinations") provide evidence that apparitions serve as "vehicles of consciousness."

In a recent extension of Price's theory, Michael Grosso suggests that the ego may become fragmented in the afterlife and that, when one's wishes and desires are played out, one may eventually achieve the sort of transpersonal state experienced by mystics. Grosso attributes the repetitive, rudimentary forms of behavior frequently exhibited by ghostly apparitions to such fragmentation of the personality.[81]

The well-known American psychologist (and parapsychologist) Gardner Murphy also proposed that the mind might survive death in a fragmentary state in a type of collective consciousness. However, Murphy noted that the idea that the individual mind will survive death in an intact condition presupposes that the individual mind is a rigid, encapsulated entity. Instead, Murphy argued, the individual mind, being merely an aspect of a larger field of consciousness, may take on new qualities and form new structural relationships, no longer clinging to its narrow, biologically-oriented form of organization. He quotes Nietzsche's remark that the ego is a "grammatical illusion," and notes that the Buddhists deny the existence of a personal soul.[82] William Roll has cited instances involving the apparent fusion of memories from different people in mediumistic communications and in past-life memories reported by children as giving further support to Murphy's contention that personalities may undergo fragmentation, fusion and reorganization after death.[83] The reader will recognize of course that in these discussions of the details of the afterlife, we have left the world of hard (and even soft) science and entered the realm of pure speculation.

Roll's theory of "psi fields." A final version of collective mind theory has been proposed by William Roll.[84] Roll contends that physical objects contain "psi fields," or localized memory traces of events happening in their vicinity. He further postulates that the system of psi fields constitutes a type of collective mind he calls a "psi structure." He suggests that individual minds are not entirely separate entities but a merely parts of this psi structure. He explains place-related effects, such as hauntings in which a ghost is seen performing some repetitive act in a particular location in a house, as being due to the activation of the psi fields associated with a particular location or object.

Conclusions

As can be seen, despite the occasional contentions of some skeptics, parapsychologists are active theorizers. One of the most exciting developments in the past two decades has been the growing realization that psi phenomena need not be in conflict with established laws of science. The past decade has seen the experimental confirmation of the principle of nonlocality in quantum mechanics and the growing realization of the importance of that principle for a theory of psi phenomena. At present, theorizing in parapsychology is held back by the lack of a reliable data base and repeatable psi effects upon which a powerful theory of psi might be constructed and refined. Thus, many of the theories in this chapter represent mere presentations of "theoretical environments" within which more specific theories yielding more powerful experimental predictions might be constructed.

This chapter has been concerned primarily with theories aimed at explaining how psi information might be transmitted. In the next chapter, we will examine theories directed at understanding how a (possibly nonmaterial) collective or individual mind could interact with the physical brain. In succeeding chapters, we will examine the issue of whether such a mind (or portion thereof) could survive the death of that brain. We will also examine the parapsychological evidence for such survival, in the form of ghosts, past-life memories, near-death experiences, and various other phenomena.

8. Mind and Matter

We now turn an examination of the relationship between the conscious mind and the physical brain. This discussion will provide a framework that will enable us later to address the question of whether there might be an immaterial aspect to the mind, a soul as it were, that might be able to survive the destruction of the physical body at death. We will consider philosophical analyses of the so-called mind-body problem, as well as the neurophysiological evidence bearing on the question of whether there is an immaterial mind that exists independently of the physical brain system. Following this chapter, we will examine the parapsychological evidence for the continued existence of minds or spirits after death. This evidence consists, among other things, of encounters with apparitions and ghosts, communications ostensibly received from the deceased through mediums and dreams, near-death experiences, and cases suggestive of reincarnation and possession. Finally, the possible roles of immaterial minds in a physical universe will be discussed. The question of whether such minds played any role in the creation of life or in the direction of the course of evolution will be considered, together with the evidence that the universe itself may be a deliberate creation of the mind. We begin with a look at the mind-body problem.

Historical Roots

Before launching into a discussion of modern views on the mind-body problem, it is helpful to consider the historical processes that gave rise to those views. In particular, an historical perspective will enable us to understand the almost religious vehemence with which some positions are held.

In the history of human thought up until surprisingly recent times, it was much more common to attribute mental or psychological properties to seemingly inanimate matter than it is today. Jonathan Shear, the editor of the newly founded *Journal of Consciousness Studies*, notes that the problem of accounting for the existence of conscious experience that confronts modern science was not a problem for the ancient Greeks, as they viewed the material world as being imbued with mind, which served as a force governing the behavior of matter.[1] Aristotle, for instance, taught that the natural state of any body was one of rest. He taught that the crystalline spheres which carried the planets and stars on their celestial voyages in his cosmology were associated with incorporeal "movers" that provided the needed force to maintain their motion. He viewed these movers as being spiritual in nature and conceived of the relation of a mover to its sphere as "akin to that of a soul to its body."[2]

Aristotle's view was given a Christian interpretation in the middle ages, with his "movers" being equated with the angels described in the Scriptures. Aristotle also attributed psychological properties to baser matter, ascribing the tendency for a terrestrial object to fall to the Earth to its "aspiration" to reach its natural place.

Even as late as 1600, William Gilbert, an English physician and the founder of the scientific study of magnetic phenomena, proclaimed that the Earth has a magnetic soul analogous to the "magnetic soul" that Gilbert believed governed the behavior of lodestones. According to Gilbert, the rotation of the Earth and the inclination of its axis of rotation with respect to the sun were both caused by a desire on the part of the Earth's soul to avoid extreme temperatures and to cause seasonal variations. Almost two centuries later, in 1777, the English chemist Joseph Priestley asserted that physical matter was akin to "spiritual and immaterial beings" because of its properties of attraction and repulsion.

These animistic views of matter gradually crumbled under the onslaught of scientific advances. The law of the conservation of angular momentum (earlier called the doctrine of "impetus") led John Philoponos in the sixth century and William of Ockham in the fourteenth to deny the need to assume the existence of angels to keep the planetary spheres in motion. After all, if you spin a top, it keeps spinning by itself. In rejecting these angels, William of Ockham was led to formulate his famous injunction "not to multiply entities beyond necessity," which has since become known as "Ockham's Razor." In fact, Ockham's Razor, which was originally formulated to justify the exclusion of a class of spiritual beings (Aristotle's angelic movers) is still one of the primary justifications used by modern scientists and philosophers to deny the existence of a realm of mental experience that is independent of physical events in the brain. With regard to Ockham's original application of his principle, the historian of science Herbert Butterfield sees the impetus doctrine (in the form of the modern laws of conservation of momentum) as the primary factor underlying the banishment of a spiritual realm from scientific accounts of the world and the establishment in seventeenth century of the view of the universe as material clockwork-like mechanism.[3]

Once the picture of the physical universe as a soulless machine gained ascendancy, not only did matter get stripped of its mental and spiritual aspects, so did living organisms. For instance, while Ernest Haeckel used an analogy between the growth of salt crystals and that of living cells to proclaim that all matter had a spiritual aspect, his contemporary Carl Nageli used precisely the same analogy to deny that biological cells were associated with a spiritual force, instead arguing that their growth was due to simple mechanical forces. The chemical synthesis of organic compounds in the laboratory, exemplified by Friederich Wöhler's synthesis of urea in 1828, further undermined the vitalistic philosophies that insisted that a spiritual force governed biological processes. Antoine Lavoisier had earlier demonstrated that the ratio of emitted heat to carbon dioxide was the same for candle flames as it was for animals, suggesting that respiration was a purely mechanical process. While vitalism is not dead, its few modern advocates such as Arthur Koestler[4] have been regarded as fringe thinkers by the scientific establishment.

One of the contributors to this mechanistic cosmology was, paradoxically enough, the seventeenth century philosopher and mathematician Rene Descartes, who is widely regarded as being the prototype of the modern dualist (a dualist being one who regards the realms of mind and matter as having independent reality). Among the phenomena that had most strongly indicated a mental aspect to matter were those suggestive of the operation of action-at-a-distance, such as gravitation and magnetism. Descartes was able to eliminate this stumbling block on the road to a totally mechanistic outlook by proposing theories of magnetism (the vortex theory) and gravitation (the plenum theory) that avoided the problem of action-at-a-distance by assuming that these two types of force were transmitted through a physical medium.

Descartes extended his mechanistic philosophy to encompass living creatures as well as inanimate matter. He viewed animals as mere machines. He did not, however, question the existence of minds in humans; indeed, he thought one's primary and most direct knowledge was of one's own mind. He viewed mind as a totally different kind of entity from matter. In Descartes' view, one's mind (or ego) was indivisible and hence lacked a basic character of matter—that of extension in space. Thus, the mind inhabited a different plane of existence from the physical world and could not be said to have a spatial location.

Despite their different natures, Descartes proposed that the mind interacted with the physical body by deflecting the motion of the "animal spirits" flowing through the brain. He thought the pineal gland was the area of the brain in which this mind-matter interaction took place (as the pineal gland was the one structure that was not duplicated in the cerebral hemispheres and thus seemed appropriate to house a unitary and indivisible mind). Because Descartes' law of inertia held merely that the total quantity of motion in a system remains constant (but not necessarily its *direction*), he proposed that the soul acted upon the body by altering the direction of motion of the animal spirits, while not changing the intensity of that motion. The mathematician

G.W. Leibniz, however, demonstrated that Descartes was in error and that directionality was conserved in the law of momentum. Thus Leibniz demonstrated that the physical body (as modeled by Descartes) was a deterministic system. There was therefore no room left for an influence of the mind on the body, and the mind was totally excluded from influence on the physical world. (It should be noted that mind retained a place in Leibniz' own "monad" cosmology, although that cosmology never gained ascendancy in Western thought.) Once again, an application of the law of inertia led to the exclusion of the spiritual realm from scientific models of the world, only this time it was not angels being banished from the heavens, but the human soul itself being banished from its body. Indeed the historian of science Richard Westfall sees the rigid exclusion of the psychic from physical nature as the "permanent legacy" of the seventeenth century.[5]

At this point it should be reemphasized that, since the emergence of the theory of quantum mechanics early in this century, the brain is no longer viewed as a deterministic system. Thus, the argument from determinism no longer works, and there is now the possibility that an immaterial mind could interact with a physical brain by selecting which quantum state the brain enters out of the many states that are possible at any given time. The philosopher Michael Lockwood has noted that the prejudice in favor of matter was grounded in the apparent solidity of the former in the Newtonian worldview. Lockwood points out that the solidity of matter has disappeared in the theory of quantum mechanics (material particles exist as probability waves in an abstract mathematical space until they are observed) and that mind and matter are now both equally mysterious.[6]

The tenacity with which some scientists resist the idea of an autonomous realm of mind is perhaps understandable in light of history. The emerging mechanistic picture of the world was fiercely resisted by the religious establishment, notable examples being the condemnation of Galileo for the crime of propounding the heliocentric (sun-centered) model of the solar system and the resistance to the theory of biological evolution that is still being mounted by Christian fundamentalists. Thus, any mention of an immaterial soul may raise fears of a descent back into religious irrationalism (and a consequent lack of funding) on the part of many scientists.

Let us now turn to an examination of modern views on, and "solutions" of, the mind-brain problem.

Monistic Philosophies

Monistic solutions to the mind-brain problem are those that postulate that the universe is composed of only one type of "stuff." That "stuff" is usually taken to be mind, matter, or some sort of "tertium quid" having both mental and physical properties. Monism stands in contrast to dualism and pluralism, which comprise those philosophical positions that postulate the existence of two or more distinctly different types of "stuff," with one of them typically being mind and another being matter.

Idealism. The monistic position that contends that the world is composed solely of minds and mental events goes by the name of idealism. According to idealists, all that exists is mental experience. People consciously or unconsciously construct the hypothesis of a physical world in order to account for certain regularities in their sensory experience, but this is only a convenient fiction. The contention that the physical world may be an illusion is logically irrefutable. For instance, you may think you are a human being holding a book on the mind-brain problem in your hand, whereas in fact you may be a nucleon-based life form on the surface of a neutron star who has gone into the analogue of a movie theater where strong pion fields have been applied to your brain both to induce amnesia for your real existence and to create in you the illusion that you are some two-legged elongated oxygen-breathing carbon-based being on a remote planetary body for the sole purposes of entertainment. More simply, you could be merely dreaming or hallucinating. Following the Taoist philosopher Chuang Tzu, the reader might legitimately wonder whether she or he might be a butterfly temporarily dreaming about being a human being reading a sentence about butterfly dreams. I can remember arguing with someone against this position. I maintained that I could not be dreaming because of the clarity and consistency of my sensory experience. Imagine my surprise when I woke up. (This actually happened to me.)

All you can be certain of is your own existence. Seeking certain knowledge, Descartes found that he could not doubt his own existence as a thinking being. In perhaps his most famous quote, he was led to exclaim, "I think, therefore I am." All you can be absolutely certain of is your own existence and that you are now thinking certain thoughts, remembering certain memories, feeling certain feelings and sensing certain sensations. The inferences you make about your external environment based on these mental events may not be valid, as you may be hallucinating, remembering falsely, having groundless feelings and thinking delusional thoughts. The doctrine that only one's self exists or can be proven to exist is a special case of idealism that goes by the name of solipsism.

The various agencies presumed by idealists to be responsible for producing the illusion of the physical world have included God (in the view of the prototypical idealist, the eighteenth century philosopher Bishop George Berkeley, for whom Berkeley University was named), a collective mind or collective unconscious, and the illusion-producing state of craving and ignorance (according to certain schools of Buddhism).

The reply of most modern scientists and philosophers of science to idealism is that scientific theories that postulate the existence of an objective physical world have produced more exact predictions about possible human observations than have idealistic theories and therefore should be preferred over the latter for that reason. (Such theories are even covertly preferred by most solipsists, who seem strangely reluctant to step in front of illusory oncoming trains. Dr. Samuel Johnson said of idealism, "I refute it thus," and then he proceeded to kick a rock with his foot. Johnson's "refutation," while actually proving nothing, did show his dedication to the anti-idealist cause.)

Idealism is not merely an historical curiosity, but even has its advocates today. Within parapsychology, for instance, Edgar Mitchell, a former astronaut and moon-voyager, has suggested that an idealistic philosophy may have to be adopted in order to account for psychokinetic effects.[7] More recently, the physicist Amit Goswami has contended that an idealist conception of the world is required in order to render modern theories of physics, in particular quantum mechanics, coherent.[8]

Radical Materialism. Radical materialism is the polar opposite of idealism. Radical materialists deny the existence of mental events, insisting that the world of physical matter is the only reality. Incredibly enough, this philosophy held sway in the discipline of psychology itself in the early part of this century (at least in the United States). Behaviorism emerged as the dominant force in psychology in this country as a reaction against the fallibility of the method of introspection that predominated in the earliest days of psychological investigation. Behavior was publicly observable and scientifically measurable, whereas the vague mental images that form, say, a particular individual's idea of the number seven are not. Some of the leaders of the behaviorist movement, such as John Watson and the earlier versions of B.F. Skinner, went so far as to deny the existence of mental events altogether.[9] This denial of course flies in the face of the fact that the reader and I (if I am not a figment of the reader's imagination) have directly experienced such mental events as sensations, thoughts, feelings and memories. Skinner's position essentially contains its own refutation. Skinner could not consistently claim that he believed that mental events do not exist, as that belief would itself constitute a mental event. Therefore by his own theory (and reportedly by his own contention), Skinner's expressions of belief in the doctrine of radical materialism were merely forms of physical behavior than he had been rewarded for displaying in the past (through royalties, academic honoraria, etc.). If the books produced by Skinner are in fact merely the product of conditioned typewriter-pecking responses, there is no need to take these books seriously. It should be noted that Skinner did eventually retreat from this early radical version of his theory.

Materialism is not dead as a philosophy in modern cognitive neuroscience, however. The philosopher Paul Churchland has recently proposed doing away with "folk psychology" (talk of mental events such as beliefs and desires) in all human discourse.[10] He would replace "folk psychology" with a strictly neural account of behavior. Thus, instead of a wife telling her husband that she is really angry at him, she would say instead, "The neurons in my amygdala seem to be firing at an unacceptably high rate."

Churchland has in fact gone so far as to assert that truth might cease to be an aim of science! This assertion is implicitly based on the assumption that the concept of truth presupposes the existence of propositions capable of being true or false, which in turn presupposes the existence of mental events such as thoughts, ideas and beliefs that are expressed in such propositions. Churchland proposes that scientific theories should no longer be expressed in terms of sentences but rather in terms of patterns of connections among neurons (or among the pseudoneurons in a computerized "neural net," as discussed below). But now we are right back where we started. Unless human knowledge is to be given up entirely, Churchland must at least be able to entertain propositions such as "neural net *A* diagnoses diseases more accurately than does neural net *B*." Such propositions, however express beliefs. If Churchland seriously wishes to give up the "folk psychological" concept of belief, then his philosophy self-destructs in the same way that Skinner's did.

Skinner, incidentally, was by no means the last modern thinker to deny the existence of private conscious experience, or "qualia" in the terminology of philosophers. The prominent materialist philosopher Daniel Dennett has recently concluded that "contrary to what seems obvious at first blush, there simply are no qualia at all."[11] Dennett is, however, mistaken. Apparently unlike Dennett, I have personally experienced several of them, of varying degrees of pleasantness. Perhaps the reader has as well.

Quasi-dualistic materialism. More sensible versions of materialism concede the existence of mental events, but contend that mental events arise solely from physical events and that a complete scientific description of the world can be given in terms of physical processes alone. In one version of this theory, mental events are thought to be brain events experienced from the "inside." The view goes by the names "central state materialism" and "neural identity" theory, among others. A related doctrine is double aspect theory. Double aspect theorists contend that mental and physical events are merely two aspects of a single underlying reality. As the vast majority of double aspect theorists implicitly or explicitly assume that this single underlying reality is essentially physical matter, this theory is basically equivalent to the previous two. A similar doctrine is panpsychism, which asserts that all matter, not just living organisms, has a mental aspect. A prominent recent proponent of this position is the philosopher David Ray Griffin, although he prefers to call his doctrine "panexperientialism" rather than "panpsychism," as he does not contend that rocks and other inanimate collections of material particles possess a highly unified and structured consciousness, but rather ascribes only vague "feeling-responses" to them.[12] Panpsychism carries the advantage that one does not need to explain the sudden emergence of consciousness in higher life forms, as consciousness is inherent in matter from the start. (It should, however, be noted that panpsychism still faces the difficulty of accounting for the emergence of a unified mind and global consciousness out of a myriad of psychic elements, as was pointed out long ago by William James and, more recently, by William Seager.[13])

While we are on the subject of consciousness in rocks, the reader may be vaguely recalling hearing something about consciousness in plants a few years ago. What you may be recalling is Cleve Backster's claim to have detected a "primary perception" in plants (and in all life for that matter). Backster is a polygraph (lie detector) expert, and one day he got the idea of wiring up his philodendron plant to see if he could measure the flow of water through its leaves. (Polygraph machines work by measuring the electrical resistance of a person's skin. When the person perspires, the resistance goes down. So it is really a sweat, or anxiety, detector rather than a lie detector.) After the water experiment, Backster got the idea of burning the plant with a match to see what the effect would be. As soon as the idea popped into Backster's head, the plant became extremely agitated, according to the polygraph record, almost as if it were reading Backster's mind. Backster then had someone brutally assault the philodendron's companion (another plant). Later the philodendron was able to pick out this botanicidal maniac from a lineup by manifesting severe anxiety in his presence, but remaining calm in the presence of other people.

Backster then got the idea of terminating (killing) brine shrimp in the room adjacent to the plant. Predictably enough, the plant manifested severe anxiety when its brine shrimp compatriots were being boiled to death, but remained calm when an empty saline solution was dumped into the steaming cauldron.[14] Unfortunately, other scientists were by and large unable to replicate Backster's rather striking results. Also, consciousness in plants was a bit much politically for even parapsychologists to swallow. So Backster's primary perception was never really accepted as a legitimate effect by the parapsychological community. As for Backster, the last I recall hearing of him, he was trying to scare the living daylights out of some cups of yogurt (yogurt does after all contain a live bacterial culture).

But I digress severely. Let us get back to the subject by examining the philosophical position of epiphenomenalism. Epiphenomenalism is technically a form of dualism, insofar as it grants separate reality to the realms of mind and matter; however, I will classify epiphenomenalism as a form of quasi-dualistic materialism, as it denies that mental events have any influence whatsoever on the physical world. Mental events are considered to be mere "epiphenomena" of physical events in the sense that, while mental events are caused by physical events, they are themselves incapable of causing or influencing physical events. A prominent advocate of epiphenomenalism was the biologist T.H. Huxley, noted for his tireless defenses of Darwin's theory of evolution.

Several writers, including Roger Penrose[15] and Karl Popper and John Eccles[16] have noted that epiphenomenalism in fact goes counter to Darwinism. Why should a conscious mind have evolved, they ask, if it did not play an active role in benefiting the organism? Also, epiphenomenalism is a self-destructive theory in the same way that radical materialism is. Epiphenomenalists discuss mental events. Presumably this behavior is caused in part by the existence of (someone's) mental experience, otherwise epiphenomenalism could not claim to be a theory of mental experience. Thus, the theory of epiphenomenalism is refuted by the fact of its own existence.

The late Heinz Pagels raised the question of whether the universe could be a giant computer, much as a personal computer screen can become transformed into a mini-universe with quasi-organisms evolving on it when a program realizing mathematician John Conway's "game of life" is run on it.[17] This idea had previously been suggested by Ed Fredkin of M.I.T. and explicitly endorsed by Tomasso Toffoli.[18] If this suggestion has any validity, we cannot equate ourselves with the godlike programmers who created the universe and assume that we have simply each become entranced in the life of one of our three-dimensional creations (which we have come to regard as our physical body). Because of the arguments against epiphenomenalism, we cannot be mere spectators in the world. Our consciousnesses have a more active role in the universe than that.

The philosophical positions that I have grouped together under the heading of quasi-dualistic materialism would seem to be equivalent to one another as scientific theories, insofar as they all apparently make the same scientific predictions (mainly that no violations of the known laws of physics will occur in the brain and that no successful predictions regarding the behavior of the brain can be generated from theories involving nonphysical entities such as souls or minds that could not in principle at least be derived from theories referring solely to physical entities and processes). It is commonly held, both by parapsychologists and skeptics, that psi phenomena are inexplicable on the basis of current physical theories. J.B. Rhine in particular was highly skeptical that psi phenomena could be explained on the basis of any physicalistic theory. In fact, Rhine suggested that psi was nonphysical in nature, due to the lack of dependence of experimental psi-scoring rates on spatial or temporal separations, physical barriers between the percipient and the target, and the physical nature of the target, as well as due to the apparent backward causation in time involved in precognition (and, now we might add, retroactive PK). At one point, he postulated the existence of "nonphysical energy,"[19] a concept that John Beloff considered to be oxymoronic.[20]

For this reason, it is often believed that the existence of psi phenomena would falsify physicalism (where "physicalism" denotes the class of theories encompassing radical materialism and quasi-dualistic materialism). As the vast majority of working scientists subscribe to some form of physicalistic solution to the mind-body problem, it should not be surprising that they would choose to reject the claims of parapsychology, insofar as those claims tend to threaten their worldview. In fact, in a recent scathing attack on parapsychology, Nicholas Humphrey clearly stated that the questions of the existence of souls and of the existence of paranormal powers are not independent issues and that the possession of a soul would imply the existence of such powers.[21] On the other side of the fence, as psi phenomena suggest the existence of a nonphysical aspect to the mind, many people who would prefer to believe in the existence of an immortal soul may tend to adopt a belief in psi phenomena in support of their position. Indeed, John Beloff even asserted, in a Presidential Address to the Parapsychological Association, that the existence of an afterlife is contingent on the existence of psi, in seeming agreement with Humphrey's position.[22] This is undoubtedly too strong an assertion, however, as it is quite conceivable that a mind or soul could survive death even if the living person (or surviving trace) did not possess the powers of ESP and PK.

Actually, even if it is assumed that the explanation of psi phenomena will require the postulation of entities and principles beyond those currently known to physicalistic science, it may be a mere issue of terminology whether such entities are to be considered material or nonmaterial. If the former, the physicalist can claim victory; if the latter, the dualist can claim the same. Obviously, if mind and matter interact, they form one united system. Whether one chooses to call that system the physical universe may be a matter of semantics rather than substance. (Some of the theoretical concepts already employed by physicists, such as the quantum-mechanical wave function discussed in Chapter 7, already seem more mindlike than material in any event.)

Strangely enough, J.B. Rhine himself disavowed any position of dualism. John Beloff traces Rhine's eschewal of dualism to his difficulty in seeing how such dissimilar things as mind and matter could interact, although Beloff himself sees no reason why a cause must necessarily be of the same nature as its effect.[23] Beloff suggests that Rhine's position may have been motivated by a desire to avoid charges of supernaturalism as well as a desire to leave the door open for an ultimate cosmology that would embrace both mind and matter. Beloff notes that Rhine recognized that psi might potentially be given an explanation in terms of quantum mechanics and that Rhine only wished to state the incompatibility of psi with "conventional" physics. Interestingly enough, Frederick Dommeyer has classified Rhine as a double-aspect theorist, presumably referring to a version of double aspect theory in which the common substance underlying mental and physical events is something other than matter as currently understood.[24]

Several other parapsychological theorists have proposed versions of the double aspect theory. Edmund Gurney, one of the early pioneers of psychical research, proposed that some third form of existence or "tertium quid," in addition to mind and matter, would be required in order to explain mental phenomena and to bridge the gap between mind and brain.[25] In more recent times, Carroll Nash has proposed a double aspect theory to explain psi phenomena.[26] Nash proposes that mind and matter are each aspects of some tertium quid, or neutral substance, that is not governed by space, time or causality, thus allowing psi to occur (as well as providing the basis for mystical experiences). Nash's theory does not, however, appear to be sufficiently developed to enable testable predictions to be derived from it.

Consciousness in computers and robots. Many people argue that, if a computer can duplicate human thought processes, there is no need to postulate the existence of an immaterial mind or soul to explain human thought, as human-manufactured computers are presumably not endowed with such ethereal entities as souls or minds (even if they are made in Japan). Other writers, such as Roger Penrose, David Layzer and John Searle, have argued that, even if computers were to prove capable of simulating human behavior, this would not imply that computers possessed awareness or had conscious experiences. Rather, they see the biochemical "wetware" of the human brain as having specific properties necessary for the production of consciousness that the hardware of a typical digital computer lacks.[27] On the other hand, their assertions that the particular properties of biological wetware are necessary for the generation of conscious experience are not in general supported by any convincing argument. It would be desirable, therefore, to have a more or less objective test to determine whether a computer or robot is conscious. As the reader will recall from Chapter 7, the mathematician Alan Turing proposed an operational definition of consciousness in computers in the form of an imitation game (which has since become known as the Turing test).[28] If a human being communicating with a computer and another human being through a teletype machine (or, these days, a computer monitor) cannot tell which is the computer and which is the human being, then the computer should be deemed conscious (that is, if you are willing to ascribe consciousness to the human being on the basis of her behavior, you should extend the same courtesy to the computer).

Could a computer successfully pass the Turing test? Computers operate by following algorithms (fixed mechanical procedures for solving a problem or producing output). The well-known mathematician and physicist Roger Penrose, however, has argued that human thought must not rely exclusively on such algorithms.[29] Penrose bases his contention that human thought must have a nonalgorithmic component in part on mathematician Kurt Gödel's famous incompleteness theorem. In 1931, Gödel shocked the mathematical world by demonstrating that there exist statements within any reasonably powerful mathematical axiom system that are true but which can never be proved to be true within the axiom system itself. To oversimplify slightly, such a statement might read as follows: "This theorem is not provable." Let us call this statement Theorem X. If Theorem X were provable, a contradiction would result, as Theorem X asserts its own unprovability. Therefore, if the mathematical axiom system is consistent, Theorem X could never be proven. Consequently, Theorem X is true, as it simply asserts its own unprovability. Computers, being driven by algorithms, are equivalent to mathematical axiom systems. Hence, a computer would be unable to perceive the truth of its own Theorem X, as it would only regard as true those statements which it could prove. Humans, on the other hand, are readily able to perceive the truth of such statements as Theorem X. Hence, Penrose argues, human thought is not algorithmic and therefore could not be simulated by an algorithmic computer. The chief difference between the computer and the human in this regard might be that the human can understand the *meaning* of the statements involved, whereas computers just blindly manipulate symbols according to prescribed rules without any idea of what those symbols might mean.

It may be objected that, even if a computer could simulate human thought, humans quite possibly possess psi abilities that may be indicative of a spiritual or immaterial aspect to human beings. Computers, being mere machines, would presumably be incapable of demonstrating such psi powers. Actually, Turing himself considered this objection in his original proposal of the imitation game. He suggested that computers might be able to manifest, or least simulate, psi powers if a random event generator (REG) were included in the computer's design.[30] Thus, in a telepathy experiment, the sender or the experimenter could use her psychic powers to influence the REG in such a way as to make it appear that the computer has ESP. Various psychokinetic tasks posed to the computer might be performed inadvertently by experimenter psi (especially if the experimenter was rooting for the computer). Thus, to all appearances, the computer would have psi powers. To pursue this line of thought even further, it would be interesting to speculate what would happen if a large number of quantum-mechanically based REGs were installed in the computer. If minds are to be equated with the "hidden variables" that govern the outcome of quantum decisions, perhaps such a largely nondeterministic computer would be able to acquire a mind. Of course, it would no longer be the sort of deterministic, algorithm-following sort of computer that is known as a Turing machine. Instead, it might be something approaching a silicon-based life form.

Penrose himself has recently argued that, as human awareness must be noncomputational in nature and as current laws of physics are essentially computational systems, new principles of physics may be required to explain humans' capacity to achieve direct insight into mathematical problems and to understand the meaning of language. He notes that the expert computer chess-playing program Deep Thought failed to solve a simple chess problem that required "global awareness" to solve, and points to this failure as further evidence that human thought processes are nonalgorithmic. He cites the ability of humans to perceive the truth of Gödel's Incompleteness Theorem as evidence that the mind is not a Turing machine (that is a digital computer), although he notes that Turing himself continued to adhere to the view of the human mind as a digital computer. On the other hand, Penrose observes that Kurt Gödel maintained that the mind was not identical to the physical brain, as Gödel felt that the physical brain would necessarily be a computationally-based system. Gödel was thus a dualist. As we shall see, Penrose has come to view consciousness as intimately connected to nonlocal quantum processes in the brain. He sees such noncomputable quantum processes as being a prerequisite for consciousness. Any system based entirely on simple computation must be nonconscious in Penrose's view.[31] Paul Churchland, perhaps the foremost defender of radical materialism in the modern era, has recently expressed agreement with Penrose's view that human reasoning is nonalgorithmic. Churchland does not, however, see such nonalgorithmic reasoning as emerging from arcane quantum mechanical processes, but rather from the continuous, analog nature of the human brain (as compared to Turing machines, which operate by entering one discrete state after another).[32]

Philosopher John Searle has argued that even if a computer were to successfully simulate human behavior, this would not imply consciousness on the part of the computer.[33] As an analogy, he considers the case of a person who does not speak Chinese who sits alone in a room with a book of rules instructing him how to respond to strings of Chinese characters. While a speaker of Chinese may think he is engaging in a dialogue with this person by swapping notes back and forth under the door to the room, the person inside the room does not in fact understand what the Chinese speaker is saying or what he himself is saying, as he does not know what the symbols *mean*. Similarly, Searle argues, computers are engaged in a purely syntactic manipulation of symbols and have no idea of what those symbols mean. In his later publications, Searle does concede that a robot might be said to have semantic and not just merely syntactical understanding of linguistic symbols if the robot were provided with sensing devices (such as TV cameras) and motor apparatus (such as robot arms). In such a case, the robot could develop a sensory "awareness" of the outside world and could gain an inkling of "insight" into the fact that words refer to objects and events in an outside world.

In the end, the real test of consciousness in automata such as robots and computers may be to wait to see if such machines spontaneously express curiosity and wonderment about their own inner experience, much as human philosophers of mind do. Presumably, a nonconscious computer would not develop a preoccupation with the machine equivalent of the mind-body problem.

So much for theory. How successful have such attempts at simulating human thought in computers been? The traditional approach to artificial intelligence (AI), in which a computer's central processor operates on a set of data in a step-by-step manner following the prescribed rules and procedures inherent in a computer program, has been successful only in certain highly circumscribed areas, such as chess-playing and theorem-proving, which lend themselves to a such a serial, step-by-step rule-following approach. This traditional AI approach has been much less successful in "fuzzier" areas, such as the manipulation and perception of three-dimensional objects and language comprehension. A new approach has recently come to the forefront in the artificial intelligence community, which goes by the names "parallel distributed processing" and "connectionism." The connectionist approach abandons the use of a central processor that performs operations one step at a time in a prescribed manner. Instead, the computer adopts a "parallel processing" approach modeled loosely on processes occurring in the brain. In connectionist approaches, the computer is programmed with a set of artificial "neurons" or nodes. Upon "firing," each neuron or node may inhibit or excite other neurons or nodes in the computer network. Whether a particular neuron fires or not depends on the net amounts of excitatory and inhibitory stimulation it receives from other nerves in the network. In a sensory recognition task, the sensory input is defined to be the pattern of excitation in a set of neurons designated as "sensory neurons." The computer's response is defined in terms of the pattern of activity of a set of "output" neurons. Depending on the correctness of the response, a "tutor" program external to the network adjusts the "synaptic" weights (that is, the degrees to which each neuron will excite or inhibit its fellow neurons) in such a way as to increase the accuracy of the response on the next trial.

Andy Clark notes that connectionist models have been very successful in tasks involving low-level pattern recognition and motor output, but seem ill-suited to dealing with serial tasks such as logical deductions and language production. He suggests that different computational architectures may be needed to accomplish different types of tasks. He notes that sudden flashes of insight in human problem solving may be naturally explainable in terms of connectionist models, but observes that such flashes of insight are usually considered to be the result of unconscious rather than conscious processes. In general, the limited informational capacity, serial-processing approach of traditional AI is quite similar to the activity of the conscious mind as viewed in cognitive psychology, whereas the processes involved in connectionist models bear a greater similarity to brain processes that are usually regarded as taking place at an unconscious level.[34]

Thus, the dichotomy between the traditional, serial-processing approach to AI and the connectionist approach is highly analogous to the dichotomy between the conscious mind and the physical brain. In fact, Michael Lockwood has explicitly compared consciousness to a serial computer "sitting on top" of a parallel-processing connectionist device and acting as an executive system whose purpose is to avoid or resolve impasses in the connectionist machine.[35] He notes that the cognitive psychologist Philip Johnson-Laird has contended that parallel processing in brains may be controlled by executive serial-processing systems, and he agrees with Johnson-Laird that such executive systems are the "proper domain of consciousness."[36]

To the extent that connectionist models succeed in duplicating human behavior, one might assume that human behavior could be explained in terms of the activity of the human brain without recourse to positing any conscious mind existing apart from the physical neurons in the brain. Such duplication has yet to be achieved, however. In the first place, connectionist models have thus far at least failed to master the serial reasoning tasks, such as theorem proving and chess playing, that we normally assume are accomplished through the application of conscious thought. In the second place, the external "tutor" program that adjusts the synaptic weights is a purposive entity that lies outside of the network itself. Jack Cowan and David Sharp, for instance, express extreme skepticism that the processes used to alter the synaptic weights in connectionist AI models could be employed in the brain.[37] There are other important differences between the processes employed in connectionist AI and those likely to be employed by real neural nets in physical brains. Even connectionism enthusiast Paul Churchland concedes that computer "neural nets" have severe deficiencies as models of actual brains.[38] For instance, the axons of real neurons have a fixed excitatory or inhibitory effect on all subsequent neurons, not a varied and modifiable one as in computer net models. Churchland also notes that even the recent generation of computers still flunk the Turing test, citing a recent contest sponsored by the General Dynamics Corporation as an example of such failure.[39]

We cannot rule out dualism based on attempts to simulate human intelligence in computers to date. *Space Odyssey*'s HAL is not yet with us (unless you count the computers that attempt to engage us in phone conversations during dinner).

Dualistic Philosophies

We are thus led to consider dualist positions, which grant independent reality to both mental and physical events. We will begin with parallelism.

Parallelism. Parallelism is a peculiar form of dualism in that it insists that the realms of mind and matter are totally separate and do not interact at all. One of the foremost advocates of this doctrine was the seventeenth century mathematician and philosopher Gottfried Willhelm Leibniz, who asserted that God had placed the physical and mental realms in "preestablished harmony" so that they are forever in correspondence with one another, much as two synchronized clocks continue to display the same time as one another. Parallelism seems to have one more realm than it needs. After all, the reason that we postulate the existence of a physical world in the first place is to explain certain regularities in our sensory experience. If the physical world is not the cause of our sensations, there is really no reason to postulate its existence at all. Which brings up...

Interactionism. Interactionists, as their name implies, assume that the mental and physical realms do in fact interact with one another. Unlike epiphenomenalism, in interactionism the causal highway is a two-way street. Not only do events in the physical realm cause mental events, but mental events are capable of influencing physical events as well. As we have mentioned, since the advent of the theory of quantum mechanics, the brain is no longer considered to be a completely deterministic system and therefore could be open to influence from a mental realm. (In this context, however, it should be noted that some die-hard materialists such as philosopher Daniel Dennett continue to reject dualism on the basis of arguments involving the outmoded concept of a deterministic brain system.[40]) In fact, the brain seems almost designed in such a way as to maximize its receptivity to such influence from a nonmaterial mind. Neurophysiologist John Eccles has called the brain just "the sort of a machine a 'ghost' could operate," as its functioning is dependent on minute electrical potentials and the motions of neurotransmitter molecules and calcium ions.[41] Several prominent physicists, including Niels Bohr, Arthur Eddington, Henry Margenau, Euan Squires and Henry Stapp, have explicitly proposed that the mind interacts with the brain by influencing the outcome of quantum processes within the brain.[42] Roger Penrose has suggested that the "oneness" or "global" quality of consciousness may be related to nonlocal quantum connections between neural processes in the brain, and he further notes that neurons, unlike the elements of deterministic computers, are subject to quantum mechanical influences.[43] In the most recent version of Penrose's theory, he proposes that water molecules in the microtubules composing the cytoskeletons of widely separated neurons could exist in a quantum-mechanically coherent state. As the configuration of such cytoskeletons could influence the synaptic connections between neurons, this would provide a nonlocal means of unifying neural activity over wide regions of the brain. In fact, Penrose equates the operation of free will with quantum mechanical decisions influencing the configuration of such microtubules. It should, however, be noted that Penrose objects to the dualistic view that an immaterial mind external to the physical brain system can influence the outcomes of quantum mechanical processes in the brain. Rather than being caused by conscious awareness, Penrose proposes that quantum mechanical state vector reduction occurs when the energy difference between the alternative physical outcomes becomes sufficiently great.[44] Penrose's theory is based in part on Stuart Hameroff's proposal that the cytoskeletal microtubules within neurons may be centrally involved in the computational activity of the brain. Hameroff, incidentally, concurs with Penrose's view that conscious experience may involve nonlocal quantum connections between microtubules in widely separated neurons. Hameroff thinks that such connections may help to bind diverse neural activity into unified perceptions and experiences and to provide a unified sense of the self. He also sees such connections as providing the indeterminism necessary for the operation of "free will."[45]

In particular, Penrose has contended that water molecules in widely separated microtubules could exist in a quantum-mechanically coherent state and that nonlocally correlated changes in cytoskeleton configurations could alter synaptic connections between neurons. He sees such conformational changes as being intimately associated with the experience of "free will."[46] Recently, Rick Grush and Patricia Churchland have argued that microtubules are not in close enough proximity to the synaptic complex to influence synaptic transmission. They also note that the gout drug colchicine depolymerizes microtubules, disrupting any quantum mechanical coherence that might be present, but is not associated with any loss of consciousness.[47] In reply to Grush and Churchland, Penrose and Hameroff counter that very little colchicine enters the brain and that most brain microtubules are hardened and do not undergo cycles of polymerization and depolymerization. They also note that the drug does in fact cause impairments in learning and memory.[48]

David Hodgson has seconded Penrose's assertion that consciousness is intimately dependent on nonlocal connections between spatially separated brain events. In his view such connections help forge a united perception of an object from its separate features. He conjectures that nature had to provide such nonlocal connections in order for consciousness to exist. He further contends that only indeterministic systems are associated with consciousness, as conscious minds would be of no use to a mechanistic system.[49] Physicist A.J. Leggett has even suggested that new quantum principles may be needed to describe the behavior of complex systems such as brains.[50] Penrose agrees with this position of Leggett and proposes that new laws of physics will be required to explain noncomputational brain activity.[51]

There has even been a recent attempt to subject the theory that nonlocal quantum processes undergird conscious thought to an experimental test. Nunn, Clarke, and Blott found that when a record was made of the electrical activity of one of the brain's hemispheres, performance on psychological tasks involving that hemisphere was enhanced. Presumably, the making of an EEG recording assisted in collapsing quantum mechanical state vectors, resulting in more efficient cognitive performance.[52]

Having laid the basic groundwork, we will now consider a variety of specific theories as to how mind-brain interaction might be accomplished.

Thouless and Wiesner's "Shin" theory. The parapsychologists Robert Thouless and B.P. Wiesner proposed an "internal psi" model of mind-brain interaction.[53] In referring to the mind, they use the Hebrew letter "Shin" in order to avoid the metaphysical baggage involved in the use of the word "soul." They propose that the mind becomes aware of brain states by "clairvoyantly" monitoring neural activity. Volitional activity is accomplished through the "psychokinetic" influence of neural events. They see psi phenomena such as ESP and PK as rare, externalized forms of the mind's normal interactions with the brain. In fact, they propose two types of telepathy: gamma-telepathy, in which a Shin clairvoyantly monitors the activity of a brain other than its own, and kappa-telepathy, in which a Shin psychokinetically influences a brain other than its own.

There is a smattering of parapsychological evidence that has some relevance to Thouless and Wiesner's theory. Charles Honorton and Lawrence Tremmel, for instance, conducted a study in which they found that success in a PK task was positively correlated with the subject's ability to control his own brain waves. They interpret their finding as providing support for Thouless and Wiesner's internal psi model of mind-brain interaction.[54] On the other hand, if it is assumed that the Shin has a limited attentional capacity, one might anticipate that subjects would be successful in a PK task precisely when their attention was not devoted to controlling their brain waves, and that therefore a negative correlation would be expected. Just such a prediction was in fact made by D. Scott Rogo,[55] citing Roll's finding of a high incidence of epilepsy among presumed poltergeist agents[56] in support of the view that successful PK is accompanied by the disruption of normal brain processes. It should also be noted that a study by Mario Varvoglis and Donald McCarthy failed to replicate Honorton and Tremmel's results. Indeed, Varvoglis and McCarthy found that significant PK effects occurred only during trials in which the subjects performed poorly on the brain-wave control task.[57]

Other evidence that the mind might be capable of influencing brain activity is provided by Baumann, Stewart and Roll's finding that humans could psychokinetically influence the firing rate of the pacemaker neuron of the marine snail *Aplysia*[58] and Rein's finding that activity of monoamine oxidase, an enzyme regulating neurotransmitter concentrations, could be influenced through psychokinesis.[59] Neither of these studies was methodologically perfect, however.

Evidence from telepathy experiments that percipients perceive specific neurological events in the brains of the senders would give support to Thouless and Wiesner's theory of telepathy. Rene Warcollier did report evidence of what he called "dissociation" in his experiments on the telepathic reception of drawings.[60] This dissociation consisted of the percipient's drawing fragments of the target (such as isolated corners of a line drawing), suggesting that the percipient may have been responding to individual eye fixations on the part of the sender or even to "feature analyzers" in the sender's brain.

John Beloff has expressed doubt that someone could read the idiosyncratic "neurological code" employed by someone else's brain.[61] Beloff's objection would suggest that telepathic interaction must take place at a higher, mental level, rather than involving the direct reading of another person's brain state. Incidentally, Beloff himself has proposed a model of mind-brain interaction very similar to that of Thouless and Wiesner, except that Beloff further conjectures that the mind or Shin might survive the death of the brain with some of its memories intact.[62]

Some further support for Thouless and Wiesner's theory, in particular for the concept of kappa-telepathy, is provided by the rather voluminous literature reporting successful attempts to influence the behavior of living organisms using psi (which is sometimes interpreted as evidence of psychokinesis and sometimes as evidence of telepathy).

Several purely neurological findings, such as the results of split-brain research, pose severe difficulties for Thouless and Wiesner's theory of mind-brain interaction. A discussion of those findings will be postponed until after the theories of Eccles and Penfield have been discussed.

Eccles' theory of mind-brain interaction. Over a period of many years, Sir John Eccles has developed a rather elaborate model of mind-brain interaction. Eccles is a renowned neurophysiologist, who in 1963 shared the Nobel prize in medicine and physiology with his coworkers A.L. Hodgkin and A.F. Huxley; the prize was awarded for their studies of the axons of the giant squid, establishing the membrane theory of nerve conduction and demonstrating the exchange of sodium and potassium ions across the membrane (which has come to be recognized as the basic mechanism of nerve impulses).

Eccles has progressively elaborated his dualistic model in a series of publications spanning several decades.[63] He feels that it is necessary to postulate the existence of a mind separate from the brain in order to explain the integration of mental activity. In particular, Eccles feels that the integrated perception of objects and visually presented scenes cannot be explained in terms of known neurological processes, in view of the fact that the nervous impulses related to visual experiences appear to be fragmented and sent to divergent areas of the brain. For instance, Christof Koch and Francis Crick count from 30 to 40 different cortical areas specializing in different aspects of visual processing.[64] Similarly, Wilson, Scalaidhe and Goldman-Rakic have recently described the separation of the neurons dealing with the spatial location and identity (color and shape) of an object in the prefrontal cortex of the brain of a monkey.[65] Thus, the perception of any single object involves the firing of neurons in widely dispersed areas of the brain. It is difficult to understand how this neural activity can possibly result in a unified perception of an object, a conundrum Koch and Crick call the "binding problem."[66] According to Stacia Friedman-Hill, Lynn Robertson and Anne Triesman, a breakdown of this perceptual unity was apparent in a recently described patient who miscombined colors and shapes from different objects and who was unable to judge the locations of objects. This patient had bilateral lesions in the parietal-occipital areas of the brain, suggesting that these brain regions may be centrally involved in generating unified perceptions of experience.[67] Crick himself ascribes the unity of perception to rhythmic oscillations in the brain resulting in the synchronous firing of large populations of neurons.[68] Two other neurophysiologists, Gerald Edelman and Giulio Jononi, contend that the binding of perceptions and the unity of experience is achieved thorough reentrant signaling pathways in the brain.[69]

Eccles, on the other hand, sees the integration of neural activity as the *raison d'être* of an immaterial mind, and he suggests that the evolution of consciousness may have paralleled the emergence of the visual processing mechanism. He endorses William James' conjecture that brains may have had to acquire conscious minds because they had grown too complex to control themselves.

Eccles proposes that another role of consciousness is to assist in the solving of nonroutine problems (as opposed to the execution of overlearned and routine skills such as tying one's shoes); Eccles' view of the role of consciousness is similar to that of many cognitive psychologists in this regard.

Eccles contends that the mind interacts with only certain groups (or "modules") of neurons, which he calls open neurons. He uses the term "liaison brain" to refer to the regions of the brain containing these open modules, and he asserts that this liaison brain lies in the cerebral cortex rather than in the deeper areas of the middle brain. In support of this site, he cites experimental results indicating that cats who have had their cerebral cortex removed behave as if they were mindless automata.[70]

Until fairly recently, Eccles maintained that the liaison brain was generally located in the left cerebral hemisphere, due to the fact that language ability is usually located in that hemisphere and the fact that split-brain patients typically report (from the left hemisphere where their language skills are located) that they have experienced no discontinuity in their sense of self following their commisurotomy (an operation that involves severing the corpus callosum, a bundle of nerve fibers that connect the two hemispheres of the brain and provide the primary means for communication between them).

Some evidence in favor of Eccles' theory that the left brain is the site of consciousness is provided by Efron's finding that flashes presented to the left and right visual fields were judged to be simultaneous only when the flash on the left occurred several thousandths of a second before the one on the right, suggesting that the judgment of simultaneity was made on the basis of the simultaneous arrival of the neural messages at a site in the left hemisphere. (Strangely enough, information about the right visual field is sent directly to the left hemisphere and information about the left visual field to the right.)[71]

Another piece of evidence in favor of locating the liaison brain in the left hemisphere is the fact that migraine attacks and brain injuries are more often associated with a loss of consciousness when they occur in the left hemisphere than when they occur in the right.[72]

In his earlier writings, Eccles tended to see linguistic ability as a prerequisite for self-consciousness, and he consequently denied self-consciousness to most nonhuman animals and even to the right hemisphere of the human brain following commisurotomy. He has since recanted this position in his later writings, citing Gallup's research demonstrating self-recognition by chimpanzees when confronted by their images in a mirror (they cleaned spots off their faces)[73] and research by Sperry, Zaidel and Zaidel demonstrating the ability of the right hemisphere in split-brain patients to recognize pictures of themselves (the patients, not the hemispheres!).[74] Eccles does continue to restrict consciousness to birds and mammals, the brains of lower animals such as bees and frogs being too small to support consciousness in his view. (Interestingly Eccles has assigned consciousness to precisely those animals that sleep. Could there be some significance to this?)

In Eccles' earlier writings, he expressed doubt that influences at the quantum level would be sufficient to explain the influence of the mind on the brain, as he felt that quantum events would be too random to account for the "precisely causal events" in the mind-brain interaction. In his later writings, he changed his mind, observing in particular that the exocytosis of synaptic vesicles (a primary mechanism in the transmission of nervous impulses from one neuron to another) involves energies within the range of the Heisenberg Uncertainty Principle of quantum mechanics (and thus would allow the mind to influence the brain by determining the outcomes of quantum decisions). Although Eccles has cagily avoided referring to parapsychology in most of his writings, as least on one occasion he has used the word "psychokinesis" to describe the mind's action on the brain.[75]

The prominent philosopher of science Karl Popper, with whom Eccles wrote his most encyclopedic volume, *The Mind and Its Brain*, also endorsed a quantum-mechanically based theory of mind-brain interaction; however, at one point in the book Popper suggests that the mind may have its own source of (presumably physical) energy. Under this view, the mind would be a sort of quasiphysical object that might be capable of greater influence on the brain than that allowed by the Heisenberg Uncertainty Principle of quantum mechanics. Popper even went so far as to assert that the law of energy is only "statistically valid."[76] Thus, the conscious mind proposed by Popper is a powerful one indeed.

Penfield's theory of mind-brain interaction. A second prominent neurophysiologist to propose a dualistic model of mind-brain interaction was Wilder Penfield. The most complete exposition of his model is given in his posthumously published book *The Mystery of the Mind*.[77] Unlike Eccles, Penfield does not locate the site of mind-brain interaction in the cerebral cortex, but rather in the evolutionarily older region of the higher brain stem (diencephalon). (Such a site would make evolutionary sense if immaterial minds are to be attributed to more "primitive" organisms that lack a neocortex.) As one piece of evidence in favor of this localization, Penfield cites the fact that injury to this site typically removes consciousness and results in a coma. Interestingly, Penfield does not believe that the site of mind-brain interaction lies in the reticular activating system of the brain stem, despite the fact that injury to this area also produces unconsciousness. This is due in large part to the fact that Penfield assigns a central role to the diencephalon in the integration of brain activity. In particular, he cites the vast number of two-way connections between the diencephalon and the cerebral cortex as evidence for such a central role. In a recent essay, the late Robert Thomson agreed with Penfield that the higher brain stem may be centrally involved in integrating behavior. Thomson reviews research indicating that injuries to this region produce deficits in a wide range of learning and problem-solving tasks, and he also reviews evidence indicating that memories may be stored in this region.[78] The physicist Nick Herbert locates the site of consciousness a bit further down, in the reticular formation of the brain stem. Herbert sees this area as having a central role in the integration of sensory information and the regulation of behavior. He sees the cortex as a peripheral device that is not associated with consciousness.[79]

John Eccles explicitly takes issues with Penfield's proposed site of mind-brain interaction, noting that injury to the brain stem merely removes the background excitation of the cerebral cortex that is necessary for consciousness to occur.[80] As evidence against Eccles' localization of the site of mind-brain interaction in the cerebral cortex, Penfield cites the fact that large portions of the cerebral cortex can be removed without loss of consciousness.

As further evidence in support of his proposed site of interaction, Penfield cites the fact that epileptic seizures in the higher brain stem cause a person to behave as a mindless automaton, carrying out preprogrammed motor acts without a later memory of them. Penfield sees conscious attention as a prerequisite to the storing of memories. In this, he agrees with Eccles, who cites an experiment by Held and Hein demonstrating that active exploration of the environment is associated with learning in kittens, whereas passive exploration (being carried around a room) is not.[81] However, in cases of multiple personality, secondary personalities seem to be capable of storing memories when the primary personality is distracted or unconscious (although such memories are not generally accessible to the primary personality).

Similar phenomena are described by Ernest Hilgard in proposing his "hidden observer" or "neodissociation" theory of hypnosis.[82] Specifically, Hilgard was often able to converse with subconscious portions of a hypnotized subject's mind. Frequently, such subconscious personalities or "hidden observers" were able to report memories of events of which the hypnotized person had no conscious knowledge. For instance, Hilgard hypnotized a subject and told her she would experience no pain when one of her hands was immersed in ice water. While the subject reported no pain, Hilgard was able to converse with a subconscious personality that did remember experiencing the painful stimulus. It should also be noted that Carl Jung contended that memories of unattended events are stored in the personal unconscious. (Of course, attention by some unconscious personality or "protopersonality" may indeed prove necessary for memory formation.)

As evidence that the conscious mind lies outside of the brain mechanism, Penfield cites the fact that movements or other activity produced by electrical stimulation of the brain are experienced as ego-alien and involuntary. For example, if Penfield applied an electrical stimulus to a patient's brain causing her to raise her arm, she typically experienced the raising of the arm to occur independently of her will. Electrical stimulation of the brain never resulted in a sense of volition. (Of course, a materialist could object that this merely proves that the brain can discriminate arm movements initiated by it in an unmolested state from those caused by the application of an outside electrical impulse). Penfield specifically declined to use the word "immaterial" to describe the mind, perhaps because he viewed such a term as implying a total separation between mind and matter.

Other views on mind-brain interaction. Many other theorists have forwarded their own hypotheses regarding the nature and location of mind-brain interaction. The number of sites proposed is legion, and at times it seems that no area of the brain will prove to be exempt from being designated as the site of the soul. V.S. Ramachandran sees the frontal lobes as the likeliest candidate for the site of mind-brain interaction, partially due to the fact that persons with frontal lobe lesions frequently report a loss of coherence and continuity in their sense of self.[83] Joseph LeDoux equates consciousness with language use and thus associates it with the linguistic apparatus of the brain. He therefore denies consciousness to the right hemisphere in split-brain patients unless it possesses a linguistic capacity, in which case LeDoux would ascribe a dual consciousness to the patient.[84] John O'Keefe sees consciousness as primarily concerned with the construction of mental representations of the world. He would therefore locate consciousness in the septohippocampal region of the brain, insofar as the neurophysiological evidence suggests that "cognitive maps" may be located in this area (certain neurons in a rat's hippocampus may fire when the rat is in a particular location). O'Keefe also notes that conscious attention is necessary for the storage of episodes and narratives in memory, and certainly the hippocampus must be intact in order that such memories be stored. Patients with damage to the hippocampal region are generally unable to form new episodic memories. Such a patient may for instance believe he is still a soldier in Korea, having formed no memories of events occurring in the years since he received his head injury.

O'Keefe further notes that consciousness is especially involved in dealing with novel events. The conscious mind, he asserts, selects actions to be carried out, but is not involved in the details of these action programs (such as the specific steps involved in tying a shoe). These action programs instead tend to be automatic and occur outside of awareness. He does note that consciousness is involved in the initial learning of such programs. Conscious attention is also activated when the result of a motor action is unexpected and deviates from the fixed action plan. He observes that certain neurons in the hippocampal area tend to fire when an organism is confronted with a novel situation, which he takes as further support for the hippocampus as the site of consciousness.[85]

Like O'Keefe, David Oakley also asserts that the conscious mind is intimately involved with the creation of cognitive representations of the world. He notes that the hippocampus and neocortex must be intact for such representations to emerge, as opposed to simple conditioned responses.[86] In an article written with Lesley Eames, Oakley suggests that two or more domains of consciousness may coexist within a single person.[87] Oakley and Eames note, for instance, that associative learning occurred separately for each of the alternate personalities in the "Jonah" case of multiple personality, whereas Pavlovian conditioning, which they view as noncortical and automatic, was shared among the different personalities.[88] They also attribute a dual consciousness to split brain patients, although they see "self-awareness" as usually being restricted to the left hemisphere.

Benjamin Libet sees the supplementary motor area (SMA) of the cerebral cortex as being one of the primary areas that is involved in voluntary acts.[89] In this he agrees with Eccles, who at one point went so far as to say that "there is strong support for hypothesis that the SMA is the sole recipient area of the brain for mental intentions that lead to voluntary movements."[90] Libet notes that patients with damaged supplementary motor areas are often incapable of spontaneous voluntary movement; while they may listlessly respond to suggestions from others, they seldom initiate movements on their own. In this sense their will is curtailed. Libet's view is underscored by Goldberg's observation that lesions of the supplementary motor area lead to repetitive hand movements, such as buttoning and unbuttoning a shirt, that are experienced as ego-alien and occurring independently of the subject's will.[91] Libet further observes that blood flows into the supplementary motor area when movements are merely being contemplated.

Libet's own experiments indicate that subjects' decisions to initiate motor movements (flexing the hand) typically do not occur until 350 milliseconds after a readiness potential had begun to build in the brain, indicating that the brain itself had already been preparing for movement at the time of the subject's experienced decision. Libet notes, however, that mind-brain interaction must be a two-way street, and he found that subjects could change their mind about flexing their hands during the final 150 milliseconds preceding the actual physical act. He also found that this veto decision seemed to coincide in time with a drop in the voltage of the readiness potential. Libet infers from this that the conscious mind has the ability to block an already initiated movement or to let it occur. In this view, the brain is seen as generating courses of action, while the mind or a "free will" decides on the options. He sees the inhibition of action as one of the central roles of a conscious mind.

Libet has just recently proposed the existence of a "conscious mind field" (CMF), which he sees as being produced by brain activity. The CMF is not capable of being detected by physical measuring devices, nor is it reducible to neural processes; nevertheless, Libet proposes that the CMF is capable of exerting a causal influence on brain processes and that it provides the means whereby diverse neural activity can give rise to unified perceptions and experiences. Libet contends that his view of the CMF is compatible with a variety of different philosophical positions on the mind-body problem.[92]

The staunch defender of materialism Paul Churchland has recently proposed the intralaminar nucleus of the thalamus as the brain site responsible for producing a "unified consciousness." (Yes, now even Churchland uses the word "consciousness" in a nonpejorative sense). Churchland bases his claim on the fact that this brain site possesses two-way projections to diverse areas of the brain as well as the fact that the various senses are represented polymodally in this area. He notes that his colleague Antonio Damasio has nominated the right parietal lobe of the brain for a similar role, as this area must be intact in order for a continuous sense of the self to exist.[93]

Finally, Jean Burns has suggested that the synchronous firing of large assemblies of neurons underlies conscious experience and forms the interface for mind-brain interaction. Burns' theory is based on brain wave records and recordings from single neurons showing that such synchronous firings are involved in acts of conscious perception.[94] Burns' view in this regard is very similar to that of Koch and Crick, discussed above.

As the reader can see, a myriad of different ideas have been proposed as to how mind-brain interaction might be accomplished and where such interaction might take place in the brain.

Implications of split-brain research. The results of research with split-brain patients pose difficulties for a naive interpretation of any theory in which a single immaterial mind is assumed to interact in a global manner with large areas of the brain. At this point, we had better backtrack and describe these results for the reader unfamiliar with such research. In some cases of intractable epilepsy, a drastic surgical procedure involving the severing of the neural connections between the two cerebral hemispheres may be performed in order to stop electrical seizures of the brain from spreading from one hemisphere to the other. This procedure involves cutting the fibers of the corpus callosum, a bundle of nerves directly connecting the two hemispheres of the brain. This operation is called a commisurotomy or callosectomy. "Split-brain preparation" is a somewhat dehumanizing term that is sometimes used to refer to human beings that have undergone such a procedure. We will call them simply "split-brain patients." The act of severing the corpus callosum seems to result in a person with two separate spheres of consciousness, one residing in the right hemisphere and one residing in the left hemisphere. If one were to have such a patient visually fixate a point on a movie screen and then flash a picture of a hammer in his left visual field and a picture of a pencil in his right visual field, the two hemispheres would have different ideas about what was shown on the screen. If you asked the patient what he saw, he would usually say "a pencil," because the brain structures involved in the production of language generally reside in the left cerebral hemisphere and information from the right visual field is funneled into the left hemisphere. On the other hand, if you asked the patient to pick up the object that he saw on the screen with his left hand (which strangely enough is controlled by his right hemisphere), he would pick up the hammer. (His right hand may very well be reaching out and trying to guide the left hand to the pencil, however.) Similarly, if you blindfolded him and gave him a chesspiece to hold in his left hand, he would not be able to describe verbally what object he had been holding (as the sensory information from the left hand is fed to the right hemisphere and linguistic ability is located in the left). He would, however, be able to identify the chesspiece by using his left hand to pick it out from an array of objects on a table.

These findings pose grave difficulties for a naive theory of mind-brain interaction of the Thouless and Wiesner type. Under Thouless and Wiesner's theory, the patient's Shin should be able to overcome the above communication gap. Through clairvoyant perception of the sensory information in the right hemisphere and psychokinetic influence of the language centers in the left hemisphere, a split-brain patient should be able to give a verbal description of an object held in the left hand. That such an effect is not observed would seem to constitute devastating evidence against Thouless and Wiesner's theory. Two means of saving the theory are apparent, however. First, it could be assumed that the mind's influence on the brain is restricted to the facilitation and inhibition of the transmission of information across synapses. (Synapses are microscopic gaps between neurons. When a neuron fires, it releases chemicals called neurotransmitters that travel across the synapse. When the neurotransmitters reach the postsynaptic neuron, they may bind to receptors on its surface. These neurotransmitters may either increase or decrease the probability that the postsynaptic neuron will fire.) Under this version of Thouless and Wiesner's theory, the mind would be unable to integrate the activity of the brain in the absence of the corpus callosum and might be assumed to experience two alternating or parallel, but independent, streams of consciousness.

In this context it should be noted that Eccles cited split-brain research as evidence against Penfield's proposal that mind-brain interaction occurs in the higher brain stem or diencephalon, insofar as the connections between the diencephalon and the cerebral hemispheres are not severed in a commisuro-tomy.[95] Robert Thomson notes that the results of split-brain research pose a real problem for his own proposal that the higher brain stem is the area in which central integration of the brain's activities takes place.[96]

The fact that the deep connections in the brain stem and limbic system are not cut in a callosectomy indicates that some neural connections between the hemispheres do survive this procedure. Donald MacKay has noted that emotional reactions (which are governed by the limbic system in the deep middle regions of the brain) on the whole tend to be unified between the two hemispheres in split-brain patients (although it should be conceded that the generation of emotional reactions is not usually thought to be a conscious activity).[97] The fact that some neural communication still exists between the hemispheres makes it a little more plausible that some residual extraphysical communication might exist as well.

A second means of saving Thouless and Wiesner's theory would be to assume that the mind (Shin) is restricted to interacting with only a localized region of the brain (as in the theories of Eccles and Penfield) or that more than one Shin might be associated with the human brain, each having its own localized area of interaction or assuming a different role in the overall func-tioning of the personality. In earlier versions of Eccles' theory, for instance, it was assumed that the mind's interaction with the brain is localized in the left hemisphere and that the right hemisphere is not conscious after a callosec-tomy. There is, however, good reason to attribute some degree of conscious-ness to the right hemisphere of a split-brain patient, as that hemisphere is fre-quently capable of comprehending and responding to oral instructions and occasionally capable of communicating through the use of such devices as a Scrabble set. Furthermore, several instances of apparent motivational conflict between the hemispheres have been reported, including one instance in which the hemispheres expressed different job preferences.[98] Eccles does concede that many prominent split-brain researchers, including Pucetti, Sperry, Bogen and Gazzaniga, have postulated the existence of two self-conscious minds in split-brain patients. (Gazzaniga has since retreated from this view. He has recently argued against a doubling of consciousness in split-brain patients, as right hemispheres lacking a verbal capacity are generally unable to engage in problem-solving or to make inferences about causation. Thus, he see a cen-tral capacity of humans as lacking in the right hemispheres of such patients.[99])

In his recently proposed theory of conscious mind fields, Benjamin Libet speculates that there may be two CMFs in split-brain patients. Interestingly, he proposes that his CMF theory might be tested experimentally by surgically isolating a portion of the cerebral cortex that is scheduled to be removed in a brain operation to see if activity in such isolated tissue could give rise to a verbal report.[100] One would have thought this question has already been answered in the negative by the results of split-brain research.

One way out of the split-brain difficulty might be to propose that the right hemisphere is associated with its own Shin. It might be assumed that this Shin is acquired by the right hemisphere at the time of the callosectomy, or it might be assumed that the right hemisphere was always associated with a second Shin, which was in a subordinate relationship with the Shin of the left hemisphere prior to the callosectomy. Evidence in favor of the latter interpretation is provided by Hilgard's observation that highly hypnotizable persons tend to shift their eyes to the left more often than do less hypnotizable persons.[101] As left-shifting of the eyes is often thought to be associated with activation of the right hemisphere of the brain, this could be interpreted as evidence for a second Shin in the right hemisphere corresponding to Hilgard's "hidden observer" (the subconscious personality presumed by Hilgard to be responsible for hypnotic effects, such as acting out posthypnotic suggestions for which the subject has amnesia).

Polly Henninger has noted that 37 percent of multiple personality patients have alternate personalities of differing handedness, which is far above the usual frequency of left-handedness and ambidexterity in the general population. She suggests that dual personalities may be associated with different hemispheres of the brain, or at least involve differing dominance and activation patterns of the hemispheres. She further suggests that the right hemisphere may be the site of the "cognitive unconscious" and the repository of repressed thoughts and feelings.[102] Certainly, her hypothesis would be consonant with the observation that patients with damage to their right hemispheres often feel a sense of elation, whereas those with damage to their left hemispheres feel depressed.

It might even be reasonable to assume that there are more than two Shins associated with a normal human brain. William McDougall, for instance, proposed that the normal human mind is composed of a hierarchy of "coconscious personalities," each carrying out its own separate function. McDougall used Morton Prince's term "coconscious" rather than the usual terms "subconscious" or "unconscious" to describe such secondary personalities in order to emphasize their self-awareness. If genuine, cases of ostensible multiple personality may represent instances in which one or more of these subordinate personalities has rebelled against the primary, executive personality. Indeed, many lines of psychological research, including studies of subliminal perception, posthypnotic suggestion, preattentive filters, multiple personalities and automatic motor performance, indicate that the human mind is capable of conducting a great deal of sophisticated mental activity, including sentence construction and comprehension, as well as complex motor acts, outside of the awareness of the primary personality.

Take for instance the phenomenon of "blindsight," in which cortically blind subjects can respond appropriately to visually presented stimuli even though they have no conscious experience of seeing those stimuli. Cortical blindness refers to blindness that is a result of damage to the visual cortex in the occipital lobes at the rear of the brain. (Yes, reader, the area of the brain that deals with vision is at the rear of the brain. It must begin to seem that whoever wired up the brain must have had a surplus supply of cable!) Even though the eyes of such patients may be perfectly normal, they may be blind in part of their visual field because of such damage to their visual cortex. When you present a small dot of light to such patients in the blind areas of their visual fields, they will say that they saw nothing. If you ask them to just take a guess by pointing at where the dot of light might have been, they frequently point right at the exact location that the dot occupied. If you present erotic pictures to such a patient in the blind area of his or her visual field, the patient may blush or giggle or say things like, "That's quite a machine you've got there, Doc!" They will still, however, deny having consciously seen anything. Interpretations of words may be biased by information presented in the blind area of the visual field, and eye movements may be altered by such stimuli.[103] Most researchers think that blindsight is caused by a secondary visual center that lies in a subcortical area of the brain known as the superior colliculus (although Francis Crick has recently noted that other areas must be involved as well, as blindsight sometimes involves responsiveness to color differences and there are no color sensitive neurons in the superior colliculus[104]). It would be tempting to think that a secondary center of consciousness or Shin was associated with this secondary visual center. On the other hand, some writers, such as Owen Flanagan and Anthony Marcel, have argued against any attribution of full consciousness to this secondary center, insofar as information acquired through blindsight is not generally acted upon. For instance, the patient may be thirsty, but will not respond to the sight of a water fountain presented to the blind area of her visual field.[105] It would be possible to argue that this secondary center cannot move the patient's body of its own accord as it is a subordinate personality or "module." Actually, most researchers feel that the purpose of this secondary center is to guide eye movements, and perhaps this is not a role that one would want to associate with consciousness.

Psychologists have also discovered in recent years the existence of two different memory systems: a procedural memory system that is involved in the learning of skills, and a declarative memory system that is involved in the learning of facts. Damage to the hippocampal area of the brain can result in a loss of the ability to form new episodic memories. Thus, a patient that has incurred such damage may be unable to remember any of the events that have occurred during the past few years. He will not know the name of the doctor who has treated him during that time and will greet him each day as if meeting a new person. Strangely enough, such a patient can be taught to solve a puzzle or play a game to the point that he develops any expert level of competence. Nevertheless, each day as he is presented with the game or puzzle, he will deny ever having seen it before. He can acquire new skills but cannot form memories of events. In one case a psychologist shook hands with such a patient and in doing so pricked the patient's hand with a pin. Later, although she failed to recognize the psychologist, she refused to shake his hand. She said she thought it might be unpleasant but could not say why. Thus, it seemed that a part of her that was outside of her conscious awareness retained a memory for this event.[106] Again, it would be possible to assert that only an unconscious stimulus-response association was stored and that such a reaction need not involve a coconscious subpersonality of the patient.

The doctrine that the human personality is composed of several subminds goes back in the Western tradition at least as far as Aristotle, who postulated the existence of "vegetative soul," a "sensitive soul," and a "rational soul" in each person. It has been revived in the "Massachusetts modularism" of Jerry Fodor, who views the mind as split into modular "computational" components.[107] Perhaps this position's most enthusiastic recent advocate has been Michael Gazzaniga, who rejects the doctrine of a unitary consciousness in favor of the view that the mind is composed of a collection of independently-functioning modules that he describes as "coconscious."[108] As evidence for such a modular view, Gazzaniga cites post-hypnotic suggestion, apparent unconscious (or coconscious) problem-solving activity (in which the solution to a complex problem suddenly emerges full-blown into consciousness), blindsight, the existence of separate procedural and declarative memory systems, and split-brain research. Gazzaniga tends to equate the "conscious self" with the module that is in control of the language centers of the brain, and he refers to this module as the "executive module." He cites many instances in which the executive module uses confabulation to explain behavior that was in fact generated by other modules. For instance, a person who acts under a post-hypnotic suggestion to close a window may claim that he was cold. Gazzaniga also cites several instances of confabulation by the verbal left hemisphere to explain actions performed in response to directions given to the right hemisphere in split-brain patients. It might not be far-fetched to postulate that all or most modules might likewise maintain the illusion that they were the sole center of consciousness or sole controller of the body. A "unitarian" approach to the soul might still be maintained in the sense that, while a person may be composed of several centers of consciousness, each of these is itself unitary and indivisible.

One final, rather bizarre fact that is of relevance to the present discussion is that the cerebral hemispheres of dolphins sleep at separate times.[109] This suggests that these aquatic animals may also have at least two centers of consciousness, whose activity is even more decoupled than is the case with humans.

In conclusion, it is possible to construct dualistic models that are capable of dealing with the results of split-brain research, although they all involve a retreat from the naive dualism proposed by Descartes. Split-brain research is very heartening to those materialists who insist that we are nothing but our physical bodies. However, as we shall see in Chapter 12, there are a few severe conceptual problems involved with the notion that one's physical body is identical to one's self. I will postpone my final arguments against physicalism until then.

In the meantime, if an immaterial mind does in fact exist, could it survive the death of the physical body and live on in some sort of afterlife? The next four chapters take up this question, beginning with the parapsychological evidence in favor of survival.

9. Smoke and Mirrors; Dreams and Ghosts

If the conscious mind or self (or as we have just seen, selves) is to be regarded as something other than a mere side-effect of physical brain activity, it becomes legitimate to wonder what happens to the mind or self when a person's physical body dies and the physical brain no longer exists. There is a subfield of parapsychology called survival research that is concerned with examining the various forms of evidence suggesting that some portion of one's personality might survive the death of one's physical body. This type of research was a central concern of the early founders of the Society for Psychical Research, many of whom sought to disprove the materialistic philosophy based on Newtonian physics that had gained ascendancy in intellectual circles toward the latter part of the nineteenth century. As we have seen, the prevailing scientific picture of the world in that period seemed to exclude the soul as depicted in the Western religious tradition as well as any other type of immaterial mind. Due to the existence of seemingly reasonable skeptical objections to much of the evidence obtained in favor of such survival of death, most contemporary professional parapsychologists are not involved in such traditional survival research, although there does exist a small minority of professional workers who continue to make the survival problem their primary research focus.

The evidence for the existence of discarnate entities that are apparently the surviving traces of formerly living persons falls into several general categories. The first type of evidence comes from the practice of mediumship, in which a purportedly discarnate personality is apparently able to communicate with the living through the intermediate agency of a paranormally gifted living person called a medium. In the case of physical mediumship, the communication from the deceased takes the form of physical phenomena, such as the materialization of objects, apparently tangible apparitions or materializations of the deceased, or the apparently paranormal movement of objects or shaking of tables. A second form of mediumship is mental mediumship, in which a discarnate personality is seemingly able to converse with living human beings. This communication may take several forms. In some instances, the personality of the deceased communicator apparently takes over the body of the medium and speaks directly with the medium's clients by use of the medium's own vocal apparatus. In other cases the communication may be achieved through automatic writing (in which the medium's hand writes messages of which the medium is ostensibly unaware) or through specially designed communication devices such as Ouija boards. Sometimes no direct communication is involved, but rather the medium may merely relay messages from the deceased. Occasionally (albeit rarely in modern times) communication is achieved through "direct voice," meaning that the deceased person's voice appears to emanate from a location spatially distant from any living person or at least independently of the vocal apparatus of any living person.

Appearances in dreams constitute a second way in which the dead may manifest themselves to the living. Of course the mere fact that a deceased person appears in one's dream does not constitute compelling evidence of that person's continuing existence, any more than a dream of a Martian invasion constitutes conclusive evidence of Martians. There are, however, cases on record in which deceased persons have communicated information in such dreams and in which that information was apparently unknown to any living person at the time of the dream but was subsequently verified as accurate.

Closely related to dreams are "hallucinatory" experiences such as apparitions, hauntings, deathbed visions, out-of-body experiences and near-death experiences. Apparitional experiences, which have been previously discussed in Chapter 2, include cases in which dead or dying persons appear to someone in a vision. Such a vision is sometimes interpreted as an appearance of the ghost or spirit of the appearing person. Occasionally, information is communicated to the percipient in such cases that would not normally be available to her (in cases of crisis apparitions, for instance, the information is frequently simply that the appearing person has died). In cases of hauntings, apparitions and sounds are experienced repeatedly at a specific location, such as a house. Often such apparitions and sounds are perceived by more than one person, rendering the hypothesis that these apparitions are due to mental illness or a temporary psychopathological state on the part of the percipient less plausible. In some instances, the apparition is said to resemble a deceased person who was formerly associated with the location.

Some research indicates that dying persons frequently report visions of deceased relatives and friends who have apparently come to conduct them into the postmortem state. Such apparitions are termed "deathbed visions." Closely related to deathbed visions are near-death experiences, in which persons who lose consciousness during an accident or illness (and whose vital signs occasionally deteriorate to the point that they are pronounced clinically dead) report upon resuscitation experiences suggestive of a visit to a postmortem state. These experiences often include apparent out-of-body travel, journeys through a tunnel, encounters with deceased friends and relatives, and a conference with a guru-like "being-of-light." Panoramic reviews of one's past life are also commonly reported. Near-death experiences are suggestive of the survival of the human personality from both a first-person and a third-person perspective, insofar as they include visions of the deceased (much as in the case of deathbed visions) as well as involving a personal experience of the postmortem state, including the apparent separation from the physical body inherent in out-of-body experiences and the perception of fantastic otherworldly landscapes characterized by brilliant unearthly colors and apparently inhabited by the spirits of the deceased.

Additional evidence for survival is provided by cases suggestive of reincarnation. This evidence takes several forms. In some cases, the evidence for reincarnation is obtained from a psychic or medium who is able to "read" a client's past lives through paranormal means and is able to describe details of those lives to the client. In other cases, a person may report details of past lives after undergoing hypnotic age-regression to a time before his or her birth. The evidence in both of these categories is weak, because in the vast majority of cases the information provided by the psychic or obtained through hypnotic regression is either unverifiable due to the paucity of historical records or else is not verified simply because no attempt is made to verify it.

A stronger form of evidence is provided by cases in which children spontaneously recall a previous life (usually in the recent past) and attempts at verification reveal that the child has accurately related many details of the life of the claimed former personality that the child apparently had no normal means of knowing. Closely related to reincarnation cases are cases in which a person is apparently possessed by the spirit of a deceased person or "obsessed" (that is, influenced) by such a spirit. Because of the complexity of the evidence for reincarnation and the philosophical arguments for and against the doctrine of rebirth, we will devote a separate chapter to reincarnation.

Finally, there are a few strange and highly dubious categories of evidence for survival, including instances in which spirits have been apparently captured on film and in which the voices of the departed have been allegedly recorded on audiotape. There have also been attempts to photograph and estimate the weight of the soul as it departs at death. Finally and most strangely, there have been cases in which the dead have apparently dialed up the living on the telephone. This idiosyncratic category of evidence will also be covered in a separate chapter. Let us begin, however, by examining the more orthodox evidence for survival arising from mediumship.

Mediumship

The belief that it is possible to contact the dead through the intermediary of a living person forms a part of many formal and informal religious traditions. Ian Wilson notes that rites for contacting the dead existed in ancient Greece and observes that the Biblical tradition has Saul contacting the deceased Samuel through the mediumship of the witch of Endor.[1] Spiritualistic seances go back at least as far as 1000 A.D. in the Norse tradition, and mediumship was intimately associated with the phenomenon of animal magnetism or mesmerism (now called hypnosis) in the first half of the nineteenth century.[2] Mediumship has of course always been associated with shamanistic religions, possibly even into prehistoric times. Nevertheless, in most people's minds mediumship is most clearly associated with the Spiritualist tradition that began to flourish in America and England during the second half of the nineteenth century and which is still alive in a much muted form today.

The birth of the modern Spiritualist movement is usually traced to the Fox sisters, who claimed to be able to communicate with the spirits of the deceased through mysteriously produced rapping sounds. The Fox sisters' phenomena began with a series of raps that occurred over a time period beginning in 1847 in their childhood home in Hydesville, New York. The raps appeared to answer questions, and, when an alphabetic code was worked out, claimed to originate from the spirit of a peddler who was murdered in the house. A body was found buried in the cellar of the house, and the Fox sisters became celebrities. They subsequently developed a stage act in which they produced rapping messages from the deceased in front of large audiences. The sisters later became alcoholics, and one of them confessed that she had fraudulently produced the rapping noises by popping the joint of her big toe (although she later retracted this confession). By this time, mediumship had become a growth industry, and Spiritualism developed as a religious movement centered around mediumistic phenomena. The heyday of Spiritualism is past, although the recent mania for "channelled" advice from the beyond in the United States clearly has its roots in the mediumistic tradition.

Physical mediumship. When anomalous physical phenomena seemingly connected with the spirits of the dead are manifested in the presence of a human intermediary or medium, one is said to be dealing with "physical mediumship." Such phenomena are typically obtained in the context of a seance, in which a group of people seeking contact with the dead, called "sitters," gather in the presence of a medium. Frequently, but not invariably, the medium enters a trance state as part of the ritual of contacting the dead. The phenomena obtained may include materializations or "apports" of objects (that is, the seeming appearance of objects out of thin air), the production of ectoplasm (an alleged wispy or ghostlike substance which may form the material for the physical reconstruction of the body of an appearing dead person), the production of strange sounds, including raps, the anomalous movement of objects, including the tilting of the seance table, and the anomalous appearance of written messages, such as chalkwriting on a board of slate. This list is not meant to be exhaustive, and many other types of phenomena may be manifested.

Many physical mediums have been detected in fraud. The medium Mina Crandon, for instance, was allegedly able to obtain many physical phenomena, among them the production of wax fingerprints of her dead brother Walter. Fraud was revealed when E.E. Dudley was able to ascertain that a sample of such fingerprints were actually those of the medium's very much alive dentist.[3]

In another celebrated case, a medium named Florence Cook was allegedly able to produce a materialization of the highly attractive body of a spirit named Katie King while Cook herself was tied to a chair inside a "cabinet." On one occasion (and in violation of the etiquette of seance behavior), a sitter named George Sitwell grabbed the materialized form of Katie King. The cabinet was then thrown open, and the medium's chair was found to be empty, the ropes slipped, and the medium's clothes to be lying in disarray about the cabinet. Cook had herself portrayed Katie King.[4]

While the above two exposures of fraudulent mediums took place in the nineteenth century, fraudulent mediums continue to be exposed in recent times. In an incident similar to the Katie King fiasco, several spirits at the Facet of Divinity Church (endorsed by death and dying expert Elizabeth Kübler-Ross) were found to be very much alive and kicking after they had taken the extraordinary step of having sexual relations with worshipers in need of "comfort" from the beyond.[5] Melvin Harris describes the exposure of the medium Paul McElhaney. One of the features of McElhaney's act was the apparent materialization of carnations; however, inspection of his possessions revealed that he had hidden the carnations to be materialized inside a tape recorder prior to the seance.[6]

Because of the high incidence of fraud, most parapsychologists today cast a wary eye at physical mediumship. There continues to be debate about the genuineness of some phenomena, but in general the observational conditions for physical mediumship have been quite poor. Ectoplasm, for instance, was conveniently asserted to be sensitive to light, necessitating a darkened room in order to avoid injury to the medium (or, more likely, the medium's reputation). The apparent levitation of D.D. Home outside of an upper story window is one incident that is still argued to be genuine by some psychical researchers; however, this alleged levitation took place under very poor observational conditions, including total darkness.[7]

Mental mediumship. In mental mediumship, messages are purportedly received from the dead through the agency of a medium. In some cases these messages may be relayed through the process of automatic writing, whereby the medium's hand writes messages of which the medium claims no knowledge and for which she claims no responsibility. Occasionally, a device such as a Ouija board or planchette is used to facilitate the production of such unconsciously received messages. Alternatively, the medium may be "possessed" by the spirits of the dead, who then communicate directly through the vocal apparatus of the medium. Such possession is often produced by the medium's entering a trance state. More rarely, the voice of the postmortem personality is heard to emanate from a point in space unoccupied by any person. This form of mediumship is called "direct voice." One of the lesser known projects of Thomas Edison was the development of an ideal megaphone or "trumpet" through which the dead could speak in this manner.

In trance mediumship, the medium is often possessed by a "control" spirit, who acts as "master of ceremonies" during the seance. Such control spirits may introduce new discarnate personalities, who then may displace the control in terms of possession of the medium's body. In many instances, the control is a childlike figure, such as Feda, the little Indian girl who served as the control for the medium Gladys Osborne Leonard. In some cases, such as that of Mrs. Leonora Piper's control Phinuit, who claimed to be a French physician serving royalty, the control spirit appears to be a totally fictional character. Most psychical researchers have come to view such control spirits as little more than secondary personalities of the mediums. One notable exception was George Pellew, a deceased friend of the psychical researcher Richard Hodgson, who displaced Phinuit as Mrs. Piper's control during the 1890s. Purportedly, "Pellew" was able to recognize 30 friends and relatives of George Pellew, adding some credence to the former's claim to be the surviving shade of the latter. However, the archskeptic C.E.M. Hansel has pointed out that Pellew's family denied the authenticity of the communications from "Pellew."[8]

Sometimes information is provided by such ostensible deceased communicators which is accurate and which the medium would have no normal means of knowing. For a period of time the spirit of the deceased psychical researcher Richard Hodgson served as Mrs. Piper's control. As reported by William James,[9] on one occasion "Hodgson" reminded a sitter of an anecdote Hodgson had related via letter to the sitter before his death. The anecdote involved a starving couple who were praying for food. The couple's prayers were overheard by a passing atheist. The atheist dropped some bread down a chimney and heard the couple thanking God. When the atheist revealed himself as the couple's benefactor, the wife replied, "Well the Lord sent it even if the devil brought it."

During the sitting with Mrs. Piper, the Hodgson control asked, "Do you remember a story I told you and how you laughed about the man and woman praying?"

The sitter replied, "Oh and the devil was in it. Of course I do."

"Hodgson" then added, "Yes the devil, they told him it was the Lord who sent it even if the devil brought it ... About the food that was given them ... I want you to know who is speaking."

The provision of such seemingly accurate messages by alleged deceased communicators has rendered some parapsychologists more favorably disposed toward mental mediumship than they are toward physical mediumship. There are, however, ways in which a medium can gain information about deceased persons without directly communicating with the spirits of the dead. Some fraudulent mediums may conduct research on the lives of persons likely to consult them. The medium Arthur Ford, for instance, was discovered to have kept elaborate files on prospective sitters. Ray Hyman has described techniques whereby a medium or psychic can give a "cold reading" for a client he does not know by deliberately using vague statements, which are then progressively refined based on feedback from the client until an apparently accurate body of information has been communicated.[10]

Mediumistic communications may also include information that is derived from obituary notices and other written records. Sometimes such information is apparently used unconsciously by a seemingly honest medium, through a process known as cryptomnesia. In a case of cryptomnesia, a person may read an obituary notice in a newspaper and then later "receive" this information from the apparent surviving spirit of the deceased while playing with a Ouija board. In such cases, the medium or Ouija board operator may have forgotten having ever seen the obituary notice, although this information has presumably been retained at an unconscious level and is being used subconsciously to construct the "communication" from the deceased. Ian Stevenson and John Beloff have described several cases in which all the information provided by a "drop in" communicator (a spirit who emerges uninvited during a seance) had previously been published in an obituary notice or other single written source.[11] In one case, Stevenson was able to demonstrate that the obituary notice was on the same page of the newspaper as the crossword puzzle which the Ouija board operator worked daily.

Ravaldini, Biondi and Stevenson have recently described an apparent instance of communication by a Sicilian priest who had been murdered in Canton, Ohio, through a medium in Italy.[12] This communicator was one of the drop-in variety insofar as he was unknown to any of the sitters present at the mediumistic session. The communication contained several accurate details, including a description of the murder, but these details corresponded to information that had previously been published in obituary notices. The authors argue against an explanation in terms of cryptomnesia on the basis of the fact that "Ohio" was misspelled as "Chio" in one of the obituaries in an Italian newspaper. They argue that "Canton, Chio" would be more likely to be interpreted as "Canton, China" than as "Canton, Ohio" by an Italian medium, although this would hardly seem to constitute an airtight case against cryptomnesia. Also, as M.H. Coleman notes, as twenty years had elapsed since the priest's death, there was ample opportunity for alternate means of information transmission to occur.[13]

Another possibility, if one is willing to grant the existence of psi, is that mediums may be able to use their ESP faculties to gather information about the deceased from the minds of the sitters present or from other persons or written records scattered throughout the world. In its extreme form, this has become known as the "super-ESP" hypothesis. (Of course, if one extends this hypothesis to include direct retrocognitive telepathy with the previously existing mind of the deceased, the super-ESP hypothesis begins to merge with the survival hypothesis. If one grants that the minds of deceased persons can be accessed telepathically after their death, then those minds in at least some sense can be said to exist after death, inasmuch as their contents continue to be accessible through retrocognitive telepathy.) In one amusing application of the super-ESP theory, the psychologist G. Stanley Hall constructed a biography for a fictional niece named Bessie Beals. He then received communications from Bessie Beals through Mrs. Piper that related some of the information in the fictional biography. It is surprising that Mrs. Piper could acquire this information through ESP but remain unaware of its fraudulent nature. (In this context, it should be noted that Raymond Bayless and E.E. McAdams have argued that a real person named Bessie Beals may have existed.[14])

Finally, recent evidence indicates that some seance records have been fraudulently altered. Melvin Harris has charged that the British researcher S.G. Soal, who is known to have altered some of the data in his experimental work in parapsychology, altered transcripts of at least one seance in which he participated.[15] The case in question involved a communication from the supposedly deceased spirit of Gordon Davis, a friend of Soal's, who turned out to be very much alive at the time of the communication. The medium involved was Blanche Cooper. Through Cooper, "Davis" provided an accurate description of a house that the real Gordon Davis would move into well after the seance was held. Harris notes that Davis' future house was located near Soal's own residence. He charges that Soal may have looked in the window of the house to gain information as to its appearance, which he then inserted into the transcript of the prior seance. One of these details was that of a statue of a black bird sitting on Davis's piano. However, a duplicate copy of the seance in question, in Soal's own handwriting, had been sent to the Reverend A.T. Fryer, a fact that Soal had apparently forgotten when he altered his copy of the document. The duplicate transcript held by Fryer showed no references either to Davis or to a statue of a black bird. While obviously not proof of survival, the Gordon Davis case had stood for years as a prominent example of psi phenomena occurring in the context of mediumship.

Due to the counterexplanations of fraud, "cold reading" techniques, and the possible ability of mediums to gather information about deceased persons through psi, few parapsychologists today would be willing to conclude that the survival of death of the human personality has been demonstrated through the study of mediumship.

Dreams

Occasionally, deceased persons appear in dreams. Usually, of course, such figures can be dismissed as images constructed by the dreamer's subconscious mind. On rare occasions, however, such deceased persons may communicate information to the dreamer that neither the dreamer nor any other living person had any apparent normal means of knowing. In one famous and oft-cited case, known as the Chaffin will case,[16] a father communicated the existence of an alternative will to one of his sons in a dream. Under the original will, one of the dreamer's brothers had inherited the father's farm and the rest of the family had inherited nothing. Based on information given to him in his dream, the son was able to locate a second will in his father's handwriting, in which the property was distributed more equally. This will was admitted to probate. A cynic could dismiss this case as fraud combined with forgery, especially as the dreamer had much to gain by perpetrating such a fraud. In fact, Ian Wilson has noted that most of the witnesses in the Chaffin will case were family members who stood to profit from the new will.[17] Less cynically, one might assume that the dreamer learned of the will's existence and location through clairvoyance or that he had picked up cues as to the will's existence from his father's behavior before death.

George Zorab has compiled a collection of cases of the "Chaffin will type."[18] In one such case, a bookkeeper in Holland had been accused of embezzling approximately 1,800 guilders and died before his name could be cleared. After the bookkeeper's death, his son had a dream in which a white figure appeared to him and said, "Look in the ledger at the dates." Upon checking, it was found that his father had included the date at the top of a column in one of his additions. It is quite possible that the son may have unconsciously noted the identity between the disputed amount and the date and that this fact entered his conscious awareness in the form of the dream in question. There are many examples on record of such problem-solving activity in dreams, a notable one being Elias Howe's invention of the sewing machine, which was based in part on a dream Howe had in which a group of cannibals were about to eat him. In this dream some of the cannibals thrust spears at Howe. These spears had holes in them near their tips, which suggested to Howe that he should put the hole near the point of the needle in his sewing machine rather than at the base of the needle. Another example of such problem-solving activity in dreams is provided by August Kekule's discovery of the ringlike structure of the benzene molecule, which was presented to him in the form of a dream in which benzene molecules were transformed into a group of dancing snakes that suddenly took their tails into their own mouths.

Because of the existence of such counterexplanations as those discussed above, the existing evidence from dreams cannot be taken as definitive evidence of the survival of the human personality of death.

Apparitions

Another category of spontaneous psi experiences that are often taken as evidence for the survival of human personality of death consists of apparitional experiences. The sighting of apparitions or "ghosts" is not as uncommon as one might think. In John Palmer's mail survey of the greater Charlottesville, Virginia, area, 17 percent of the respondents reported having seen an apparition.[19] A Gallup poll indicated that about 9 percent of the population of Britain believe that they have seen a ghost.[20]

Erlendur Haraldsson conducted a detailed survey relating to apparitional experience in Iceland.[21] Of the 902 respondents in Haraldsson's survey, 31 percent affirmed having experienced the presence of a deceased person. Detailed interviews with 100 of the respondents who reported such experiences indicated that 16 percent of the experiences involved the mere feeling of the deceased person's presence, 70 percent involved a visual hallucination, 24 percent included an auditory experience, 7 percent a tactile experience, and 5 percent an olfactory sensation. One-third of the cases occurred when the percipient was falling asleep, which indicated to Haraldsson that hypnagogic imagery was frequently involved in the experience. In 23 percent of the cases the appearing person had died violently, which Haraldsson notes is a disproportionately high number. In 43 percent of the cases, more than one person was present at the time of the apparition, and in one-third of these cases it was claimed that the apparition was collectively perceived.

A recent survey modeled after the early S.P.R.'s "Census of Hallucinations"[22] has been reported by D.J. West.[23] As in the original census, volunteers interviewed their acquaintances regarding apparitional experiences. Of 1,129 distributed questionnaires, 840 were returned, with 14.6 percent of the respondents reporting an experience with hallucination of a human figure. Discounting dubious cases, West concludes that 11.3 percent of the respondents reported "genuine" hallucinations, which he notes compares favorably to the figure of 10 percent obtained by the early S.P.R. Only 9 of the 840 respondents reported detailed, apparently psi-related hallucinations, a figure that is also comparable to the proportion obtained in the earlier survey.

It is very common for people to experience the presence of a deceased spouse. A study in Wales indicated that 43 percent of widows and widowers had seen an apparition of their dead spouses, and a second survey indicated that nearly 60 percent of the widows in the greater Los Angeles area had experienced the presence of their deceased spouse.[24] Of course, the fact that a bereaved widow has a vision of her deceased husband does not imply that she has accurately perceived the presence of her husband's now disembodied spirit. The vision could simply be a grief-induced hallucination.

Occasionally, however, such postmortem apparitions transmit information to the percipient which the percipient had no apparent normal means of knowing. In the case of crisis apparitions, the information transmitted is usually simply that the appearing person has died or been injured. As we have previously remarked, such apparitions could be simply ESP-induced hallucinations, and therefore they cannot be taken as providing definitive evidence of the spirit of the appearing person has survived death.

On the other hand, not all cases involving information transmission fit into the crisis apparition category. For instance, Stanislav Grof describes two cases in which the participants in LSD sessions apparently received accurate information from the dead.[25] The first case involved an LSD session in America, in which the participant "saw" a deceased person who gave him the name and address of his parents in Moravia. When the parents were contacted at the address in Moravia, they stated that they had a son who had died three weeks prior to the LSD session.

In Grof's second case, the wife of Grof's colleague Walter Pahnke, who had died in a scuba diving accident, experienced an LSD-induced vision of her deceased husband. The apparition requested her to return a book located in the attic of her house. She claimed to have had no prior knowledge of the book or its location, but she was able to find it and return it.

Of course, neither of these cases constitute definitive evidence of survival. In fact, both could be due to cryptomnesia, or hidden memory. Possibly the first percipient may have read an obituary notice for the dead Moravian youth, but had forgotten that he had read it. Similarly, Mrs. Pahnke may have had a subconscious memory of the borrowed book. Counterexplanations in terms of ESP are also possible.

One apparitional experience that is frequently cited as providing evidence of survival is that of the "Red Scratch" case.[26] The percipient in this case was a traveling salesman, who was staying in a hotel room. At one point he looked up from recording his orders and saw an apparition of his sister, who had died nine years previously, sitting beside him at the table. As he addressed her and moved toward her, she disappeared. Later, telling his parents about the apparition, he mentioned a red scratch that he had seen on the side of the girl's face. At that point his mother nearly fainted, then arose trembling and stated her belief in the survival of her daughter's spirit, as she had in fact made such a scratch on her daughter's face at her funeral while attending to the body. She covered up the scratch with makeup and had told no one about it. It is, however, easily imaginable that the makeup job was not perfect and that the son may have noticed the scratch at the time of the funeral. Alternatively, he may have subconsciously overheard his mother talking in her sleep about the incident soon after the funeral (or, possibly, derived the information telepathically from her). Once again, this case does not provide conclusive evidence of survival.

Hauntings

Haunting cases involve repeated anomalous events, usually associated with a particular location or object. Very often, apparitions or "ghosts" are sighted. Sometimes several witnesses will claim to have seen apparitions at the location over a period of time. Some of the apparitions may be collectively perceived. Occasionally anomalous sounds are heard, including raps, footsteps and voices. Sensations of cold and strange odors are sometimes reported. Occasionally, anomalous movements of objects are associated with hauntings, although cases in which this feature is prominent are usually classified as poltergeist cases. As mentioned in Chapter 3, Gauld and Cornell found hauntings and poltergeist cases to constitute two fairly distinctive "clusters" of phenomena in their statistical analysis of such cases. Hauntings have been recorded throughout the ages. The Roman writer Pliny the Younger, for instance, reported a haunting case in the first century A.D.

Certain types of haunting phenomena may be due to the effects of suggestion and to the misattribution of normal sounds to paranormal causes. A frightened person alone in a house with a reputation for being haunted may misinterpret a normal settling noise as a paranormal rap or a ghostly footstep. The resulting shivers of fear may be responsible for sensations of cold.

The repeated sighting of apparitions by multiple witnesses is of course less easy to explain as the misinterpretation of normal stimuli or as due to psychopathology on the part of the percipient. There is thus a greater temptation in such cases to attribute the recurring vision to the surviving spirit of a deceased person.

Let us examine a fairly typical haunting case that was investigated by Teresa Cameron and William Roll.[27] This case involved repeated sightings of an apparition of a male figure, who was usually described as about six feet tall, weighing 190 pounds, and typically wearing a brown suit, in a radio station in Virginia over a time period from October of 1980 through April of 1981. The figure was usually seen in a standing position, and the sightings occurred in a hallway near the women's restroom or in the doors leading off the hallway. Five employees witnessed the apparition. Three of the employees had heard stories about ghosts in the station, but had treated these stories in a joking manner. Evidently, a former employee had reported many sightings of apparitions, both inside and outside the building. This employee reportedly had severe psychological problems and left her employment under strained circumstances. She did not respond to Cameron and Roll's inquiries or grant an interview.

The first sighting during the time period in question was by William Morrison, an engineer and carpenter. After an initial fleeting glance, Morrison saw a male figure wearing a brown suit from a distance of about twenty feet. He said the figure appeared to take a few steps while he was looking at it, although he did not recall seeing any legs or feet.

Carolyn McDougall, a 30-year-old continuity director at the station, heard papers "riffling" as she came out of the ladies' room. She then saw a male figure wearing a brown jacket standing in a doorway. She stated that she saw only "down to the start of his pants." She did not recall seeing any face, legs or feet on the figure. Although her experience occurred a day or two after Morrison's sighting, she did not hear of Morrison's experience until after her own vision. Both of these sightings occurred in October of 1980.

In April of 1981, Gloria Johnson, a receptionist at the station, was coming out of the ladies' room when she saw a transparent male figure wearing a dark suit moving (but neither walking nor "gliding") down the hallway. She had heard nothing about prior sightings at the station before she had her experience, and she had begun her employment in December of 1980.

A 30-year-old engineer named Henry Eaton saw a strange male seated at a fellow employee's desk. He turned to reach for his own chair in order to sit down, and by the time he redirected his attention to the unknown figure it had vanished. This sighting occurred on the same day as the vision of Gloria Johnson, but he did not mention it until Miss Johnson burst into the room to describe her own sighting. He had previously heard stories about ghosts in the building.

Jack Sneider, a 21-year-old announcer on the evening shift, twice saw a strange male figure when no one else was presumably in the building, these sightings taking place in November and December of 1980.

Cameron and Roll had the witnesses take Wilson and Barber's Inventory of Childhood Memories and Imaginings (ICMI). Based on these scores and interview data, Cameron and Roll conclude that three of the witnesses may have been psychologically predisposed to having apparitional experiences. Carolyn McDougall obtained a very high score on the ICMI, indicative of a fantasy-prone personality. She is also a self-described psychic who has had other apparitional experiences and has reported seeing UFOs. Gloria Johnson had previously seen an apparition of her grandfather and had experienced a recurrent apparition in her childhood. Henry Eaton obtained a high score on the ICMI and has been diagnosed as manic-depressive. Thus, these three witnesses may have had various forms of psychopathology, or at least fantasy-prone personalities, that may have rendered them prone to having apparitional experiences.

Cameron and Roll note that Eaton and Morrison both had visual problems and that Morrison and Sneider saw the visions at night and in poorly lit areas. Morrison also reported feeling quite fatigued on the night of his sighting. Having previously heard stories of ghosts in the station, these witnesses might have been primed to interpret ambiguous stimuli experienced under poor observational conditions as ghostly phenomena. (While Sneider had reportedly not heard such stories prior to his experiences, these stories may have colored his retrospective interpretation of ambiguous events.)

One piece of evidence supporting the paranormality hypothesis, Cameron and Roll conclude, is the tight clustering in time of Morrison's and McDougall's experiences as well as of Johnson's and Eaton's experiences. As to agency, McDougall and Morrison thought that the apparitions resembled Charles Michaux, a former employee of the station who had died in 1978. Michaux had been fired under stressful conditions before the Christmas of 1977, causing a fight to break out among the remaining employees during the annual Christmas party. Michaux died of a heart attack shortly thereafter. Obviously, however, the evidence from this case, like the evidence from most hauntings, does not constitute a clear cut case for any type of paranormal process, much less the survival of a discarnate spirit.

Even animals can sometimes appear as ghosts. My next door neighbor had the experience of repeatedly seeing a cocker spaniel lying on a particular step in her stairway or under a desk built into the wall. When she mentioned this to the former owner of the house, he told her that at the time he lived in the house he had a pet cocker spaniel that used to like to sleep in precisely those locations.

There have been a few attempts to study hauntings scientifically. One method, used by Michaeleen Maher and her coworkers,[28] involves dividing up a house into many different zones. A number of psychics, or "sensitives," then state which zones they feel are associated with ghostly phenomena and attempt to describe any apparitions that might have been seen. A set of control subjects or skeptics then do the same. While the results have been mixed, in some cases the psychics' descriptions of the ghostly phenomena corresponded more closely to the witnesses' accounts than did the skeptics' descriptions. This, however, proves nothing, as certain locations in the house may naturally suggest ghostly presences, thus accounting for the fact that both the psychics and the actual witnesses assumed that ghosts would be present at these locations. Similarly, certain houses may suggest certain types of ghosts. Thus, correspondences between witnesses' and outsiders' descriptions of the location and nature of ghosts cannot be taken as proving anything about the paranormality of the phenomena. Similarly, if the psychics were to provide descriptions that corresponded more closely to witnesses' accounts than the control subjects or skeptics did, this would again prove nothing. Psychics and people who see ghosts may merely tend to think alike. Also, self-proclaimed sensitives who frequently investigate hauntings may have gathered a great deal of knowledge relating to where people will report seeing ghosts.

There have been a few attempts to detect physical anomalies at haunting locations, but these have generally failed to yield any sort of consistent effect. One intriguing finding was recently reported by Dean Radin and William Roll.[29] They found the activity of a Geiger counter to be significantly increased when placed in an area of space said by a psychic to be currently occupied by a ghost, suggesting that this ghost may have been in some sense "radioactive." They speculate that the psychic may have been able to sense local regions of increased radioactivity, such as pockets of radon gas, or that she may have influenced the results by moving a radioactive piece of jewelry closer to the Geiger counter during the tests. Two of the investigators also witnessed a luminous blob in a room that the psychic claimed was occupied by a ghost, further suggesting the existence of some sort of physical anomaly in the environment.

Hornell Hart has noted that the fragmentary, repetitive nature of most apparitions' behavior does not seem consistent with the hypothesis that apparitions are indications of the fully surviving consciousness of the deceased.[30] Several other theories of haunting apparitions, including those of Myers, Tyrrell and Roll, have already been discussed in Chapters 3 and 7, and so we will not repeat those discussions here.

The evidence for survival provided by haunting cases, while suggestive, is not particularly strong. In many cases, a skeptic could maintain that the apparitional figures are simply hallucinations, perhaps caused by fatigue or some sort of pathological state in the witnesses. Also, normal settling noises and other sounds may be misinterpreted as ghostly phenomena in a house with a reputation for being haunted. It should also be realized that haunting cases, in the narrow sense of the repeated sighting of apparitions in a single location by several witnesses, are much, much more rarely reported than are spontaneous psi experiences. Thus, hauntings might more easily be attributed to psychopathology or fraud than spontaneous psi cases could be.

Near-Death Experiences

Some people who have come close to dying, such as in cases of cardiac arrest or being knocked unconscious during an automobile accident, but who have been revived after a period of apparent unconsciousness report an encounter with an apparently nonphysical or postmortem realm. Such experiences are called "near-death experiences" (NDEs) and were brought to the attention of the general public through the publication in 1975 of Raymond Moody's best-selling book *Life-after-Life*.[31] Moody lists the following characteristics of the NDE: loud ringing or buzzing noises, sensations of traveling down a tunnel-like passage, out-of-body experiences, viewing the physical body from an external vantage point, emotional upheavals, sensations that one possesses a quasi-physical astral body, encounters with the apparitions of deceased relatives and friends, an encounter with a "being of light" who serves as a spiritual guide (frequently interpreted as a Christ-like being in the West), undergoing an evaluation of one's life, experiencing a panoramic review of one's life, approaching a barrier or border, being told that one must go back (that is, return to one's physical body and rejoin the realm of the living), not wishing to return, experiencing deep feelings of joy and peace, experiencing a reunion with the physical body, and having experiences of an ineffable nature (e.g., sensations of color or mystical union that cannot be described in words.)

Of the fifteen elements listed above, Moody notes that usually eight or more are reported by a typical NDEr, although no single case in his collection included more than 12 of the above 15 characteristics. He further notes that no single item of the 15 is included in every single NDE account.

Several surveys relating to NDEs have been carried out. The data indicate that somewhere around one half of the people who have been revived from a state of clinical death claim to have experienced an NDE, a remarkably high figure.[32]

Kenneth Ring conducted a study of 102 persons who had experienced NDEs in order to determine how frequently various elements of the NDE, as described by Moody, occurred.[33] He found that 60 percent of his respondents reported feelings of peace and contentment during their NDEs, 33 percent reported an out-of-body experience, 23 percent reported sensations of entering a region of darkness or traveling down a tunnel, 20 percent sensed a (typically benevolent) presence who aided them in reviewing and evaluating their lives, 17 percent reported seeing a light to which they were drawn, and 10 percent experienced seeing a world of "preternatural beauty."

The skeptical view of NDEs is of course that they simply represent hallucinations, dreams and fantasies constructed by the mind under conditions of physical trauma or stress. Various neurophysiological causes for such hallucinations have been proposed, including seizures in the temporal lobes of the brain,[34] lack of oxygen to the brain,[35] the release of endorphins in the brain,[36] and the random firing of cells in the visual cortex of the brain.[37] Ronald Siegel has also noted that tunnel-like imagery is one of the eight common "form constants" of hallucinations induced by LSD.[38] In Chapter 4, we discussed theories attributing the out-of-body component of the NDE to states of depersonalization, a denial of death and a reliving of the birth trauma.

As with the other categories of evidence for survival, the primary evidence that NDEs are not simply fantasies or hallucinations is provided by cases in which patients become anomalously aware of information during an NDE when they apparently had no normal means of acquiring such information. In many cases, this information pertains to events at the scene of an accident or during a surgical procedure that the patient witnesses from a vantage point above the body, while the body itself is apparently unconscious. For instance, a patient undergoing cardiac arrest may describe events occurring during the resuscitation procedure. If the procedure itself is simply described, it is possible that the patient is merely demonstrating knowledge of resuscitation procedures she has gleaned from watching television shows, etc. If specific idiosyncratic events in the vicinity of the patient's body are described, it is quite possible that the patient, despite her apparent unconsciousness, retained enough awareness and sensory ability to perceive the described events, Indeed, there is a wide body of evidence that patients retain some sensory capacity even under conditions of deep surgical anesthesia.[39]

It is less easy to explain cases in which the patient reports awareness of events occurring at locations remote from the body during the NDE, such as the case of the woman who saw a tennis shoe on a window ledge in the hospital during an NDE, which was discussed in Chapter 4. Such cases are exceedingly rare, however. There is some data indicating that NDErs tend to have fantasy-prone personalities,[40] which would give further support to the theory that NDEs simply represent fantasies and hallucinations.

Deathbed Visions

Closely related to the near-death experience is the phenomenon of deathbed visions, in which dying patients apparently see apparitions of deceased relatives and friends, who appear at their bedside for the seeming purpose of conducting the dying person into the afterlife. In fact, out-of-body experiences and deathbed visions could conceivably be regarded as unusual NDEs in which only one component of the NDE occurs. One feature that distinguishes deathbed visions from typical NDEs is that the patient is not generally in a state of unconsciousness or "clinical death" at the time of the experience. Deathbed visions have been studied by William Barrett in the 1920s and the team of Karlis Osis and Erlendur Haraldsson in the 1960s and 1970s.[41] Osis and Haraldsson collected their data from surveys of doctors and nurses in the United States and India regarding their recollections of any visions reported by dying patients. In the United States, hallucinated figures were primarily of deceased persons (70 percent), the rest being split between living persons (17 percent) and religious figures (13 percent). In India, a much higher percentage of religious figures was reported (50 percent), with deceased persons representing only 29 percent of the hallucinations, and living persons 21 percent. In approximately three-fourths of the cases in both countries, the purpose for the apparitional figure's appearance was interpreted to be to escort the dying person into the afterlife. In both countries, the percentage of patients reporting such apparitions declined as the clarity of consciousness, as measured by the drugs administered and the presence of fever, declined. Osis and Haraldsson take this as evidence that such apparitions do not represent mere hallucinations engendered by psychopathological states; on the other hand, it could equally well be argued that persons in an impaired state of consciousness may be less able to communicate coherently about such an apparitional experience.

One type of deathbed vision case that is a little more difficult to attribute to a simple hallucinatory process occurs when a deceased person appears to a dying patient who had no knowledge that the appearing person had died. Karlis Osis quotes the following case from William Barrett's investigations[42]:

On Jan. 12, 1924, a Mrs. B. was dying in a hospital in England. Her sister Vida had died on Dec. 25, 1923, but her illness and death had been carefully kept from Mrs. B because of her own serious illness. As Mrs. B. was sinking, she said: 'It is all so dark, I cannot see.' A moment later her face brightened and she exclaimed: 'Oh it is lovely and bright; you cannot see as I can.' A little later she said: 'I can see father, he wants me, he is so lonely.' then with a rather puzzled expression: "He has Vida with him,' turning to her mother—'Vida is with him!' A few moments later she died.

On the other hand, Michael Grosso has noted that such "Peak in Darien" cases (as they are called) are extremely rare.[43]

We now turn to the evidence for reincarnation, which constitutes perhaps the strongest form of parapsychological evidence for survival.

10. Reincarnation

We may lead more than one life. There is a body of parapsychological evidence that suggests that a process of reincarnation may take place, in which a mind or soul may survive the death of the physical body and be reborn in a new physical body. This evidence is roughly of three kinds. The first category of evidence consists of "readings" by psychics and other spiritual advisers, who are allegedly able to use their psychic abilities to gather information about the past lives or former incarnations of their clients. Perhaps the best known of such psychics was the psychic diagnostician Edgar Cayce, who frequently described the past lives of patients who consulted him for medical advice. Past lives as described by Cayce often involved such exotic locales as the lost continent of Atlantis and other planets. A second line of evidence arises from the technique of hypnotic age regression, in which a hypnotized subject is led backward in time to his or her childhood and then regressed even further backward in time to previous lives. Psychological and medical problems are often ascribed by past-life hypnotherapists to events that occurred in the patient's previous incarnations and that became known through such past-life hypnotic regression techniques. A third form of evidence for reincarnation consists of spontaneous reports by young children of memories relating to previous lives. In such cases, which occur mainly in cultures having a strong religious belief in reincarnation, the child typically claims to be the reincarnation of a person who had died within the past few years. The child may exhibit knowledge of that previous life which is difficult to explain on the basis of the child's experiences in his or her present life. The child may also manifest personality traits and behaviors consistent with those of the claimed former personality. These behaviors are sometimes at variance with the behavioral norms of the culture in which the child is being raised. As we shall see, this type of case provides the strongest evidence for reincarnation of any of the three categories of evidence discussed above.

Philosophical Background

Many cultures around the world subscribe to a belief in reincarnation. A partial list of such cultures would include the ancient Egyptians, Hindus, Buddhists, Jains, large numbers of Druse and Shiite Moslems, and several shamanistic traditions, including those of the native tribes of northwestern North America, the Trobriand Islanders, Australian aborigines, and the Ainu of northern Japan. Many prominent thinkers in the Western tradition have also been reincarnationists, among them Pythagorus, Plato, Walt Whitman, Henry David Thoreau, Ralph Waldo Emerson, Henry Ford and Charles Lindberg. The French philosopher Voltaire is responsible for the memorable quote "It is no more surprising to be born twice than it is to be born once."

Within the Judeo-Christian tradition, a different view has held, namely that we live but one life. Some sects adhere to the doctrine that the bodies of everyone who ever lived will be physically resurrected on the Day of Judgment. Many sects within the Judeo-Christian tradition hold that eternal damnation or salvation is dependent on acts committed within this one physical incarnation, a stern doctrine indeed. It is interesting to note that the early Christian Gnostics, including such figures as Origen in the third century A.D., taught the doctrine of reincarnation. Reincarnationist beliefs within the Christian tradition were finally suppressed, however, by an ecumenical council held in 553 A.D. Despite the banning of reincarnation as heresy, many people within the Western culture continue to believe in reincarnation. A recent Gallup poll of American adults indicated that 21 percent believed in reincarnation, with another 22 percent indicating that they were "not sure" whether reincarnation occurs or not.[1]

It is perhaps not surprising that the belief in reincarnation is so widespread. The reincarnationist cycle of birth, death and rebirth bears many similarities to other naturally occurring cycles, such as the annual changes of the seasons and the daily cycle of light and darkness. Just as our bodies incorporate atoms that were once parts of the bodies of other people, so it might not be too surprising if our bodies also harbored souls which once resided in the bodies of other persons. Another advantage of the reincarnation process is that it renders our present incarnate state less puzzling. Under the official Judeo-Christian view, one lives but one human lifetime, which is but a flicker of an eyelash when compared to the 15 billion years or so that have elapsed since the creation of our current universe in the Big Bang as well as the eons that lie ahead before the eventual recollapse of the universe at the time of the Big Crunch (or, alternatively, until its more quiet end in a "heat death"). Because our lives are such infinitesimal spans when compared to the age of the universe, each conscious person must marvel at the fact that this present moment in time just happens to be one of the moments when he or she exists, as, if a moment were to be chosen at random from the history of the universe, the probability that any person would exist at that time would be essentially zero. The fact that the moment which has somehow mysteriously been selected to be "now" is also a moment at which the reader is conscious must surely seem like a miracle if the single life hypothesis is true. The fact that "now" happens to be a moment when you are conscious would become much less surprising under the hypothesis of reincarnation, as "now" would only have to correspond to any moment in a potentially endless succession of lives rather than a single life. If one were to allow the possibility of incarnation in nonhuman life forms, or even on other planets or in other universes, it becomes more and more probable that a particular person (that is, soul) would be conscious "now."

Several objections have been raised to the idea of reincarnation. One, which was raised by the third century Christian philosopher Tertullian and has recently been reiterated by the philosopher Paul Edwards, is based on population explosion.[2] There are many more human beings alive today than have lived at any time in the past. Thus, it is claimed, there would not be enough souls to animate each new human body, as the number of bodies must surely outrun the number of reincarnating souls. This objection could easily be met by assuming that souls that were once housed in nonhuman beings could reincarnate as humans. (It might not be surprising that kids like dinosaurs so much if you assume they spent one hundred million years incarnated in their bodies.) If the animal population is not large enough, it may be that souls can be drawn from other planets (assuming that interstellar travel would not constitute any great difficulty for a soul existing outside of physical spacetime) or even from other decaying universes. (One of the explanations for the Anthropic Principle, the fact that the laws and conditions of our universe seem to be very delicately balanced to support the existence of life, is that many universes are created and we of necessity exist in a universe capable of supporting life. The Anthropic Principle will be discussed in greater detail in Chapter 13.)

A second objection to reincarnation is that we have no memory of our previous lives. Actually, that may not always be the case. Much of the parapsychological evidence for reincarnation, to be discussed below, consists of instances in which persons have in fact claimed to remember details of their previous lives. Reincarnation could of course occur without any transfer of memory from one incarnation to another. As will be discussed in Chapter 12, a considerable body of evidence exists that memories are either physically stored in the brain or at least intimately dependent on certain brain structures. It would be difficult therefore to imagine that memories could in general survive the dissolution of the physical brain at death. On the other hand, we do not remember the events of many previous days of our lives, although we did in fact live through them. Our system of memories changes over time, with some memories decaying and new ones being formed. Our essential selves, on the other hand, seem to remain unchanged over time. We are not identical with any particular set of memories. Thus, it would be easily conceivable that one's self could be reincarnated in a new body, while retaining no memory of one's previous life. Several writers, including Ken Wilber and the author, have in fact suggested that reincarnation might occur in just such a memoryless manner.[3]

The parapsychologist D.F. Lawden has recently proposed that minds or consciousnesses experience the passage of time only when incarnated in a physical body.[4] After death, Lawden proposes, the mind would exist in a timeless, mystical state of identification with the entire spacetime continuum. This mystical state of union with the cosmos as a whole is unstable according to Lawden, and so the mind's attention once again contracts to a single stream of consciousness and one is reborn into a new physical body. In Lawden's view, the order among successive rebirths may not correspond to their order in physical time due to the timeless nature of the state between incarnations. Thus, one's "next life" may be in the Middle Ages, or one might be born again in the twentieth century and encounter one's present self as a friend. If one were to extend Lawden's theory to encompass the alternate universes inherent in Hugh Everett's "many worlds" interpretation of quantum mechanics, one could even imagine being reborn as one's present self, but eventually experiencing a different life history as one travels up a different branch of the tree of possible futures!

A somewhat similar view has recently been proposed by Carroll Nash. Nash postulates the existence of a postmortem condition in which one's mind exists in a timeless state and is capable of seeing all the events of one's life (one's "worldline") at once. He proposes that this experience may form the basis of the "life reviews" frequently reported by persons undergoing near-death experiences. He further suggests that one might become bored with one's own worldline and thus might be drawn to experience other worldlines as well. In Nash's opinion, this common sharing of pain and pleasures would resolve some of the inequities of our earthly lives and would unify all minds in a single consciousness.[5]

Both Lawden's and Nash's hypotheses are of course purely speculative. Lawden explicitly notes the similarity of some of his views to those of the Hindu-Buddhist tradition. In the Indian Vedic tradition, God or Brahman (the one Self of the universe) becomes bored with his solitary existence and splits himself into all the creatures of the earth. The Hindu tradition has it that one's progression from incarnation to incarnation depends on one's level of moral development. Persons of high spiritual development are rewarded by being reborn into more favorable conditions, while miscreants may be punished for their misdeeds in the circumstances of their next lives through a process known as karma. According to Hindu philosophy, the goal of spiritual development is to realize the identity between one's individual self *(atman)* and the universal Self of the cosmos *(Brahman)*. In Buddhism, the goal of spiritual development is to reduce one's own suffering (and that of others) through the extinction of the cravings and desires that give rise to suffering (to the extent that they are invariably unfulfilled). The final aim is to achieve a state of total extinction of desire known as nirvana. Nirvana is essentially a state of extinction of the self. Despite Buddhists' belief in reincarnation, the Buddhist doctrine of *anatta* is essentially a denial of the existence of a permanent self. Ken Wilber notes that while Buddhism denies a permanent existence to the individual soul or self, it does grant a "relative existence" to the soul.[6] Indeed, the doctrine of *anatta* seems directed primarily against the idea that personality patterns and traits have a permanent existence. Thus, seekers of enlightenment should not cling to their present mental states. Rather, each such seeker should see himself or herself as pure consciousness and awareness, something separate from the personality traits, memories, feelings and sensations that may form the objects of desire or clinging, preventing one from reaching a state of enlightenment. The similarities between Eastern views regarding the extinction of self and union with a World Soul and Lawden's and Nash's views discussed above should be apparent (indeed, Lawden explicitly comments on these similarities).

An interesting element of Hindu and Buddhist doctrine is the concept of the kalpa, the great cycle beginning with the creation of the world through the splitting of Brahman and ending with the annihilation of the world (which is then created anew). One kalpa was thought to last 4.3 billion years, which is extraordinarily close to the 10 to 15 billion years modern physicists believe have elapsed since the creation of the universe in the Big Bang.

The parapsychological evidence is equivocal regarding the existence of the Hindu and Buddhist principle of karma, wherein one is rewarded or punished for the deeds of one's past lives in the circumstances of one's present life. As will be seen, the evidence from psychic readings and hypnotic regression suggests the existence of such a principle, but these cases do not provide the strongest evidence for reincarnation. The more compelling evidence from spontaneous recall of past life memories does not in general suggest the existence of any moral karmic principle governing the assignment of incarnations. It is now time to examine in detail the parapsychological evidence for reincarnation.

Psychic Readings

One form of evidence for reincarnation consists of instances in which a professional psychic describes details of the alleged past lives of a client who has consulted the psychic for spiritual or medical advice. If the psychic has displayed evidence of paranormal ability by accurately describing details of the client's life that the psychic had no apparent normal means of knowing, then the client and other observers may be inclined to accept the psychic's description of the client's past lives as accurate knowledge obtained through the same extrasensory abilities the psychic employed in describing the more mundane (yet at the same time more verifiable) details of the client's present life.

By far the most famous collection of such past life readings was provided by the psychic diagnostician Edgar Cayce, who has been discussed earlier in connection with psychic healing. Cayce, it will be recalled, was allegedly able to enter a trance and diagnose people's illnesses, given only their names and addresses. What is of interest in the present context is that Cayce frequently traced the cause of the illness to events occurring in a previous life of the patient. Often the illness seemed to be a means of paying a karmic debt. After entering his trance, Cayce would describe consulting the "akashic records," in which the details of everyone's past lives are recorded. Cayce was initially surprised at the Hinduistic nature of his readings, which indicated the operation of a karmic principle governing reincarnation that was quite at variance with Cayce's own fundamentalist Christian upbringing. Cayce's past life readings have been popularized in many books[7] and form the basis for a great many people's belief in reincarnation.

The following is a typical Cayce reading. This particular reading was given for a client who was suffering from a bone cancer in her hip. Cayce traces this condition to the client's having laughed at the suffering of the Christian gladiators in a past life during Nero's reign in Rome. In reading the text of Cayce's remarks, the reader should bear in mind that Cayce typically used the phrase "the entity" in referring to the client, or more precisely, the client's soul. The reading is as follows[8]:

During the period in Nero's reign in Rome, in the latter portion of the same, the entity was then in the household of Parthesias—and one in whose company many became followers of, adherents to, those called Christians in the period, and during those persecutions in the arena when there were physical combats. The entity was as a spectator of such combats, and under the influence of those who made light of them; though the entity felt in self that there was more to that held by such individuals, as exhibited in the arena, but the entity— to carry that which was held as necessary with the companionship of those about the same—laughed at the injury received by one of the girls in the arena, and suffered in mental anguish when she later—or became cognizant of—the physical suffering brought to the body of that individual during the rest of the sojourn.

As the reader can gauge from the above passage, Cayce's readings are not primarily remembered for the literary value of their prose. The main shortcoming of Cayce's readings, and of psychics' past-life readings in general, as evidence for reincarnation is that there has usually been little or no attempt to verify that the persons who formed the described past incarnations ever existed. Such attempts as have been made have been largely futile due to the extreme scarcity of records pertaining to the lives of most people who lived even as recently as one century ago. Thus, there is little reason to believe that such readings represent anything more than the psychic's fantasies. In the case of Cayce, this is doubly true insofar as Cayce frequently described past lives on the lost continent of Atlantis, the existence of which would contradict a vast body of geophysical evidence, as well as on such planets as Mercury and Jupiter, which are hardly likely to support life. At least some of what Cayce said about past lives has to be erroneous; possibly all of it is.

Hypnotic Age Regression

A great deal of interest in reincarnation was stirred up in the 1950s with the publication of the "Bridey Murphy" case by Morey Bernstein, a business-man and amateur hypnotist.[9] Bernstein's subject was a Colorado housewife named Virginia Tighe. Bernstein used the technique of hypnotic age regres-sion to take Tighe back to the time of her early childhood. Then he suggested that she could go even further back in time, beyond her birth, where she would find herself in "some other scene, in some other place, [and] in some other time." At this point Tighe began to describe another life as Bridget (Bridey) Murphy, an Irish girl living in Cork and Belfast during the early part of the nineteenth century. While in the Bridey Murphy persona, Tighe used several Irish expressions, such as "lough" to refer to a lake, "linen" to refer to a hand-kerchief and "flat" to refer to a platter. At one point, she even danced an Irish jig. She also correctly named two Belfast grocery stores and accurately stated that a big rope company and a tobacco house were operating in Belfast at the time in question.

The details of her life as Bridey Murphy were not verifiable due to the scarcity of records. Two of her statements were challenged. She had stated that Bridey's husband, Brian McCarthy, had taught law at Queen's University in Belfast. *Life* magazine charged that there was no such institution, but the existence of Queen's University was later proven. "Bridey" also asserted that she had a metal bed. *Life* charged that such beds were not introduced until at least 1850, but the psychical researcher Eric Dingwall was able to locate an advertisement for metal beds in Bridey's home town of Cork in 1830, and the philosopher C.J. Ducasse was able to show that iron beds existed even in the eighteenth century.[10] A more devastating criticism was delivered by the *Chicago American*. That newspaper asserted that a woman named Bridie Murphy Corkell had lived across the street from Virginia Tighe when she was a little girl and suggested that an unconscious memory of this woman formed the underpinnings of Tighe's construction of the Bridey Murphy persona under hypnosis. Curiously, Mrs. Corkell was the mother of the editor of the Sun-day edition of the *Chicago American*. There proved to be some difficulty in ver-ifying that her maiden name was Murphy, so this detail may be questionable.

In any event, the Bridey Murphy case, despite its powerful role in creating a reincarnation "flap," is surprisingly weak in terms of detailed statements made by Tighe that were subsequently verified. This weakness will prove to be a characteristic of the hypnotic regression evidence in general as we shall see.

In recent years, hypnotic regression to past lives has become a growth industry in many areas of the United States. Several versions of "past lives therapy" have flourished, in which it is claimed that patients' medical and psychological problems can be alleviated when the patients discharge pent-up emotions by reexperiencing traumatic events they suffered through in their prior incarnations.[11] Many other people have undergone hypnotic regression to past lives outside of any therapeutic context. The main problem with the body of evidence that has emerged from hypnotic regression is that there has been little or no attempt on the part of the investigators involved in these cases to verify any of the details contained in these descriptions of past lives. Usually, there is not even an attempt to ascertain that the person described as a former incarnation of the subject actually existed! Thus, for the bulk of these cases, there is no compelling reason to regard these descriptions of past lives as anything other than the product of the subjects' imaginations.

In a few rare cases, some details contained in past life descriptions obtained through hypnotic regression have been verified. Linda Tazari, for instance, reports a case in which a woman recounted a life in Spain during the sixteenth century.[12] The woman provided the names of several members of the Inquisition and their victims. She also accurately described buildings used by the Inquisitors and gave the correct dates of publication of several documents. Several obscure English documents and Spanish language sources had to be consulted in order to verify this information, so it is unlikely that the subject would have had easy access to this information.

In most such cases, however, it is difficult to rule out the possibility that the subject could have acquired the information given in a past-life description through normal channels. In fact, in several instances, it has been shown that all the details provided in a past-life description were contained in a single written source, which makes it appear plausible that the subject's knowledge of these details could be explained by the phenomenon of cryptomnesia, or unconscious memory of reading the source in question. Melvin Harris describes two such cases.[13] In the first, a woman described a previous life in Britain during the third century. Every detail in her description was found to be contained in Louis de Wohl's novel *The Living Wood*. In the second case, hypnosis was used to regress the subject back to the times when she first learned of the details given in her past life descriptions. Under hypnosis, she was in fact able to recall reading the books that provided the material from which she constructed her past life accounts. Jonathan Venn cites a case in which a hypnotically regressed subject gave the date of a witchcraft trial as 1556, whereas the real date was 1566. The erroneous date had appeared in several books, one of which may have been the source of the subject's material. Venn also provides a statistical analysis of a single case, in which he found that statements that related to commonly available records were more likely to be true than those that related to less accessible records.[14]

For all these reasons, hypnotic regression cases provide less than compelling evidence for reincarnation.

Spontaneous Recall

The strongest evidence for reincarnation is provided, at least at the present time, by cases in which young children spontaneously report memories of previous lives. The most prolific investigator of such cases has been Ian Stevenson, a professor of psychiatry at the University of Virginia, who has generated a prodigious number of publications on the subject.[15] While Stevenson labored alone in the reincarnation vineyards for years, several other researchers have recently joined the fray.[16]

A typical case of such spontaneous recall, reported by two of Stevenson's associates, Satwant Pasricha and David Barker, involved a boy in India named Rakesh Gaur.[17] In May of 1974, when Rakesh was a little more than four-years-old, he began to speak of a previous life in which he had been a carpenter named Bithal Das, who had been electrocuted at the age of 35. He claimed that he had lived in the village of Tonk, which was about 225 kilometers distant and that he had two sons named Babu and Bhanwar Lal. He stated that he had been a carpenter and was of the carpenter caste (a step down from his current status as a member of the Brahman caste). Rakesh in fact displayed a great deal of interest in carpentry as a child. He said that he had a well near his house and that he had hidden 1500 rupees at a certain location in his house. All of the above statements proved to be accurate descriptions of the circumstances of a carpenter in Tonk named Bithal Das, who had in fact died of electrocution. One erroneous statement that Rakesh did make was that Bithal Das' wife's name was Keshar, whereas in fact it was Radha.

One day in July 1976, Rakesh recognized the driver of a bus from Tonk, calling him by name. He related his past life memories to this bus driver, who then contacted the family of Bithal Das, the ostensible previous incarnation. Rakesh's family then made arrangements to visit Tonk. Upon arriving in the city, Rakesh pointed to an electrical pole, stating that he had died while working on that pole. This statement later proved to be erroneous, as Bithal Das had in fact died when he contacted a live wire while clearing the blockage in a water drain with an iron bar. Rakesh did recognize Bithal Das' son Bhanwar and his widow Radha in an area near the post office, in fact picking Radha out from among a group of women. When Bhanwar asked Rakesh what his name used to be, Rakesh replied "Arun." This would seem to be an error, but Pasricha points out that this was in fact a name Rakesh had been called when he was younger and that Rakesh may have misunderstood the question. Rakesh did provide a fairly accurate and detailed description of the house Bithal Das had occupied during his life in response to further questioning by Bhanwar Lal.

One of the weaknesses of the above case, as pointed out by one of its investigators, David Barker, is that no written records of Rakesh's statements were made prior to his visit to Tonk, and that therefore one has to rely on the memory of various witnesses as to what Rakesh actually said.

Reincarnation cases are not as rare as one might expect. As of 1990, Ian Stevenson's collection included approximately 2500 such cases. In a systematic survey of Northern India, Barker and Pasricha found an incidence rate of nineteen reincarnation cases per thousand inhabitants.[18] In his mail survey of the population of the greater Charlottesville area, John Palmer found that somewhere between eight and nine percent of the respondents claimed to have memories of a past life, although Palmer did not attempt to verify the details of these memories.[19] Stevenson reports that male subjects outnumber female subjects by a ratio of two to one in his case collection,[20] and James Matlock reported a similar ratio of male to female subjects in a separate analysis of published cases.[21]

Stevenson notes that in 35 percent of his reincarnation cases, the child is born with a birthmark or birth defect that seems significantly related to events in the life of the claimed previous personality.[22] Frequently such birthmarks correspond to wounds incurred at the time of a violent death. In one such case, the subject was born with a long birthmark around his neck that seemed to correspond to the wounds received by the person whose life the subject claimed to remember; that person had died of a slit throat.[23]

Stevenson suggests that such birth defects may be psychologically induced. He presents evidence that some birthmarks and birth defects may be caused by maternal fright.[24] In several anecdotal reports, a woman who had seen an injury or a deformity later gave birth to a child with a similar mark or deformity. Stevenson also cites a case in which in which a man murdered another man and then cut off his limbs with a sword. The victim's mother cursed the murderer's wife. Her child was subsequently born without arms and with deformities of the feet. Based on this evidence, Stevenson suggests that birthmarks and birth defects may be psychically induced.

Another feature of reincarnation cases is the announcing dream, in which a pregnant woman may dream of a deceased relative or acquaintance who informs her of his intention to be reborn as her child. Of the twenty-four cases that Stevenson investigated among the Haida Indians of British Columbia, fourteen were characterized by announcing dreams. In one of Stevenson's Haida cases, a tribal elder had said that he wished to be born with only one hand so that he could avoid manual labor. After his death, his grandchild was born without a hand on his right arm.

Many of Stevenson's subjects displayed skills and interests that seem to represent a continuation of skills and interests developed in the claimed previous life. Rakesh Gaur's interest in carpentry in the case discussed above would constitute an example of this phenomenon. Also, many subjects display phobias that seem related to their past life memories. One of Stevenson's cases involved a boy who recalled a past life in which he had been killed when a van crashed into the abutment of a bridge. The child displayed a fear of that particular bridge and of automobiles in general.[25] Stevenson notes that such phobias, which occur in about one third of his cases,[26] seem in most instances to relate to the manner of death of the previous personality. He has even gone so far as to contend that unusual phobias, talents, and interests in general (including transsexualism) may have their roots in past life experiences, whether they are remembered or not.

Cases in which a person manifests a skill which he or she had no opportunity to acquire in the present life provides further evidence for reincarnation. The same holds true for mediumship. If a medium with no apparent mathematical skills is possessed by the spirit of a deceased mathematician and is able to solve randomly chosen partial differential equations, this would constitute a strong case for survival, as it is unlikely that a medium could acquire such a complex skill through telepathy.

In a handful of cases, a medium or person remembering a past life has been able to speak in a language which he or she had no opportunity to learn normally, a phenomenon known as xenoglossy. The principal investigator of the phenomenon of xenoglossy has been Ian Stevenson.[27] In one of Stevenson's cases, a woman who had been hypnotically regressed to a previous life spoke in German, a language that she did not know in her normal waking state.[28] Some skepticism was expressed by German-speaking observers as to whether the subject really understood what she was saying in this case. D. Scott Rogo has also contended that this subject attempted on at least one occasion to fake knowledge of German by consulting a dictionary. In any event, Rogo asserts, her knowledge of German was rudimentary and she was unable to keep track of long speeches and complex phrases.[29]

Another case, investigated by Stevenson and Pasricha,[30] is quite unusual in that it resembles a case of possession more than a typical reincarnation case. (The phenomenon of possession will be described in greater detail below.) In this case, an Indian woman first spoke of memories of a previous life when she was in her thirties. Her body was apparently completely taken over by the personality of the previous incarnation. Her primary personality had amnesia for events occurring when the previous personality was in control of the body, and the previous personality had amnesia for events occurring when the primary personality was in control of the body, although this mutual amnesia was not entirely complete. When the previous personality was manifesting, the subject spoke Bengali, a language Stevenson and Pasricha claim she had no opportunity to learn. Six native speakers verified that she was fluent in Bengali while in the previous personality state. In a recent independent investigation of the case, V.V. Akolkar was able to determine that this subject did in fact have some training in Bengali, which of course diminishes the evidence for xenoglossy considerably.[31]

Sarah Thomason has argued that two of Stevenson's cases fail to provide evidence for true, responsive xenoglossy (in which a subject can hold a two-way conversation in the language) as opposed to recitative xenoglossy (in which the subject may simply recite a phrase or word he may have previously memorized or may simply parrot back words presented to him by the questioner). Thomason claims that Stevenson's subjects show an extremely limited vocabulary, that they provide only short answers, which often consist of mere repetition of phrases, when questions are posed to them, and that they make simple mistakes that are probably due to the fact that the subject understands only one or two words in a sentence.[32]

In general, the evidence for xenoglossy is quite fragmentary. Xenoglossy cases are extremely rare, and only three cases have received thorough investigation, all by Stevenson. At least two of these three cases are extremely weak, and in any event it would seem to be an impossible task to demonstrate conclusively that an adult subject never had enough exposure to a given foreign language to enable him to produce a few simple phrases.

In an extraordinarily large number of spontaneous recall cases, the previous life ended in a violent death. Such deaths occur in well over half of Stevenson's cases.[33] James Matlock observes that this represents a substantial elevation over the rate of violent deaths in the general population, which stands at five percent.[34] Stevenson notes that the details of a violent death are frequently the most prominent memories in such cases. In instances of homicide, the murderer's name is frequently recalled, and occasionally events that the previous personality would have no way of knowing are nevertheless recalled (such as the process whereby an object came to fall on one's head, resulting in death). Stevenson further notes that even cases in which the death of the previous personality was nonviolent frequently involve sudden death or unfinished business (such as when a mother of young children dies or when the subject reports dying as a child in the previous life). Stevenson believes that such unfinished business can result in past life memories being more likely to emerge in the next incarnation and can also lead to a shorter time interval before reincarnation than might otherwise be the case. In fact, he presents evidence that cases involving a violent death involve a shorter time interval before rebirth than cases involving a nonviolent death.[35] The average time interval between lives is, incidentally, only 15 months in Stevenson's cases.

Stevenson offers a few speculations regarding the process of reincarnation based on his research.[36] He suggests that between lives the personality exists as a discarnate trace called a "psychophore." The psychophore retains images relating to the previous life. These images are then capable of being described once the child whose body becomes associated with the psychophore develops the ability to speak. Stevenson further notes that his cases provide little support for the hypothesis that a moral principle of karma guides the reincarnation process.

Criticisms of spontaneous recall cases. Critics have attacked the evidence for reincarnation based on spontaneous recall on several fronts. First and foremost among these criticisms is the possibility that the child may have acquired the information about the previous life through normal means and consciously or unconsciously used this information to construct a past-life fantasy or hoax. Certainly in cases in which the recalled past life is that of a deceased member of the subject's family the possibility for sensory transmission of information is enormous. In other cases, the subject's present family may have had contact with or knowledge of the family of his claimed former incarnation. In fact, in only about one-quarter of such cases are the two families unknown to each other.[37] Also, the high proportion of violent deaths cases in Stevenson's collection raises the suspicion that the death of the prior personality may have received much formal and informal publicity, rendering it even more likely that the subject could have been exposed to information relating to the death through normal channels.

For a parapsychologist willing to admit the existence of psi, ESP constitutes another channel whereby the subject may have acquired information relating to the claimed past life. In such a scenario, the subject would then use the information consciously or unconsciously to impersonate the prior personality or to construct a past life fantasy (which a confused subject might actually believe). Stevenson counters this charge by noting that his subjects evidence no extraordinary extrasensory abilities apart from the reincarnation memories themselves. He also points to the behavioral and emotional components of such cases (such as the manifestation of skills or phobias relating to a past life), which he claims are not so easily explainable on the basis of ESP.[38] In this context, it is interesting to note that in one of the three cases extensively investigated by Antonia Mills, the subject did in fact display extrasensory awareness (including precognitive awareness) of events happening to the family of the previous personality after the case had developed.[39]

Another possibility is that reincarnation cases may be consciously perpetrated hoaxes. Stevenson himself has detected several such cases.[40] Ian Wilson has argued that a disproportionately large number of Stevenson's cases consist of poor children remembering wealthy lives. He contends that these cases may represent a scheme to bilk money from the family of the claimed former incarnation.[41] In fact, however, the evidence does not indicate any great tendency for subjects to recall past lives under better conditions than their present one.[42]

One weakness of most reincarnation cases is that no written record is made of the child's statements regarding his alleged past life prior to the attempted verification of those statements. This allows the possibility that the child and his family may mingle their memories of what the child said with what they have subsequently learned about the previous personality through meeting and interviewing the family, consulting records, and so forth. Stevenson even introduced the term "paramnesia" to describe such memory distortion, and he himself thinks that the easiest way to attack his research would be on the basis of the unreliability of witnesses' memories.[43] In fact, in only about one percent of Stevenson's cases were written records made of the child's statements prior to attempts to verify them. On the other hand, some of these cases, such as the case of Bishen Chand,[44] are fairly impressive in terms of the number of accurate details contained in the child's statements.

One concern regarding Stevenson's reincarnation cases is that such cases may be manufactured as a result of parental or cultural encouragement. Certainly, the vast majority of Stevenson's cases arise in cultures that already subscribe to a belief in reincarnation, such as the Hindu population of India, Druse Moslems, or the Tlinget Indians of Alaska. Also, the features of such cases may vary across cultures. For instance, announcing dreams and rebirth within the same family are far more common among the Native American tribes of the Northwest than among the Hindus of India.[45] Stevenson suggests that nascent cases may be suppressed in cultures hostile to reincarnation.[46] He further notes that such cultures provide no cognitive framework in which such memories could be made intelligible.

Possession and Obsession

Closely related to reincarnation cases are cases in which a person's normal personality is apparently temporarily or (much more rarely) permanently displaced by the personality of a deceased human being (or other entity). This phenomenon is known as possession. A milder form of this syndrome occurs when a person merely seems to be under the influence or partial control of a discarnate personality, without the person's primary personality being displaced. Such cases are commonly termed instances of "obsession."

One of the classic cases of possession has come to be called the "Watseka Wonder." It was first reported in a pamphlet by the self-proclaimed minister E.W. Stevens, who in fact may have been one of the prime instigators of the phenomena.[47] The subject of this case was a thirteen-year-old girl named Lurancy Vennum, who in 1877 fell into a "trance," or an apparently hysterical illness, in which she apparently became possessed by several "spirits," including the personality of a sullen elderly woman and a young man who claimed to have lost his life after running away from home. One of the Vennums' neighbors, Asa Roff, whose own daughter had died twelve years previously, convinced the Vennums to allow E.W. Stevens, a "magnetic healer" and "minister," to see Lurancy. Stevens hypnotized the girl and suggested she replace the unpleasant personalities currently possessing her with a more pleasant personality. Lurancy then suggested a list of control spirits, including the deceased Mary Roff, and the Roffs, who were present, readily agreed to have their daughter serve as control. After becoming possessed by the spirit of Mary Roff, Lurancy lost all traces of her former personality, did not recognize members of her biological family, and insisted on living with the Roffs. She lived with the Roffs for a little more than three months. During that time, she recalled many events in the life of Mary Roff in conversations with the Roffs, including the details of a trip to Texas in 1857 and the names of many friends and acquaintances of the Roffs from the time preceding Lurancy's birth. She also on one occasion pointed to a collar, saying she had tatted it (which was true as applied to Mary). She did not recall any of the details of her former life as Lurancy Vennum during the three months in question. Finally, Lurancy's old personality reemerged, and she returned to the home of her biological family, although the Mary Roff personality would emerge from time to time during visits between Lurancy and the Roffs.

There are several problems with this case. First, the Roff personality was virtually suggested to a psychologically troubled young adolescent by the hypnotist minister (who also served as the main chronicler of the case). She may have seized on the Mary Roff personality as a means of temporarily escaping a troubled home life. Watseka, Illinois, was a small town, and Lurancy probably had ample opportunity to learn some of the details of Mary Roff's life, especially as Mary had become insane at the time of her early and mysterious death and so may have been the subject of much town gossip. Also, as Rodger Anderson points out,[48] the Roffs and the Vennums had been near neighbors when Lurancy was seven. The Roff boy was Lurancy's age and hence a probable playmate, thus affording Lurancy another opportunity to learn some of the details of the Roffs' history. Finally, there is always the possibility that Lurancy may have simply repeated details she heard in earlier conversations among the Roffs and that she may have recognized a child's handiwork in the tatted collar and made the obvious inference that it was Mary's sewing. For all these reasons, despite its centrality in the popular literature on parapsychology, the Watseka Wonder does not present an especially strong case for possession.

Several of Ian Stevenson's reincarnation cases might be better interpreted as cases of possession, including the xenoglossy case discussed above. Stevenson's collection also contains several cases in which the a child's normal personality seemed to be supplanted by the personality of a deceased person well after the child's birth. In fact, Stevenson himself has suggested that cases of this type might be better explained in terms of possession rather than reincarnation.[49]

Of course, cases of ostensible possession occur frequently in religious contexts, such as when a practitioner of voodoo is possessed or "ridden" by a god or when a ritual of exorcism is performed to cure an apparent case of demonic possession within the context of Christianity. In the vast majority of such cases, however, the possessing entity does not seem to be identifiable with any specific living or dead person, nor is there much in the way of solid evidence for the paranormal acquisition of information. This being the case, it would seem reasonable to assume that such cases of possession are the result of suggestion, the product of attention-seeking role playing, or constitute an especially bizarre form of multiple personality.

In cases of obsession, the subject's personality is not supplanted by the surviving spirit of a deceased person, but is apparently under the influence of such a spirit. Perhaps the best described case of obsession in the annals of psychical research was investigated by the American researcher James Hyslop.[50] The case involved a goldsmith named Frederic L. Thompson, who was suddenly seized by a desire to sketch and paint in oils during the summer and autumn of 1905. Thompson even remarked to his wife that he felt he was an artist named Robert Swain Gifford. Thompson had met Gifford only a few times and knew little about his work. Gifford had died in 1905. Thompson's pictures, which consisted largely of seascapes, were found to correspond closely to Gifford's work. Upon visiting the Elizabeth Islands and Naushon Island in Buzzard's Bay, where Gifford had done most of his painting, Thompson discovered several scenes that closely resembled paintings he had recently generated under the influence of the Gifford persona. At one point, Thompson heard a voice telling him to look on the other side of a tree. Upon doing so, Thompson discovered Gifford's initials carved there, together with the date 1902. Thompson did in fact live in New Bedford for a period of time during his childhood, but he claimed never to have visited the Elizabeth Islands during this time.

Some of the shortcomings of this case include the fact that the subject himself served as one of the principal investigators of the case. Also, it would not strain one's credulity too much to imagine that similarities between two collections of seascapes might arise purely by chance. A skeptic could maintain that Thompson may have identified with Gifford for some strange psychological reason and carried that identification to the point that he fancied himself possessed by Gifford.

A more recent case of obsession was described by D. Scott Rogo. In this case, a man was cured of transvestism after a female spirit who was apparently controlling his behavior was expelled through a rite of exorcism.[51] This case does not provide particularly compelling evidence of obsession, however, as the female spirit was never identified with any specific living or dead person. Also, it is not uncommon for transvestites to talk about expressing their female personas and to distinguish such personas from their everyday male selves.

The strongest evidence for reincarnation or possession remains Ian Stevenson's reincarnation cases. Even those cases have their shortcomings. As we shall see in Chapter 12, however, it is extremely unlikely that you could leave your physical brain behind and still retain all the memories, thoughts and feelings that have plagued you through this life. Reincarnation need not involve memory. As the ancient Greeks thought, we may drink of the river of Lethe and remember no more.

11. Into the Twilight Zone

We will now examine several rather colorful (and sometimes rather bizarre) forms of evidence for survival. They all fall into the categories of attempts to measure and record the activities of discarnate spirits with physical devices. These include attempts to weigh the soul, to photograph ghosts, and to record the voices of the deceased.

Weighing the Soul

In a rather macabre experiment shortly after the turn of the century, Duncan MacDougall, a physician at Massachusetts General Hospital, attempted to measure the mass of the souls of terminally ill patients as they died upon a bed resting on a delicately balanced beam scale. Usable data were obtained from four such patients and the results indicated a weight loss of between 3/8 and 3/4 of an ounce at the time of death. In a second experiment, no detectable weight loss at the time of death was detected in 15 dogs.[1] The American psychical researcher Hereward Carrington argued that air loss from the lungs could account for up to five grams of the weight loss (or about one quarter of the weight loss reported by MacDougall).[2] On the other hand, Donald Carpenter has contended in a recent review of MacDougall's studies that no such weight loss would occur if the air in the lungs is at the ambient pressure.[3] MacDougall in fact tested the effect of expelling the air in the lungs and found it to have no impact on the patient's weight. Voiding of solids and fluids should have had no effect, as these would presumably be captured in the bed. In a definitive (although one is tempted to say breezy) analysis, Carpenter concludes that expulsion of gases through flatulence can account for at most one gram of weight loss.

Following up on MacDougall's research, H.L. Twining claimed to detect a weight loss of between one and two milligrams at the time of death in mice that were killed with cyanide. This weight loss was, however, prevented if the mouse was sealed in a tube, and Twining ascribed the change in weight to loss of moisture.[4]

Snapshots of Spirits

There have been many attempts to detect the soul visually as well as to weigh it. Closely related to the just discussed experiments of Twining is one such attempt at visual detection of the soul by a physicist named R.A. Watters in the 1930s.[4] In an experiment not likely to win the approval of today's advocates of animal rights, Watters decapitated animals, including frogs and mice, and claimed to have photographed forms bearing a resemblance to the animals in a cloud chamber of the type used to detect subatomic particles. Watters later came to attribute this effect to the emission of chemicals from the animal's bodies. When this possibility was eliminated, the cloud chamber apparitions ceased to appear.[5]

Alleged photographs of spirits played a prominent role in the early history of psychical research. The French researcher Hyppolite Baraduc produced photographs of what appeared to be luminous globes hovering over his wife and son at the times of their deaths.[6] Several people claimed to have taken pictures of ghosts, but these all too inevitably turned out to be hoaxes involving double exposures of film. Sir Arthur Conan Doyle, the creator of Sherlock Holmes, even published a book in which he accepted two young ladies' claim to have photographed fairies.[7] The fairies, however, turned out to be almost exact copies of illustrations from a popular children's book augmented with wings. Thus it appears that the "fairies" were mere cardboard cutouts (as they frankly appear to be in the photographs), and it seems that the girls were playing a prank on Doyle.

Psychics frequently report seeing "auras" or luminous glows surrounding people. Sometimes such auras are interpreted as being caused by the astral body's extending beyond the confines of the physical body. Several attempts to detect auras through physical measuring devices have been reported. One of the first was Walter Kilner's invention of dicyanin goggles which he claimed enabled the viewer to see the auras surrounding people.[8] Unfortunately, it seems that the auras visible through Kilner's goggles were due to the differential refraction of ordinary light rays. Luminous halos or coronas surrounding living objects appear in pictures obtained through Kirlian photography, in which a high voltage electrical field is applied to an object in direct contact with photographic film. In the early 1970s, many people interpreted these coronas and halos as representing pictures of auras, astral bodies, or some other form of "vital energy." Since that time, it has been rather conclusively demonstrated that such Kirlian auras are caused by known chemical and electrical processes. The nature of the aura obtained in the photograph is dependent on mundane physical variables such as the amount of water in the specimen, the pressure exerted by the specimen on the film, salt concentrations, and other variables. The aura is the result of simple electrical corona discharge and does not reflect any "psychical energy."[9]

At one point, it was argued that the "phantom leaf effect," in which the Kirlian image of a whole leaf remains even after part of the leaf has been destroyed, points to the existence of a nonphysical energy body capable of being photographed through the Kirlian process. Many investigators have found this effect difficult to replicate,[10] and at least one replication has been withdrawn due to suspected fraud on the part of a member of the investigating team.[11] Arleen Watkins and William Bickel have also pointed out that the phantom leaf effect can be the result of placing the partial leaf in the same position on the film that the whole leaf originally occupied. As the moisture pattern from the original, whole leaf may remain on the film, a Kirlian photograph depicting an intact leaf may result.[12] Also, Kirlian auras have been photographed around inanimate objects such as coins. Surely, dimes do not have astral bodies and nickels do not have souls.

Tuning in to Valhalla

A few people have actually claimed to be able to pick up broadcasts from the afterlife using tape-recording equipment. Some of these investigators have taped the signal received at a radio frequency over which no station is broadcasting, while others have simply turned on a microphone in a presumably quiet environment without any radio hookup at all. This technique was invented independently by Attila von Szalay and Friedrich Jurgenson in the late 1950s and early 1960s.[13] A great deal of "research" using this technique was conducted by Konstantin Raudive, who reported his results in a popular book entitled *Breakthrough* in 1971.[14]

This body of research has been roundly criticized and condemned by the parapsychological research community. E. Lester Smith argued that Raudive was so eager to hear voices in ambiguous sounds that he was able to decipher signals from the beyond in what was really random radio static. In support of this idea, he noted that the same sorts of errors that Raudive usually made when he spoke German were being made by the spirits of the dead whose voices he claimed to have captured on audiotape. In fact, Smith noted that other observers often had to be "trained" for months by Raudive before they too could hear the voices of the departed on Raudive's tapes,[15] much as the subjects of the kingdom were eventually able to see the emperor's new clothes. The British researcher David Ellis visited Raudive's laboratory in an effort to confirm his results, but was unable to hear the voices. His impression was that Raudive seemed to be interpreting nonvocal sounds as voices. Ellis has also pointed out that the earlier electronic voice researcher Friedrich Jurgenson admitted to having "functional hallucinations," which consisted of hearing voices in natural sounds, after he discontinued his own tape experiments.[16]

Stray radio signals could also have played a role in generating some of the voices. Ellis was able to determine that a sequence of phrases in several different languages purportedly directed to Raudive by the denizens of the afterlife was actually an announcement in English broadcast by Radio Luxemborg. Smith also suggested that stray radio signals were responsible for many of Raudive's voices. He notes that Raudive's willingness to use any language and to accept ungrammatical utterances from the beyond make it quite likely that Raudive's voices were such stray speech fragments. Jurgen Keil was able to identify a 37-word passage in German on the tapes, but notes that Raudive used five languages to decode the passage and did not recognize the fact that it was entirely in German.[17] Thus, if these were voices from another dimension, their advice might have lost something in the translation.

E. Lester Smith even suggested that Raudive's eagerness to hear from the expired may have led him to use ventriloquism unconsciously to produce the voices on tape, and Gerd Hövelman has likewise postulated that Jurgenson's and Raudive's voices might be the product of unconscious whispering on the part of people present during the tape-recording process.[18]

Raymond Bayless and the late D. Scott Rogo have even published a collection of cases in which people have claimed to have received phone calls from the dead.[19] Their study, however, was widely criticized in the parapsychological community for its generally sloppy and credulous nature.[20] Nonetheless, one waits with bated breath for the next development in electronic communication from the beyond. To my knowledge, the dead must not have a fax machine at their disposal nor do they seem to have much in the way of an e-mail sending capability (possibly this may await the demise of Bill Gates).

We will now turn to more somber matters, as we attempt to answer the ultimate question confronting all of us: what happens to us when we die?

12. The Mind's Fate Upon Death

Who are we? What are we? We emerge, seemingly from nothingness, into the physical world. Is it to nothingness that we return? Are we our physical bodies? Our personalities? Or are we a field of pure consciousness through which our thoughts, sensations and emotions flutter like so many butterflies?

Much of the parapsychological evidence for the survival of death, including that from mediumship and reincarnation cases, suggests that the mind is able to survive death with large portions of its memories, skills and personality intact. There is, however, an overwhelming amount of evidence that one's emotions, patterns of behavior and cognitive skills are intimately tied to the state of one's brain. For instance, damage to the right hemisphere of the brain can turn a depressed musician into a happy-go-lucky, tone-deaf individual. Damage to the frontal lobes of the brain can turn an upright citizen into a raincoat-opening exhibitionist. Surely the removal of one's entire brain at death would change one's state of consciousness profoundly!

Memory also appears to be intimately dependent on brain structures. There is an abundance of evidence that damage to the hippocampal and thalamic areas of the brain can destroy one's ability to store new long term memories. People with such a condition live in a kind of dream state. They will not recognize the nurse who has been taking care of them daily for years, but will greet him each time as if meeting someone new. There is also an increasing amount of evidence that some memories may be stored in localized regions of the brain and may be erased when these areas are damaged. For instance, in a bilingual patient who speaks, say, English and Greek, it is possible to interfere with his inability to speak Greek by electrically disrupting one area of his brain and to interfere with his ability to speak English by disrupting another area.[1] Michael Gazzaniga describes a case in which a localized brain lesion rendered a woman incapable of naming the color of red fruits, although she could name the color of non-red fruits such as bananas as well as of red objects such as fire engines.[2] In another case, a very circumscribed brain lesion rendered a patient unable to name colors altogether.[3] Localized memory traces have also been demonstrated in nonhuman subjects. Memory for a conditioned eyeblink response has, for instance, been shown to reside in the cerebellum of the rabbit.[4] There is also a considerable body of evidence that the storage of memories is dependent on changes in the synaptic connections among the neurons of the brain.[5]

Even the avowed dualist Sir John Eccles believes that long term memories are stored as changes in synaptic connections between neurons. Eccles does, however, feel compelled to postulate the existence of a second, non-physical memory system in which "recognition memory" (which monitors the correctness of recalled information) resides, even though he maintains that memories of the details of the events in one's life are physically stored in the brain and hence lost at death.[6] Ian Stevenson likewise proposes that there are two memory stores, one physical and one nonphysical. He suggests that, although brain mechanisms may control access to all memories before death, this does not prove that the memory traces themselves are physical.[7]

The parapsychologist Alan Gauld has also questioned whether memories are stored as physical traces in the brain, noting that memories are sometimes gradually recovered after brain damage.[8] David Lund makes the argument that the brain may be the transmitter rather than the generator of consciousness, a view that goes back to William James.[9] Under this analogy, a damaged brain may simply be unable to receive the signal from an intact consciousness. On the other hand, Barry Beyerstein has argued that a nonphysical mind should be able to compensate for the effects of brain damage. Why, he asks, can the mind allegedly separate from the body in an out-of-body experience and perceive the environment if it cannot overcome perceptual deficits caused by brain damage (such as the cortical blindness discussed in Chapter 8)?[10]

What Is the Self?

Obviously, the physical body does not survive the death of the physical body. As we have just seen, it appears unlikely that our memories and personalities could survive the dissolution of our physical brains. What, however, constitutes our essential selves? Are we our bodies? Our personalities and memories? Or are we something less than these yet at the same time something infinitely more?

Many philosophers see the physical body as an essential part of one's self. In Terence Penelhum's view, for instance, it makes no sense to talk about people surviving their deaths in some sort of disembodied state. If such a disembodied ghost were to communicate through a medium and relate memories of the person's life, this would prove nothing according to Penelhum, as memories might be illusory. He thinks that people can only be identified on the basis of their physical bodies and that therefore it makes no sense to talk about people surviving the deaths of their bodies.[11] Of course, physical appearances can also be deceptive. Someone could disguise herself as someone else for instance; thus, it is not clear that physical appearance is a foolproof means of identifying a person either. Peter Geach is another philosopher who maintains that personality traits and memories are not a sufficient basis to identify a person. He compares the transfer of personality traits and memories from one body to another, such as might occur in one of Stevenson's reincarnation cases, to the spreading of a disease.[12]

The noted philosopher Antony Flew also contends that immaterial souls would not be identifiable. In Flew's opinion, the idea that a person survives death can only be made intelligible if you assume that people possess some sort of quasi-physical astral body, on the basis of which they could be identified. Flew views the ideas of disembodied survival and incorporeal souls as incoherent notions. He maintains that the word "person" refers to a flesh and blood creature and that it therefore makes no sense to talk of a person surviving the death of his physical body.[13]

All of these writers contend that some sort of physical body is necessary in order to establish the continuity of personal identity. It is not clear why we should put so much more stock in physical appearance than in mental appearance. Let us suppose, however, that we are indeed our physical bodies. We then must confront the fact that each of us inhabits a different body from day to day. Each day our bodies incorporate new atoms from the food we eat. Old atoms are constantly being sluffed off in our daily micturation and defecation episodes, in our dandruff and each time we exhale. Your body today and your body of ten years ago have very few atoms in common. You inhabit a different body today from the body you inhabited ten years ago. If you are the same self, you have survived the dissolution of your old physical body. Perhaps you can survive the dissolution of your present body at death as well.

If you are not the particular collection of physical particles that make up your present physical body, perhaps you are the particular *pattern* of molecules that make up your present body. You would then remain the same person even if the physical particles that make up your body changed, so long as the general pattern remained the same. This is the basis of the famous beaming technique in the *Star Trek* television and movie series. In *Star Trek*, one can "beam" to a new location by undergoing a process in which one's physical body is atomized, information about the pattern of the physical particles that make up one's body is sent to a distant location, and a new body is reassembled (presumably out of new atoms) at the second location. Peter Oppenheimer and Derek Parfit have independently concluded that this beaming process would result in the death of everyone who used it as a form of transportation, followed by the construction of a replica of the person at the destination site. This replica may not be the original person any more than identical twins are the same person as each other.[14] To make this example more compelling, assume that more than one copy of the person is assembled at the destination site. (This happens from time to time in *Star Trek*. Remember the evil Kirk and the wimpy Kirk episode?) Surely it would be difficult to believe that one's self could simultaneously inhabit all the replicas of one's physical body that are constructed at the destination site; a conscious self cannot have several separate and independent streams of consciousness occurring at the same time.

Rather than equating the self with the collection of atoms or pattern of material particles that make up a person's body, many philosophers have equated the self with the system of memories, thoughts, emotions and behavior patterns that make up one's personality. Thus, one's self would not be dependent on the existence of any particular body. This view would allow for the possibility that a person could reincarnate or possess the body of a medium after death. Also, if we were able to build a computer or robot that perfectly simulated your personality, we would have to say that your self continued to exist in the computer or robot, because you are nothing more nor less than your personality. In fact, several writers, including Hans Moravec and G. Fjermedal, have proposed that it would be possible to achieve personal immortality by "downloading" one's memories into a computer or robot. Your self would then live on in the computer or robot that is simulating your personality.[15] The physicist Frank Tipler has even recently argued that we will all be resurrected by being simulated on a giant computer at the end of time.[16] Once again, however, there is nothing in principle stopping someone from constructing a computer or robot to simulate your personality while you are still alive. Surely it would be absurd to think that your self would then reside both in the computer and in your physical body. The computer or robot is just a replica of you. It is not you. You are not your personality traits and behavior patterns.

As we discussed above, due to the intimate dependency of your personality and behavior patterns on the state of your brain, it appears unlikely that your thoughts, emotions and memories could remain unchanged following the dissolution of your brain at death. But you are not your thoughts, emotions and memories any more than you are your physical body. Like the atoms that make up your physical body, your thoughts, emotions and memories are continually changing. If you are the same self that you were five years ago, you cannot be identical to a particular constellation of thoughts, feelings and memories, as your personality has changed over the years (unless the reader has just emerged from cryogenic storage). It is, of course, always possible that you are not the same self. It may be that each night when you go to sleep your soul wanders off aimlessly and is "sucked into" another body as it wakes up. If that is true, your soul may only have been residing in your present body since this morning. The reason you think you have inhabited it for a long time is that the physical brain of the body you currently inhabit contains memories for events in the distant past. You therefore remember spending many years in this body, but the memories are an illusion; instead, you have spent those years flitting from body to body like a hapless ball in a pinball machine.

Actually, even though we seem to be located in our brains, our true selves may not be located there at all. We (modern Westerners at least) experience ourselves as being located in our heads. (Actually, this view of our selves is to some extent a scientific hypothesis. The Ancient Greek philosophers Democritus, Empedocles and Aristotle located the seat of intelligence in the heart, not the brain. William Harvey, the man who discovered how blood circulates in the human body, saw the blood itself as the seat of the soul. The brain itself was once thought to be an organ whose primary function was to cool the blood.)

In his science fiction story "Where am I?", the philosopher Daniel Dennett concocts a scenario in which sensory information is transmitted directly to a person's brain from a robot located at a distant location. The person's brain also controls the motions of the robot. Thus, the person would see what the robot "sees," and when the person commands his own arm to move, the robot's arm would move instead. Assuming that the person's brain has been "unplugged" from its own sensory organs, there is no doubt that the person would experience himself as located in the body of the robot and not as a disembodied brain floating in a laboratory tank at a remote location. Thus, we may not be located where we think we are (that is, in our brains). We may not be "located" in physical space at all.

If you are the same self you remember being several years ago, it is clear that you cannot be the particular physical body you presently inhabit. Nor can you be the present collection of thoughts, emotions and memories that seem to make up your personality. Instead, you are the thinker of your thoughts, the senser of your sensations, the feeler of your feelings, and the rememberer of your memories, rather than being the thoughts, sensations, feelings and memories themselves. You are a field of pure consciousness and are not the contents of consciousness. You are the experiencer, not what is experienced. We experience our feelings, our physical bodies. They are not us. They are what we experience.

We do somehow seem to be attached to, or at least associated with, a particular brain. How this comes about is a mystery. But we cannot be the brain.

There are philosophers who deny the existence of a continuing self altogether. Both Daniel Dennett and Susan Blackmore deny the existence of a continuing field of consciousness, or "Cartesian theater" as they call it.[17] Stephen Priest has countered Descartes' argument that "I think therefore I am" by asserting that thoughts do not imply the existence of a thinker.[18] Even William James argued that there may be no substantial soul, but only an ongoing stream of consciousness.[19] James' view has recently been echoed by Thomas Clark, who contends that a person is simply an assemblage of "qualia" or experiences and denies the existence of a self separate from the experiences themselves.[20]

The basic problem with this denial of the existence of the self is that one cannot have a stream of consciousness without a riverbed for it to flow through. One of the foremost modern deniers of the self is the philosopher Derek Parfit. In Parfit's opinion, in each person there is only a continuing series of thoughts, sensations, memories and feelings, with no continuing self to experience them. But in order to explain the unity and continuity of experience, Parfit is forced to assert that these thoughts, sensations and memories are experienced by the same "state of awareness."[21] But this state of awareness is nothing more or less than the self or soul, assuming one is willing to equate the self with a field of pure consciousness.

As we have argued, you are not your physical body. If you are a particular physical body, it would be most unlikely that you would exist now. The probability that the specific combination of genes that govern the makeup of your particular body would have ever come together is vanishingly small. The probability that "now" happens to be a moment in the history of the universe in which that body is alive is also vanishingly small. If you are a specific body, it is extremely unlikely that you would have ever existed, much less exist at the present time. But here you are. Also, due to the replacement of atoms in your body, you have already survived the death of several physical bodies. Perhaps the self can survive the destruction of its present physical body at death as well. After all, as Voltaire pointed out, it is no more surprising to be born twice than it is to be born once. If you assume that you were not alive before your birth, that did not seem to prevent you from being alive now. Thus, being dead in the future need not prevent you from emerging from nonlife into life once again. Death may even serve a purpose in enabling one to escape the rut of one's present life and to begin life anew.

Next we consider the question of whether conscious minds may have played a truly grand role in the creation and design of life and of the very cosmos itself.

13. Mind and Cosmos

Several writers have suggested that conscious minds may play a truly grand role in the universe, perhaps even being responsible for the creation and design of living beings and the creation and design of the very physical universe itself. Strangely enough, the evidence is most compelling for the most grandiose of the these claims, namely that the universe may have been designed by a conscious agent or agents. Let us begin, however, by examining the less cosmological assertion that minds may have played a role in the emergence of life and in directing the course of evolution.

The Creation of Life

According to currently accepted scientific wisdom, life emerged from random chemical reactions in the early stages of the Earth's development. Several prominent scientists have, however, expressed skepticism that the random mixing of chemicals could produce the complex, self-replicating entities we call living beings. Among these scientists are two British knights, Sir Francis Crick, a co-winner of the Nobel prize for the discovery of the structure of DNA molecules, and Sir Fred Hoyle, a noted astronomer. Both Crick and Hoyle have proposed that life evolved in outer space and then migrated to Earth.[1] Outer space is a lot roomier than the Earth and consequently affords life more opportunity to evolve randomly. Given the vast reaches of space and innumerable planetary systems, even the most improbable events, such as the creation of living beings from the random mixing of chemicals, are bound to occur. Hoyle has even suggested that certain disease epidemics are caused by viruses descending to Earth from outer space. In some cases, Hoyle contends, these viruses may insert their genes into the genomes of terrestrial animals, altering the course of biological evolution.

Both Michael Hart and Richard Dawkins have also argued that it is extremely improbable that life will evolve in any given planetary system. However, because of the large number of planetary systems in the universe, they argue, life is bound to emerge in some of them. In fact, Hart argues that the

207

existing evidence indicates that our universe is spatially infinite, so that all possible forms of life will emerge. Both Dawkins and Hart agree that because of the extremely low probability that life will emerge randomly in any given planetary system, life would be expected to be extremely sparsely distributed in the universe.[2] Perhaps this is why we see so little evidence of extraterrestrial civilizations in our local area of the universe (notwithstanding the repeated abduction and sexual molestation by the bald-headed, bug-eyed UFO pilots of such horror fiction writers as Whitley Strieber).

John Casti has observed that life depends crucially on the accurate self-replication of molecular systems. He further observes that one cannot get reliable replication without large RNA molecules and that one cannot get large RNA molecules without a reliable replication system, thus producing a "Catch-22" situation, rendering it implausible that life could evolve randomly.[3] Sidney Fox, on the other hand, has proposed that the first life forms consisted of microspheres composed of spontaneously forming thermal proteins. In Fox's view DNA and RNA molecules emerged later in the course of evolution.[4] Just recently, Julius Rebek and his coworkers at M.I.T. have succeeded in synthesizing very simple self-replicating molecules, showing that self-replication need not involve RNA or DNA and may be achieved by quite simple molecules that are likely to arise randomly in a "prebiotic soup" on the early Earth.[5] Thus, it seems by no means impossible that life could have emerged from random chemical reactions either on Earth or in outer space, and so we are not compelled to assume that conscious minds must have played a role in the creation of the first self-replicating life forms. Later in this chapter, however, we will see that the physical universe itself seems to be delicately designed to allow the possibility of life's emerging in it. Perhaps a conscious agent or agents had a hand in designing the very laws of nature and in setting the initial conditions of our universe.

Directed Evolution

As we discussed in Chapter 8, until fairly recent times, even orthodox biologists assumed that some sort of psychical energy or vital force animated living creatures. We have already traced the retreat of this doctrine of vitalism in the face of scientific advances such as the synthesis of the biological molecules urea and glucose in the laboratory. Still, the philosophy of vitalism is not dead and retains some adherents today. For instance, in the early 1960s, the philosopher C.J. Ducasse of Brown University proposed a solution to the mind-body problem that he called "hypophenomenalism," in which the mind is viewed as animating the body.[6] Under this doctrine, the mind is responsible for maintaining the life of the body.

The Australian biologist Charles Birch has contended that the mind cannot be reduced to brain activity and that mental events such as ideas and emotions may influence physical events in the body, such as the behavior of molecules. He further proposes that minds may be able to influence the outcome of seemingly "random events" in the process of biological evolution.[7] (As we have already seen, Carroll Nash obtained evidence that human subjects could use their psychokinetic powers to influence the rate at which bacterial genes mutate.[8])

Sir John Eccles has recently gone so far as to maintain that there exists a divine guidance over the course of evolution.[9] The physicist O. Costa de Beauregard has postulated that the direction of biological evolution is directed from the future through the emission of advanced waves that travel backward in time.[10] Another modern vitalist is consciousness researcher Willis Harman, who contends that there exists a "self-organizing" force governing living beings that cannot be explained on the basis of the principles of physics.[11]

One of the most enthusiastic proponents of the doctrine that purposive influences guide the course of biological evolution in recent years was the popular science writer Arthur Koestler.[12] Koestler provided several examples of evolutionary development that he felt could not be accounted for by the neo–Darwinian theory that evolution proceeds through random mutations in genes. One of these examples was that of the sixth finger of the giant panda. Koestler argued that the finger would have been useless unless it was equipped with its own nerves, blood supply and system of muscles. Koestler felt that this confluence of events was unlikely to occur by chance. Koestler's view appears to be based on the assumption that a separate mutation would be required for each system. When one considers how frequently domestic cats are born with extra toes, Koestler's argument seems to fall apart. Evidently, viable supernumerary digits can arise without the divine coordination of a host of separate mutations.

Similarly, Koestler argues that the evolution of birds required the "simultaneous transformation of scales into feathers, solid bones into hollow tubes, the outgrowth of air sacs into various parts of the body, the development of shoulder muscles and bones to athletic proportions, and so forth."[13] Once again it is only Koestler's assumption that these transformations had to be simultaneous and discrete rather than nonsimultaneous and gradual. That Koestler's assumption is in fact false is readily apparent upon an examination of the Jurassic bird *Archeopteryx*, which represents a transitional form between the reptiles and birds in the course of evolution. *Archeopteryx* had small wings (which were used mainly for gliding), clawed fingers (which were presumably used for climbing), teeth and feathers, but no hollow bones.

Koestler asserted that mutations are almost always trivial or harmful and thus could not serve to further the course of evolution. He cited the example of mutations that change the color of a plant, contending that such mutations were so trivial that they could not have any evolutionary significance. However, such a mutation could increase a plant's fertility by making it more attractive to bees or could increase the plant's longevity if the color change resulted in the plant's resembling a poisonous species. Similar mutations affecting the color of an animal might confer camouflage benefits or increased attractiveness to the opposite sex.

As further evidence that evolution is guided by some sort of purposeful force rather than being the result of random mutations, Koestler cited the example of mutant eyeless flies, which, when inbred, gave rise to several flies with normal eyes after a few generations. An advocate of neo–Darwinism can readily cope with this finding, however. The neo–Darwinist can simply assert that the mutation responsible for the eyeless condition was unstable and that the gene backmutated to its normal form. Also, as William Day points out, the emergence of a gene having a new function in the course of evolution is usually preceded by the duplication of the old gene, so that copies of the old gene are preserved in the animal's DNA should something go awry with the new gene.[14]

Another piece of evidence for a purposive influence guiding the course of evolution educed by Koestler was the fact that the isolated marsupial animals of Australia evolved into similar types of animals as did the placental animals elsewhere on the Earth. The neo–Darwinist can, however, readily retort that similar environmental "niches" will tend to favor the evolution of similar types of animals.

Koestler argued for a modified form of Lamarck's theory of the inheritance of acquired characteristics. As evidence in favor of his theory, he cited the fact that the skin on the soles of the feet of the human embryo is thickened, which he thought reflected the acquisition of calluses by prior generations of walking humans. On the other hand, it would be quite easy for the neo–Darwinist to cope with this observation by pointing out that mutations favoring thick skins on the soles of the feet will be favored by natural selection, as thin-soled children may not be able to flee from predators over long distances. In summary, Koestler did not provide much in the way of compelling evidence to challenge the neo–Darwinian position.

Another recent writer to challenge the neo–Darwinian theory is biochemist Rupert Sheldrake, who proposes that embryological development is guided through "morphic resonance."[15] Sheldrake proposes, for instance, that a bear embryo will be guided in its development through "resonating" with the "morphic fields" of all the bears that have preceded it into the world. Each creature tends to resonate with similar creatures that have existed in the past. Susan Blackmore has pointed out that Sheldrake's theory is circular insofar as Sheldrake explains the similarity of two creatures in terms of resonance and the resonance between two creatures on the basis of their similarity.[16] Similarly, it is difficult to see how morphic resonance could account for the process of evolution and the emergence of novel forms of life, as morphic resonance would confine creatures to repeating previous patterns of biological development.

Sheldrake even proposes that telepathy is due to morphic resonance between similar brains. He also contends that memory is due to morphic resonance with one's own past brain states and hypothesizes that we could survive death with our memories intact, as memories are not stored in the physical brain but are the result of morphic resonance.

There is virtually no evidence for the "morphic fields" that Sheldrake proposes govern the phenomenon of morphic resonance, and only a smattering of evidence for the morphic resonance effect itself. Most of the latter evidence results from a handful of studies that are methodologically flawed in one respect or another. In one typical study, for example, it was found that a real Japanese nursery rhyme was easier for English-speaking subjects to learn than a newly composed nursery rhyme. Sheldrake interpreted this as being due to morphic resonance with the minds of all the Japanese people who had previously learned the nursery rhyme. However, as Sue Blackmore pointed out,[17] the rhyme may have been popular in the first place because it was particularly "catchy" and easy to learn. (Sheldrake himself acknowledged Blackmore's point in this regard.[18]) A similar methodological defect occurs in most of the other studies that have been conducted on morphic resonance.[19] Biologists have been quick to condemn Sheldrake's theory as being baseless and have pointed out that orthodox biological and physical processes can account for most of the biological effects Sheldrake ascribes to morphic resonance. Not much of a case can be made for nonphysical influences on biological evolution on the basis of the extremely shaky evidence for Sheldrake's morphic resonance effect.

Finally, it should be noted that there has been a recent flap in the scientific literature over the possible existence of directed mutation in *E. coli* bacteria. The team of Cairns, Overbaugh and Miller have found that a mutant form of this bacterium that is unable to metabolize lactose mutated back to the normal form when placed on a medium containing high concentrations of lactose, suggesting that the mutations tended to occur in a direction favorable to the organism. Similarly, B.G. Hall found that bacteria that are unable to synthesize the amino acids tryptophan and cysteine mutate in such a way as to be able to synthesize these amino acids when they are unavailable in the environment. Very recent findings suggest that starvation does indeed affect the types of mutation that occur, although it has yet to be determined that the mutations occur in a purposeful rather than random manner.[20]

There is thus no compelling evidence for an influence of mind on the creation of life or the direction of biological evolution. There is a bit more of a suggestion of a role for the mind in the creation of the universe itself, however, as we shall now see.

Mind as Deity

The universe we inhabit seems very delicately designed to support the existence of living creatures and hence of conscious minds. This suggests that the universe may have been created by a conscious Being or beings to serve as some sort of cosmic amusement park. The fact that the universe seems designed to support the existence of intelligent beings has been commented on by many physicists, who have coined the term "anthropic principle" to denote this element of apparent design in the universe.

As the physicist Paul Davies points out, if the rate of expansion of the universe immediately after its creation in the Big Bang had differed even slightly from its actual value, life as we know it could not exist. Had the rate of expansion been infinitesimally slower, all matter would have collapsed into black holes shortly after the creation of the universe. Had the rate been slightly faster, the matter density would have been too small to allow galaxies to form. Davies also points out that matter seems to be very uniformly distributed throughout the galaxy. If the mass distribution had been less homogeneous, the gaseous clouds needed to form stars, planetary systems and living beings would not have existed, and most of the mass in the universe would have been consumed in black holes.[21]

Roger Penrose has pointed out that the universe was created in a very highly ordered state that would not be expected to occur by chance.[22]

The laws of physics themselves seem to be delicately contrived to allow for the emergence of life. In *The Anthropic Cosmological Principle*, John Barrow and Frank Tipler note that even minuscule variations from the existing ratios of the strength of the nuclear force to the electromagnetic force, of the total number of photons to the total number of protons in the universe, and of the mass of the electron to the mass of the proton would have rendered the universe incapable of supporting life. They further contend that the existing abundances and properties of the chemical elements are especially suitable for the emergence of life, noting in particular that the most abundant chemicals, such as water and carbon dioxide, seem optimally suited to supporting life.[23] John Gribbin and Martin Rees point out that the so-called "weak force" that governs radioactive decay must be extremely fine-tuned in order for stars to shed matter in great quantities during supernova explosions.[24] (Our bodies are composed of elements that were forged in the interior of stars and then released in supernova explosions. As Carl Sagan was fond of saying, we are all "starfolk.") George Greenstein has observed that even a difference of one part in 100 billion in the electrical charges of the electron and the proton would cause physical objects to fly apart due to electrical repulsion among their parts. Greenstein further notes that if the ratio of the masses of the proton and the neutron were reversed, protons would decay into neutrons and even simple elements such as hydrogen would not exist (and hence neither would life).[25]

Even the number of dimensions of space seems uniquely suited to supporting the existence of life. Planetary orbits would be unstable if space had more than three dimensions,[26] and Greenstein has pointed out that a universe of at least three dimensions may be required in order that brains with highly complex connections among their neurons can exist (which may be necessary for consciousness).[27]

John Barrow and Frank Tipler have speculated that physicist John Wheeler's ideas about a "participatory universe" might be extended to encompass the universe as a whole.[28] In Wheeler's view, events only become real when they are observed by a conscious being. If this view is extended to encompass the creation of the universe itself, the universe could only be real if it were observed by at least one conscious being, hence any real universe must be able to support the existence of conscious observers. The physicist Edward Tryon has proposed that the creation of the universe may actually have been a quantum fluctuation. He further observes that the total energy of the universe may be equal to zero, as negative gravitational potential energies may balance out the positive energies of physical particles. If the total energy of the universe is zero, then there is no limit on how long the universe might exist under the Heisenberg Uncertainty Principle of quantum mechanics.[29] Thus, the universe may be the ultimate "free lunch." If the universe is a quantum fluctuation that can only become real through being observed, as Wheeler thinks, then the creation of the universe might have been the ultimate act of retroactive PK! (Wheeler himself would abhor this particular interpretation of his theory, as he is an ardent opponent of parapsychology.)

Mind, viewed as the creator of the physical world, is literally deified. If the intelligence that created the physical world is somehow to be identified with the souls that now inhabit it, then that intelligence is unlike the post–Newtonian Christian God who stands remote from his creation once it is complete. It resembles much more the Vedic picture of the Universal Self that divides into the minds of the myriad creatures of the world, which derives from the Brhadaranyaka Upanisad. The philosopher Alan Watts was fond of comparing this Indian view of creation to God playing hide-and-seek with himself in the physical world.

W.T. Stace has argued that the pure ego of each individual being (*atman*) must be identical to the universal ego (*Brahman*), as both are simply fields of pure consciousness. He suggests that this identity is intuitively recognized in mystical experiences in which a person feels herself to be at one with the World and with God. He notes that scientific and mathematical concepts are based on dissection of the world into atomistic concepts, and he proposes that the reason why mystical experiences are "ineffable," or impossible to describe in words, lies in the inability of scientific language to describe a nonatomistic or holistic reality.[30]

The philosopher Colin McGinn has recently observed that the mind is frequently conceived as being nonspatial in nature and that some type of non-spatial order must have preceded the creation of space in the Big Bang. He suggests that this nonspatial order may still persist and may form the basis of consciousness.[31]

Of course, a creative intelligence need not be benign. The early Christian Gnostics viewed the creator of the world as a malevolent demiurge who wished to trap spirits in matter and to prevent their return to a state of dis-embodied divine being. Also, as Joseph Campbell pointed out, the second century Christian philosopher Marcion viewed the god of the Old Testament as an evil being responsible for imprisoning spirits in matter.[32]

There are ways of accounting for the evidence for the anthropic principle without assuming that the universe was designed by a creative intelligence. Barrow and Tipler note that if one accepts Tryon's view that the creation of the universe was a quantum fluctuation, then Hugh Everett's many worlds interpretation of quantum mechanics would imply that all possible universes must be created.[33] Each universe might have its own set of initial conditions, and the laws of physics might crystallize out into different forms in each universe. As conscious observers, we must of course be living in one of the universes that is capable of hosting conscious beings. But this does not mean that a conscious agent designed the universe, as all possible universes must occur.

M.A. Markov has hypothesized that universes may spawn "daughter universes" which become separate from the "mother universe."[34] Indeed, there has been speculation that it might be possible for a mad scientist to create such a universe in his own basement. This would lead to another version of the many universes theory. Another possibility, which has been extensively discussed by George Gale, is that of an oscillating universe.[35] If the amount of matter of our universe is sufficiently large, then we are living in what is known as a "closed universe," that is a universe that is destined to recollapse in a "Big Crunch." The Big Crunch is a time-reversed version of the Big Bang, in which all the matter of the universe becomes compressed in a spacetime singularity, or black hole. Because the known laws of physics break down in a singularity, several physicists have proposed that the universe will be reborn after the Big Crunch in a process known as the "Big Bounce." The new version of the universe will have different initial conditions and possibly even different laws of physics from the previous universe. During many of these cycles, the universe may be incapable of supporting life as we know it, but we by definition inhabit a cycle that is conducive to our existence. Thus, it seems to us that the universe has been especially designed to support life, whereas in fact it has not. In passing, we should note that this model of an oscillating universe bears a certain resemblance to the cyclic views of time held by the ancient Greeks, such as Plato, Aristotle and Pythagoras, as well as to the great cosmological cycles called *kalpas* in Hindu philosophy.

A spatial rather than temporal version of the many worlds hypothesis is offered by A.D. Linde.[36] He suggests that the laws of physics may have assumed different forms in different regions of our own universe. We of course live in a region where the laws of physics are conducive to our existence.

In this context, it should be noted that most of the arguments with regard to the anthropic principle have centered around whether or not the sort of carbon-based life with which we are familiar could exist in a particular universe. However, might not radically different universes give rise to different forms of life? Perhaps we have not even been able to conceive of the types of life that might arise in such radically altered universes.

The anthropic principle seems to strike a note of euphoria in many people. Certainly, if the universe has been designed to support conscious observers (or if those observers created the universe themselves), a certain elation may be experienced at the idea that one's existence is not as precarious and fragile as one might have thought and that one may be a great deal more powerful than appearances would indicate. However, if the universe is designed to house conscious beings, one could easily argue that, from the existing evidence, the universe appears more likely to be designed as a torture chamber than as a playground for the gods. The moral implications are also less clear than many would suppose. The conception that we are all parts of one Universal Self could just as easily lead us to mistreat others ("I'm only hurting myself—a victimless crime") or to commit murder ("he'll just get reincarnated anyway") or to treat all humans as siblings (an attempted nonsexist translation of "all men are brothers"). Also, if conscious observers created the universe, the question then arises as to who or what created them as well as any "preuniverse" they may have inhabited. One thus arrives at the usual intractable infinite regress that accompanies explanations of the Creation in terms of a Creator. Certainly at this stage of our inquiry, a more manageable question, and one perhaps more amenable to scientific investigation, is that of the relationship of the conscious mind to the physical brain. Given the current state of our knowledge, this is as (or more) profound and exciting a question as that of the role of conscious agents in creating the universe itself.

14. In Conclusion

The world can no longer be viewed as a collection of isolated atomic particles careening about in an uncoordinated and meaningless manner. This atomistic cosmology is dead, although many laymen and all too many scientists have yet to grasp that fact.

The data of parapsychology suggest that we possess mental abilities that cannot be explained on the basis of current theories of physics. It appears that human beings are more than just physical bodies and that conscious minds may play a truly fundamental role in the universe. We are not separate encapsulated egos. We are each other.

We are not our physical bodies. Each of us has already shed several such bodies the way a snake sheds its skin. We play a more fundamental role in the world than the temporary agglutinations of material particles that comprise our physical selves. Consciousness may be even prior to space and time themselves. For the time being, however, we might as well lie back and enjoy the show. Somebody went to a lot of trouble to put it on for us.

Chapter Notes

Chapter 2.
Spontaneous Psi

1. This case is taken from Rhine (1961), p. 55.
2. Owen (1964).
3. Gurney, Myers & Podmore (1886a), p. 194.
4. *Ibid.*, p. 194.
5. Virtanen (1990).
6. Gurney, Myers & Podmore (1886a), pp. 187-189.
7. Stevenson (1970b), pp. 49-50.
8. Rhine (1977), p. 71.
9. Rhine (1961), pp. 43-44.
10. *Ibid.*, pp. 49-50.
11. Schwarz (1980), pp. 247-248.
12. Stanford (1974, 1990a).
13. Rhine (1961), p. 243.
14. *Ibid.*, p. 244.
15. Wilson (1987), p. 183.
16. Rhine (1961), pp. 245-246.
17. Rhine (1963).
18. Rhine (1981).
19. Virtanen (1990).
20. Rinaldi & Piccinni (1982).
21. Gurney, Myers & Podmore (1886a), p. 144.
22. Sidgwick et al. (1894).
23. Tyrrell (1953).
24. Hart (1956).
25. Haraldsson (1991, August).
26. Myers (1903).
27. Gurney, Myers & Podmore (1886a, 1886b).
28. See Tyrrell (1953) and Price (1939, 1940, 1948, 1953, 1959).
29. Osis (1981).
30. Rhine (1962).
31. Rhine (1981), Schouten (1982).

32. See Schouten (1979, 1981, 1982) and Rhine (1978, 1981).
33. See Schouten (1979, 1981, 1982).
34. Persinger (1985; 1986; 1987; 1988, August); Persinger & Krippner (1987, 1989); Persinger & Schaut (1987).
35. See Adams (1986, 1987); Bierman & Van Gelderen (1994, August); Broughton & Higgins (1994, August); Carpenter (1995, August); Dalton & Stevens (1995); Dalton & Utts (1995, August); Gissurarson (1992); Krippner (1994); Krippner & Persinger (1993, August); Radin (1992, August); Radin & Bisaga (1991, August); Radin, McAlpine & Cunningham (1994); Spottiswoode (1993, August); Tart (1987, 1998a, 1988b); Williams, Roe, Upchurch & Lawrence (1994, August); and Zilberman (1991, 1995).
36. See Persinger (1988, August) and Persinger & Krippner (1989).
37. See Radin, McAlpine & Cunningham (1994) and Adair (1991).
38. Persinger (1979).
39. Tyrrell (1946).
40. Rhine (1978, 1981).
41. Rao (1986).
42. Ehrenwald (1977, 1978).
43. Bergson (1914).
44. Torrey (1992).
45. Freud (1963).
46. Irwin(1989).
47. Broughton (1991).
48. Sidgwick et al. (1894).

49. Rinaldi & Piccinini (1982).
50. Schouten (1979, 1984).
51. Ullman (1987).
52. Cox (1956).
53. Taylor (1980).
54. Schriever (1987).
55. Sondow (1988).
56. Schouten (1981).
57. See Hall, McFeaters & Loftus (1987); Loftus (1981); Loftus & Greene (1980); and Loftus, Miller & Burns (1978).
58. Harris (1986).
59. Hearne (1984).
60. Tyrrell (1953).
61. Haight (1979).
62. Rhine, 1970, p. 150.
63. Palmer (1979); McClenon (1990).
64. Efron (1963).
65. Rhine (1961).
66. Stevenson (1987).
67. Fisher (1984).
68. Rhine & Feather (1962).

Chapter 3.
Chasing the Poltergeist

1. Roll (1977a).
2. Bender (1968).
3. Hastings (1978).
4. Roll (1977a, 1977b, 1978a, 1978b, 1982b).
5. Palmer (1979).
6. Gauld & Cornell (1979).
7. Zorab & MacKenzie (1980).
8. Rogo (1977).
9. Pierce (1973).
10. Stevenson (1972a).
11. Irwin (1994).
12. Roll & Tringale (1983).
13. Roll (1978a).
14. Roll & Montagno (1983).
15. Irwin (1994).

16. Fodor (1964).
17. Rogo (1974).
18. Owen (1978).
19. Taboas (1980, 1984); Taboas & Alvarado (1981).
20. Roll (1969, 1972).
21. Roll (1977a).
22. Randi (1985).
23. Roll (1993, August).
24. Frazier (1995)
25. Roll (1977a, 1977b).
26. Gauld & Cornell (1979).
27. Roll (1977b).
28. Munson (1987).
29. Lambert (1955).
30. Gauld & Cornell (1979).
31. Roll, Burdick, & Joines (1973).
32. Persinger & Cameron (1986).

Chapter 4.
Astral Wanderings

1. Blackmore (1982a), p. 9.
2. Grof (1990).
3. Taken from Myers (1903).
4. Gauld (1982), pp. 222-223.
5. Grosso (1976).
6. Mitchell (1981).
7. Tyrrell (1953), p. 144.
8. MacKenzie (1971), pp. 82.
9. Mitchell (1981), p. 106.
10. Blackmore (1982a), p. 12.
11. Osis & Haraldsson (1977c).
12. Mitchell (1981).
13. Crookall (1970).
14. See Muldoon & Carrington (1929), for instance.
15. Mitchell (1981).
16. Muldoon & Carrington (1929).
17. Roll (1982b).
18. Anderson (1981).
19. Ehrenwald (1974).
20. Noyes (1972).
21. Myers, Austrin, Grisso & Nickeson (1983); Smith & Irwin (1981).
22. Rogo (1978); Sagan (1977); Honegger (1983).
23. Blackmore (1983a).
24. Palmer (1978, 1986).
25. Blackmore (1984b).
26. Blackmore (1983c).
27. Munro & Persinger (1992).
28. Hart (1954); Green (1967); Blackmore (1978, 1982b, 1982c, 1984a);

Palmer (1979); Myers, Austrin, Grisso & Nickeson (1983); Irwin 1980); Tart (1971).
29. Haraldsson, Gudmusdottir, Ragnarsson & Johnsson (1977).
30. Kohr (1980).
31. Blackmore (1984a).
32. Alvarado (1984).
33. Shiels (1978).
34. Palmer & Vassar (1974); Irwin (1979, 1980, 1986); Cook & Irwin (1983); Blackmore (1982c, 1983c, 1986b).
35. Cook & Irwin (1983); Blackmore (1983c, 1986b).
36. Irwin (1980, 1981); Myers, Austrin, Grisson & Nickeson (1983); Wilson & Barber (1982); Stanford (1987), but see also Gabbard, Jones & Twemlow (1980).
37. Blackmore (1982b, 1982c, 1983a, 1984a, 1986a, 1986b); Irwin (1986); Stanford (1990b).
38. Stanford (1990b).
39. Mitchell (1981).
40. Palmer & Vassar (1974).
41. Palmer & Lieberman 1975).
42. Smith & Irwin (1981).
43. Tart (1968).
44. Blackmore (1982c).
45. Tart (1967, 1969).
46. Mitchell (1981).
47. Osis & McCormick (1980).
48. Morris (1974); Morris, Harary, Janis, Hartwell & Roll (1978).

Chapter 5.
Healers, Shamans, Saints and Seers.

1. Cunliffe (1980).
2. Booth (1986).
3. Emery (1996).
4. Frazier & Randi (1986); Lyons & Truzzi (1991); Nickell (1994).
5. Christopher (1970), p. 106.
6. Kurtz (1986), p. 262.
7. Blackmore (1983b).
8. Roney-Dougal (1991, August).
9. Rubin & Honorton (1971); Thalbourne, Delin, Barlow & Steen (1992-1993).

10. Harris (1986); Hoebens (1982, 1986a, 1986b).
11. Lyons & Truzzi (1991).
12. See Wiseman, West & Stemman (1996) for a review of such studies.
13. Kaufman (1979).
14. Hansen (1982).
15. Betz (1995a, 1995b).
16. Krippner (1980).
17. Seligman (1975).
18. See Ader (1981).
19. Haraldsson & Olafsson (1980).
20. Randi (1987).
21. In Edge, Morris, Palmer & Rush (1986).
22. Randi (1979).
23. Randi (1987).
24. See Fuller (1974).
25. Nolen (1975).
26. Granone (1972).
27. Hoy (1981).
28. Lincoln & Wood (1979).
29. Azuma & Stevenson (1987).
30. Grad (1977).
31. Grad, Cadoret & Paul (1961).
32. Watkins & Watkins (1971); Watkins, Watkins, & Wells (1973); Wells & Klein (1972); Wells & Watkins (1975).
33. Wirth, Johnson, Harvath & MacGregor (1992).
34. Snel & Van der Sijde (1990-1991).
35. Wirth (1989, August; 1990), but see also the nonsignificant study of the effect of healing and prayer on diabetes mellitus by Wirth & Mitchell (1994).
36. Grad (1963, 1964); MacDonald, Hickman & Dakin (1977); Solfvin (1982); Saklani (1988a, 1988b, 1989, August, 1990, 1992, August); Scofield & Hodges (1991).
37. Grad (1964, 1965); Dean (1983a, 1983b); Dean & Brahme (1975); Grad & Dean (1984); Schwartz, De Mattei, Brahme & Spottiswoode (1987); Saklani (1988a, 1988b); Rein & McCraty (1994), but see also Fenwick & Hopkins (1986)
38. Smith (1968, 1972); Edge (1980b).

39. Barry (1968a, 1968b);
Tedder & Monty (1981).
40. Nash (1984b).
41. Dolin, Davydov, Moro-
zova & Shumov (1993,
August).
42. Braud & Schlitz (1983,
1988); Braud, Schlitz,
Collins & Klitch (1985);
Dolin, Dymov & Khatch-
enkov (1993, August).
Radin, Taylor & Braud
(1993, August).
43. Baumann, Stewart & Roll
(1986).
44. Braud (1988, August,
1990); Braud, Davis &
Wood (1979).
45. Braud, Schlitz & Schmidt
(1990).
46. Nash (1984b); Saklani
(1988a, 1988b).
47. Grad, Cadoret & Paul
(1961).
48. Watkins & Watkins
(1971); Rein (1986); Wirth
(1989, August; 1990).
49. Motoyama (1978).
50. Stokes (1980).
51. Sjolund, Terenius &
Erikson (1977).
52. Bowers (1979).
53. Haynes (1984).
54. Reichbart (1976).
55. Reichbart (1978).
56. Brookes-Smith (1973).
57. Winkelman (1983).
58. McKee (1982).
59. Giesler (1985).
60. Saklani (1988a, 1988b).
61. Dennett (1985); Leikind
& McCarthy (1985).
62. Barker (1979).
63. Nickell & Fisher (1987).
64. See Rogo (1981) and
White (1982).
65. Schwarz (1980).
66. Alvarado (1987).
67. Alvarado (1983).
68. Rogo (1977).
69. David-Neel (1971).
70. White (1985, 1990).

Chapter 6.
Is Psi Real?

1. Bell (1964).
2. Richet (1884, December;
1888).
3. Troland (1917); Coover
(1917); Estabrooks (1927).
4. Dessoir (1889).
5. Rhine & Pratt (1954).

6. Schmidt (1969).
7. See Sinclair (1930/1962)
and Warcollier (1948/1963).
8. Puthoff & Targ (1979);
Targ & Puthoff (1977);
Targ, Puthoff & May
(1979).
9. Targ, Puthoff & May
(1979), p. 88.
10. Ullman, Krippner &
Vaughn (1973).
11. Ullman, Krippner &
Vaughn (1973), p. 131.
12. Ullman, Krippner &
Vaughn (1973), p. 131.
13. Schmidt (1970).
14. Braud (1979).
15. Schmidt (1975a, 1975b,
1984).
16. See Schmidt (1976, 1981,
1983, 1986, 1993); Terry &
Schmidt (1978); Gruber
(1980); Schmidt, Morris &
Rudolph (1986); and
Schmidt & Schlitz (1988,
August).
17. Rhine (1974).
18. Wiesner & Thouless
(1942); Thouless & Wiesner
(1948).
19. Beloff (1979).
20. Both quotations are taken
from Collins & Pinch
(1979), p. 244.
21. Taken from Feuer (1974),
p. 253.
22. Feuer (1974), p. 254.
23. Fox (1988), p. 45.
24. Beloff (1983).
25. Alcock (1981).
26. Tart (1982).
27. Tart & Lebore (1986).
28. Irwin (1985).
29. Baker (1990).
30. Hovland, Janis & Kelly
(1953).
31. Festinger (1957).
32. Randi (1980).
33. Marks & Kammann
(1980).
34. Abelson & Rosenberg
(1958).
35. See Asch (1958); Schacter
(1951); and Milgrim (1963,
1968).
36. See Rokeach (1960).
37. Marshall (1990).
38. Don, Warren, McDo-
nough & Collura (1988).
39. Gardner (1981) writing
about the experiment
reported in Tart (1976).
40. Diaconis (1978).
41. Tart (1976).

42. Puthoff, Targ & Tart
(1980).
43. Marks & Kammann
(1978, 1980).
44. Tart, Puthoff & Targ
(1980).
45. Marks & Scott (1986).
46. Bisaha & Dunne (1979).
47. Marks (1986).
48. Schlitz & Gruber (1980).
49. Schlitz & Gruber (1981).
50. Hyman (1986).
51. Child, Kanthamani &
Sweeney (1977).
52. Palmer (1983, 1984);
Palmer & Kramer (1986).
53. Akers (1984).
54. Egely (1986).
55. Taylor (1980).
56. Barry (1968a, 1968b).
57. Richmond (1952).
58. Johnson (1982).
59. Pleass & Dey (1987).
60. Palmer & Lieberman
(1976).
61. Nash (1982).
62. Palmer & Lieberman
(1975).
63. Palmer & Vassar (1974).
64. Honorton, Ferrari & Bem
(1990, August).
65. Krishna & Rao (1991,
August).
66. Akers (1984).
67. Tyrrell (1936).
68. Blackmore (1984c) com-
menting on Spinelli (1978).
69. Sinclair (1930/1962) and
Warcollier (1948/1964).
70. Targ & Puthoff (1977).
71. Jahn & Dunne (1987).
72. Hansen, Utts & Mark-
wick (1991, August).
73. Akers (1984).
74. Brown (1953, 1955, 1957);
Gilmore (1989); Alcock
(1981).
75. Hardy, Harvie & Koestler
(1975); Koestler (1978).
76. Alcock (1981); Calkins
(1980); Girden (1978); Moss
& Butler (1978); Gilmore
(1989).
77. Alcock (1984), p. 317.
78. Hansel (1980) on Schmidt
(1969).
79. Akers (1984, 1985).
80. Akers (1984).
81. Hyman (1983).
82. Stenger (1990) comment-
ing on Targ & Puthoff
(1977).
83. Akers (1984)
84. Alcock (1981).

85. Stanford (1982).
86. Blackmore (1980).
87. Hansel (1966, 1980).
88. Gurney (1888-1889).
89. Hansel (1966, 1980).
90. Hansel (1966, 1980).
91. Stevenson (1967).
92. Irwin (1994).
93. Hasted (1981).
94. Gardner (1986).
95. Pamplin & Collins (1975).
96. Randi (1983a, 1983b, 1986).
97. Eisenbud (1967, 1977a, 1977b, 1982); Eisenbud, Pratt & Stevenson (1981).
98. Akers (1984).
99. Soal & Bateman (1954).
100. Scott and Haskell (1974).
101. Markwick (1978).
102. Hansel (1980).
103. Pratt & Woodruff (1939).
104. Broad & Wade (1982); Kohn (1986).
105. Gardner (1986).
106. Kennedy & Taddonio (1976); Kennedy (1994a, 1994b).
107. Schmidt (1970).
108. See Parker (1977) & Sargent (1980).
109. See Weiner & Zingrone (1986) and White (1976) for a review of such evidence.
110. Millar (1978).
111. Leggett (1987b).
112. Griffin (1988a).
113. Beloff (1984).
114. Beloff (1984).
115. Walti (1990).
116. Gardner (1991).
117. Honorton (1985); Hyman (1985).
118. Honorton & Ferrari (1989); Schechter (1984); Braud (1985); Braud, Schlitz & Schmidt (1990); Radin, May Thomson (1986); Radin & Ferrari (1991); Watt (1991, August); Honorton, Ferrari & Bem (1990, August); Milton (1993, August; 1994, August); Haraldsson & Houtkooper (1994, August); Stanford & Stein (1994).
119. Radin, May & Thomson (1986).

Chapter 7.
Time, Space and Mind.

1. Rao (1977).
2. Flew (1989).
3. See Morris (1983) for a discussion.
4. Popper (1959).
5. Bohm & Peat (1987).
6. Turing (1964).
7. Harman (1993).
8. Tart (1972).
9. See Feyerbend (1981), Dolby (1979), Collins & Pinch (1982), and Woolgar (1988), for example.
10. Schmeidler (1972).
11. Wheeler (1962).
12. Parker (1991).
13. Murphy (1964).
14. Toben & Wolf (1982).
15. Morris (1990).
16. Friedman (1991).
17. Gödel (1949a, 1949b).
18. Tipler (1974).
19. Herbert (1988).
20. Morris & Thorne (1988); Morris, Thorne & Yurtsever (1988).
21. See Lemonich (May 13, 1991), Peterson (1994) and Travis (1992) for a discussion of the controversies surrounding Gott time machines.
22. Halpern (1992).
23. Targ, Puthoff & May (1979); Rauscher (1979, 1983a, 1983b); Ramon & Rauscher (1980).
24. Rucker (1984).
25. Zöllner (1901).
26. Ouspensky (1912/1970, 1931/1971).
27. Rhine (1955).
28. Rhine (1961), pp. 198-199.
29. Dunne (1938).
30. Broad (1953, 1978); Lawden (1982).
31. Mundle (1964).
32. Everett (1957).
33. One of the earliest proponents of an "electromagnetic" theory of psi was Joseph Glanvill, a contemporary of Newton, who proposed that telepathic exchanges were caused by the vibrations of the "ether." See Jaki (1969). More modern proponents of electromagnetic theories of psi include Kazhinsky

(1962), Taylor (1975), and Becker (1990, 1992).
34. Hammond (1952) and Ruderfer (1968, 1980).
35. Vasiliev (1976); Targ & Puthoff (1977); Ullman & Krippner (1969).
36. Kogan (1968); Persinger (1979).
37. See Puthoff & Targ (1979).
38. Osis (1965); Dunne & Jahn (1992).
39. Schlitz & Gruber (1980, 1981); Markwick & Beloff (1983); Tedder & Monty (1981); Tedder & Braud (1981); Tedder & Bloor (1982), to name a few.
40. Due to the law of conservation of momentum, such a process is forbidden in empty space, but may occur in the presence of matter, as pointed out by Leggett (1987b).
41. Ruderfer (1974); Dobbs (1965, 1967).
42. Feinberg (1975).
43. Stokes (1985); Bell (1986); Hiley (1986).
44. Clay & Crouch (1974).
45. Herbert (1988).
46. Schouten (1982).
47. See Green (1960) and Orme (1974).
48. Sondow (1982).
49. Schouten (1991, August).
50. Rinaldi & Piccinini (1952).
51. Tart (1983).
52. Honorton & Ferrari (1989).
53. Schriever (1987).
54. Sondow (1988).
55. Haight (1979).
56. Schouten (1981).
57. Aspect, Dalibard and Roger (1982).
58. See Stokes (1987) or Stokes (1991) for instance.
59. Radin (1989).
60. Edge (1980a, 1985).
61. Braude (1986); Roll (1987).
62. Penrose (1987a, 1989, 1994).
63. Eccles (1979, 1980); Popper & Eccles (1977).
64. Bohm (1980); Bohm & Peat (1987).
65. Pribram (1971, 1978).
66. Rao (1978).
67. Darling (1995).

68. See Roll (1982b); Villars (1983); Nash (1983, 1984a); and Giroldini (1986), for instance.
69. Mattuck (1977, 1982, 1984); Schmidt (1975a, 1975b, 1984); and Walker (1975, 1984).
70. See Stokes (1987) or Stokes (1991), for instance.
71. Roll (1988).
72. Beloff (1978).
73. Rogo (1977).
74. Schatzman (1980).
75. Goodsort (1981).
76. David-Neel (1971).
77. Tyrrell (1953), p. 119.
78. James (1909/1960).
79. Myers (1903).
80. Price (1939, 1940, 1948, 1953, 1959, 1961).
81. Grosso (1979).
82. Murphy (1945, 1973).
83. Roll (1982a, 1984).
84. Roll (1961, 1964, 1966, 1979, 1981, 1982a, 1982b, 1983).

Chapter 8.
Mind and Matter.

1. Shear (1995)
2. Mason (1962), p. 42.
3. Butterfield (1957).
4. Koestler (1972, 1978).
5. Westfall (1977).
6. Lockwood (1989).
7. Mitchell (1979).
8. Goswami (1993).
9. See Skinner (1953), for instance.
10. Churchland (1989, 1995).
11. Dennett (1988), p. 74.
12. Griffin (1988a, 1988b, 1994).
13. Seager (1995)
14. Backster (1968).
15. Penrose (1987b).
16. Popper & Eccles (1977).
17. Pagels (1988).
18. Toffoli (1982).
19. Rhine (1972).
20. Beloff (1981).
21. Humphrey (1996), p. 64.
22. Beloff (1983).
23. Beloff (1981).
24. Dommeyer (1982).
25. Gurney (1887).
26. Nash (1976).
27. Penrose (1987b), Layzer (1990), Searle (1990, January).
28. Turing (1950).

29. Penrose (1987b, 1989, 1994).
30. Turing (1950).
31. Penrose (1994); Clark (1994).
32. Churchland (1995).
33. Searle (1987; 1990, January).
34. Clark (1989).
35. Lockwood (1989).
36. Lockwood (1989), p. 124.
37. Cowan & Sharp (1988).
38. Churchland (1989).
39. Churchland (1995).
40. Dennett (1991).
41. Eccles (1953), p. 285.
42. Bohr (1958); Eddington (1935), Margenau (1984); Squires (1990); Stapp (1992).
43. Penrose (1987a).
44. Penrose (1994).
45. Hameroff (1994).
46. Penrose (1994).
47. Grush & Churchland (1995).
48. Penrose & Hameroff (1995).
49. Hodgson (1991).
50. Leggett (1987a).
51. Penrose (1994).
52. Nunn, Clark & Blott (1994).
53. Thouless & Wiesner (1948).
54. Honorton & Tremmel (1979).
55. Rogo (1980).
56. Roll (1978a).
57. Varvoglis & McCarthy (1982).
58. Baumann, Stewart & Roll (1986).
59. Rein (1986).
60. Warcollier (1948/1963).
61. Beloff (1980).
62. Beloff (1990).
63. Eccles (1953, 1970, 1977, 1979, 1980, 1983, 1987, 1989); Eccles & Robinson (1984); Popper & Eccles (1977).
64. Koch & Crick (1991).
65. Wilson, Scalaidhe & Goldman-Rakic (1993).
66. Koch & Crick (1991).
67. Friedman-Hill, Robertson & Triesman (1995).
68. Crick (1994).
69. Edelman & Jononi (1995).
70. Bard (1968).
71. Efron (1963).
72. See Miller (1990).

73. Gallup (1977).
74. Sperry, Zaidel & Zaidel (1979).
75. Eccles (1977).
76. Popper & Eccles (1977), p. 541.
77. Penfield (1975).
78. Thomson (1993).
79. Herbert (1993).
80. Popper & Eccles (1977).
81. Eccles (1979) discussing Held & Hein (1963).
82. Hilgard (1977).
83. Ramachandran (1980).
84. LeDoux (1985).
85. O'Keefe (1985).
86. Oakley (1985a, 1985b).
87. Oakely & Eames (1985).
88. Ludwig, Brandsma, Wilbur, Bendfeldt & Jameson (1972).
89. Libet (1989, 1991).
90. Eccles (1983), p. 45.
91. Goldberg (1985).
92. Libet (1994).
93. Churchland (1995).
94. Burns (1993).
95. Popper & Eccles (1977).
96. Thomson (1993).
97. MacKay (1980).
98. Harth (1982), p. 191.
99. Gazzaniga (1992).
100. Libet (1994).
101. Hilgard (1977), p. 111.
102. Henninger (1992).
103. Marcel (1988); Rafal, Smith, Krantz, Cohen & Brennan (1990).
104. Crick (1994).
105. Marcel (1988); Flanagan (1992).
106. Cowey (1991); Reber (1992).
107. Fodor (1983).
108. Gazzaniga (1985, 1989).
109. Churchland (1986).

Chapter 9.
Smoke and Mirrors;
Dreams and Ghosts.

1. Wilson (1987).
2. Leahey and Leahey (1983).
3. Hansel (1980), p. 77.
4. See Oppenheim (1985) for more details.
5. Randi (1980), p. 9.
6. Harris (1986).
7. Jenkins (1982).
8. Hansel (1966).
9. James (1910).
10. Hyman (1977).

11. Stevenson (1978); Stevenson & Beloff (1980).
12. Ravaldini, Biondi & Stevenson (1990).
13. Coleman (1991).
14. McAdams & Bayless (1981).
15. Harris (1986).
16. Described in Myers (1903).
17. Wilson (1987).
18. Zorab (1962).
19. Palmer (1979).
20. Gallup (1982).
21. Haraldsson (1981).
22. Sidgwick et al. (1894).
23. West (1990).
24. Rees (1971); Kalish and Reynolds (1974).
25. Grof (1990).
26. Myers (1903).
27. Cameron & Roll (1983).
28. Maher & Schmeidler (1975); Maher & Hansen (1992a, August; 1992b, 1995); Roll, Maher & Brown (1992, August).
29. Radin & Roll (1994, August).
30. Hart (1959).
31. Moody (1975).
32. Sabom (1982); Pasricha (1993, 1995); Ring (1980).
33. Ring (1979, 1980).
34. Thorton (1984); Wilson (1928); Carr (1982); and Persinger (1983).
35. Rodin (1980) and Schnaper (1980).
36. Shaver (1986); Blackmore (1993).
37. Blackmore (1991b, 1992); Siegel (1980).
38. Siegel (1977).
39. Bennett, Davis & Giannini (1985); Goldmann, Shah & Hebden (1987); Evans & Richardson (1988); Furlong (1990); Pearson (1961); Kihlstrom, Schachter, Cork, Hurt & Behr (1990); Millar & Watkinson (1983).
40. Twemlow & Gabbard (1984); Council, Greyson & Huff (1986, August).
41. Barrett (1926); Osis (1961); Osis & Haraldsson (1977a, 1977b).
42. Quotation taken from Osis (1961), p. 16.
43. Grosso (1981).

Chapter 10.
Reincarnation.

1. Gallup & Newport (1992).
2. Edwards (1992); Tertullian (1992).
3. Stokes (1982, 1987); Wilber (1990).
4. Lawden (1989).
5. Nash (1995).
6. Wilber (1990).
7. Cermina (1967); Stearn (1967); Woodward (1971), for instance.
8. Woodward (1971), p. 61.
9. Bernstein (1956).
10. Ducasse (1961).
11. See Goldberg (1982), Wambaugh (1978) and Weiss (1988).
12. Tazari (1990).
13. Harris (1986).
14. Venn (1986).
15. Cook, Pasricha, Samararatne, Maung & Stevenson (1983); Pasricha & Stevenson (1979); Stevenson (1960a, 1960b, 1966, 1970a, 1972b, 1973, 1974a, 1974b, 1974c, 1975, 1977a, 1977b, 1977c, 1980, 1983a, 1983b, 1986, 1987, 1988a, 1998b, 1989, 1990, 1993); Stevenson & Chadha (1988); Stevenson & Pasricha (1979, 1980); Stevenson, Pasricha & Samararatne (1988).
16. Pasricha & Barker (1981); Pasricha (19992a, 1992b); Akolkar (1992); Keil (1991); Mills, Haraldsson & Keil (1994).
17. Pasricha & Barker (1981).
18. Barker & Pasricha (1979).
19. Palmer (1979).
20. Stevenson (1986).
21. Matlock (1989, August).
22. Stevenson (1993).
23. Stevenson (1974c).
24. Stevenson (1988a, 1989, 1992).
25. Stevenson (1990).
26. Cook et al. (1983).
27. Stevenson (1974d, 1976, 1984); Stevenson & Pasricha (1979, 1980).
28. Stevenson (1976).
29. Rogo (1987).
30. Stevenson & Pasricha (1980).
31. Akolkar (1992).
32. Thomason (1987).

33. Stevenson (1987).
34. Matlock (1990).
35. Stevenson & Chadha (1988).
36. Stevenson (1987).
37. Stevenson (1986); Cook (1986).
38. Stevenson (1987).
39. Mills (1989).
40. Stevenson, Pasricha & Samraratne (1988).
41. Wilson (1987, 1988).
42. Matlock (1990); Pasricha (1978); Mills (1989).
43. Stevenson (1977b, 1987).
44. Stevenson (1972b).
45. Stevenson (1987, 1990).
46. Stevenson (1974b).
47. Stevens (1887).
48. Anderson (1980).
49. Stevenson (1987), p. 124.
50. Hyslop (1909).
51. Rogo (1989).

Chapter 11.
Into the Twilight Zone.

1. MacDougall (1907a, 1907b).
2. Carrington (1907).
3. Carpenter (1984).
4. Twining (1915).
5. Watters (1935).
6. Carrington (1921).
7. Doyle (1921).
8. Kilner (1920).
9. Burton, Joines & Stevens (1975); Robinson, Maeir, O'Hallaren, Daniels & Staehel (1975); Montandon (1977); Pehek, Kyler & Faust (1976); Watkins & Bickel (1986, 1989).
10. Hubacher & Moss (1976); Watkins & Bickel (1986).
11. Kejariwal, Chattopadhya & Choudhury (1983).
12. Watkins & Bickel (1986).
13. See Jurgenson (1964), Bayless (1959), and Bayless (1980).
14. Raudive (1971).
15. Smith (1972, 1974).
16. Ellis (1973).
17. Keil (1980).
18. Hovelman (1982).
19. Rogo & Bayless (1979).
20. See Hardy (1979), for instance.

Chapter 12. *The Mind's Fate Upon Death.*

1. Ojemann (1983).
2. Gazzaniga (1989).
3. Kinsbourne & Warrington (1964).
4. See Squire (1987) and Krupa, Thompson & Thompson (1993).
5. See Squire (1987), Baringa (1990), Zhong & Wu (1990), Rose (1992), and Fanselow (1993).
6. Eccles (1979); Eccles & Robinson (1984).
7. Stevenson (1981).
8. Gauld (1982).
9. Lund (1985); James (1898/ 1992).
10. Beyerstein (1987).
11. Penelhum (1987).
12. Geach (1987).
13. Flew (1987, 1991).
14. Oppenheimer (1986); Parfit (1987).
15. Fjermedal (1987); Moravec (1988).
16. Tipler (1994).
17. Dennett (1991); Blackmore (1991a, 1993).
18. Priest (1991).
19. James (1890/1992).
20. Clark (1995).
21. Parfit (1987).

Chapter 13. *Mind and Cosmos.*

1. Crick (1981); Hoyle (1983); Hoyle & Wickramasinghe (1981, 1988).
2. Hart (1990); Dawkins (1987).
3. Casti (1989).
4. Fox (1988).
5. See Pool (1990), Amato (1994), and Feng, Park & Rebek (1992).
6. Ducasse (1961).
7. Birch (1988).
8. Nash (1984b).
9. Eccles (1989).
10. de Beauregard (1979).
11. Harman (1993).
12. Koestler (1967, 1972, 1978).
13. Koestler (1978), p. 175.
14. Day (1984).
15. Sheldrake (1981, 1983a 1983b, 1988a, 1988b, 1990).
16. Blackmore (1985b).
17. Blackmore (1985a).
18. Sheldrake (1983a, 1988b).
19. See Stokes (1995) for a more thorough discussion of the methodological flaws in the research purporting to support Sheldrake's theory.
20. Stahl (1990); Thaler (1994); Culotta (1994).
21. Davies (1983).
22. Penrose (1986).
23. Barrow & Tipler (1986).
24. Griffin & Rees (1989).
25. Greenstein (1988).
26. Barrow & Tipler (1986); Gribbin & Rees (1989); Greenstein (1988).
27. Greenstein (1988).
28. Barrow & Tipler (1986).
29. Tryon (1973).
30. Stace (1960).
31. McGinn (1995).
32. Campbell (1964).
33. Barrow & Tipler (1986).
34. Markov (1985).
35. Gale (1990).
36. Linde (1985).

Bibliography

Abelson, R.P., & Rosenberg, M.J. (1988). Symbolic psychologic: A model of attitudinal cognition. *Behavioral Science, 3*, 1–13.

Adair, R.K. (1991). Constraints on biological effects of weak extremely-low-frequency electromagnetic fields. *Physical Review A, 43*, 1039–1048.

Adams, M.H. (1986). Variability in remote-viewing performance: Possible relationship to the geomagnetic field. In D.H. Weiner & D.I. Radin (Eds.), *Research in parapsychology, 1985* (p. 25). Metuchen, NJ: Scarecrow Press.

Adams, M.H. (1987). Persistent temporal relationship of ganzfeld results to geomagnetic activity. Appropriateness of using standard geomagnetic indices. In D.H. Weiner & R.D. Nelson (Eds.), *Research in parapsychology, 1986* (p. 78). Metuchen, NJ: Scarecrow Press.

Ader, R. (1981). *Psychoimmunology.* New York: Academic Press.

Akers, C. (1984). Methodological criticisms of parapsychology. In S. Krippner (Ed.), *Advances in parapsychological research, Volume 4* (pp. 112–164). Jefferson, NC: McFarland.

Akers, C. (1985). Can meta-analysis resolve the ESP controversy? in P. Kurtz (Ed.), *A skeptic's handbook of parapsychology* (pp. 611–627). Buffalo, NY: Prometheus Books.

Akolkar, V.V. (1992). Search for Sharada: Report of a case and its investigation. *Journal of the American Society for Psychical Research, 86*, 206–247.

Alcock, J.E. (1981). *Parapsychology: science or magic?* New York: Pergamon Press.

Alcock, J.E. (1984). Parapsychology's past eight years. A lack of progress report. *Skeptical Inquirer, 8*, 312 320.

Alvadaro, C.S. (1983). Paranormal faces: The Belmez case. *Theta, 11*, 38–41.

Alvarado, C.S. (1984). Phenomenological aspects of out-of body experiences: A report of three studies. *Journal of the American Society for Psychical Research, 78*, 219 240.

Alvarado, C.S. (1987). Observations of luminous phenomena around the human body: A review. *Journal of the Society for Psychical Research, 54*, 38–60.

Amato, I. (1992). Capturing chemical evolution in a jar. *Science, 255*, 800.

Anderson, R.I. (1980). The Watseka Wonder: A critical re-evaluation. *Theta, 8*(4), 6–10.

Anderson, R.I. (1981). Contemporary survival research: A critical review. *Parapsychology Review, 12*(5), 8–13.

Asch, S.E. (1958). Effects of group pressure upon the modification and distortion of judgments. In E. Maccoby, T. Newcomb & E. Hartley (Eds.), *Readings in social psychology* (pp. 174–183). New York: Holt, Rhinehart & Winston.

Aspect, A.J., Dalibard, J., & Roger, G. (1982). Experimental test of Bell's inequalities using time varying analyzers. *Physical Review Letters, 49*, 1804–1807.

Azuma, N., & Stevenson, I. (1987). Difficulties confronting investigators of "psychic surgery" in the Phillipines. *Parapsychology Review, 18*(2), 6–8.

Backster, C. (1968). Evidence of a primary perception in plant life. *International Journal of Parapsychology, 10*, 329–348.

Baker, R.A. (1990). *They call it hypnosis.* Buffalo, NY: Prometheus Books.

Bard, P. (1968). Postural coordination and locomotion and their central control. In V.B. Mountcastle (Ed.), *Medical physiology* (pp. 1750–1770). St Louis, MO: Mosby CV.

Baringa, M. (1990). The tide of memory, turning. *Science, 248*, 1603–1605.

Barker, D.R. (1979). Psi phenomena in Tibetan culture. In W.G. Roll (Ed.), *Research in parapsychology, 1978* (pp. 52–54). Metuchen, NJ: Scarecrow Press.

Barker, D.R., & Pasricha, S. (1979). Reincarnation cases in Fatehabad: A systematic survey in North India. *Journal of Asian and African Studies, 14,* 231–240.

Barrett, W. (1926). *Death-bed visions.* London: Methuen.

Barrow, J.D., & Tipler, F.S. (1986). *The anthropic cosmological principle.* New York: Oxford University Press.

Barry, J. (1968a). General and comparative study of the psychokinetic effect on fungus culture. *Journal of Parapsychology, 32,* 237–243.

Barry, J. (1968b). PK on fungus growth. *Journal of Parapsychology, 32,* 55. (Abstract.)

Baumann, S., Stewart, J.L., & Roll, W.G. (1986). Preliminary results from the use of two novel detectors for psychokinesis. In D.H. Weiner & D.I. Radin (Eds.), *Research in parapsychology, 1985* (pp. 59–62). Metuchen, NJ: Scarecrow Press.

Bayless, R. (1959). [Letter to the Editor.] *Journal of the American Society for Psychical Research, 40,* 35–38.

Bayless, R. (1980). Voices and raps: Tape-recorded psychokinesis. *Theta, 8*(2), 8–10.

Becker, R.O. (1990). The relationship between bioelectromagnetics and psychic phenomena. *ASPR Newsletter, XVI,* 11–14.

Becker, R.O. (1992). Electromagnetism and psi phenomena. *Journal of the American Society for Psychical Research, 86,* 1–17.

Bell, J.S. (1964). On the Einstein-Podolsky-Rosen paradox. *Physics, 1,* 195–200.

Bell, J.S. (1986). [Transcript of radio interview.] In P.C.W. Davies & J.R. Brown (Eds.), *The ghost in the atom* (pp. 45–57). New York: Cambridge University Press.

Beloff, J. (1978). Explaining the paranormal with epilogue—1977. In J. Ludwig (Ed.), *Philosophy and parapsychology* (pp. 353–370). Buffalo, NY: Prometheus Books.

Beloff, J. (1979). The categories of psi: The case for retention. *European Journal of Parapsychology, 3,* 69–77.

Beloff, J. (1980). Could there be a physical explanation for psi? *Journal of the Society for Psychical Research, 50,* 263–272.

Beloff, J. (1981). J.B. Rhine on the nature of psi. *Journal of Parapsychology, 45,* 41–54.

Beloff, J. (1983). Three open questions. In W.G. Roll, J. Beloff & R.A. White (Eds.), *Research in parapsychology, 1982* (pp. 315–327). Metuchen, NJ: Scarecrow Press.

Beloff, J. (1984). Research strategies for dealing with unstable phenomena. *Parapsychology Review, 15*(1), 1–7.

Beloff, J. (1990). *The relentless question: Reflections on the paranormal.* Jefferson, NC: McFarland & Co.

Bender, H. (1968). Physikalische untersuchung des spufalles in Rosenheim 1975. *Zeitschrift fur parapsychologie und Grenzebiete der Psychologie, ll,* 113–131.

Bennett, H.L., Davis, H.S. & Giannini, J.A. (1985). Non verbal response to intraoperative conversation. *British Journal of Anaesthesia, 57,* 174–179.

Bergson, H. (1914). Presidential address to the Society for Psychical Research (1913). *Proceedings of the Society for Psychical Research, 27,* 157–175.

Bernstein, M. (1956). *The search for Bridey Murphy.* Garden City, NY: Doubleday.

Betz, H-D. (1995a). Unconventional water detection: field test of the dowsing technique in dry zones: Part I. *Journal of Scientific Exploration, 9,* 1–43.

Betz, H-D. (1995b). Unconventional water detection: field test of the dowsing technique in dry zones: Part 2. Journal *of Scientific Exploration, 9,* 159–189.

Beyerstein, B.L. (1987). The brain and consciousness: Implications for psi phenomena. *Skeptical Inquirer, 12,* 163–173.

Bierman, D.J., & Van Gelderen, W.J.M. (1994, August). Geomagnetic activity and PK on a low and high trial-rate RNG. Paper presented at the 37th annual convention of the Parapsychological Association. Amsterdam, the Netherlands.

Birch, C. (1988). The postmodern challenge to biology. In D.R. Griffith (Ed.), *The reenchantment of science* (pp. 69–78). Albany, NY: State University of New York Press.

Bisaha, J., & Dunne, B.J. (1979). Multiple subject and long-distance precognitive remote viewing of geographical locations. In C.T. Tart, H. E. Puthoff, & R. Targ (Eds.), *Mind at large* (pp. 107–124). New York: Praeger.

Blackmore, S. J. (1978). Parapsychology and out-of-body experiences. London: Society for Psychical Research.

Blackmore, S.J. (1980). The extent of selective reporting ESP ganzfeld studies. *European Journal of Parapsychology, 3,* 213–219.

Blackmore, S.J. (1982a). *Beyond the body.* London: Heinemann.

Blackmore, S.J. (1982b). Have you ever had an OBE: The wording of the question. *Journal of the Society for Psychical Research, 51,* 292–302.

Blackmore, S.J. (1982c). Out-of-body experiences, lucid dreams and imagery: Two surveys. *Journal of the American Society for Psychical Research, 76*, 301–317.

Blackmore, S.J. (1983a). Birth and the OBE: An unhelpful analogy. *Journal of the American Society for Psychical Research, 77*, 229– 238.

Blackmore, S.J. (1983b). Divination with tarot cards: An empirical study. *Journal of the Society for Psychical Research, 52*, 97–101.

Blackmore, S.J. (1983c). Imagery and the OBE. In W.G. Roll & R.A. White (Eds.), *Research in parapsychology, 1982* (pp. 231–232). Metuchen, NJ: Scarecrow Press.

Blackmore, S.J. (1984a). A postal survey of OBEs and other experiences. In R.A. White & R.S. Broughton (Eds.), *Research in parapsychology, 1983* (pp. 57–61). Metuchen, NJ: Scarecrow Press.

Blackmore, S.J. (1984b). A psychological theory of the out-of-body experience. *Journal of Parapsychology, 48*, 201–218.

Blackmore, S.J. (1984c). ESP in young children: A critique of the Spinelli evidence. *Journal of the Society for Psychical Research, 52*, 311– 315.

Blackmore, S.J. (1985a). Is this the secret of life? *Fate, 38*(9), 32–42.

Blackmore, S.J. (1985b). Rupert Sheldrake's *New science of life*: Science, parascience or pseudoscience? *Parapsychology Review, 16*(3), 6–8.

Blackmore, S.J. (1986a). Spontaneous and deliberate OBEs: A questionnaire survey. *The Journal of the Society for Psychical Research, 53*, 218–224.

Blackmore, S.J. (1986b). Where am I: Perspectives in imagery, memory and the OBE. In D.H. Weiner and D.I. Radin (Eds.), *Research in parapsychology, 1987* (pp. 108–111). Metuchen, NJ: Scarecrow Press.

Blackmore, S.J. (1991a). Beyond the self: The escape in reincarnation in Buddhism and psychology. In A.S. Berger & J. Berger (Eds), *Reincarnation: Fact or Fable?* (pp. 117–129). London, England: Aquarian Press.

Blackmore, S.J. (1991b). Near-death experiences: In or out of the body? *Skeptical Inquirer, 16*, 33–45.

Blackmore, S.J. (1992). Glimpse of an afterlife or just the dying brain? *Psi Researcher*, No. 6., 2–3.

Blackmore, S.J. (1993). *Dying to live*. Buffalo, NY: Prometheus Books.

Bohm, D. (1980). Wholeness and the implicate order. London: Routledge & Kegan Paul.

Bohm, D., & Peat, F.D. (1987). *Science, order and creativity*. New York: Bantam.

Bohr, N. (1958). *Atomic physics and human knowledge*. New York: Wiley and Sons.

Booth, J. (1986). *Psychic paradoxes*. Buffalo, NY: Prometheus Books.

Bowers, J.Z. (1979). Reception of acupuncture by the scientific community: From scorn to a degree of interest. In S.H. Mauskopf (Ed.), *The reception of unconventional science* (pp. 91–104). Boulder, CO: Westview Press.

Braud, W.G. (1979). Conformance behavior involving living systems. In W.G. Roll (Ed.), *Research in parapsychology, 1978* (pp. 111–115). Metuchen, NJ: Scarecrow Press.

Braud, W.G. (1985). The two faces of psi: Psi revealed and psi observed. In B. Shapin & L. Coly (Eds.), *The repeatability problem in parapsychology*. New York: Parapsychology Foundation.

Braud, W.G. (1988, August). Distant influence of rate of hemolysis of human red blood cells. Paper presented at the 31st annual convention of the Parapsychological Association, Montreal, Canada.

Braud, W.G. (1990). Distant mental influence of rate of hemolysis of human red blood cells. *Journal of the American Society for Psychical Research, 84*, 1–24.

Braud, W.G., Davis, G., & Wood, R. (1979). Experiments with Matthew Manning. *Journal of the Society for Psychical Research, 50*, 199–223.

Braud, W.G., & Schlitz, M.J. (1983). Psychokinetic influence on electrodermal activity. *Journal of Parapsychology, 47*, 95–117.

Braud, W.G., & Schlitz, M.J. (1989). Rule of possible intuitive data sorting in electrodermal biological psychokinesis (Bio-PK). *Journal of the American Society for Psychical Research, 83*, 289–302.

Braud, W.G., Schlitz, M.J., Collins, J., & Klitch, H. (1985) Further studies of the bio-PK effect: Feedback, blocking, generality/specificity. In R.A. White & J. Solfvin (Eds.), *Research in parapsychology, 1984* (pp. 45–48). Metuchen, NJ: Scarecrow Press.

Braud, W.G., Schlitz, M., & Schmidt, H. (1990). Remote mental influence of animate and inanimate target systems: A method of comparison and preliminary findings. In L.A. Henkel & J. Palmer (Eds.), *Research in parapsychology, 1989* (pp. 42–47). Metuchen, NJ: Scarecrow Press.

Braude, S.E. (1986). *The limits of influence*. London: Routledge & Kegan Paul.

Broad, C.D. (1953). *Religion, philosophy and*

psychical research. New York: Harcourt, Brace & Co.

Broad, C.D. (1978). The philosophical implications of foreknowledge. In J. Ludwig (Ed.), *Philosophy and Parapsychology* (pp. 287–312). Buffalo, NY: Prometheus Books.

Broad, W., & Wade, N. (1982). *Betrayers of the truth.* New York: Simon & Schuster.

Brookes-Smith, C. (1973). Data-tape recorded experimental PK phenomena. *Journal of the Society for Psychical Research, 47,* 69–89.

Broughton, R.S. (1991). *Parapsychology: The controversial science.* New York: Random House.

Broughton, R.S., & Higgins, C.A. (1994, August). An investigation of micro-PK and geomagnetism. Paper presented at the thirty-seventh annual convention of the Parapsychological Association. Amsterdam, the Netherlands.

Brown, G. Spencer (1953). Statistical significance in psychical research. *Nature, 172,* 154–156.

Brown, G. Spencer (1955). Psychical research as a test of probability theory. *Proceedings of the First International Conference of Parapsychological Studies* (pp. 5–6). New York: Parapsychology Foundation.

Brown, G. Spencer (1957). *Probability and statistical inference.* London: Longman, Green & Co.

Burns, J.E. (1993). Current hypotheses about the nature of the mind-brain relationship and their relationship to findings in parapsychology. In K.R. Rao (Ed.), *Cultivating consciousness: Enhancing human potential, wellness and healing* (pp. 139–148). Westport, CT: Praeger.

Burton, L., Joines, W. & Stevens, B. (1975). Kirlian photography and its relevance to parapsychological research. In J.D. Morris, W.G. Roll & R.L. Morris (Eds.), *Research in parapsychology, 1974* (pp. 107–112). Metuchen, NJ: Scarecrow Press.

Butterfield, H. (1957). *The origins of modern science.* New York: MacMillan.

Calkins, J.L. (1980). Comments by James Calkins. *Zetetic Scholar, No. 6,* 77–81.

Cameron, T., & Roll, W.G. (1983). An investigation of apparitional experiences. *Theta, 11,* 74–78.

Campbell, J. (1964). *The masks of God: Oriental philosophy.* New York: Penguin Books.

Carpenter, D.G. (1984). Weighing the soul at death: Some methodological and theoretical considerations. *Theta, 12,* 12–16.

Carpenter, J.C. (1995, August). Small group interaction as a medium for ESP response. Paper presented at the 38th annual convention of the Parapsychological Association. Durham, NC.

Carr, D. (1982). Pathophysiology of stress-induced limbic lobe dysfunction: A hypothesis for NDEs. *Anabiosis, 2,* 75–89.

Carrington, H. (1907). On Dr. MacDougall's experiments. *Journal of the American Society for Psychical Research, 1,* 276–283.

Carrington, H. (1921). *The problems of psychical research.* New York: Dodd, Mead.

Casti, J. (1984). *Paradigms lost.* New York: William Morrow & Co.

Cerminara, G. (1967). *Many mansions.* New York: Signet.

Child, I.L., Kanthamani, H.H., & Sweeney, V. (1977). A simplified experiment in dream telepathy. In J.D. Morris, W.G. Roll & R.L. Morris (Eds.), *Research in parapsychology, 1976* (pp. 91–93). Methuchen, NJ: Scarecrow Press.

Christopher, M. (1970). *ESP, seers and psychics.* New York: Crowell.

Churchland, P.M. (1989). *A neurocomputational perspective.* Cambridge, MA: MIT Press.

Churchland, P.M. (1995). *The engine of reason, the seat of the soul: A philosophical journey into the brain.* Cambridge, MA: MIT Press.

Churchland, P.S. (1986). *Neurophilosophy.* Cambridge, MA: MIT Press.

Clark, A. (1989). *Microcognition: Philosophy, cognitive science and parallel distributed processing.* Cambridge, MA: MIT Press.

Clark, J. (1994). [Interview of Roger Penrose.] *Journal of Consciousness Studies, 1,* 17–24.

Clark, T.W. (1995). Function and phenomenology: Closing the explanatory gap. *Journal of Consciousness Studies, 2,* 241–254.

Clay, R.W., & Crouch, P.C. (1974). Possible observation of tachyons associated with extensive air showers. *Nature, 248,* 28.

Coleman, M.H. (1991). [Letter to the Editor.] *Journal of the Society for Psychical Research, 57,* 434–435.

Collins, H., & Pinch, T. (1979). The construction of the paranormal: Nothing unscientific is happening. In R. Wallis (Ed.), *On the margins of science* (pp. 237–269). (Sociological Review Monograph 27). Keele: Stoke-on-Trent, England: Brooks.

Collins, H., & Pinch, T. (1982). *Frames of meaning: the social construction of extraordinary science.* London: Routledge & Kegan Paul

Cook, A.M. & Irwin, H.J. (1983). Visuospatial skills and the out-of-body experience. *Journal of Parapsychology, 47,* 23–35.

Cook, E.W. (1986). Research on reincarnation type cases: Present status and suggestions for future research. In K.R. Rao (Ed.), *Case studies in parapsychology* (pp. 87–96). Jefferson, NC: McFarland.

Cook, E.W., Pasricha, S., Samararatne, G., Maung, U.W., & Stevenson, I. (1983). A review and analysis of "unsolved" cases of the reincarnation type. II. Comparison of features of solved and unsolved cases. *Journal of the American Society for Psychical Research, 77,* 115–135.

Coover, J.E. (1971). Experiments in psychical research at Leland Stanford Junior University. *Psychical Research Monograph No 1.* Stanford, CA: Leland Stanford Junior University Publications.

Council, J.R., Greyson, B., & Huff, K.D. (1986, August). Fantasy-proneness, hypnotizability, and reports of paranormal experiences. Paper presented at the annual convention of the American Psychological Association.

Cowan, J.D., & Sharp, D.H. (1988). Neural nets and artificial intelligence. In S.R. Graubard (Ed.), *The artificial intelligence debate* (pp. 85–121). Cambridge, MA: MIT Press.

Cowey, A. (1991). Grasping the essentials. *Nature, 349,* 102–103.

Cox, W.E. (1956). Precognition: An analysis, II. *Journal of the Society for Psychical Research, 50,* 99–109.

Crick, F. (1981). *Life itself.* New York: Simon & Schuster.

Crick, F. (1994). *The astonishing hypothesis: The scientific search for the soul.* New York: Charles Scribner's Sons.

Crookall, R.J. (1970). *Out-of-the-body experiences.* Hyde Park, NY: University Books.

Culotta, E. (1994). A boost for "adaptive" mutation. *Science, 265,* 318–319.

Cunliffe, J. (1980). 1970: It wasn't a good year for psychics. *Skeptical Inquirer, 5*(1), 7–10.

Dalton, K., Stevens, P (1995, August). The Edinburgh autoganzfeld and geomagnetism. Paper presented at the 38th annual convention of the Parapsychological Association. Durham, NC.

Dalton, K., & Utts, J. (1995, August). Sex pairing, target type and geomagnetism in the PRL automated ganzfeld series. Paper presented at the 38th annual convention of the Parapsychological Association. Durham, NC.

Darling, D. (1995). *Soul search.* New York: Villard Books.

Dawkins, R. (1987). *The blind watchmaker.* New York: Norton.

David-Neel, A. (1971). *Magic and mystery in Tibet.* New York: Dover.

Davies, P. (1983). *God and the new physics.* New York: Simon and Schuster.

Day, W. (1984). *Genesis on planet Earth.* New Haven: Yale University Press.

Dean, D. (1983a). An examination of infrared and ultra-violet technique to test for changes in water following the laying on of hands. Unpublished doctoral dissertation. Humanistic Psychology Institute, San Francisco.

Dean, D. (1983b). Infrared measurements of healer-treated water. In W.G. Roll, J. Beloff & R.A. White (Eds.), *Research in parapsychology, 1982* (pp. 100–101). Metuchen, NJ: Scarecrow Press.

Dean, D., & Brame, E. (1975). Physical changes in water by laying-on-of-hands. Proceedings of the Second International Congress of Psychotronic Research. Paris: Institute Metapsychique International.

de Beauregard, O.C. (1979). Quantum paradoxes and Aristotle's twofold information concept. In C.T. Tart, H.E. Puthoff and R. Targ (Eds.), *Mind at large* (pp. 175–187). New York: Praeger.

Dennett, D.C. (1988). 'Quining qualia.' In A.J. Marcel & E. Bisiach (Eds.), *Consciousness in contemporary science* (pp. 42–77). Oxford, England: Oxford University Press.

Dennett, D.C. (1991). *Consciousness explained.* Boston: Little, Brown & Co.

Dennett, M.R. (1985). Firewalking: Reality or illusion? *Skeptical Inquirer, 10,* 37–40.

Dessoir, M. (1889). Die parapsychologie. *Sphinx, 7,* 341–344.

Diaconis, P. (1978). Statistical problems in ESP research. *Science, 201,* 131–136.

Dobbs, H. (1965). Time and extrasensory perception. *Proceedings of the Society for Psychical Research, 54,* 249–361.

Dobbs, H. (1967). The feasibility of a physical theory of ESP. In J. Smythies (Ed.), *Science and ESP* (pp. 225–254). New York: Humanities Press.

Dolby, R. (1979). Reflections on deviant science. In R. Wallis (Ed.), *On the margins of science: The social reconstruction of rejected knowledge (Sociological Review Monograph 27)* (pp. 9–47). Stoke-on-Trent, England: Brooks.

Dolin, Y.S., Davydov, V.A., Morzova, E.V., &

Shumov, D.V. (1993, August). Studies of a remote mental effect on plants with electrophysiological recording. Paper presented at the 36th annual convention of the Parapsychological Association. Toronto, Canada.

Dolin, Y.S., Dymov, V.I., & Khatchenkov, N.N. (1993, August). Preliminary study of a human operator's effect on the psychophysiological state of another individual with EEG recording. Paper presented at the 36th annual convention of the Parapsychological Association. Toronto, Canada.

Dommeyer, F. (1982). J.B. Rhine and philosophy. In K.R. Rao (Ed.), *J.B. Rhine: On the frontiers of science* (pp. 117–133). Jefferson, NC: McFarland.

Don, N.S., Warren, C.A., McDonough, B.E. & Collura, T.F. (1988). Event-related brain potential and a phenomenological model of psi-conducive states. In D.H. Weiner & R.L. Morris (Eds.), *Research in parapsychology, 1987* (pp. 72–76). Metuchen, NJ: Scarecrow Press.

Doyle, A.C. (1921). *The coming of the fairies.* London: Hodder & Stoughton.

Ducasse, C.J. (1961). *The belief in a life after death.* Springfield, IL: Thomas.

Dunne, B.J. & Jahn, R.G. (1992). Experiments in remote human/machine interaction. *Journal of Scientific Exploration, 6,* 311–312.

Dunne, J.W. (1938). *An experiment with time.* New York: MacMillan.

Eccles, J.C. (1953). *The neurophysiological basis of mind.* Oxford: Clarendon.

Eccles, J.C. (1970). *Facing reality.* New York: Springer Verlag.

Eccles, J.C. (1977). The human person in its two-way relationship to the brain. In J.D. Moris, W.G. Roll and R.L Morris (Eds.), *Research in parapsychology, 1976* (pp. 251 262). Metuchen, NJ: Scarecrow Press.

Eccles, J.C. (1979). *The human mystery.* New York: Springer International.

Eccles, J.C. (1980). *The human psyche.* New York: Springer International.

Eccles, J.C. (1983). Voluntary movement, freedom of the will, moral responsibility. *Perkins Journal, 36*(4), 40–48.

Eccles, J.C. (1987). Brain and mind, two or one? In C. Blakemore and S. Greenfield (Eds.), *Mindwaves: Thoughts on intelligence identity and consciousness* (pp. 293–304). New York: Basil Blackwell.

Eccles, J.C. (1989) *Evolution of the brain: Creation of the self.* New York: Routledge.

Eccles, J.C., & Robinson, D. (1984). *The won-der of being human.* New York: The Free Press.

Eddington, A.S. (1935). *New pathways in science.* Cambridge, England: Cambridge University Press.

Edelman, G.M., & Jononi, G. (1995). Neural darwinism: The brain as a selectional system. In J. Cornwall (Ed.), *Nature's imagination* (pp. 78–100). New York: Oxford University Press.

Edge, H.L. (1980a). Activity metaphysics and the survival problem. *Theta, 8*(3), 5–8.

Edge, H.L. (1980b). The effect of laying-on-of-hands on an enzyme: An attempted replication. In W.G. Roll (Ed.), *Research in parapsychology, 1979* (pp. 137–139). Metuchen, NJ: Scarecrow Press.

Edge, H.L. (1985). Parapsychology and atomism. *Journal of the Society for Psychical Research, 53,* 78–86.

Edge, H.L., Morris, R.L., Palmer, J., & Rush, J.H. (1986). *Foundations of parapsychology.* Boston, MA: Routledge & Kegan Paul.

Edwards, P. (1992). Introduction. In P. Edwards (Ed). *Immortality* (pp. 1–70). New York: Macmillan.

Efron, R. (1963). The effect of handedness on the perception of simultaneity and temporal order. *Brain, 86,* 261.

Efron, R. (1963). Temporal perception, aphasia and déjà vu. *Brain, 86,* 403–424.

Egely, G. (1986). A pilot study of PK on liquids. In D.H. Weiner & D.I. Radin (Eds.), *Research in parapsychology, 1985* (pp. 62–66). Metuchen, NJ: Scarecrow Press.

Ehrenwald, J. (1974). Out-of-body experiences and the denial of death. *Journal of Nervous and Mental Disease, 159,* 227–233.

Ehrenwald, J. (1977). Psi phenomena and brain research. In B.B. Wolman (Ed.), *Handbook of parapsychology* (pp. 716–729). New York: Van Nostrand Reinhold.

Ehrenwald, J.(1978). *The ESP experience.* New York: Basic Books.

Eisenbud, J. (1967). *The world of Ted Serios.* New York: Morrow & Co.

Eisenbud, J. (1977a). Observations on a possible new thoughtographic talent. *Journal of the American Society for Psychical Research, 71,* 299–304.

Eisenbud, J. (1977b). Paranormal photography. In B.B. Wolman (Ed.), *Handbook of parapsychology* (pp. 382–413). New York: Van Nostrand Reinhold.

Eisenbud, J. (1982). Some investigations of claims of PK effects on metal and film by Sasuaki Kiyota. I. The Denver series. *Jour-*

nal of the American Society for Psychical Research, 76, 218–233.

Eisenbud, J., Pratt, J.G., & Stevenson, I. (1981). Distortions in the photographs of Ted Serios. *Journal of the American Society for Psychical Research*, 75, 143–153.

Ellis, D.J. (1973). Does the tape recorder hold the key to survival? *Theta*, No. 38, 1–3.

Emery, C.E. (1996). Psychics missed it big (again) in 1995. *Skeptical Inquirer*, 26(1), 5–6.

Estabrooks, G.H. (1927). *A contribution to experimental telepathy*. Boston: Boston Society for Psychical Research.

Evans, C. & Richardson, P.H. (1988). Improved recovery and reduced postoperative stay after therapeutic suggestions, during general anesthesia. *Lancet, 8609*, 491–193.

Everett, H. (1957). 'Relative state' formulation of quantum mechanics. *Reviews of Modern Physics, 39*, 454–462.

Fanselow, M.S. (1993). Associations and memories: The role of NMDA receptors and long-term potentiation. *Current Directions in Psychological Science, 2*, 152–156.

Feinberg, G. (1975). Precognition—a memory of things future. In L. Oteri, (Ed.), *Quantum physics and parapsychology* (pp. 54–73). New York: Parapsychology Foundation.

Feng, Q., Park, T.K. & Rebek, J. (1992). Crossover reaction between synthetic replicators yield active and inactive recombinants. *Science, 256*, 1179–1180.

Fenwick, P., & Hopkins, R. (1986). An examination of the effects of healing on water. *Journal of the Society for Psychical Research, 53*, 387–390.

Festinger, L. (1957). *A theory of cognitive dissonance*. Evanston, IL: Row Press.

Feuer, L. (1974). *Einstein and the generations of science*. New York: Basic Books.

Feyerbend, P. (1981). How to defend society against science. In I. Hacking (Ed.), *Scientific revolutions* (pp. 156–167). New York: Oxford University Press.

Fisher, J. (1984). *The case for reincarnation*. New York: Bantam Books.

Fjermedal, G. (1987). *The tomorrow makers*. New York: MacMillan.

Flanagan, O. (1992). *Consciousness reconsidered*. Cambridge, MA: MIT Press.

Flew, A. (1987). Is there a case for bodied survival? In A. Flew (Ed.), *Readings in the philosophical problems of parapsychology* (pp. 347–361). Buffalo, NY: Prometheus Books.

Flew, A. (1989). The problem of evidencing the improbable and the impossible. In G.K.

Zollschan, J.F. Schumaker & G.F. Walsh (Eds.), *Exploring the paranormal* (pp. 313–327). Dorset, England: Prism Press.

Flew, A. (1991). Transmigration and reincarnation. In A.S. Berger & J. Berger (Eds.), *Reincarnation: Fact or fable?* (pp. 101–116). London, England: The Aquarian Press.

Fodor, J.A. (1983). *The modularity of mind*. Cambridge, MA: MIT Press/Bradford Books.

Fodor, N. (1964). *Between two worlds*. West Nyack, NY: Parker Publishing.

Fox, S. (1988). *The emergence of life*. New York: Basic Books.

Frazier, K. (1995). 'Columbus poltergeist' Tina Resch imprisoned in daughter's murder. *Skeptical Inquirer, 19*(2), 3.

Frazier, K., & Randi, J. (1986). Prediction after the fact: Lessons of the Tamara Rand hoax. In K. Frazier (Ed.), *Science confronts the paranormal* (pp. 211–214).

Freud, S. (1963). *Studies in parapsychology*. New York: Collier.

Friedman, J.L. (1991). Evading the cosmic censor. *Nature, 351*, 269–270.

Friedman-Hill, S.R., Robertson, L.C., & Triesman, A. (1995). Parietal contributions to visual feature binding: Evidence from a patient with bilateral lesions. *Science, 269*, 853 855.

Fuller, J.G. (1974). *Arigo: Surgeon of the rusty knife*. New York: Thomas Crowell Co.

Furlong, M.W. (1990). A randomized double blind study of positive suggestions presented during anaesthesia. In B. Bonke, W. Fitch & K. Millar (Eds.), *Memory and awareness in anaesthesia* (pp. 170–175). Lisse/Amsterdam: Swetzs & Zeitlinger.

Gabbard, G. Jones, F. & Twemlow, S. (1980). The out-of-body experience: iii. Differential diagnosis. Paper presented at the 1980 annual meeting of the American Psychiatric Association. San Francisco, California.

Gale, G. (1990). Cosmological fecundity: Theories of multiple universes. In J. Leslie (Ed.), *Physical cosmology and philosophy* (pp. 189–206). New York: MacMillan.

Gallup, G.G. (1977). Self-recognition in primates. *American Psychologist, 32*, 329–335.

Gallup, G.H. (1982). Among British people belief in the paranormal increasing. *Emerging Trends* (Princeton Religion Research Center), 4, 5.

Gallup, G.H., & Newport, F. (1992). Belief in paranormal phenomena among adult Americans. *Skeptical Inquirer, 15*, 137–146.

Gardner, M. (1981). *Science: Good, bad and bogus*. Buffalo, NY: Prometheus Books.

Gardner, M. (1986). Magicians in the psi lab: Many misconceptions. In K. Frazier (Ed.), *Science confronts the paranormal* (pp. 170–175). Buffalo, NY: Prometheus Books.

Gardner, M. (1991). How to fabricate a PPO. *Journal of the Society for Psychical Research*, *58*, 43–57.

Gauld, A. (1982). *Mediumship and survival*. London: Paladin Books.

Gauld, A., & Cornell, A.D. (1979). *Poltergeists*. London: Routledge & Kegan Paul.

Gazzaniga, M.S. (1985). *The social brain: Discovering the networks of the mind*. New York: Basic Books.

Gazzaniga, M.S. (1989). Organization of the human brain. *Science*, *245*, 947–852.

Gazzaniga, M.S. (1992). *Nature's mind*. New York: HarperCollins.

Geach, P. (1987). Reincarnation. In A. Flew (Ed.), *Readings in the philosophical problems of parapsychology* (pp. 327–337). Buffalo, NY: Prometheus Books.

Giesler, P.V. (1985). Differential micro-PK effects among Afro-Brazilian Caboclo and Candomble cultists using trance-significant symbols as targets. In R.A. White & J. Solfvin (Eds.), *Research in parapsychology, 1984* (pp. 14–17). Metuchen, NJ: Scarecrow Press.

Gilmore, J.B. (1989). Randomness and the search for psi. *Journal of Parapsychology, 53*, 307–340.

Girden, E. (1978). Parapsychology. In E.C. Carterette and M.P. Friedman (Eds.), *Handbook of perception, Volume 10* (pp. 385–412). New York: Academic Press.

Giroldini, W. (1986). A physical theory for paranormal phenomena. *European Journal of Parapsychology, 6*, 151 165.

Gissurarson, L.R. (1992). The psychokinesis effect: Geomagnetic influence, age and sex differences. *Journal of Scientific Exploration, 6*, 157–165.

Gödel, K. (1949a). An example of a new type of cosmological solution of Einstein's field equations of gravitation. *Reviews of Modern Physics, 21*, 447–450.

Gödel, K. (1949b). A remark about the relationship between relativity theory and idealistic philosophy. In P.A. Schlipp (Ed.), *Albert Einstein: Philosopher-Scientist* (pp. 555–562). Evanston, IL: Library of Living Philosophers.

Goldberg, B. (1982). *Past lives, future lives*. New York: Random House.

Goldberg, G. (1985). Supplementary motor area structure and function: Review and hypothesis. *Behavioral and Brain Sciences, 8*, 189–230.

Goldmann, L., Shah, M., & Hebden, M. (1987). Memory and cardiac anaesthesia. *Anaesthesia, 42*, 596–603.

Goodsort, T.C. (Pseudonym). [Rogo, D.S.] (1981). [Review of *The story of Ruth*.] *Journal of the American Society for Psychical Research, 75*, 186–191.

Goswami, A. (1993). *The self-aware universe: How consciousness creates the material world*. New York: Tarcher/Putnam.

Grad, B. (1963). A telekinetic effect on plant growth. *International Journal of Parapsychology, 5*, 117–133.

Grad, B. (1964). A telekinetic effect on plant growth. II. Experiments involving treatment of saline in stoppered bottles. *International Journal of Parapsychology, 6*, 473–498.

Grad, B. (1965). Laying on of hands: A review of experiments with plants and animals. *Journal of the American Society for Psychical Research, 59*, 95–129.

Grad, B.(1977). Laboratory evidence of "laying-on-of hands." In N.M. Regush (Ed.), *Frontiers of healing* (pp. 203–213). New York: Avon Books.

Grad, B., Cadoret, R.J. & Paul, G.I. (1961). The influence of an unorthodox method of treatment of wound healing in mice. *International Journal of Parapsychology, 3*(2), 5–24.

Grad, B., & Dean, D. (1984). Independent confirmation of infrared healer effects. In R.A. White & R.S. Broughton (Eds.), *Research in parapsychology, 1983* (pp. 81–83). Metuchen, NJ: Scarecrow Press.

Granone, F. (1972). Guaritorie chirurghi-medium filippini. *Rassegna d. Ipnosie Medicina Psicosomatica, 8*, 99–119.

Green, C.E. (1960). Analysis of spontaneous cases. *Proceedings of the Society for Psychical Research, 53*, 97–161.

Green, C.E. (1967). Ecsomatic experiences and related phenomena. *Journal of the Society for Psychical Research, 44*, 111–130.

Greenstein, G. (1988). *The symbiotic universe*. New York: William Morrow & Co.

Gribbin, J., & Rees, M. (1989). *Cosmic coincidences*. New York: Bantam Books.

Griffin, D.R. (1988a). Introduction: The reenchantment of science. In D.R. Griffin (Ed.), *The reenchantment of science* (pp. 1–46). Albany: State University of New York Press.

Griffin, D.R. (1988b). Of minds and molecules: Postmodern medicine in a psychosomatic universe. In D.R. Griffin (Ed.), *The reenchantment of science* (pp. 141–163). Albany, New York: State University of New York Press.

Griffin, D.R. (1994). Dualism, materialism, idealism and psi. *Journal of the American Society for Psychical Research, 88,* 23–29.

Grof, S. (1990). Survival after death: Observations from modern consciousness research. In G. Doore (Ed.), *What survives? Contemporary explorations of life after death* (pp. 22–33). Los Angeles: Tarcher.

Grosso, M. (1976). Some variations of outbody experiences. *Journal of the American Society for Psychical Research, 70,* 179–193.

Grosso, M. (1979). The survival of personality in a mind-dependent world. *Journal of the American Society for Psychical Research, 73,* 367–380.

Grosso, M. (1981). Toward an explanation of near-death phenomena. *Journal of the American Society for Psychical Research, 75,* 37–60.

Gruber, E. (1980). Conforming of prerecorded group behavior with disposed observers. In W.G. Roll (Ed.), *Research in parapsychology, 1979* (pp. 134–136). Metuchen, NJ: Scarecrow Press.

Grush, R., & Churchland, P.S. (1995). Gaps in Penrose's toilings. *Journal of Consciousness Studies, 2,* 10–29.

Gurney, E. (1887). *Tertium quid: Chapters on various disputed questions.* London: Kegan Paul.

Gurney, E. (1888–1889). Note relating to some of the published experiments in thought-transference. *Proceedings of the Society for Psychical Research, 5,* 269–270.

Gurney, E., Myers, F.W.H., and Podmore, F. (1886a). *Phantasms of the living. Volume I.* London: Trübner.

Gurney, E., Myers, F.W.H., and Podmore, F. (1886b). *Phantasms of the living. Volume II.* London: Trübner.

Haight, J. (1979). Spontaneous psi cases: A survey and preliminary study of ESP, attitude and personality relationships. *Journal of Parapsychology, 43,* 179–203.

Hall, D.F., McFeaters, S.J., Loftus, E.F. (1987). Alterations in recollection of unusual and unexpected events. *Journal of Scientific Exploration, 1,* 3–10.

Halpern, P. (1992). *Cosmic wormholes: The search for interstellar shortcuts.* New York: Dutton.

Hameroff, S.R. (1994). Quantum coherence in microtubules: A neural basis for emergent consciousness. *Journal of Consciousness Studies, 1,* 91–118.

Hammond, A. (1952). A note on telepathic communication. *Proceedings of the I.R.E., 40,* 605.

Hansel, C.E.M. (1966). *ESP: A scientific evaluation.* New York: Charles Scribner's Sons.

Hansel, C.E.M. (1980). *ESP and parapsychology: A critical re-evaluation.* Buffalo, NY: Prometheus.

Hansen, G.P. (1982). Dowsing: A review of experimental research. *Journal of the Society for Psychical Research, 51,* 343–367.

Hansen, G.P., Utts, J. & Markwick, B. (1991, August). Statistical and methodological problems of the PEAR remote viewing experiments. Paper presented at the 34th annual convention of the Parapsychological Association. Heidelberg, Germany.

Haraldsson, E. (1981). Apparitions of the dead: A representative survey in Iceland. In W.G. Roll & J. Beloff (Eds.), *Research in parapsychology, 1980* (pp. 3–5). Metuchen, NJ: Scarecrow Press.

Haraldsson, E. (1991, August). Apparitions of the dead. Analyses of a new collection of 350 reports. Paper presented at the 34th annual convention of the Parapsychological Association. Heidelberg, Germany.

Haraldsson, E., Gudmundsdottir, A., Ragnarsson, J.L., & Johnsson, S. (1977). National survey of psychical experiences and attitudes toward the paranormal in Iceland. In J.D. Morris, W.G. Roll & R.L. Morris (Eds.), *Research in parapsychology, 1976* (pp. 182–186). Metuchen, NJ: Scarecrow Press.

Haraldsson, E., & Houtkooper, J.M. (1994, August). Perceptual defensiveness, personality and belief. Meta-analysis, experimenter and decline effects. Paper presented at the 37th annual convention of the Parapsychological Association. Amsterdam, the Netherlands.

Haraldsson, E., & Olafsson, O. (1980). A survey of psychic healing in Iceland. *The Christian Parapsychologist, 3,* 276–279.

Hardy, A., Harvie, R., & Koestler, A. (1975). *The challenge of chance.* New York: Vintage Books.

Hardy, J. (1979). [Review of *Phone calls from the dead.*] *Parapsychology Review, 10*(4), 11–12.

Harman, W.W. (1993). Does further progress in consciousness research await a reassessment of the metaphysical foundations of modern science? In K.R. Rao (Ed.), *Cultivating consciousness: Enhancing human potential wellness and healing* (pp. 11–23). Westport, CT: Praeger.

Harris, M. (1986). *Investigating the unexplained*. Buffalo, NY: Prometheus Books.

Hart, H. (1954). ESP projection: Spontaneous cases and the experimental method. *Journal of the American Society for Psychical Research, 48*, 121–146.

Hart, H. (1956). Six theories about apparitions. *Proceedings of the Society for Psychical Research, 50*, 153–239.

Hart, H. (1959). *The enigma of survival*. Springfield, IL: Charles C. Thomas.

Hart, M.H. (1990). Atmospheric evolution, the Drake equation, and DNA: Sparse life in an infinite universe. In J. Leslie (Ed.), *Physical cosmology and philosophy* (pp. 256–266). New York: MacMillan.

Harth, E. (1982). *Windows on the mind: Reflections on the physical basis of consciousness*. New York: Morrow.

Hasted, J. (1981). *The metal benders*. London: Routledge & Kegan Paul.

Hastings, A. (1978). The Oakland poltergeist. *Journal of the American Society for Psychical Research, 72*, 233–256.

Haynes, R. (1984). Levitation. *Parapsychology Review, 15*(4), 13–15.

Hearne, K.M.T. (1984). A survey of reported precognitions and of those who have them. *Journal of the Society for Psychical Research, 52*, 261–270.

Held, R., & Hein, A. (1963). Movement-produced stimulation in the development of visually guided behavior. *Journal of Comparative and Physiological Psychology, 56*, 872–876.

Henninger, P. (1992). Conditional handedness: Changes in multiple personality disordered subject reflect shift in hemispheric dominance. *Consciousness and Cognition, 1*, 265–287.

Herbert, N. (1988). *Faster than light: Superluminal loopholes in physics*. New York: NAL Books.

Herbert, N. (1993). *Elemental mind*. New York: Dutton.

Hiley, B. (1986). [Transcript of radio interview.] In P.C.W. Davies & J.R. Brown (Eds.), *The ghost in the atom* (pp. 135–148). New York: Cambridge University Press.

Hilgard, E. (1977). *Divided consciousness*. New York: Wiley.

Hodgson, D. (1991). *The mind matters*. New York: Oxford University Press.

Hoebens, P.H. (1982). Mystery men from Holland. II. The strange case of Gerard Croiset. *Zetetic Scholar, 9*, 21–32.

Hoebens, P.H. (1986a). Croiset and Professor Tenhaeff: Discrepancies in claims of clairvoyance. In K. Frazier (Ed.), *Science confronts the paranormal* (pp. 133–141). Buffalo, NY: Prometheus Books.

Hoebens, P.H. (1986b). Gerard Croiset: Investigations of the Mozart of "psychic sleuths." In K. Frazier (Ed.), *Science confronts the paranormal* (pp. 122–123). Buffalo, NY: Prometheus Books.

Honegger, B. (1983). The OBE as a near-birth experience. In W.G. Roll, J. Beloff, & R.A. White (Eds.), *Research in parapsychology, 1982* (pp. 230–231). Metuchen, NJ: Scarecrow Press.

Honorton, C. (1985). Meta-analysis of psi ganzfeld research: A response to Ray Hyman. *Journal of Parapsychology, 49*, 51–91.

Honorton, C., & Ferrari, D.C. (1989). Meta-analysis of forced-choice precognition experiments. *Journal of Parapsychology, 53*, 281–308.

Honorton, C., Ferrari, D.C., & Bem, D.J. (1990, August). Extraversion and ESP performance: A meta-analysis and a new confirmation. Paper presented at the 33rd annual convention of the Parapsychological Association. Chevy Chase, MD.

Honorton, C., & Tremmel, L. (1979). Psi correlates of volition: A preliminary test of Eccles' "neurophysiological hypothesis" of mind-brain interaction. In W.G. Roll (Ed.), *Research in parapsychology, 1978* (pp. 36–38). Metuchen, NJ: Scarecrow Press.

Hövelman, G.H. (1982). Involuntary whisperings, conversational analysis, and electronic voice phenomena. *Theta, 10*, 54–55.

Hovland, C., Janis, I.L., & Kelly, H. (1953). *Communication and persuasion*. New Haven: Yale University Press.

Hoy, D. (1981). Psychic surgery: Hoax or hope? *Zetetic Scholar, 8*, 37–46.

Hoyle, F. (1983). *The intelligent universe*. New York: Holt, Rhinehart & Winston.

Hoyle, F., & Wickramasinghe, C. (1981). *Evolution from space*. New York: Simon & Schuster.

Hoyle, F., & Wickramasinghe, C. (1988). *Cosmic life-force*. New York: Paragon House.

Hubacher, J., & Moss, T. (1976). The "phantom leaf" effect as revealed through Kirlian photography. *Psychoenergetic Systems, 1*, 223–232.

Humphrey, N. (1996). *Leaps of faith*. New York. Basic Books.

Hyman, R. (1977). "Cold reading": How to convince strangers that you know all about them. *Zetetic (Skeptical Inquirer)*, *1*(2), 18–37.

Hyman, R. (1983). Does the ganzfeld experiment answer the critics' objections? In W.G. Roll, J. Beloff, & R.A. White (Eds.), *Research in parapsychology, 1982* (pp. 21–23). Metuchen, NJ: Scarecrow Press.

Hyman, R. (1985). The ganzfeld psi experiment: A critical appraisal. *Journal of Parapsychology*, *49*, 3–49.

Hyman, R. (1986). Outracing the evidence: The muddled mind race. In K. Frazier (Ed.), *Science confronts the paranormal* (pp. 91–108). Buffalo, NY: Prometheus Books.

Hyslop, J.H. (1909). A case of veridical hallucinations. *Proceedings of the American Society for Psychical Research*, *3*, 1–469.

Irwin, H.J. (1979). Coding preferences and the form of spontaneous extrasensory experiences. *Journal of Parapsychology*, *43*, 205–220.

Irwin, H.J. (1980). Out of the body down under: Some cognitive characteristics of Australian students reporting OBEs. *Journal of the Society for Psychical Research*, *50*, 448–459.

Irwin, H.J. (1981). Some psychological dimensions of the out of-body experience. *Parapsychology Review*, *12*(4), 1–6.

Irwin, H.J. (1985). Fear of psi and attitude toward parapsychological research. *Parapsychology Review*, *16*(6), 1–9.

Irwin, H.J. (1986). Perceptual perspective of visual imagery in OBEs, dreams and reminiscence. *Journal of the Society for Psychical Research*, *53*, 210–217.

Irwin, H.J. (1989). *An introduction to parapsychology*. Jefferson, NC: McFarland & Co.

Irwin, H.J. (1994). *An introduction to parapsychology* (second edition). Jefferson, NC: McFarland & Co.

Jahn, R.G., & Dunne, B.J. (1987). *Margins of reality*. New York: Harcourt, Brace, Jovanovich.

Jaki, S. (1969). *Brain, mind and computers*. South Bend, Indiana: Gateway Editions.

James, W. (1890/1992). On the theory of the soul. In P. Edwards (Ed.), *Immortality* (pp. 177–183). New York: Macmillan.

James, W. (1898/1992). Consciousness, the brain and immortality. In P. Edwards (Ed.), *Immortality* (pp. 282–291). New York: Macmillan.

James, W. (1909/1960). The final impressions of a psychical researcher. In G. Murphy & R.O. Ballou (Eds.), *William James on psychical research* (pp. 309–325). New York: The Viking Press.

James, W. (1910). Report on Mrs. Piper's Hodgson control. *Proceedings of the Society for Psychical Research*, *23*, 2–121.

Jenkins, E. (1982). *The shadow and the light*. North Pomfret, VT: Hamish Hamilton.

Johnson, M. (1982). An attempt to select for psi ability in *paramecium aurelia*. *Journal of the Society for Psychical Research*, *51*, 272–282.

Jurgenson, F. (1964). *Rosterna fran Rymden*. Stockholm: Faxon & Lindstrom.

Kalish, R.A., & Reynolds, D.K. (1974). Widows view death: A brief research note. *Omega*, *5*, 187–192.

Kaufman, A.B. (1979). A critical look at the phenomenon of dowsing. *Parapsychology Review*, *10*(6), 20–22.

Kazhinsky, B. (1962). *Biologicheskaya Radiosvyaz*. Kizv: Ukranian Academy of Sciences.

Keil, J. (1980). The voice on tape phenomena: Limitations and possibilities. *European Journal of Parapsychology*, *3*, 287–296.

Keil, J. (1991). New cases in Burma, Thailand and Turkey: A limited field study replication of some aspects of Ian Stevenson's research. *Journal of Scientific Exploration*, *5*, 27–59.

Kejariwal, P., Chattopadhya, A., & Choudhury, J.K. (1983). Some observations of the phantom leaf effect. In W.G. Roll, J. Beloff & R.A. White (Eds.). *Research in parapsychology, 1982* (pp. 110–111). Metuchen, NJ: Scarecrow Press.

Kennedy, J.E. (1994a). Exploring the limits of science and beyond. Research strategy and status. *Journal of Parapsychology*, *58*, 59–77.

Kennedy, J.E. (1994b). Methods to investigate goal oriented psi. Paper submitted to the *Journal of Parapsychology*.

Kennedy, J.E., and Taddonio, J.L. (1976). Experimenter effects in parapsychological research. *Journal of Parapsychology*, *40*, 1–33.

Kihlstrom, J.F., Schachter, D.L., Cork, R.C., Hurt, C.A., & Behr, S. E. (1990). Implicit and explicit memory following surgical anaesthesia. *Psychological Science*, *1*, 303–306.

Kilner, W.J. (1920). *The human atmosphere*. London: Kegan Paul.

Kinsbourne, M. & Warrington, E. (1964). Observations on color agnosia. *Journal of*

Neurobiology, Neurosurgery and Psychiatry, 27, 296–299.

Koch, C., & Crick, F. (1991). Understanding awareness at the neuronal level. *Behavioral and Brain Sciences, 4*, 683–685.

Koestler, A. (1967). *The ghost in the machine.* New York: Macmillan.

Koestler, A. (1972). *The roots of coincidence.* New York: Random House.

Koestler, A. (1978). *Janus.* New York: Random House.

Kogan, I.M. (1968). Information theory analysis of telepathic communication experiments. *Radio Engineering, 23*, 122–130.

Kohn, A. (1986). *False prophets.* New York: Basil Blackwell.

Kohr, R.L. (1980). A survey of psi experiments among members of a special population. *Journal of the American Society for Psychical Research, 74*, 395–411.

Krippner, S. (1980). A suggested typology of folk healing and its relevance for parapsychological investigation. *Journal of the Society for Psychical Research, 50*, 491–500.

Krippner, S. (1994). Enhancement of accuracy of telepathic dreams during periods of decreased geomagnetic activity. Paper presented at the 13th annual meeting of the Society for Scientific Exploration. Austin, Texas.

Krippner, S., & Persinger, M.A. (1993, August). Enhancement of accuracy of telepathic dreams during periods of decreased geomagnetic activity: The William E. experiments. Paper presented at the 36th annual convention of the Parapsychological Association. Toronto, Canada.

Krishna, S.R. & Rao, K.R. (1991, August). The effect of feedback on subjects' responses to a personality questionnaire. Paper presented at the 34th annual convention of the Parapsychological Association. Heidelberg, Germany.

Krupa, D.J., Thompson, J.K., & Thompson, R.F. (1993). Localization of a memory trace in the mammalian brain. *Science, 260*, 989–991.

Kurtz, P. (1986). *The transcendental temptation.* Buffalo, NY: Prometheus Books.

Lambert, G.W. (1955). Poltergeists: A physical theory. *Journal of the Society for Psychical Research, 38*, 49–71.

Lawden, D.F. (1982). Psychical research and physics. In I. Grattan-Guinness (Ed.), *Psychical Research* (pp. 335 343). Wellingborough, England: The Aquarian Press.

Lawden, D.F. (1989). Some thoughts on birth and death. *Journal of the Society for Psychical Research, 56*, 39–43.

Layzer, D. (1990). *Cosmogenesis.* New York: Oxford University Press.

Leahey, T.H. & Leahey, G.E. (1983). *Psychology's occult doubles.* Chicago: Nelson-Hall.

LeDoux, J.E. (1985). Brain, mind and language. In D.A. Oakley (Ed.), *Mind and brain* (pp. 197-216). New York: Methuen.

Leggett, A.J. (1987a). Reflection on the quantum measurement paradox. In B.J. Hiley & D.F. Peat (Eds.), *Quantum implications: Essays in honour of David Bohm* (pp. 85–104). London: Routledge & Kegan Paul.

Leggett, A.J. (1987b). *The problems of physics.* New York: Oxford University Press.

Leikind, B.J., & McCarthy, W.J. (1985). An investigation of firewalking. *Skeptical Inquirer, 10*, 23–34.

Lemonich, M.D. (May 13, 1992). How to go back in time. *Time*, 74.

Libet, B. (1989). Neural destiny: Does the brain have a mind of its own? *The Sciences, 29*(2), 32–35.

Libet, B. (1991). Conscious functions and brain processes. *Behavioral and Brain Sciences, 14*, 685–686.

Libet, B. (1994). A testable field theory of mind-brain interaction. *Journal of Consciousness Studies, 1*, 119–126.

Lincoln, P.J., & Wood, N.J. (1979). Psychic surgery: A serological investigation. *The Lancet, i*, 1197–1198.

Linde, A. (1985). The universe: Inflation out of chaos. *New Scientist, 105* (March 7), 11–18.

Lockwood, M. (1989). *Mind, brain and the quantum.* Cambridge, MA: Basil Blackwell.

Loftus, E.F. (1981). Mentalmorphosis: Alterations in memory produced by bonding of new information to old. In J.B. Long & A.J. Baddeley (Eds.), *Attention and performance. IX.* Hillsdale, NJ: Erlbaum.

Loftus, E.F., & Greene, E. (1980). Warning: Even memory for faces may be contagious. *Law and Human Behavior, 4*, 323 334.

Loftus, E.F., Miller, D.G., & Burns, H.J. (1978). Semantic integration of verbal information into visual memory. *Journal of Experimental Psychology: Human Learning and Memory, 4*, 19–31.

Ludwig, A.M., Brandsma, J.M., Wilbur, C.B., Bendfeldt, E., & Jameson, D.H. (1972). The objective study of a multiple personality: Or are two heads better than one? *Archives of General Psychiatry, 26*, 298–310.

Lund, D.H. (1985). *Death and consciousness.* Jefferson, NC: McFarland.

Lyons, A., & Truzzi, M. (1991). *The blue sense.* New York: Warner Books.

MacDonald, R.G., Hickman, J.L., & Dakin, H.S. (1977). Preliminary physical measurements of psychophysiological effects associated with three alleged psychic healers. In J.D. Morris, W.G. Roll, & R.L. Morris (Eds.), *Research in parapsychology, 1976* (pp. 74–76). Metuchen, NJ: Scarecrow Press.

MacDougall, D. (1907a). Hypothesis concerning soul substance together with experimental evidence of the existence of such substance. *American Medicine, 2*(4), 240–243.

MacDougall, D. (1907b). Hypothesis concerning soul substance together with experimental evidence of the existence of such substance. *Journal of the American Society for Psychical Research, 1,* 237–244.

MacKay, D. (1980). Conscious agency with split and unsplit brains. In B. Josephson & V. Ramachandran (Eds.), *Consciousness and the physical world.* New York: Pergamon Press. 95–113.

MacKenzie, A. (1971). *Apparitions and ghosts.* New York: Popular Library.

Maher, M.C., & Hansen, G.P. (1992a, August). Quantitative investigation of a "haunted castle" in New Jersey. Paper presented at the 35th annual convention of the Parapsychological Association. Las Vegas, NV.

Maher, M.C., & Hansen, G.P. (1992b). Quantitative investigation of a reported haunting using several detection techniques. *Journal of the American Society for Psychical Research, 86,* 347–374.

Maher, M.C., & Hansen, G.P. (1995). Quantitative investigation of a "haunted castle" in New Jersey. *Journal of the American Society for Psychical Research, 89,* 19–50.

Maher, M.C., & Schmeidler, G.R. (1975). Quantitative investigation of a recurrent apparition. *Journal of the American Society for Psychical Research, 69,* 341–352.

Marcel, A.J. (1988). Phenomenal experience and functionalism. In A.J. Marcel & E. Bisiach (Eds). *Consciousness in contemporary science* (pp. 121–158). New York: Oxford university Press.

Margenau, H. (1984). *The miracle of existence.* Woodbridge, CT: Ox Bow Press.

Markov. M.A. (1985). Entropy in an oscillating universe in the assumption of universe 'splitting' into numerous smaller 'daughter universes.' In M.A. Markov, V.A. Berezin, & V.P. Frolov (Eds.), *Proceedings of the third seminar on quantum gravity.* Moscow: World Scientific.

Marks, D.F. (1986). Remote viewing revisited. In K. Frazier (Ed.), *Science confronts the paranormal* (pp. 110–121). Buffalo, NY: Prometheus Books.

Marks, D.F., & Kammann, R. (1978). Information transmission in remote viewing experiments. *Nature, 274,* 680–681.

Marks, D.F., & Kammann, R. (1980). *The psychology of the psychic.* Buffalo, NY: Prometheus Books.

Marks, D.F., & Scott, C. (1986). Remote viewing exposed. *Nature, 319,* 444.

Markwick, B. (1978). The Soal-Goldney experiments with Basil Shackleton: New evidence of data manipulation. *Proceedings of the Society for Psychical Research, 56,* 250–277.

Markwick, B., & Beloff, J. (1983). Dream states and ESP: A distance experiment with a single subject. In W.G. Roll, J. Beloff, & R.A. White (Eds.) *Research in parapsychology, 1982* (pp. 228–230). Metuchen, NJ: Scarecrow Press.

Marshall, E. (1990). Science beyond the pale. *Science, 249,* 14–16.

Mason, S. (1962). *A history of the sciences.* New York: Macmillan.

Matlock, J.G. (1989, August). The relation of the subject's age to external cueing in spontaneous past life memory cases: A study of published cases. Paper presented at the 32nd annual convention of the Parapsychological Association. San Diego, CA.

Matlock, J.G. (1990). Past life memory case studies. In S. Krippner (Ed.), *Advances in parapsychological research, Volume 6* (pp. 184–267). Jefferson, NC: McFarland.

Mattuck, R.D. (1977). Random fluctuation theory of psychokinesis: Thermal noise model. In J.D. Morris, W.G. Roll, and R.L. Morris (Eds.), *Research in parapsychology, 1976* (pp. 191–195). Metuchen, NJ: Scarecrow Press.

Mattuck, R.D. (1982). A model of the interaction between consciousness and matter using Bohm-Bub hidden variables. In W.G. Roll, R.L. Morris and R.A. White (Eds.), *Research in parapsychology, 1981* (pp. 146–147). Metuchen, NJ: Scarecrow Press.

Mattuck, R.D. (1984). A quantum mechanical theory of the interaction of consciousness with matter. In M. Cazenave (Ed.),

Science and consciousness (pp. 45–65). New York: Pergamon Press.

McAdams, E.E., & Bayless, R. (1981). *The case for life after death.* Chicago: Nelson Hall.

McClenon, J. (1990). A preliminary report on African-American anomalous experiences in northeast North Carolina. *Parapsychology Review, 21*(1), 1–4.

McGinn, C. (1995). Consciousness and space. *Journal of Consciousness Studies, 2,* 220–230.

McKee, R.L. (1982). Psi related beliefs among the rural people of Swaziland. *Parapsychology Review, 13*(3), 11–16.

Milgrim, S. (1963). Behavioral study of obedience. *Journal of Abnormal and Social Psychology, 67,* 371–378.

Milgrim, S. (1968). Some conditions of obedience and disobedience to authority. *International Journal of Psychiatry, 6,* 259–276.

Millar, B. (1978). The observational theories: A primer. *European Journal of Parapsychology, 2,* 304–332.

Millar, K., & Watkinson, N. (1983). Recognition of words presented during general anaesthesia. *Ergonomics, 6,* 585–594.

Miller, L. (1990). *Inner natures: Brain, self and personality.* New York: Ballantine Books.

Mills, A. (1989). A replication study: Three cases of children in Northern India who are said to remember a previous life. *Journal of Scientific Exploration, 3,* 133–184.

Mills, A., Haraldsson, E., & Keil, H.H.J. (1994). Replication studies of cases suggestive of reincarnation by three independent investigators. *Journal of the American Society for Psychical Research, 88,* 207–219.

Milton, J. (1993, August). A meta-analysis of waking state of consciousness, free-response ESP studies. Paper presented at the 36th annual convention of the Parapsychological Association. Toronto, Canada.

Milton, J. (1994, August). Mass-ESP: A meta-analysis of mass media recruitment ESP studies. Paper presented at the 37th annual convention of the Parapsychological Association. Amsterdam, the Netherlands.

Mitchell, E. (1979). A look at the exceptional. In C.T. Tart, H.E. Puthoff and R. Targ (Eds.), *Mind at large* (pp. 2–10). New York: Praeger.

Mitchell, J.L. (1981). *Out-of-body experiences: A handbook.* Jefferson, NC: McFarland.

Montandon, H.E. (1977). Psychophysiological aspects of the Kirlian phenomenon: A confirmatory study. *Journal of the Society for Psychical Research, 71,* 45–49.

Moody, R.A. (1975). *Life after life.* New York: Bantam Books.

Moravec, H. (1988). *Mind children: The future of robot and human intelligence.* Cambridge, MA: Harvard University Press.

Morris, M., & Thorne, K. (1988). Wormholes in space-time and their use for interstellar travel. *American Journal of Physics, 56*(5), 395.

Morris, M., Thorne, K., & Yurtsever, U. (1988). Wormholes, time machines and the weak energy condition. *Physical Review Letters, 61,* 1446.

Morris, R. (1983). *Dismantling the universe.* New York: Simon & Schuster.

Morris, R. (1990). *The edges of science.* New York: Prentice Hall.

Morris, R.L. (1974). PRF research on out-of-body experiences. *Theta,* No. 41, 1–3.

Morris, R.L., Harary, S.B., Janis, J., Hartwell, J., & Roll, W.G. (1978). Studies of communication during out-of-body experiences. *Journal of the American Society for Psychical Research, 72,* 1–21.

Moss, S., & Butler, D.C. (1978). The scientific credibility of ESP. *Perceptual and Motor Skills, 46,* 1063–1074.

Motoyama, H. (1978). *Science and the evolution of consciousness.* Brookline, MA: Autumn Press.

Muldoon, S.J., & Carrington, H. (1929). *The projection of the astral body.* London: Rider & Co.

Mundle, C.W.K. (1964). Does the concept of precognition make sense? *International Journal of Parapsychology, 6,* 179–198.

Munro, C., & Persinger, M.A. (1992). Relative right temporal lobe theta activity correlates with Vingiano's Hemispheric Quotient and the "sensed presence." *Perceptual and Motor Skills, 75,* 899–903.

Munson, R.S. (1987). Interpersonal systems and parapsychology. In D.H. Weiner & R.D. Nelson (Eds.), *Research in parapsychology, 1986* (pp. 130–135). Metuchen, NJ: Scarecrow Press.

Murphy, G. (1945). Field theory and survival. *Journal of the American Society for Psychical Research, 39,* 181–209.

Murphy, G. (1964). Lawfulness vs. caprice: Is there a law of psychic phenomena? *Journal of the American Society for Psychical Research, 65,* 3–16.

Murphy, G. (1973). A Caringtonian approach to Ian Stevenson's *Twenty cases suggestive of reincarnation. Journal of the American Society for Psychical Research, 67,* 117–129.

Myers, F.H.W. (1903). *Human personality and its survival of death.* London: Longmans.

Myers, S.A., Austrin, H.R., Grisso, J.T., & Nickeson, R.C. (1983). Personality characteristics as related to the out-of-the-body experience. *Journal of Parapsychology, 47,* 131–144.

Nash, C.B. (1976) Psi and the mind-body problem. *Journal of the Society for Psychical Research, 48,* 267–270.

Nash, C.B. (1982). Psychokinetic control of bacterial growth. In W.G. Roll, R.L. Morris, & R.A. White (Eds.), *Research in parapsychology, 1981* (pp. 61–64). Metuchen, NJ: Scarecrow Press.

Nash, C.B. (1983). An extrasensory observational theory. *Journal of the Society for Psychical Research, 52,* 113–116.

Nash, C.B. (1984a). Quantum physics and parapsychology. *Parapsychology Review, 15*(3), 4–6.

Nash, C.B. (1984b). Test of psychokinetic control of bacterial mutation. *Journal of the American Society for Psychical Research, 78,* 145–152.

Nash, C.B. (1995). Personal survival of death by worldlines. *Journal of the Society for Psychical Research, 60,* 317–321.

Nickell, J. (1994). *Psychic sleuths.* Buffalo, NY: Prometheus Books.

Nickell, J., & Fisher, J.F. (1987). Incredible cremations: Investigating spontaneous combustion deaths. *Skeptical Inquirer, 11,* 352–357.

Nolen, W.A. (1974). *Healing: A doctor in search of a miracle.* Greenwich, CT: Fawcett.

Noyes, R. (1972). The experience of dying. *Psychiatry, 35,* 174–184.

Nunn, C.M.H., Clarke, C.J.S., & Blott, B.H. (1994). Collapse of a quantum field may affect brain function. *Journal of Consciousness Studies, 1,* 127–139.

Oakely, D.A. (1985a) Animal awareness, consciousness, and self-image. In D.A. Oakely (Ed.), *Mind and brain* (pp. 132–151). New York: Methuen.

Oakely, D.A. (1985b). Cognition and imagery in animals. In D.A. Oakley (Ed.), *Mind and brain* (pp. 99–131). New York: Methuen.

Oakely, D.A., & Eames, L.C. (1985). The plurality of consciousness. In D.A. Oakely (Ed.), *Mind and brain* (pp. 217–251). New York: Methuen.

Ojemann, G.A. (1983). Brain organization for language from the perspective of electrical stimulation mapping. *Behavioral and Brain Sciences, 6,* 189–230.

O'Keefe, J. (1985). Is consciousness the gateway to the hippocampal cognitive map? A speculative essay on the neural basis of mind. In D.A. Oakley (Ed.), *Brain and mind* (pp. 59–98). New York: Methuen.

Oppenheim, J. (1985). *The other world: Spiritualism and psychical research in England, 1850–1914.* New York: Cambridge University Press.

Oppenheimer, P. (1986). [Letter to the Editor.] *The Sciences, 26*(2), 12.

Orme, J. (1974). Precognition and time. *Journal of the Society for Psychical Research, 47,* 351–365.

Osis, K. (1961). Deathbed observations by physicians and nurses. *Parapsychological Monographs,* No. 3. New York: Parapsychology Foundation.

Osis, K. (1965). ESP over distance: A survey of experiments published in English. *Journal of the American Society for Psychical Research, 59,* 22–42.

Osis, K. (1981). Apparitions: A new model. In W.G. Roll & J. Beloff (Eds.), *Research in parapsychology, 1980* (pp. 1–3). Metuchen, NJ: Scarecrow Press.

Osis, K., & Haraldsson, E. (1977a). *At the hour of death.* New York: Avon.

Osis, K., & Haraldsson, E. (1977b). Deathbed observations by physicians and nurses. *Journal of the American Society for Psychical Research, 71,* 237–259.

Osis, K., & Haraldsson, E. (1977c). OBEs in Indian swamis: Sai Baba and Dadaji. In J.D. Morris, W.G. Roll, & R.L. Morris (Eds.), *Research in parapsychology, 1976* (pp. 147–150). Metuchen, NJ: Scarecrow Press.

Osis, K., & McCormick, D. (1980). Kinetic effects at the ostensible location of an out-of-body projection during perceptual testing. *Journal of the American Society for Psychical Research, 74,* 319–329.

Ouspensky, P.D. (1912/1970). *Tertium organum.* New York: Random House.

Ouspensky, P.D. (1931/1971). *A new model of the universe.* New York: Random House.

Owen, A.R.G. (1964). *Can we explain the poltergeist?* New York: Garrett.

Owen, A.R.G. (1978). Poltergeist phenomena and psychokinesis. In M. Ebon (Ed.), *The Signet handbook of parapsychology* (pp. 365–374). New York: Signet.

Pagels, H. (1988). *The dreams of reason.* New York: Simon & Schuster.

Palmer, J. (1978). The out-of-body experience: A psychological theory. *Parapsychology Review, 9*(5), 19–22.

Palmer, J. (1979). A community mail survey of psychic experiences. *Journal of the American Society for Psychical Research, 73*, 221–251.

Palmer, J. (1983). Sensory contamination of free-response ESP targets: The greasy fingers hypothesis. *Journal of the American Society for Psychical Research, 77*, 101–113.

Palmer, J. (1984). Contamination of free-response ESP targets: The greasy fingers hypothesis. In R.A. White & R.S. Broughton (Eds.), *Research in psychology, 1983* (pp. 25–28). Metuchen, NJ: Scarecrow Press.

Palmer, J. (1986). [Review of *flight of mind.*] *Parapsychology Review, 17*(2), 12–15.

Palmer, J., & Kramer, W. (1986). Sensory identification of contaminated free-response ESP targets: Return of the greasy fingers hypothesis. *Journal of the American Society for Psychical Research, 80*, 265–278.

Palmer, J., & Lieberman, R. (1975). The influence of psychological set on ESP and out-of-body experiences. *Journal of the American Society for Psychical Research, 69*, 193–213.

Palmer, J., & Lieberman, R. (1976). ESP and out-of-body experiences: A further study. In J.D. Morris, W.G. Roll, & R.L. Morris (Eds.), *Research in parapsychology, 1975* (pp. 102–106). Metuchen, NJ: Scarecrow Press.

Palmer, J., & Vassar, C. (1974). ESP and out-of-the-body experiences: An exploratory study. *Journal of the American Society for Psychical Research, 68*, 257–280.

Pamplin, B. & Collins, H. (1975). Spoon bending: An experimental approach. *Nature, 257*, 8.

Parfit, D. (1987). Divided minds and the nature of persons. In C. Blakemore & S. Greenfield (Eds.), *Mindwaves: Thoughts on intelligence, identity and consciousness* (pp. 19–26). New York: Basil Blackwell.

Parker, A. (1977). Parapsychologists' personality and psi in relation to the experimenter effect. In J.D. Morris, W.G. Roll, & R.L. Morris (Eds.), *Research in parapsychology, 1976* (pp. 107–109). Metuchen, NJ: Scarecrow Press.

Parker, B. (1991). *Cosmic time travel.* New York: Plenum Press.

Pasricha, S.K. (1978). An investigation into reported cases of persons who claimed to have reincarnated. Unpublished doctoral dissertation. Bangalore University, Bangalore, India.

Pasricha, S.K. (1992a). Are reincarnation cases shaped by parental guidance? An empirical study concerning the limits of parents' influence on children. *Journal of Scientific Exploration, 6*, 167–180.

Pasricha, S.K. (1992b). *Claims of reincarnation: An empirical study of cases in India.* New Delhi: Harman Publishing House.

Pasricha, S.K. (1993). A systematic survey of near-death experiences in South India. *Journal of Scientific Exploration, 7*, 161–171.

Pasricha, S.K. (1995). Near-death experiences in South India: A systematic survey. *Journal of Scientific Exploration, 9*, 79–85.

Pasricha, S.K., & Barker, D.R. (1981). A case of the reincarnation type in India: The case of Rakesh Gaur. *European Journal of Parapsychology, 3*, 381–408.

Pasricha, S.K., & Stevenson, I. (1979). A partly independent replication of investigations of cases suggestive of reincarnation. *European Journal of Parapsychology, 3*, 51–65.

Pearson, R.E. (1961). Response to suggestion given under general anaesthesia. *American Journal of Clinical Hypnosis, 4*, 106–114.

Pehek, J.O., Kyler, H.J., & Faust, D.L. (1976). Image modulation in corona discharge photography. *Science, 194*, 263–270.

Penelhum, T. (1987). Survival and disembodied existence. In A. Flew (Ed.), *Readings in the philosophical problems of parapsychology* (pp. 338–346). Buffalo, NY: Prometheus Books.

Penfield, W. (1975). *The mystery of the mind.* Princeton, NJ: Princeton University Press.

Penrose, R. (1986). Big bangs, black holes and 'time's arrow.' In R. Flood & M. Lockwood (Eds.), *The nature of time* (pp. 36–62). New York: Basil Blackwell.

Penrose, R. (1987a). Minds, machines and mathematics. In C. Blakemore & S. Greenfield (Eds.), *Mindwaves: Thoughts on intelligence, identity and consciousness* (pp. 259–276). New York: Blackwell.

Penrose, R. (1987b). Quantum physics and conscious thought. In B.J. Hiley & F.D. Peat (Eds.), *Quantum implications: Essays in honour of David Bohm* (pp. 105–120). London: Routledge & Kegan Paul.

Penrose, R. (1989). *The emperor's new mind: Concerning computers, minds and the laws of physics.* New York: Oxford University Press.

Penrose, R. (1994). *Shadows of the mind.* New York: Oxford University Press.

Penrose, R., & Hameroff, S. (1995). What 'gaps'? Reply to Grush and Churchland. *Journal of Consciousness Studies, 2*, 98–111.

Persinger, M.A. (1979). ELF field mediation in spontaneous psi events: Direct information transfer or conditional elicitation? In C.T. Tart, H.E. Puthoff, & R. Targ (Eds.), *Mind at large* (pp. 191–204). New York: Praeger.

Persinger, M.A. (1983). Religious and mystical experiences as artifacts of temporal lobe function: A general hypothesis. *Perceptual and Motor Skills, 57,* 1255–1262.

Persinger, M.A. (1985). Geophysical variables and human behavior: Intense paranormal experiences occur during days of quiet global geomagnetic activity. *Perceptual and Motor Skills, 61,* 320–322.

Persinger, M.A. (1986). Intense subjective telepathic experiences occur during days of quiet global geomagnetic activity. In D.H. Weiner & D.I. Radin (Eds.), *Research in parapsychology, 1987* (p. 32). Metuchen, NJ: Scarecrow Press.

Persinger, M.A. (1987). Spontaneous telepathic experiences from *Phantasms of the living* and low global geomagnetic activity. *Journal of the American Society for Psychical Research, 81,* 23–36.

Persinger, M.A. (1988, August). Psi research and temporal lobe activity: The geomagnetic factor. Paper presented at the 31st annual convention of the Parapsychological Association. Montreal, Canada.

Persinger, M.A., & Cameron, R.A. (1986). Are earth faults at fault in some poltergeistlike episodes? *Journal of the American Society for Psychical Research, 80,* 49–73.

Persinger, M.A., & Krippner, S. (1987). Experimental dream telepathy—Clairvoyance and geomagnetic activity. In D.H. Weiner and R.D. Nelson (Eds.), *Research in parapsychology, 1986* (pp. 85–88). Metuchen, NJ: Scarecrow Press.

Persinger, M.A., & Krippner, S. (1989). Dream ESP experiments and geomagnetic activity. *Journal of the American Society for Psychical Research, 83,* 101–116.

Persinger, M.A., & Schaut, G.B. (1987). Geomagnetic factors in spontaneous telepathic, precognitive and postmortem experiences. In D.H. Weiner & R.D. Nelson (Eds.), *Research in parapsychology, 1986* (pp. 88–90). Metuchen, NJ: Scarecrow Press.

Peterson, I. (1994). Timely questions. *Science News, 141,* 202–203.

Pierce, H.W. (1973). RSPK phenomena observed independently by two families. *Journal of the American Society for Psychical Research, 67,* 86–101.

Pleass, C.M. & Dey, N.D. (1987). Behavioral response of microorganisms to psi stimulus.

Part II. Statistical analysis of data from *Dunaliella*. In D.H. Weiner & R.D. Nelson (Eds.), *Research in parapsychology* (pp. 20–29). Metuchen, NJ: Scarecrow Press.

Pool, R. (1990). Closing the gap between proteins and DNA. *Science, 248,* 1609.

Popper, K. (1959). *The logic of scientific discovery.* New York: Basic Books.

Popper, K., & Eccles, J. (1977). *The self and its brain.* New York: Springer International.

Pratt, J.G., & Woodruff, J.L. (1939). Size of stimulus symbols in extrasensory perception. *Journal of Parapsychology, 3,* 121–158.

Pribram, K.H. (1971). *Languages of the brain: Experimental paradoxes and principles in neuropsychology.* Englewood Cliffs, NJ: Prentice-Hall.

Pribram, K.H. (1978). Consciousness: A scientific study. *Journal of Indian Psychology, 1,* 95–118.

Price, H.H. (1939). Haunting and the "psychic ether" hypothesis: With some preliminary reflections on the present condition and possible future of psychical research. *Proceedings of the Society for Psychical Research, 45,* 307–374.

Price, H.H. (1940). Some philosophical questions about telepathy and clairvoyance. *Philosophy, 15,* 363–374.

Price, H.H. (1948). Psychical research and human personality. *Hibbert Journal,* 105–113.

Price, H.H. (1953). Survival and the idea of "another world." *Proceedings of the Society for Psychical Research, 50,* 1–125.

Price, H.H. (1959). Psychical research and human nature. *Journal of Parapsychology, 23,* 178–187.

Price, H.H. (1961). Apparitions: Two theories. *Journal of Parapsychology, 24,* 110–125.

Priest, S. (1991). *Theories of the mind.* New York: Houghton Mifflin.

Puthoff, H.E., & Targ, R. (1979). A perceptual channel for information transfer over kilometer distances: Historical perspectives and recent research. In C.T. Tart, H.E. Puthoff & R. Targ (Eds.), *Mind at large* (pp. 13–76). New York: Praeger.

Puthoff, H.E., Targ, R., & Tart, C.T. (1980). Resolution in remote-viewing studies: Mini-targets. In W.G. Roll (Ed.), *Research in parapsychology, 1979* (pp. 120–122). Metuchen, NJ: Scarecrow Press.

Radin, D.I. (1989). The Tao of psi. In L.A. Henkel & R.E. Berger (Eds.), *Research in parapsychology, 1988* (pp. 157–173). Metuchen, NJ: Scarecrow Press.

Radin, D.I. (1992, August). Beyond belief: Exploring interactions among mind, body and environment. Paper presented at the 35th annual convention of the Parapsychological Association. Las Vegas, Nevada.

Radin, D.I., & Bisaga, G.J. (1991, August). Toward a high technology of the mind: A proposed design and initial experiments. Paper presented at the 34th annual convention of the Parapsychological Association. Heidelberg, Germany.

Radin, D.I., & Ferrari, D.C. (1991). Effects of consciousness on the fall of dice: A meta-analysis. *Journal of Scientific Exploration, 5,* 61–83.

Radin, D.I., May, E.C. & Thomson, M.J. (1986). Psi experiments with random number generators: Meta-analysis Part I. In D.H. Weiner & D.I. Radin (Eds.), *Research in parapsychology, 1985* (pp. 14–17). Metuchen, NJ: Scarecrow Press.

Radin, D.I., McAlpine, S. & Cunningham, S. (1994). Geomagnetism and psi in the ganzfeld. *Journal of the Society for Psychical Research, 59,* 352–363.

Radin, D.I., & Roll, W.G. (1994, August). A radioactive ghost in a music hall. Paper presented at the 37th annual convention of the Parapsychological Association. Amsterdam, the Netherlands

Radin, D.I., Taylor, R.K., & Braude, W.G. (1993, August). Remote mental influence of electrodermal activity: A preliminary replication. Paper presented at the 36th annual convention of the Parapsychological Association. Toronto, Canada.

Rafal, R., Smith, J. Krantz, S, Cohen, A., & Brennan, C. (1990). Extrageniculate vision in hemianopic humans: Saccade inhibition by signals in the blind field. *Science, 250,* 118–120.

Ramachandran, V.S. (1980). Twins, split brains and personal identity. In B.D. Josephson & V.S. Ramachandran (Eds.), *Consciousness and the physical world* (pp. 139–163). New York: Pergamon Press.

Ramon, C. & Rauscher, E.A. (1980). Super-luminal transformations in complex Minkowski spaces. *Foundations of Physics, 10,* 661–669.

Randi, J. (1979). Edgar Cayce: The slipping prophet. *Skeptical Inquirer, 4*(1), 51–57.

Randi, J. (1980). *Flim-flam.* New York: Lippincott & Crowell.

Randi, J. (1983a). The Project Alpha experiment: Part 1. The first two years. *Skeptical Inquirer, 7*(4), 24–33.

Randi, J. (1983b). The Project Alpha experiment: Part 2. Beyond the laboratory. *Skeptical Inquirer, 8*(1), 36–45.

Randi, J. (1985). The Columbus poltergeist case: Part I. *Skeptical Inquirer, 9,* 221–235.

Randi, J. (1986). The Project Alpha experiment. In K. Frazier (Ed.), *Science confronts the paranormal* (pp. 158–165). Buffalo, NY: Prometheus Books.

Randi, J. (1987). *The faith healers.* Buffalo, NY: Prometheus Books.

Rao, K.R. (1977). On the nature of psi. *Journal of Parapsychology, 41,* 294–351.

Rao, K.R. (1978). Psi: Its place in nature. *Journal of Parapsychology, 42,* 276–303.

Rao, K.R. (1986). L.E. Rhine on psi and its place. In K.R. Rao (Ed.), *Case studies in parapsychology* (pp. 52–62). Jefferson, NC: McFarland.

Raudive, K. (1971). *Breakthrough.* New York: Taplinger.

Rauscher, E.A. (1979). Some physical models potentially applicable to remote perception. In A. Puharich (Ed.), *The Icelandic papers* (pp. 50–93). Amherst, WI: Essentia.

Rauscher, E.A. (1983a). The physics of psi phenomena in space and time. Part I. Major principles of physics, psychic phenomena, and some physical models. *Psi Research, 2*(2), 64–88.

Rauscher, E.A. (1983b). The physics of psi phenomena in space and time. Part II. Multidimensional geometric models. *Psi Research, 2*(3), 93–120.

Ravaldini, S., Biondi, M., & Stevenson, I. (1990). The case of Giusepe Riccardi: An unusual drop-in communicator in Italy. *Journal of the Society for Psychical Research, 56,* 257–264.

Reber, A.S. (1992). The cognitive unconscious: An evolutionary perspective. *Consciousness and Cognition, 1,* 93–133.

Rees, W.D. (1971). The hallucinations of widows. *British Medical Journal, 4,* 37–41.

Reichbart, R. (1976). The Navajo hand trembler: Multiple roles of the psychic in traditional Navajo society. *Journal of the American Society for Psychical Research, 70,* 381–391.

Reichbart, R. (1978). Magic and psi: Some speculations on their relationship. *Journal of the American Society for Psychical Research, 72,* 153–175.

Rein, G. (1986) A psychokinetic effect on neurotransmitter metabolism: Alterations in the degradative enzyme monoamine oxidase. In D.H. Weiner & D.I. Radin (Eds.),

Research in parapsychology, 1985 (pp. 70–80). Metuchen, NJ: Scarecrow Press.

Rein, G., & McCraty, R. (1994). Structural changes in water and DNA associated with new physiologically measurable states. Paper presented at the 13th annual meeting of the Society for Scientific Exploration. Austin, Texas.

Rhine, J.B. (1972). Parapsychology and man. *Journal of Parapsychology, 36,* 101–121.

Rhine, J.B. (1974). Telepathy and other untestable hypotheses. *Journal of Parapsychology, 38,* 215–225.

Rhine, J.B., & Feather, S.R. (1962). The study of cases of "psi-trailing" in animals. *Journal of Parapsychology, 26,* 1–22.

Rhine, J.B., & Pratt, J.G. (1954). A review of the Pearce-Pratt distance series of ESP tests. *Journal of Parapsychology, 18,* 165–177.

Rhine, L.E. (1955). Precognition and intervention. *Journal of Parapsychology, 19,* 1–34.

Rhine, L.E. (1961). *Hidden channels of the mind.* New York: William Sloane Associates.

Rhine, L.E. (1962) Psychological processes in ESP experiences. Part I. Waking experiences. *Journal of Parapsychology, 26,* 88–111.

Rhine, L.E. (1963). Spontaneous physical effects and the psi process. *Journal of Parapsychology, 27,* 84–122.

Rhine, L.E. (1970). Dr. L.E. Rhine's reply to Dr. Stevenson. [Letter to the Editor.] *Journal of Parapsychology, 34,* 149–164.

Rhine, L.E. (1977) Research methods with spontaneous cases. In B.B. Wolman (Ed.), *Handbook of parapsychology* (pp. 59–80). New York: Van Nostrand Reinhold.

Rhine, L.E. (1978). The psi process in spontaneous cases. *Journal of Parapsychology, 42,* 20–32.

Rhine, L.E. (1981). *The invisible picture: A study of psychic experiences.* Jefferson, NC: McFarland.

Richet, C. (1884, December). La Suggestion mentale et le calcul des probabilités. *Revue Philosophique.*

Richet, C. (1888). Further experiments in hypnotic lucidity or clairvoyance. *Proceedings of the Society for Psychical Research, 6,* 66–83.

Richmond, N. (1952). Two series of PK tests on paramecia. *Journal of the Society for Psychical Research, 36,* 577–588.

Rinaldi, G.M., & Piccinini, G. (1982). A survey of spontaneous cases in South Tyrol. Unpublished manuscript.

Ring, K. (1979). Further studies of the near death experience. *Theta, 7*(2), 1–3.

Ring, K. (1980). *Life at death.* New York: Coward, McCann & Geoghegan.

Robinson, J.W., Maeir, D., O'Hallaren, M., Daniels, B.S., & Staeheli, J. (1975). Unpublished report. Gonzaga University.

Rodin, E.A. (1980). The reality of near-death experiences: A perceptual perspective. *Journal of Nervous and Mental Diseases, 168,* 259–263.

Rogo, D.S. (1974). Psychotherapy and the poltergeist. *Journal of the Society for Psychical Research, 47,* 433–446.

Rogo, D.S. (1977). *The haunted universe.* New York: Signet.

Rogo, D.S. (1978). *Mind beyond the body.* New York: Penguin Books.

Rogo, D.S. (1980). Theories about PK: A critical evaluation. *Journal of the Society for Psychical Research, 50,* 359–378.

Rogo, D.S. (1981). Shamans, saints and the paranormal. *Theta, 9*(4), 2–6.

Rogo, D.S. (1987). [Letter to the Editor: The Gretchen case of responsive xenoglossy.] *Journal of Parapsychology, 51,* 364–369.

Rogo, D.S. (1989). A report on an unusual cure. *Journal of the Society for Psychical Research, 56,* 23–27.

Rogo, D.S., & Bayless, R. (1979). *Phone calls from the dead.* Engelwood Cliffs, NJ: Prentice-Hall.

Rokeach, M. (1960). *The open and closed mind.* New York: Basic Books.

Roll, W.G. (1961). The problem of precognition. *Journal of the Society for Psychical Research, 41* 115–128.

Roll, W.G. (1964). The psi field. *Proceedings of the Parapsychological Association, 1,* 32–65.

Roll, W.G. (1966). ESP and memory. *International Journal of Parapsychology, 2,* 505–521.

Roll, W.G. (1969). The Newark disturbances. *Journal of the American Society for Psychical Research, 63,* 123–174.

Roll, W.G. (1972). *The poltergeist.* New York: Signet.

Roll, W.G. (1977a). Experimenting with poltergeists? *European Journal of Parapsychology, 2,* 47–71.

Roll, W.G. (1977b). Poltergeists. In B.B. Wolman (Ed.), *Handbook of parapsychology* (pp. 382–413). New York: Van Nostrand Reinhold.

Roll, W.G. (1978a). Towards a theory for the poltergeist. *European Journal of Parapsychology, 2,* 167–200.

Roll, W.G. (1978b). Understanding the poltergeist. In W.G. Roll (Ed.), *Research in parapsychology, 1977* (pp. 183 195). Metuchen, NJ: Scarecrow Press.

Roll, W.G. (1979). Psi structures. In W.G. Roll (Ed.), *Research in parapsychology, 1978* (pp. 16–17). Metuchen, NJ: Scarecrow Press.

Roll, W.G. (1981). A memory theory for apparitions. In W.G. Roll & J. Beloff (Eds.), *Research in parapsychology, 1980* (pp. 5–7). Metuchen, NJ: Scarecrow Press.

Roll, W.G. (1982a). Memory, mediumship and reincarnation. In W.G. Roll, R.L. Morris, & R.A. White (Eds.), *Research in parapsychology, 1981* (pp. 182–187). Metuchen, NJ: Scarecrow Press.

Roll, W.G. (1982b). The changing perspective on life after death. In S. Krippner (Ed.), *Advances in parapsychological research, Volume 3* (pp. 147–291). New York: Plenum Press.

Roll, W.G. (1983). The psi structure theory of survival. In W.G. Roll, J. Beloff, & R.A. White (Eds.), *Research in parapsychology, 1982* (pp. 155–120). Metuchen, NJ: Scarecrow Press.

Roll, W.G. (1984). The psychopathological and psychophysiological theories of the RSPK agent. In R.A. White and R.S. Broughton (Eds.), *Research in parapsychology, 1983* (pp. 118–119). Metuchen, NJ: Scarecrow Press.

Roll, W.G. (1987). Psi and systems theory. In D.H. Weiner & R.D. Nelson (Eds.), *Research in parapsychology, 1986* (pp. 126–129). Metuchen, NJ: Scarecrow Press.

Roll, W.G. (1988). Psi and the phenomenology of memory. In D.H. Weiner & R.L. Morris (Eds.), *Research in parapsychology, 1987* (pp. 131–134). Metuchen, NJ: Scarecrow Press.

Roll, W.G. (1993, August). The question of RSPK vs. fraud in the case of Tina Resch. Paper presented at the 36th annual convention of the Parapsychological Association. Toronto, Canada.

Roll, W.G., Burdick, D.S., & Joines, W.T. (1973). Radial and tangential forces in the Miami poltergeist. *Journal of the American Society for Psychical Research, 67*, 267–281.

Roll, W.G., Maher, M.C., & Brown, B. (1992, August). An investigation of reported haunting occurrences in a Japanese restaurant in Georgia. Paper presented at the 35th annual convention of the Parapsychological Association. Las Vegas, Nevada.

Roll, W.G., & Montangno, E. (1983). Similarities between RSPK and psychomotor epilepsy. In W.G. Roll, J. Beloff, & R.A. White (Eds.), *Research in parapsychology,*

1982 (pp. 270–271). Metuchen, NJ: Scarecrow Press.

Roll, W.G., & Tringale. S. (1983). A haunting-type case in New England. In W.G. Roll, J. Beloff, & R.A. White (Eds.), *Research in parapsychology, 1982* (pp. 132–136). Metuchen, NJ: Scarecrow Press.

Roney-Dougal, S. (1991, August). An exploration of Blackmore's Tarot experiment in a classroom situation. Paper presented at the 34th annual convention of the Parapsychological Association. Heidelberg, Germany.

Rose, S. (1992). *The making of memory.* New York: Anchor Books.

Rubin, L., & Honorton, C. (1971). Separating the yins from the yangs: An experiment with the *I ching. Journal of Parapsychology, 35*, 313–314.

Rucker, R. (1984). *The fourth dimension: Toward a geometry of higher reality.* Boston: Houghton Mifflin.

Ruderfer, M. (1968). [Letter to the Editor.] *Journal of the American Society for Psychical Research, 62*, 84–86.

Ruderfer, M. (1974). Comments on Chari's discussion of the neutrino theory of ESP. [Letter to the Editor.] *Journal of Parapsychology, 38*, 338–340.

Ruderfer, M. (1980). Neutrino theory of psi phenomena. In B. Shapin & L. Coly (Eds.), *Communication and parapsychology* (pp. 121–149). New York: Parapsychology Foundation.

Sabom, M.B. (1982). *Recollections of death: A medical investigation.* New York: Harper & Row.

Sagan, C. (1977). *Broca's brain.* New York: Random House.

Saklani, A. (1988a). Preliminary test of PSI-ability in shamans of Garhwal Himalaya. *Journal of the Society for Psychical Research, 55*, 60–70.

Saklani, A. (1988b). Psi ability in shamans of Garhwal Himalaya. In D.H. Weiner & R.L. Morris (Eds.), *Research in parapsychology, 1987* (pp. 93–96).

Saklani, A. (1989, August). Psychokinetic effect on plant growth: Further studies. Paper presented at the 32nd annual convention of the Parapsychological Association. San Diego, California.

Saklani, A. (1990). Psychokinetic effects on plant growth: Further studies. In L.A. Henkel & J. Palmer (Eds.), *Research in parapsychology, 1989* (pp. 37–41). Metuchen, NJ: Scarecrow Press.

Saklani, A. (1991, August). Promising results in PK experiments with plants. Paper presented at the 34th annual convention of the Parapsychological Association. Heidelberg, Germany.

Saklani, A. (1992). Follow-up studies of PK effects on plant growth. *Journal of the Society for Psychical Research, 58,* 258–265.

Sargent, C. (1980). A covert test of psi abilities of psi-conducive and psi-inhibitory experimenters. In W.G. Roll (Ed.), *Research in parapsychology, 1979* (pp. 115–116). Metuchen, NJ: Scarecrow Press.

Schachter, S. (1951). Deviation, rejection and communication. *Journal of Abnormal and Social Psychology, 46,* 190–208.

Schatzman, M. (1980). *The story of Ruth.* New York: Putnam's.

Schechter, E.I. (1984). Hypnotic inductions. control conditions: Illustrating an approach to the evaluation of replicability in parapsychological data. In R.A. White & R.S. Broughton (Eds.), *Research in parapsychology, 1983* (pp. 49–52). Metuchen, NJ: Scarecrow Press.

Schlitz, M.J., & Gruber, E.R. (1980). Transcontinental remote viewing. *Journal of Parapsychology, 44,* 305–317.

Schlitz, M.J., & Gruber, E.R. (1981). Transcontinental remote viewing. *Journal of Parapsychology, 45,* 233–237.

Schmeidler, G. (1972). Respice, adspice and prospice. In W.G. Roll, R.L. Morris, and J.D. Morris (Eds.), *Proceedings of the Parapsychological Association, 1971.* Durham, NC: Parapsychological Association.

Schmidt, H. (1969). Precognition of a quantum process. *Journal of Parapsychology, 33,* 99–108.

Schmidt, H. (1970). PK tests with animals as subjects. *Journal of Parapsychology, 34,* 255–261.

Schmidt, H. (1975a). A logically consistent model of a world with psi interaction. In L. Oteri (Ed.), *Quantum physics and parapsychology* (pp. 205–228). New York: Parapsychology Foundation.

Schmidt, H. (1975b). Toward a mathematical theory of psi. *Journal of the American Society for Psychical Research, 69,* 301–319.

Schmidt, H. (1976). PK effect on pre-recorded targets. *Journal of the American Society for Psychical Research, 70,* 267–291.

Schmidt, H. (1981). PK tests with pre-recorded and pre-inspected seed numbers. *Journal of Parapsychology, 45,* 87–98.

Schmidt, H. (1984). Comparison of a teleological with a quantum mechanical theory of psi. *Journal of Parapsychology, 48,* 261–276.

Schmidt, H. (1985). Addition effect for PK on prerecorded targets. *Journal of Parapsychology, 49,* 231–248.

Schmidt, H. (1986). Human PK effort on pre-recorded random events previously observed by goldfish. In D.H. Weiner & D.I. Radin (Eds.), *Research in parapsychology, 1985* (pp. 18–21). Metuchen, NJ: Scarecrow Press.

Schmidt, H. (1993). Observation of a psychokinetic effect under highly controlled conditions. *Journal of Parapsychology, 57,* 357–372.

Schmidt, H., Morris, R.L., & Rudolph, L. (1986). Channeling evidence for PK effects to independent observers. *Journal of Parapsychology, 50,* 1–16.

Schmidt, H., & Schlitz, M.J. (1988, August). A large scale pilot PK experiment with prerecorded random events. Paper presented at the 31st annual convention of the Parapsychological Association. Montreal, Canada.

Schnaper, N. (1980). Comments germane to the paper entitled "The reality of death experiences" by Ernst Rodin. *Journal of Nervous and Mental Disease, 168,* 268–270.

Schouten, S.A. (1979). Analysis of spontaneous cases as reported in *Phantasms of the living. European Journal of Parapsychology, 2,* 408–455.

Schouten, S.A. (1981). Analyzing spontaneous cases: A replication based on the Sannwald collection. *European Journal of Parapsychology, 4,* 8–48.

Schouten, S.A. (1982). Analyzing spontaneous cases: A replication based on the Rhine collection. *European Journal of Parapsychology, 4,* 114–158.

Schouten, S.A. (1984). Applying the "worry" hypothesis to spontaneous paranormal experiences. *European Journal of Parapsychology, 5,* 221–244.

Schouten, S.A. (1991, August). History of parapsychology in the Netherlands. Paper presented at the 34th annual convention of the Parapsychological Association. Heidelberg, Germany.

Schriever, F. (1987). A 30-year "experiment with time." Evaluation of an individual case study of precognitive dreams. *European Journal of Parapsychology, 7,* 49–72.

Schwartz, S.A., De Mattei, R.J., Brame, E.G., & Spottiswoode, S.J.P. (1987). Infrared spectra alteration in water proximate to the palms of therapeutic practitioners. In D.H.

Weiner & R.D. Nelson (Eds.), *Research in parapsychology, 1986* (pp. 24–29). Metuchen, NJ: Scarecrow Press.

Schwarz, B.E. (1980). *Psychic-nexus: Psychic phenomena in psychiatry and everyday life.* New York: Van Nostrand Reinhold.

Scofield, A.M., & Hodges, R.D. (1991). Demonstration of a healing effect in the laboratory using a simple plant. *Journal of the Society for Psychical Research, 57,* 321–343.

Scott, C., & Haskell, P. (1974). Fresh light on the Shackleton experiments. *Proceedings of the Society for Psychical Research, 56,* 43–72.

Seager, W. (1995). Consciousness, information and panpsychism. *Journal of Consciousness Studies, 2,* 272–288.

Searle, J.R. (1987). Minds and brains without programs. In C. Blakemore & S. Greenfield (Eds.), *Mindwaves: Thoughts on intelligence, identity and consciousness* (pp. 209–233). New York: Basil Blackwell.

Searle, J.R. (1990, January). Is the brain's mind a computer program? *Scientific American, 262,* 26–31.

Seligman, M.E.P. (1975). *Helplessness: On depression, development and death.* San Francisco: Freeman.

Shaver, P. (1986). Consciousness without the body. [Review of *Flight of mind.*] *Contemporary Psychology, 31,* 647.

Shear, J. (1995). Editor's introduction. *Journal of Consciousness Studies, 2,* 194–199.

Sheldrake, R. (1981). *A new science of life.* Los Angeles: Tarcher.

Sheldrake, R. (1983a, October 27). Formative causation: The hypothesis supported. *New Scientist,* 279–280.

Sheldrake, R. (1983b). Morphic resonance, memory and psychical research. In W.G. Roll, J. Beloff, & R.A. White (Eds.), *Research in parapsychology, 1982* (pp. 81–85). Metuchen, NJ: Scarecrow Press.

Sheldrake, R. (1988a). The laws of nature as habits: A postmodern basis for science. In D.R. Griffin (Ed.), *The reenchantment of science* (pp. 79–86). Albany, NY: State University of New York Press.

Sheldrake, R. (1988b). *The presence of the past.* New York: Times Books.

Sheldrake, R. (1990). Can our memories survive the death of our brain? In G. Doore (Ed.), *What survives?* (pp. 111–121). Los Angeles: Tarcher.

Shiels, D. (1978). A cross-cultural study of beliefs in out of-the-body experiences, waking and sleeping. *Journal of the Society for Psychical Research, 49,* 697–741.

Sidgwick, H., Johnson, A., Myers, F.W.H., Podmore, F., & Sidgwick, E.M. (1894). Report on the census of hallucinations. *Proceedings of the Society for Psychical Research, 10,* 25–422.

Siegel, R.K. (1977). Hallucinations. *Scientific American, 23*(7), 132–140.

Siegel, R.K. (1980). The psychology of life after death. *American Psychologist, 35,* 911–931.

Sinclair, U. (1930/1962). *Mental radio.* Springfield, IL: Thomas.

Sjolund, B., Terenius, L, & Erikson, M. (1977). Increased cerebrospinal fluid levels of endorphins after electroacupuncture. *Acts Physiologica Scandanavia, 100,* 382–384.

Skinner, B.F. (1953). *Science and human behavior.* Toronto: Collier-Macmillan.

Smith, E.L. (1972). The Raudive voices— objective or subjective? A discussion. *Journal of the Society for Psychical Research, 46,* 192–200.

Smith, E.L. (1974). The Raudive voices— objective or subjective? A discussion. *Journal of the American Society for Psychical Research, 68,* 91–100.

Smith, M.J. (1968). Paranormal effects on enzyme activity. *Journal of Parapsychology, 32,* 281 (Abstract).

Smith, M.J. (1972). Paranormal effects on enzyme activity through laying on of hands. *Human Dimensions, 1*(2), 15–19.

Smith, P. & Irwin, H.J. (1981). Out-of-body experiences, needs and the experimental approach. A laboratory study. *Parapsychology Review, 12*(3), 1–4.

Snel, F.W.J.J., & Van der Sijde, P.C. (1990–1991). The effect of retro-active distance healing of *Babesia Rodhani* (rodent malaria) in rats. *European Journal of Parapsychology, 8,* 123–130.

Soal, S.G., & Bateman, F. (1954). *Modern experiments in telepathy.* New Haven, CT: Yale University Press.

Solfvin, G.F. (1982). Studies of the effects of mental healing and expectations on the growth of corn seedlings. *European Journal of Parapsychology, 4,* 284–324.

Sondow, N. (1984). Spontaneous precognitive dreams: A decline with temporal distance. In R.A. White & R.S. Broughton (Eds.), *Research in parapsychology, 1983* (pp. 75–77). Metuchen, NJ: Scarecrow Press.

Sondow, N. (1988). The decline of precognized events with the passage of time: Evidence from spontaneous dreams. *Journal of the American Society for Psychical Research, 82,* 33–51.

Sperry, R.W., Zaidel, E., & Zaidel, D. (1979). Self-recognition and social awareness in the disconnected minor hemisphere. *Neuropsychologia, 17*, 153–166.

Spinelli, E. (1978). Human development and paranormal cognition. Unpublished doctoral dissertation. University of Surrey, England.

Spottiswoode, J. (1993, August). Effect of ambient field fluctuations on performance in a free response anomalous cognition task: A pilot study. Paper presented at the 36th annual convention of the Parapsychological Association. Toronto, Canada.

Squire, L., (1987). *Memory and brain.* New York: University Press.

Squires, E. (1990). *Conscious mind in the physical world.* New York: Adam Holger.

Stace, W.T. (1960). *Mysticism and philosophy.* Los Angeles: Tarcher.

Stahl, F.W. (1990). If it smells like a unicorn. *Nature, 346,* 791.

Stanford, R.G. (1974). An experimentally testable model for spontaneous psi events. I. Extrasensory events. *Journal of the American Society for Psychical Research, 68,* 34–57.

Stanford, R.G. (1982). Is scientific parapsychology possible? (Some thoughts on James E. Alcock's *Parapsychology: Science or magic?*) *Journal of Parapsychology, 46,* 231–271.

Stanford, R.G. (1987). The out-of-body experience as an imaginal journey: The developmental perspective. *Journal of Parapsychology, 51,* 135–155.

Stanford, R.G. (1990a). A model for spontaneous psi events. In S. Krippner (Ed.), *Advances in parapsychological research, Volume 6* (pp. 54–167). Jefferson, NC: McFarland.

Stanford, R.G. (1990b). The correlation of lucid dreaming and out-of-body experience: What does it mean? In L.A. Henkel & J. Palmer (Eds.), *Research in parapsychology, 1989* (pp. 9–14). Metuchen, NJ: Scarecrow Press.

Stanford, R.G., & Stein, A.G. (1994). A meta-analysis of ESP studies contrasting hypnosis and a comparison condition. *Journal of Parapsychology, 58,* 235–269.

Stapp, H. (1992). A quantum theory of consciousness. In B. Rubik (Ed.), *The interrelationship between mind and matter* (pp. 207–217). Philadelphia, PA: The Center for Frontier Sciences.

Stearn, J. (1967). *Edgar Cayce—The sleeping prophet.* New York: Doubleday.

Stenger, V.J. (1990). *Physics and psychics.* Buffalo, NY: Prometheus Books.

Stevens, E.W. (1887). *The Watseka wonder.* Chicago: Religio-Philosophical Publishing House.

Stevenson, I. (1960a). The evidence for survival from claimed memories of former incarnations. Part I. Review of the data. *Journal of the American Society for Psychical Research, 54,* 51–71.

Stevenson, I. (1960b). The evidence for survival from claimed memories of former incarnations. Part II. Analysis of the data and suggestions for further investigations. *Journal of the American Society for Psychical Research, 54,* 95–117.

Stevenson, I. (1966). Cultural patterns in cases suggestive of reincarnation among the Tlingit Indians of southeastern Alaska. *Journal of the American Society for Psychical Research, 60,* 229–243.

Stevenson, I. (1967). An antagonist's view of parapsychology. A review of Professor Hansel's *ESP: A scientific evaluation. Journal of American Society for Psychical Research, 61,* 254–267.

Stevenson, I. (1970a). Characteristics of cases of the reincarnation type in Turkey and their comparison with cases in two other cultures. *International Journal of Comparative Sociology, 12,* 1–17.

Stevenson, I. (1970b). *Telepathic impressions.* Charlottesville, VA: University Press of Virginia.

Stevenson, I. (1972a). Are poltergeists living or are they dead? *Journal of the American Society for Psychical Research, 66,* 233–252.

Stevenson, I. (1972b). Some new cases suggestive of reincarnation. II. The case of Bishen Chand. *Journal of the American Society for Psychical Research, 66,* 375–400.

Stevenson, I. (1973). Some new cases suggestive of reincarnation. IV. The case of Ampan Petcherat. *Journal of the American Society for Psychical Research, 67,* 361–380.

Stevenson, I. (1974a). Some new cases suggestive of reincarnation. V. The case of Indika Guneratne. *Journal of the American Society for Psychical Research, 68,* 58–90.

Stevenson, I. (1974b). Some questions related to cases of the reincarnation type. *Journal of the American Society for Psychical Research, 68,* 395–416.

Stevenson, I. (1974c). *Twenty cases suggestive of reincarnation.* Charlottesville, VA: University Press of Virginia.

Stevenson, I. (1974d). Xenoglossy: A review and report of a case. *Proceedings of the American Society for Psychical Research, 31.*

Stevenson, I. (1975). *Cases of the reincarnation type. Volume 1. Ten cases in India.* Charlottesville, VA: University Press of Virginia.

Stevenson, I. (1976). A preliminary report on a new case of responsive xenoglossy: The case of Gretchen. *Journal of the American Society for Psychical Research, 70,* 65–77.

Stevenson, I. (1977a). *Cases of the reincarnation type. Volume 2. Ten cases in Sri Lanka.* Charlottesville, VA: University Press of Virginia.

Stevenson, I. (1977b). Reincarnation: Field studies and theoretical issues. In B.B. Wolman (Ed.), *Handbook of parapsychology* (pp. 631–663). New York: Van Nostrand Reinhold.

Stevenson, I. (1977c). The belief in reincarnation and cases of the reincarnation type among the Haida. *Journal of the American Society for Psychical Research, 71,* 177–189.

Stevenson, I. (1978). Some comments on automatic writing. *Journal of the American Society for Psychical Research, 73,* 315–332.

Stevenson, I. (1980). *Cases of the reincarnation type. Volume 3. Twelve cases in Lebanon and Turkey.* Charlottesville, VA: University Press of Virginia.

Stevenson, I. (1981). Can we describe the mind? In W.G. Roll & J. Beloff (Eds.), *Research in parapsychology, 1980* (pp. 130–142). Metuchen, NJ: Scarecrow Press.

Stevenson, I. (1983a). American children who claim to remember previous lives. *Journal of Nervous and Mental Disease, 171,* 742–748.

Stevenson, I. (1983b). *Cases of the reincarnation type. Volume 4. Twelve cases in Thailand and Burma.* Charlottesville, VA: University Press of Virginia.

Stevenson, I. (1984). *Unlearned language: New studies in xenoglossy.* Charlottesville, VA: University Press of Virginia.

Stevenson, I. (1986). Characteristics of cases of reincarnation among the Igbo of Nigeria. *Journal of Asian and African Studies, 20,* 13–30.

Stevenson, I. (1987). *Children who remember past lives.* Charlottesville, VA: University Press of Virginia.

Stevenson, I. (1988a). A new look at maternal impressions. Paper presented at the 12th International Conference of the Society for Psychical Research.

Stevenson, I. (1988b). Three new cases of the reincarnation type in Sri Lanka with written records made before verifications. *Journal of Scientific Exploration, 2,* 217–240.

Stevenson, I. (1989). A case of severe birth defects possibly due to cursing. *Journal of Scientific Exploration, 3,* 201–212.

Stevenson, I. (1990). Phobias in children who claim to remember previous lives. *Journal of Scientific Exploration, 4,* 243–254.

Stevenson, I. (1992). A new look at maternal impressions: An analysis of 50 published cases and reports of two recent examples. *Journal of Scientific Exploration, 6,* 353–373.

Stevenson, I. (1993). Birthmarks and birth defects corresponding to wounds on deceased persons. *Journal of Scientific Exploration, 7,* 403–410.

Stevenson, I., & Beloff, J. (1980). An analysis of some suspect drop-in communicators. *Journal of the Society for Psychical Society, 50,* 427–447.

Stevenson, I., & Chadha, N.K. (1988). Two correlates of violent death in cases of the reincarnation type. *Journal of the Society for Psychical Research, 55,* 71–79.

Stevenson, I., & Pasricha, S. (1979). A case of secondary personality with xenoglossy. *American Journal of Psychiatry, 136,* 1591–1592.

Stevenson, I., & Pasricha, S. (1980). A preliminary report on an unusual case of the reincarnation type with xenoglossy. *Journal of the American Society for Psychical Research, 74,* 331–348.

Stevenson, I., Pasricha, S., & Samararatne, G. (1988). Deception and self-deception in cases of the reincarnation type: Seven illustrative cases in Asia. *Journal of the American Society for Psychical Research, 82,* 1–31.

Stokes, D.M. (1980). [Review of *Science and the evolution of consciousness: Charkas, ki and psi* by Hiroshi Motoyama.] *Journal of Parapsychology, 44,* 274–279.

Stokes, D.M. (1982) On the relationship between mind and brain. *Parapsychology Review, 13*(6), 22–27.

Stokes, D.M. (1985). Parapsychology and its critics. In P. Kurtz (Ed.), *A skeptic's handbook of parapsychology* (pp. 379–423). Buffalo, NY: Prometheus Books.

Stokes, D.M. (1987). Theoretical parapsychology. In S. Krippner (Ed.), *Advances in parapsychological research, Volume 5* (pp. 77–189). Jefferson, NC: McFarland.

Stokes, D.M. (1991). Mathematics and parapsychology. *Journal of the American Society for Psychical Research, 85,* 251–290.

Stokes, D.M. (1995). [Review of *Research in parapsychology, 1991.*] *Journal of Parapsychology, 59,* 163–175.

Taboas, A.M. (1980). The psychopathological model of poltergeist phenomena: Some criticisms and suggestions. *Parapsychology Review*, 11(2), 24–27.

Taboas, A.M. (1984). An appraisal of the role of aggression in the central nervous system in RSPK agents. *Journal of the American Society for Psychical Research*, 78, 55–69.

Taboas, A.M., & Alvarado, C.S. (1981). Poltergeist agents: A review of recent research trends and conceptualizations. *European Journal of Parapsychology*, 4, 99–110.

Targ, R., & Puthoff, H.E. (1977). *Mind-reach: Scientists look at psychic ability*. New York: Delacorte Press.

Targ, R., Puthoff, H.E., & May, E.C. (1979). Direct perception of remote geographical locations. In C.T. Tart, H.E. Puthoff, & R. Targ (Eds.), *Mind at large* (pp. 78–106). New York: Praeger.

Tart, C.T. (1967). A second psychophysiological study of out of-body experiences in a gifted subject. *International Journal of Parapsychology*, 9, 251–258.

Tart, C.T. (1968). A psychophysiological study of out-of-the body experiences in a selected subject. *Journal of the American Society for Psychical Research*, 62, 3–27.

Tart, C.T. (1969) A further psychophysiological study of out of-the body experiences in a gifted subject. *Proceedings of the Parapsychological Association*, 6, 43–44.

Tart, C.T. (1971). On being stoned: A psychological study of marijuana intoxication. Palo Alto, CA: Science and Behavior Books.

Tart, C.T. (1972). States of consciousness and state specific sciences. *Science*, 176, 1203–1210.

Tart, C.T. (1976). *Learning to use extrasensory perception*. Chicago: University of Chicago Press.

Tart, C.T. (1982). The controversy about psi: Two psychological theories. *Journal of Parapsychology*, 46, 313–320.

Tart, C.T. (1983). Information acquisition rates in forced choice ESP experiments: Precognition does not work as well as present time ESP. *Journal of the American Society for Psychical Research*, 77, 293–310.

Tart, C.T. (1987). Geomagnetic effects in a GESP test are altered by electrical shielding. In D.H. Weiner & R.D. Nelson (Eds.), *Research in parapsychology, 1986* (pp. 90–92). Metuchen, NJ: Scarecrow Press.

Tart, C.T. (1988a). Effects of electrical shielding on GESP performance. *Journal of the American Society for Psychical Research*, 82, 129–146.

Tart, C.T. (1988b). Geomagnetic effects on GESP. Two studies. *Journal of the American Society for Psychical Research*, 82, 193–216.

Tart, C.T., & Lebore, C.M. (1986). Attitudes toward strongly functioning psi: A preliminary survey. *Journal of the American Society for Psychical Research*, 80, 161–173.

Tart, C.T., Puthoff, H.E., & Targ, R. (1980). Information transmission in remote viewing experiments. *Nature*, 204, 191.

Taylor, J. (1975). *Superminds*. New York: Warner Books.

Taylor, J. (1980). *Science and the supernatural*. New York: Dutton.

Tazari, L. (1990). An unusual case of hypnotic regression with some unexplained contents. *Journal of the American Society for Psychical Research*, 84, 309–344.

Tedder, W.H., & Bloor, J. (1982). PK influence on radioactive decay from short and long distances. In W.G. Roll, R.L. Morris, & R.A. White (Eds.), *Research in Parapsychology, 1981* (pp. 148–149). Metuchen, NJ: Scarecrow Press.

Tedder, W.H., & Braud, W.G. (1981). Long-distance nocturnal psychokinesis. In W.G. Roll & J. Beloff (Eds.), *Research in Parapsychology, 1980* (pp. 100–101). Metuchen, NJ: Scarecrow Press.

Tedder, W.H., & Monty, M.L. (1981). Exploration of long-distance PK: A conceptual replication of the influence on a biological system. In W.G. Roll & J. Beloff (Eds.), *Research in Parapsychology, 1980* (pp. 90–93). Metuchen, NJ: Scarecrow Press.

Terry, J., & Schmidt, H. (1978). Conscious and subconscious PK tests with pre-recorded targets. In W.G. Roll (Ed.), *Research in Parapsychology, 1977* (pp. 36–41). Metuchen, NJ: Scarecrow Press.

Tertullian (1992). The refutation of the Pythagorean doctrine of transmigration. In P. Edwards (Ed.), *Immortality* (pp. 88–90). New York: Macmillan.

Thalbourne, M.A., Delin, P.S., Barlow, J.A. & Steen, D.M. (1992–1993). A further attempt to separate the yins from the yangs. A replication of the Rubin-Honorton experiment with the *I ching*. *European Journal of Parapsychology*, 9, 12–23.

Thaler, D.S. (1994). The evolution of genetic intelligence. *Science*, 264, 224–225.

Thomason, S.G. (1987). Past lives remembered? *Skeptical Inquirer*, 11, 367–375.

Thomson, R. (1993). Centrencephalic theory,

the general learning system, and subcortical dementia. In F.M. Crinella & J. Yu (Eds.), *Brain mechanisms: Papers in memory of Robert Thomson. Annals of the New York Academy of Sciences, Vol. 702* (pp. 197–223). New York: New York Academy of Sciences.

Thorton, E.M. (1984). *The Freudian fallacy.* Garden City, NY: The Dial Press.

Thouless, R.H., & Wiesner, B.P. (1948). The psi process in normal and "paranormal" psychology. *Journal of Parapsychology, 12,* 192–212.

Tipler, F.J. (1974). Rotating cylinders and the possibility of global causality violation. *Physical Review, 90,* 2203.

Tipler, F.J. (1994). *The physics of immortality.* New York: Doubleday.

Toben, B., & Wolf, F. (1982). *Space-time and beyond.* New York: Bantam Books.

Toffoli, T. (1982). Physics and computation. *International Journal of Theoretical Physics, 21,* 469.

Torrey, E.F. (1992). *Freudian fraud: The malignant effect of Freud's theory on American thought and culture.* New York: Harper-Collins.

Travis, J. (1992). Could a pair of cosmic strings open a route into the past? *Science, 256,* 179–180.

Troland, L.T. (1917). *A technique for the study of telepathy and other alleged clairvoyant processes.* Albany: Brandow Publishing Co.

Tryon, E.P. (1973). Is the universe a vacuum fluctuation? *Nature, 246,* 396–397.

Turing, A. (1950) Computing machinery and intelligence. *Mind, 59,* 433–460.

Turing, A. (1964). Computing machines and intelligence. In A. Anderson (Ed.), *Minds and machines* (pp. 4–30). Englewood Cliffs: Prentice Hall.

Twemlow, S.W., & Gabbard, G.O. (1984). The influence of demographic/psychological factors and preexisting conditions on the near death experience. *Omega, 15,* 223–235.

Twining, H.L. (1915). *The physical theory of the soul.* Westgate, CA: Press of the Pacific Veteran.

Tyrrell, G.N.M. (1936). Further research in extra-sensory perception. *Proceedings of the Society for Psychical Research, 44,* 99–168.

Tyrrell, G.N.M. (1946). The modus operandi of paranormal cognition. *Proceedings of the Society for Psychical Research, 48* (Part 173), 65–120.

Tyrrell, G.N.M. (1953). *Apparitions.* New York: Macmillan.

Ullman, M. (1987). The experiential dream group. In M. Ullman & C. Limmer (Eds.), *The variety of dream experience* (pp. 1–26). New York: Continuum.

Ullman, M., & Krippner, S. (1969). A laboratory approach to the nocturnal dimension of paranormal experience. Report of a confirmatory study using the REM monitoring technique. *Biological Psychiatry, 1,* 258–270.

Ullman, M., Krippner, S., & Vaughn, A. (1973). *Dream telepathy.* New York: Macmillan.

Varvoglis, M., & McCarthy, D. (1982). Psychokinesis, intentionality and the attentional object. In W.G. Roll, R.L. Morris, and R.A. White (Eds.), *Research in parapsychology, 1981* (pp. 51–55). Metuchen, NJ: Scarecrow Press.

Vasiliev, L. (1976). *Experiments in distant influence.* New York: Dutton & Co.

Venn, J. (1986). Hypnosis and the reincarnation hypothesis: A critical review and intensive case study. *Journal of the American Society for Psychical Research, 80,* 409–425.

Villars, C. (1983). Nonlocality and ESP. *Journal of the Society for Psychical Research, 52,* 189–193.

Virtanen, L. (1990). *"That must have been ESP!" An examination of psychic experiences.* Bloomington, IN: Indiana University Press.

Walker, E.H. (1975). Foundations of paraphysical and parapsychological phenomena. In L. Oteri (Ed.), *Quantum physics and parapsychology* (pp. 1–53). New York: Parapsychology Foundation.

Walker, E.H. (1984). A review of criticisms of the quantum mechanical theory of psi phenomena. *Journal of Parapsychology, 48,* 277–332.

Wälti, B. (1990). A permanent paranormal object? *Journal of the Society for Psychical Research, 56,* 65–70.

Wambaugh, H. (1978). *Reliving past lives.* New York: Harper & Row.

Warcollier, R. (1948/1963). *Mind to mind.* New York: Collier.

Watkins, A.J., & Bickel, W.S. (1986). A study of the Kirlian effect. *Skeptical Inquirer, 10,* 245–257.

Watkins, A.J., & Bickel, W.S. (1989). The Kirlian technique: Controlling the wild cards. *Skeptical Inquirer, 13,* 172 189.

Watkins, G.K., & Watkins, A.M. (1971). Possible PK influence on the resuscitation of anesthetized mice. *Journal of Parapsychology, 35,* 257–272.

Watkins, G.K., Watkins, A.M., & Wells, R.A.

(1973). Further studies on the resuscitation of anesthetized mice. In W.G. Roll, R.L. Morris, & J.D. Morris (Eds.), *Research in parapsychology, 1972* (pp. 153–159). Metuchen, NJ: Scarecrow Press.

Watt, C.A. (1991, August). Meta-analysis of DMT-ESP studies and an experimental investigation of perceptual defence/vigilance and extrasensory perception. Paper presented at the 34th annual convention of the Parapsychological Association. Heidelberg, Germany.

Watters, R.A. (1935). Phantoms. *Journal of the American Society for Psychical Research, 29,* 68–81.

Weiner, D.H., & Zingrone, N.L. (1986). The checker effect revisited. *Journal of Parapsychology, 50,* 85–121.

Weiss, B.L. (1988). *Many lives, many masters.* New York: Simon & Schuster.

Wells, R.A., & Klein, J. (1972). A replication of a "psychic healing" paradigm. *Journal of Parapsychology, 36,* 144–149.

Wells, R.A., & Watkins, G.K. (1975). Linger effects in several PK experiments. In J.D. Morris, W.G. Roll, & R.L. Morris (Eds.), *Research in parapsychology, 1974* (pp. 143–147). Metuchen, NJ: Scarecrow Press.

West, D.J. (1990). A pilot census of hallucinations. *Proceedings of the Society for Psychical Research, 57,* 163–207.

Westfall, R. (1977). *The construction of modern science.* New York: Cambridge University Press.

Wheeler, J.A. (1962). *Geometrodynamics.* New York: Academic Press.

White, R.A. (1976). The influences of persons other than the experimenter on the subject's scores in psi experiments. *Journal of the American Society for Psychical Research, 70,* 133–166.

White, R.A. (1982). An analysis of ESP phenomena in the saints. *Parapsychology Review, 13*(1), 15–18.

White, R.A. (1985). The spontaneous, the imaginal and psi: Foundations for a depth parapsychology. In R.A. White & J. Solfvin (Eds.), *Research in parapsychology, 1984* (pp. 166–190). Metuchen, NJ: Scarecrow Press.

White, R.A. (1990). An experience–centered approach to parapsychology. *Exceptional Human Experience, 8*(1/2), 7–39.

Wiesner, B.P., & Thouless, R.H. (1942). The present position of experimental research into telepathy and other related phenomena. *Proceedings of the Society for Psychical Research, 47,* 1–19.

Wilber, K. (1990). Death, rebirth and meditation. In G. Doore (Ed.), *What survives? Contemporary explorations of life after death* (pp. 176–191). Los Angeles: Tarcher.

Williams, C., Roe, C.A., Upchurch, I., & Lawrence, T.R. (1994, August). Senders and geomagnetism in the autoganzfeld. Paper presented at the 37th annual convention of the Parapsychological Association. Amsterdam, the Netherlands.

Wilson, F.A. W., Scalaidhe, S.P.O., & Goldman-Rakic, P. (1993). Dissociation of object and spatial processing domains in primate prefrontal cortex. *Science, 210,* 1955–1958.

Wilson, I. (1987). *The after death experience.* New York: Quill.

Wilson, I. (1988). [Review of *Children who remember previous lives* by Ian Stevenson.] *Journal of the Society for Psychical Research, 55,* 227–229.

Wilson, S.C., & Barber, T.X. (1982). The fantasy-prone personality: Implications for understanding imagery, hypnosis and parapsychological phenomena. In A.A. Sheikh (Ed.), *Imagery: Current theory, research and application.* New York: Wiley.

Wilson, S.K. (1928). *Modern problems in neurology.* London: Arnold.

Winkelman, M. (1983). The anthropology of magic and parapsychological research. *Parapsychology Review, 14*(2), 13–16.

Wirth, D.P. (1989, August). Unorthodox healing: The effect of noncontact therapeutic touch on the healing rate of full thickness dermal wounds. Paper presented at the 32nd annual convention of the Parapsychological Association. San Diego, California.

Wirth, D.P. (1990). Unorthodox healing: The effect of noncontact therapeutic touch on the healing rate of full thickness dermal wounds. In L.A. Henkel & J. Palmer (Eds.), *Research in parapsychology, 1989* (pp. 47–52). Metuchen, NJ: Scarecrow Press.

Wirth, D.P., Johnson, C.A., Harvath, J.S., & MacGregor, J.A.D. (1992). The effect of alternative healing therapy on the regeneration rate of salamander forelimbs. *Journal of Scientific Exploration, 6,* 375–390.

Wirth, D.P., & Mitchell, B.J. (1994). Complementary healing therapy for patients with type I diabetes mellitus. *Journal of Scientific Exploration, 8,* 367–377.

Wiseman, R., West, D., & Stemman, R. (1996). Psychic crime detectives: A new test for measuring their successes and failures. *Skeptical Inquirer, 20,* 38–40; 58.

Woodward, M.A. (1971). *Edgar Cayce's story of karma*. New York: Berkley.

Woolgar, S. (1988). *Science: The very idea*. New York: Tavistock.

Zhong, Y., & Wu, C. (1991). Altered synaptic plasticity in *Drosophilia* memory mutants with a defective cyclic AMP cascade. *Science*, *251*, 198–201.

Zilberman, M. (1991). Effect of geomagnetic activity on true predictions density in mass numerical lotteries. *Biophysica*, *37*, 566–571. (In Russian.)

Zilberman, M. (1995). Public numerical lotteries: An international parapsychological experiment covering a decade. *Journal of the Society for Psychical Research*, *60*, 149–160.

Zöllner, J.C.F. (1901). *Transcendental physics*. Boston: Beacon of Light Publishing.

Zorab, G. (1962). Cases of the Chaffin will type and the problem of survival. *Journal of the Society for Psychical Research*, *41*, 407–416.

Zorab, G., & MacKenzie, A. (1980). A modern haunting. *Journal of the Society for Psychical Research*, *50*, 284–293.

Index